*In Praise of Tārā*

# *In Praise of Tārā*

## *Songs to the Saviouress*

***

Source texts from India and Tibet on
Buddhism's Great Goddess

SELECTED, TRANSLATED, AND INTRODUCED

*by*

MARTIN WILLSON

Wisdom Publications • Boston

Wisdom Publications
361 Newbury Street
Boston, Massachusetts 02115
United States of America

First published in 1986
This revised edition, 1996



*Library of Congress Cataloging-in-Publication Data*

Wilson, Martin, 1946-
In praise ofT>r> : songs to the Saviouress : source texts from India and Tibet on Buddhism's great Goddess / selected, translated, and introduced by Martin Wilson.
p. cm.
Originally published: London : Wisdom Publications, 1986.
Includes bibliographical references and index.
ISBN 0-86171-109-2 (alk. Paper)
1. T>r> (Goddess) I. Title
BQ4710. T3W55 1996
294.3'42114—dc20 95-43430

ISBN 0 86171 109 2
01 00 99 98 97
6 5 4 3 2

*Designed by:* L·J·SAWLiT

*Cover Art:* Khadiravani Tara (Tara of the Khadira Forest) with her two companion goddesses Marici and Ekajata; artist unknown.

Cover photo: Hiroki Fujita, courtesy of the Office of Tibet, Tokyo.

Typeset in Poetica Chancery and Adobe Garamond

Wisdom Publications' books are printed on acid-free paper and meet the guidelines for permanence and durability of the Committee on Production Guidelines for Book Longevity of the Council on Library Resources.

# *Contents*

# *Illustrations and Plates*

LINE DRAWINGS by Andy Weber



COLOUR PLATES

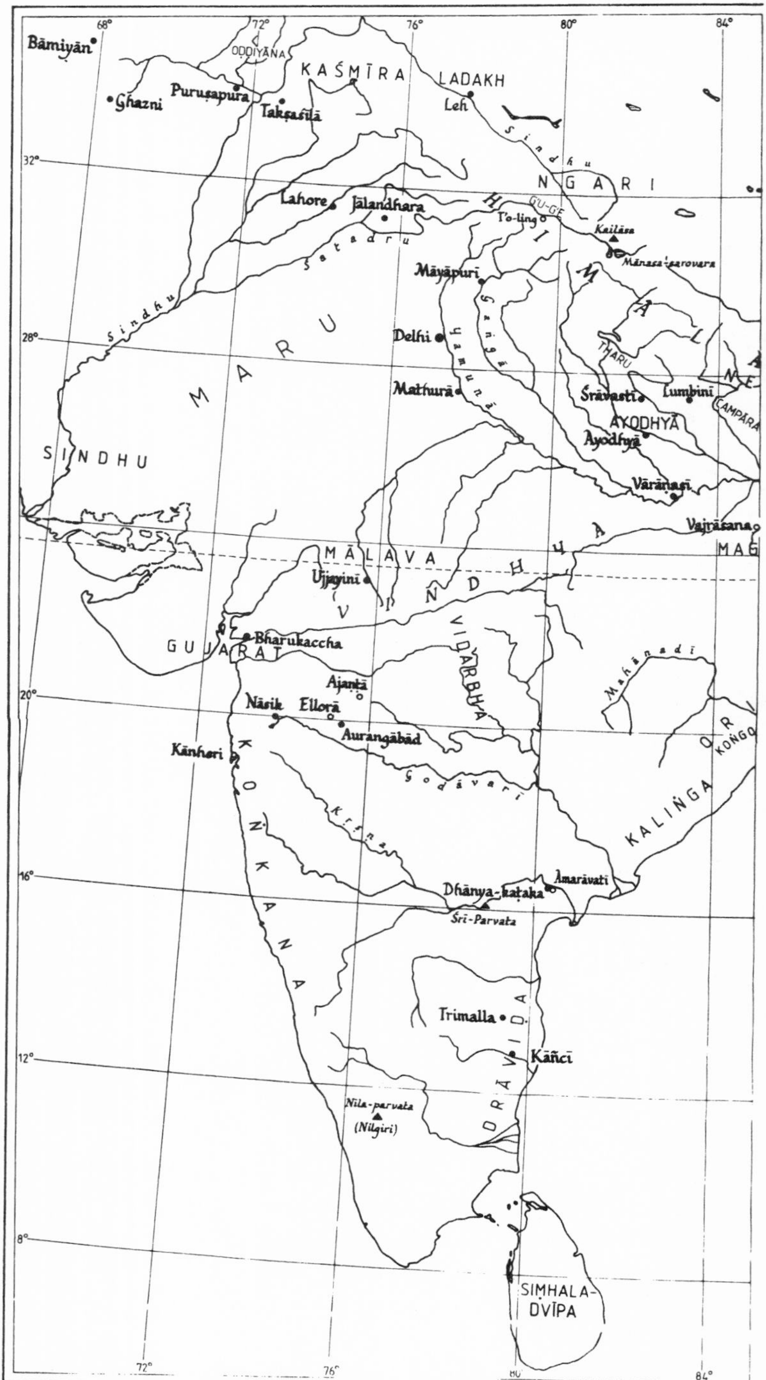

68°
72°
76°
80°
84°
32°
28°
20°
16°
12°
8°
Bāmiyān
Ghazni
Puruṣapura
Takṣaśilā
ODDIYĀNA
KAŚMĪRA
LADAKH
Leh
Sindhu
NGARI
GU-GE
T'o-ling
Kailāsa
Mānasa-sarovara
HIMĀLAYA
Lahore
Jālandhara
Śatadru
Māyāpurī
Gaṅgā
Yamunā
Delhi
Mathurā
MARU
THARU
Śrāvastī
Lumbinī
CAMPĀRAN
AYODHYĀ
Ayodhyā
Vārāṇasī
Vajrāsana
MAG
SINDHU
MĀLAVA
Ujjayinī
VINDHYA
VIDARBHA
GUJARAT
Bharukaccha
Mahānadī
Ajaṇṭā
Nāsik
Ellorā
Aurangābād
Kānheri
KONKANA
Godāvarī
Kṛṣṇa
KALIṄGA
KONGO
ORI
Amarāvatī
Dhānya-kaṭaka
Śrī-Parvata
Trimalla
DRĀVIDA
Kāñcī
Nila-parvata
(Nilgiri)
SIMHALA-DVĪPA

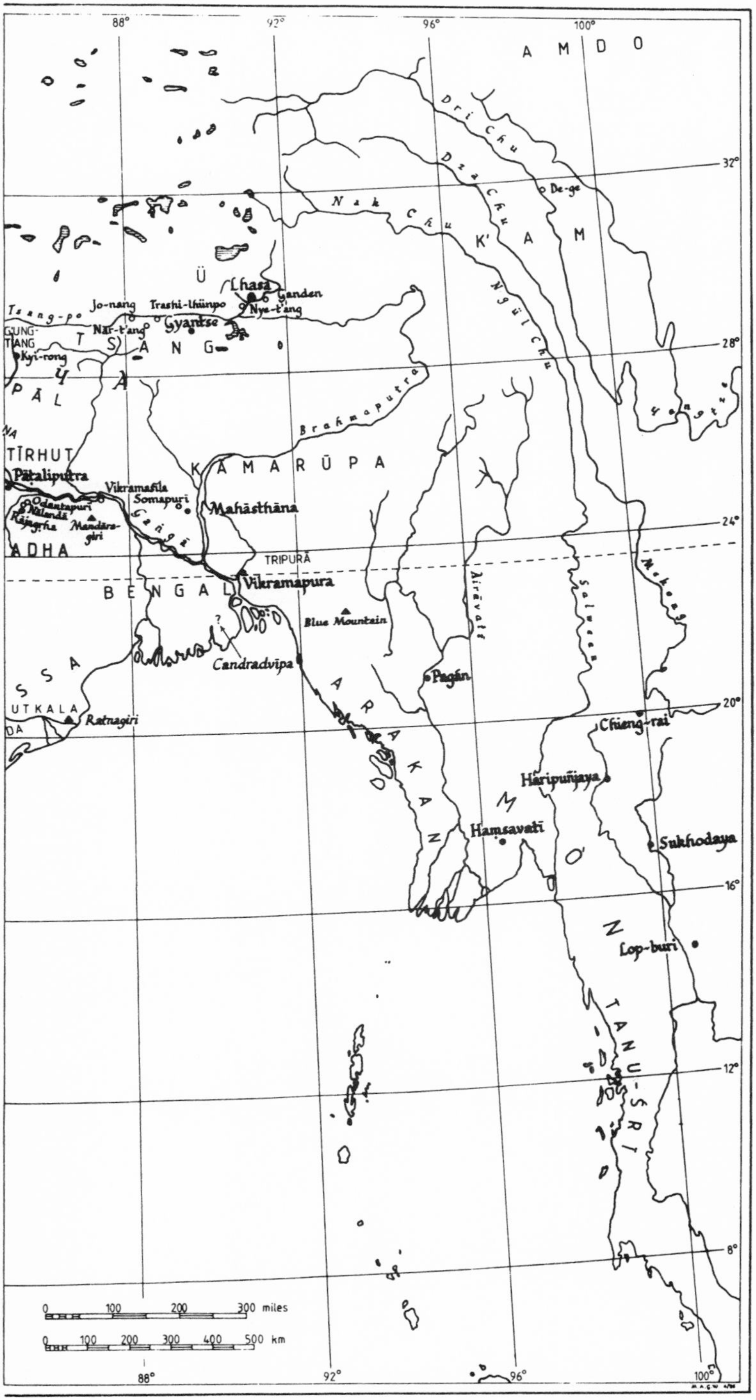

88°
92°
96°
100°
AMDO
Dri Chu
Dza Chu
De-ge
Nak Chu
K'AM
Ngül Chu
Yangtze
32°
28°
24°
20°
16°
12°
8°
Ü
Lhasa
Ganden
Nye-t'ang
Tsang-po
Jo-nang
Trashi-lhünpo
Nar-t'ang
Gyantse
GUNG-TANG
Kyi-rong
TSANG
NEPĀL
TĪRHUT
Brahmaputra
KĀMARŪPA
Pāṭaliputra
Vikramaśīla
Somapuri
Mahāsthāna
Odantapuri
Nālandā
Rājagṛha
Mandāragiri
Gaṅgā
MAGADHA
TRIPURĀ
Vikramapura
BENGAL
Blue Mountain
Candradvīpa
ORISSA
UTKALA
Ratnagiri
ARAKAN
Pagān
Airāvatī
Salween
Mekong
Chieng-rai
Haripuñjaya
Haṃsavatī
Sukhodaya
MON
Lop-buri
TANU-ŚRI
0 100 200 300 miles
0 100 200 300 400 500 km

# *Introduction*

Homage to Ārya-Tārā!

This most beloved of deities, Tārā, the Saviouress, has been exerting Her fascination on devotees for upwards of fourteen centuries, inspiring in the process some of the most attractive of Buddhist literature. This volume presents a selection, translated from Sanskrit and Tibetan. May it assist the practice of those already drawn to the *Ārya* Mother, and awaken devotion in many more!

## WHO IS TĀRĀ?

No mere legend or personified abstraction, surely, but a Perfect Buddha, a Being Awakened to Omniscience, Who has appeared to countless devotees, often saving them miraculously in desperate circumstances. Three major strands intertwine to make the Tārā we know today—Bodhisattva, Mother Goddess, and Tantric Deity.

### 1. *Tārā the Bodhisattva*

As the mental continuum of a Buddha cannot arise suddenly out of nothing, but must result from the preceding continuum of an unenlightened being, Tārā must once have been an ordinary person like ourselves, who by practising the Bodhisattva Path over an inconceivably long span of time, in birth after birth, eventually succeeded in attaining Perfect Enlightenment. The Prologue depicts Her at a crucial moment of this process, when before a Buddha of the exceedingly remote past She takes the Bodhisattva Vow, to work for the benefit of beings until *saṃsāra* is empty. Like other Bodhisattvas, She adds to this general vow Her own specific vow. Hers is particularly striking—defying the traditional teaching that She should take only male rebirths henceforth, She vows to work for others for ever in the form of a woman. This practical yet limitlessly inspiring resolution somehow makes Her seem very real and close to us of the late twentieth century, although it is supposed to have been made unimaginably long ago.

The Bodhisattva strand of Tārā's nature that issues from this vow is spun from three threads, indicated by Her three main titles.

1a. *Compassion of Lord Avalokita.* In our age, Tārā first revealed Herself to humankind as an emanation of the male Bodhisattva of Compassion, Avalokiteśvara. This is recorded in myths and substantiated by literary and archaeological evidence.[1] The usual story (pp. 123–5) is that She was born from a lotus that grew in Avalokiteśvara's tears of pity; a strange, Tantric version appears in the Prologue (p. 35). The earliest identifiable images of Tārā, dating from the sixth century, typically show Her as a member of a triad—Avalokiteśvara in the centre, with Tārā on His right, representing His Compassion, and Her sister Goddess Bhṛkuṭī on His left, representing His Wisdom.[2] In the Praises translated in this book, Tārā is hailed more than once as being the Compassion of Avalokiteśvara. Since Compassion is Avalokiteśvara's principal attribute, Tārā was by far the more important of the two Goddesses, and it was not long before She was being portrayed alone in His functions.

1b. *Mother of All the Buddhas.* Every Bodhisattva must become fully accomplished in Wisdom as well as in Compassion; in fact the only way to release from suffering is through perceiving Reality. Tārā's Wisdom is emphasized by Her title 'Mother of All the Buddhas', which equates Her with the Perfection of

Wisdom; it is a name that that Perfection has borne since the earliest Sūtras proclaiming it. Wisdom can only be feminine, because it is insight into Ultimate True Nature or Emptiness, one and indivisible, the eternal and immutable source and ground of all that is. All the Perfections that lead to Buddhahood have to be practised with Wisdom, thus it is in the womb of the Perfection of Wisdom that is nurtured the embryo of Buddhahood, conceived of the Thought of Enlightenment (*Bodhicitta*) at the time of taking the Bodhisattva Vow.

If this sounds a little abstract and remote, we should remember that we too are to be Buddhas eventually, therefore Tārā, Mother of all Buddhas of the past, present *and future*, is our own Mother also, with all the loving closeness that that implies.

1c. *Saviouress*. The name Tārā, although it could mean 'Star', is almost always interpreted as 'the Saviouress', 'She Who Leads Across'. As She Herself says in *The Hundred and Eight Names*,

> I, O Lord, shall lead [beings] across
> the great flood of their diverse fears;
> Therefore the eminent seers sing
> of me in the world by the name of Tārā.

According to the Prologue, She acquired the name through releasing innumerable sentient beings from *saṃsāra*, establishing them in the Pure Bodhisattva Stages.

But even in medieval India, only a tiny fraction of the people were really serious about seeking Liberation from *saṃsāra*. The amazing popularity of Tārā's cult was due to the worldly benefits She offered—above all, She was famous for saving from the eight great fears (or dangers), most often listed as lions, elephants, fire, snakes, robbers, imprisonment, water and the man-eating demons called *piśācas*. She appealed especially to the merchants, who in their travels were often exposed to these dangers.

The carvings in the caves of West India, at Ajaṇṭā, Aurangābād, Nāsik, Kānheri and Ellorā, show well the evolution of this function of Tārā.[3] In the sixth century, it is Avalokiteśvara alone who saves from the eight great fears. In one panel of the end of the sixth century, He is accompanied by two goddesses, presumably Tārā and Bhṛkuṭī, but it is still small replicas of the male Bodhisattva who fly to the aid of the distressed. In the seventh century, however, Tārā takes over the role, saving from the eight great fears on Her own, and rapidly becomes famous in it, as we can see from the contemporary praises by Candragomin and others and from carvings from other parts of India from the eighth century onwards. In fact, most of the songs to Tārā mention Her as Saviouress from the Eight Great Fears, if they are not built round that as their main theme, and many anecdotes (such as those collected by Tāranātha, in Part Three) testify to Her effectiveness.

The outer aspect of the eight fears is not the whole story. They can be taken symbolically, as in the song by the First Dalai Lama in Part Five, as standing for the inner fears of pride, delusion, anger, envy, wrong views, avarice, attachment and doubt. This not only makes this function of Tārā more relevant to us who see lions and elephants only at the zoo, but makes it part of Her real task as Saviouress from *Saṃsāra*.

## 2. *Tārā the Mother Goddess*

The second great strand of Tārā's personality is that She is the Buddhist form of the great Mother Goddess, Who has flourished in India from time immemorial. Many attributes of Tārā are in fact borrowed from Brahmanical forms of the Mother Goddess, especially Durgā, whose cult was already well established. They include the name of 'Saviouress' and much of Her role as rescuer from danger, besides many details of Her iconography.[4]

While Tārā is undoubtedly an Indian Mother Goddess, the Mother Goddess is universal, an expression of the Feminine archetype embedded in the minds of all of us. Because of this, Tārā strikes a resonance in the hearts even of Europeans. The Mother is no stranger to Europe's shores—even the patriarchal Romans adored Demeter, Artemis and Isis, not to mention Phrygian Cybele, until all these and others were supplanted by the Virgin Mary.[5] In Britain too, capricious Cerridwen, Arianrhod and Blodeuwedd were forced to give way to mild

Mary, but nowhere was Mary worshipped more fervently than in 'Merry England', with orgiastic rites of pagan origin that were eventually suppressed in the Puritan Revolution.[6]

Europe's Great Goddess has described herself, so Apuleius reports, as follows:

> I am she that is the natural mother of all things, mistress and governess of all the elements, the initial progeny of worlds, chief of the powers divine, queen of all that are in Hell, the principal of them that dwell in Heaven, manifested alone and under one form of all the gods and goddesses. At my will the planets of the sky, the wholesome winds of the seas, and the lamentable silences of hell be disposed; my name, my divinity is adored throughout the world, in divers manners, in variable customs, and by many names.[7]

The names she mentions include Mother of the Gods, Minerva, Venus, Diana, Proserpine, Ceres, Juno, Hecate and her 'true name', Queen Isis.

In short, she is Goddess of the Underworld, the Earth and the Heavens,[8] concerned with birth and death, love and war, the seasons, all that lives and grows, and the moon and her changes. Her typical form is that of a slender and beautiful woman, of deathly white complexion (for the New Moon), with long golden hair and blue eyes, but she also appears in red and black (or dark blue) forms (for the Full Moon and Old Moon), as an ugly hag, and in animal forms—sow, mare, owl, raven and so forth.[9]

Tārā, being Indian, naturally looks a little different from the European Goddess, and Her matchless beauty is of so transcendent an order as not to arouse attachment, but in function She has much in common with Europe's Goddess.

More generally, the Mother Goddess has been analyzed in detail by Erich Neumann, a former student of Jung's.[10] He describes the Feminine archetype as comprising an elementary character—the maternal function of containing—and a transformative character, which operates in different directions and on different planes. On the first plane is the Goddess as the Great Round, 'which is and contains the universe'. Next, on the natural plane, is the Lady of the Plants and Animals. Above this again is the Goddess of Spiritual Transformation, whose highest form of all, Neumann says, is Tārā.

These three planes correspond well with the Underworld, Earth and Heavens already mentioned, and with a standard Buddhist division of phenomena into Basis, Path and Result. To understand them, however, we must think in terms of symbols with several levels of meaning; when we have been educated always to think prosaically with only one level of meaning at a time, this can be difficult. I shall try to make it easier by distinguishing three levels explicitly as 'outer', 'inner' and 'secret', a terminology borrowed from Buddhist Tantra. On each level of each plane Tārā encompasses the functions of the Mother Goddess, though not always in the same way as the Goddess's more limited expressions; for some more primitive forms of the Goddess are scarcely more than fiends to be propitiated with bloody sacrifices, while even Kālī and Durgā, though in some aspects very exalted symbols of spiritual transformation, have been so misunderstood that human sacrifices to Durgā continued into the 1830s, while Kālī's temple in Calcutta is still a slaughterhouse.

2a. *Goddess of the Underworld.* In the narrowest sense, the underworld is the hells and the realm of the dead (known in Buddhist terminology as *pretas,* 'the departed') and the underground abode of such creatures as snakes and *nāgas.* Thus on the outer level, Tārā is Goddess of the Underworld because She can control *nāgas, pretas* and the guardians of the hells.

On the inner level, She controls the causes of these underworld states, the emotions of greed, avarice, anger and hatred.

But death implies rebirth; more widely, the underworld is the Great Round, *saṃsāra,* the state of being caught up in the round of death and rebirth under the control of defiling emotions and defiled actions. The Goddess as the Great Round is all 'the life-bearing chthonic powers of the world', not just the dark, fertile earth but the sky who 'covers her creatures on earth like a hen covering her chicks'—both the night sky that gives birth to the stars and moon, and the daytime sky that gives birth to the sun—the waters, which are her milk, and the fire of her transforming power: in fact all the elements, as well as space and time. Usually her positive, life-creating aspects predominate over the negative, destructive aspect, but she is also the ogress who holds the Tibetan Wheel of Life, shown in a monstrous form because, as Neumann says, 'wherever the antivital fanaticism of the male spiritual principle predominates, the Feminine is looked upon as negative and evil, precisely in its character of creator, sustainer and increaser of life';[11] or in Buddhist terms, because samsaric life is all suffering.

It is on the secret level, that of Tantric Buddhism, that the Goddess as Great Round is identified with Tārā. There the Great Round and Enlightenment are seen as one and the same:

> Just as is *saṃsāra*, so
> also is *Nirvāṇa* too.
> Except *saṃsāra*, there is nothing
> else that one could call *Nirvāṇa*.[12]

The elements are recognized as fully Enlightened female deities,[13] and mental defilements as the Buddhas of the Five Families;[14] to show this, the ogress of the Wheel of Life has a third, wisdom, eye and the ornaments of an Enlightened deity. If in particular you are practising Tārā, you should recognize all you see as Tārā's body (made of green light), all you hear as Her divine speech, and all your thoughts as Her divine wisdom.[15] Every particle of food you eat is Tārā, every molecule of air you breathe is Her divine energy, the house you live in is Her, when you lie down your head rests in Her lap. Thus Tārā is the Basis from which spiritual practice starts, the mud of *saṃsāra*, with all its defilements and other obscurations, in which the lotus of spiritual awakening grows.

2b. *Goddess of the Earth.* Tārā is closely connected on the outer level with the earth, the world of plants, animals and human beings. She habitually dwells in wild places such as the island of Mount Potala and the Khadira Forest (Khadira-vaṇa), abounding in all kinds of beautiful, sweet-smelling trees, flowers and other plants and happy animals and birds. Her chief symbol is a blue lotus flower (*utpala*) held in the left hand, with sometimes another in the right; as Khadiravaṇī-

Tārā She wears flowers in Her hair and even Her body is green in colour. As already stated, She is famous for subduing dangerous wild beasts such as lions, elephants and snakes, besides dangerous human beings such as robbers; like other manifestations of the Great Goddess She dominates them non-violently, without fighting them. Likewise She is known to disperse armies without killing anyone and to stay the executioner's hand.

Such properties establish Her as the Great Goddess in the aspects of Neumann's Lady of the Plants and Lady of the Beasts, iconographic types in which the Goddess is accompanied by trees, flowers, fruit, grain or other plant emblems, or by animals.

On the inner level, Tārā controls the defilements that cause human or animal rebirth, principally desire and ignorance, and the defilements symbolized by the animals, listed in 1c. In general, Neumann points out, the Goddess's domination of wild animals means She embodies spiritual forces in the human psyche that are superior to the instinctual drives represented by the animals.

The plants whose growth the Goddess nurtures generally denote spiritual growth. In European art we find the trees of life, of knowledge and of death (such as the cross), and also the wooden ship as a symbol of salvation—Tārā too is frequently described as a boatwoman, or even a boat.

By identifying with Tārā in Tantric practice one progresses spiritually, thus on the secret level Tārā is the Path of spiritual practice, the lotus plant growing up through the water towards the light.

2c. *Goddess of the Heavens.* The heavens, the regions 'above' us, comprise all superhuman states of existence. They include many grades of 'gods', noble, majestic beings purer and subtler than humans, with radiant bodies or even purely mental, without bodies; and assorted semi-divine beings such as *vidyādharas, yakṣas* and *asuras*, endowed with 'supernatural' powers. That Tārā is their Goddess is indicated by Her name, Tārā, 'star', and by the thin crescent moon She wears as a tiara; it means on the outer level that She dominates these beings and can stop them harming Her human devotees should they try to.

On the inner level, She can control in our minds all the faults to which heavenly beings are still prone, such as pride, envy, craving for existence, and subtler obscurations, and can help us realize the advanced meditational skills through which many of the divine states are achieved.

However, we can also take the heavens as extending beyond *saṃsāra* to the Pure Lands such as Sukhāvatī and to Perfect Buddhahood. Tārā is the Goddess of Spiritual Transformation. Not only can She help us be reborn in a Pure Land, but on the secret level She is Full Awakening or Enlightenment itself, the Result of following the spiritual Path, traditionally symbolized by the unfolding of the lotus flower in light and space after it has grown above the surface of the waters.

The Goddess of Spiritual Transformation, the 'Sophia' or Wisdom aspect of the Great Goddess, represents 'the generating and nourishing, protective and transforming, feminine power of the unconscious,' wherein, says Neumann, 'a wisdom is at work that is infinitely superior to the wisdom of man's waking consciousness, and that, as source of vision and symbol, of ritual and law, poetry and vision, intervenes, summoned or unsummoned, to save man and give direction to his life.'[16] It is a maternal 'wisdom of loving participation', always near and accessible. She appears, for example, as Mary, holding in her arms, as Jung pointed out, 'our greater future self';[17] but one of her main forms is as a Moon-goddess. The moon, whose connection with woman in terms of the monthly cycle is evident, is the favourite spiritual symbol of matriarchy, as a luminous body born from the darkness of night.[18] Wisdom, in fact, is just the meaning of the moon in Buddhist Tantra. There is a Tārā White as the Autumn Moon, and Tārā usually sits on a moon disk and often is backed by one as well.

The contrast between feminine moon and masculine sun is fundamental in mythology. The world over, as the Father God usurped the position of the Mother Goddess, lunar, matriarchal myths were replaced by solar, patriarchal ones. That few of us now see any more in myths than nonsensical children's tales does not alter the fact that the masculine, solar consciousness, abstract and conceptual, with its dangerous delusions of self-sufficiency, has become so overdeveloped at the expense of the feminine sphere of the mind as to put at risk the very survival of our race. As Graves puts it,[19] we are now in practice governed by the Sun-god, Apollo god of science, wielding the nuclear bomb as a thunderbolt, in an uneasy coalition with Pluto god of wealth and Mercury god of thieves. Most of us, refugees from Man's war on Nature, are forced to live as servants in Pluto's infernal realm, those squalid monuments to greed and blind ambition that we call towns and cities. Day by day the Earth's resources are futilely plundered and laid waste. Eventually the Goddess must resume Her rightful place, but the longer Her return is postponed, the less merciful will Her face be.[20]

It is missing the point to single out the Spiritually-transforming, Wisdom aspect of the Mother Goddess as the 'highest' and ignore the others. For every person in the West genuinely qualified to practise Tantra there could well be hundreds who could profitably relate to Tārā on lower planes for the present; let us not forget, for example, Her role as Lady of the Plants and Animals.

### 3. *Tārā the Tantric Deity*

The third major strand of Tārā's character is that She is a deity of Buddhist Tantra, or Vajrayāna. That is, She is a potentiality latent within every sentient being's mind, that the practitioner properly empowered by a Guru can by Tantric practice develop and learn to identify with and so eventually reach Perfection, fully realized Tārāhood.

3a. *Complete and Perfect Buddha.* The main qualification for serving as a Tantric deity is to have awakened fully to Complete and Perfect Buddhahood. Tārā is therefore a perfect Buddha, which is to say there is no fault She has failed to eliminate, however slight, and no good quality She lacks. Since qualities of Buddhas are described at great length in the Sūtras, one can easily write copiously about Tārā without fear of going astray simply by applying these descriptions to Her, though of course there must always remain infinitely many other qualities not described.[21]

Some may wonder how Tārā can be both a Bodhisattva and

a Buddha at once. Is not a Bodhisattva someone who is working towards Buddhahood but has not yet attained it, or even someone who has declined Enlightenment so as to be able to stay in *saṃsāra* and help other sentient beings? A Bodhisattva's nature is so paradoxical that the confusion is understandable. The Bodhisattva is totally dedicated to the welfare of others; although the most perfect way of helping others is to be fully Enlightened, she or he should not seek Enlightenment but should simply seek to benefit others, driving them all to Enlightenment first and herself or himself entering last of all, like a shepherd driving his flock in front of him. Although this is her aim, the result is that she attains Enlightenment quicker than ever, the law being that the last shall be first. She is then in *Nirvāṇa*, but because of her perfect Compassion does not 'enter' *Nirvāṇa* in the sense of disappearing into blissful extinction and ceasing to manifest for the benefit of sentient beings. Enlightened, she continues to perform the actions of a Bodhisattva for others' good, using the powers of a Buddha to do so as effectively as can be done; in this way she is the most perfect of Bodhisattvas.

3b. *Goddess of Action.* Although all Tantric deities are Buddhas, with identical powers, each tends to specialize in a particular field; this can be attributed to the effect of vows made before their Enlightenment. Tārā is the *karma-devī*, the Goddess of Action or Queen of the Action Family—She frequently appears in *maṇḍalas* with Her consort Amoghasiddhi, Lord of the Action Family, who like Her is green in colour.[22] Her speciality is acting with lightning swiftness to aid those in distress. In dire emergency where there is not even time to say Her ten-syllable mantra, Her devotee need only say OṂ TĀṂ SVĀHĀ, or even just think of Her, and She will be already there.

*Karma* also means a tantric rite, with which Tārā is well endowed. One of Her most popular forms is with a set of twenty-one emanations, each of whom has rites for her own special function, but there are countless other forms for different purposes. She is by no means always green, two-armed and peaceful, but according to the rite may be fierce, many-armed and of various colours. The best-known specialized form is White Tārā, who is practised for the sake of long life. Vajra-Tārā, golden in colour and with four faces and eight arms, was popular in India for rites such as driving away enemies and subjugating, though Tārā's main aspect for subjugating is the seductive red, four-armed Kurukullā. There is a special aspect of Tārā for saving from each of the eight great fears—a red, lion-faced Tārā with yellow eyes and yellow hair for saving from lions, and so on, each with Her special mantra and gestures—but in art Tārā usually performs these functions in Her ordinary green form. If you cannot find a ready-made form of Tārā for the particular rite you wish to accomplish, you need only visualize Her usual form and insert your special request into the ten-syllable mantra before the SVĀHĀ.

3c. *Feminine model for practice.* The aim of Tantric practice is actually to be the deity. In meditation one visualizes oneself with the deity's body—a body not of flesh and blood but of light—seeing the world the deity's way with the Right View of Emptiness and with overwhelming compassion towards every sentient being, and performing the deity's actions such as purifying everyone and everything so that the entire universe is a *maṇḍala* palace and Pure Land and all the beings are deities. Between meditation sessions also, one should try to feel all the time that one is the deity, and behave fittingly. If one's deity is Tārā, then, one comes to identify with Tārā, in effect to model oneself on Her.

Now Tārā is female; and not just symbolically female, according to the system of Buddhist Tantra whereby male is compassionate skilful Means and female is Wisdom of Emptiness, but female by deliberate choice in order to show that a woman's body is at least as good as a man's for benefiting sentient beings and attaining Enlightenment.

There was need for such an example. Although many virtuous women are portrayed in the scriptures, and many, both laywomen and nuns, attained Arhantship, women have generally had inferior status to men within Buddhism, though probably not so inferior as in Indian society at large in the Buddha's time.

The oldest section of the Buddhist canon, the Vinaya, records that the Buddha admitted women to ordination as nuns only with great reluctance, and subject to stringent rules making their order subordinate to that of the monks.[23]

Sūtra teachings often mention birth as a woman as something to be avoided if at all possible, since it is unconducive to spiritual practice. Men should take care not to admire the female form, and women should contemplate the advantages of being a man, create many merits, and dedicate them to being reborn male. This may well have been simply a practical counsel in relation to the social realities of the time and place, not implying any intrinsic inferiority of women; now conditions have changed, it need no longer apply. Nevertheless, it is also taught in both Hīnayāna and Mahāyāna Sūtras that the highest stages cannot be attained in a woman's form. In the Pali canon, the Buddha teaches:

> It is impossible, it cannot happen that a woman Arahant should be a Complete and Perfect Buddha, it cannot be; ... but it is possible that a man Arahant should be a Complete and Perfect Buddha, this can be.[24]

A Theravādin commentary, the *Cariyāpiṭaka Aṭṭhakathā*, teaches that a Bodhisattva's aspiration can succeed only if made by a man.[25] In a well-known Mahāyāna Sūtra, the 'Lotus Sūtra' (*Sad-dharma-puṇḍarīka*), Śāriputra claims that a woman can be neither an irreversible Bodhisattva nor a Buddha.[26] The same Sūtra and others teach that all the Bodhisattvas in Pure Lands are male.[27] Though there are one or two examples of high female Bodhisattvas, as in the *Vimalakīrti-nirdeśa-sūtra*, the overwhelming consensus of the Sūtras is that to progress beyond a certain stage on the Bodhisattva Path a female[28] is obliged to become male—either by being reborn or by instantaneous magical transformation. Among the more than a thousand Buddhas mentioned in the Sūtras, it is hard to find even one female.

The Mahāyāna Buddhist ideal is thus quite definitely male. Among Indians of two thousand years ago it could not have been otherwise. Though it might have been logical to represent high Bodhisattvas and Buddhas as sexless or hermaphrodite, reflecting the perfect harmony of masculine and feminine within their minds, in practice this would have aroused derision.

In the West, however, there is no question of telling women they should despise their female nature; and furthermore, looking at the mess the pursuit of mostly male ideas and values has got the world into, 'Battle against Nature' and all, not a few men as well as women now find it hard to believe that the ideal human being has to be male, and the thought of an all-male Pure Land often fails to arouse undiluted enthusiasm. In these circumstances the ideal of humanity represented by Tārā is more than welcome.

Although Bodhisattva images evolved from masculine-heroic to a sublime combination of inner power and compassionate softness, which strikes us as feminine,[29] Tārā could be accepted as a female Buddha only thanks to the rise of Tantra. There women are revered as the source of wisdom. Guru Padmasaṃbhava, the main introducer of Tantra to Tibet, is reported to have said:

> The basis for realizing enlightenment is a human body. Male or female—there is no great difference. But if she develops the mind bent on enlightenment, the woman's body is better.[30]

Still, even in Tantra, most of the female deities are almost anonymous consorts of the male deities; Tārā's independence is unusual. It seems to match the way She took Her Bodhisattva Vow, relying on Her own wisdom even against received tradition with all its weight of authority—a courageous example, most relevant now Buddhist teachings come laden with much tradition that need not always apply to us. It also illustrates Her completeness, that She has fully developed both the feminine and the masculine within Herself, as every practitioner, woman or man, must.

Tārā as a model of practice is extended by Her emanations or incarnations recorded as having lived in Tibet. These include the Chinese princess Kong-j'o (Chin.: Wên-ch'êng kung-chu), who in 641 married King Song-tsän gam-po of Tibet, and with his Nepalese wife converted him to Buddhism. She is credited with introducing the Buddhist traditions of painting and sculpture to Tibet, founding the Ra-mo-ch'e temple in Lhasa and many other pious works.[31] Song-tsän gam-po himself is supposed to have been an emanation of Avalokiteśvara, and his Nepalese queen one of Bhṛkuṭī. In the next century there was Ye-she Ts'o-gyäl, queen of King Tr'i-song de-tsän (755–97?) and secret consort and chief disciple of Padmasaṃbhava; She was an emanation of Sarasvatī, an aspect of Tārā. Her biography,[32] though much of it is highly esoteric, is full of inspiration. Then in 1062, or perhaps 1055, Wên-ch'êng was reborn as Ma-chik Lap-drön-ma, who according to a prophecy by Padmasaṃbhava was also a reincarnation of Ye-she Ts'o-gyäl; she achieved great fame as the founder of a Chö tradition.[33]

### *Conclusion*

This is a brief introduction to Tārā, based on hearsay and smatterings of intellectual knowledge; in fact Her nature is inexhaustible, far more profound than I can tell of, and limitlessly adaptable. Each of the three strands I have described is so rich that it can quite easily be mistaken for the whole, especially since each thread is as it were of polished gold, reflecting parts of the others. For example, a follower of Jung would concentrate on the Mother Goddess strand, while a Tibetan lama would repudiate it and find the Tantric strand all-sufficient: in his system, everything about Tārā was taught by Śākyamuni Buddha and the possibility of Hindu influence does not arise. I as a Western scholar cannot accept that view literally because of the absurdities it leads to. To see Tārā as a Mother Goddess you have to step outside the Buddhist framework, which is hard for a Tibetan, but for a Westerner coming to Tārā from outside Buddhism the Mother Goddess aspect may well be the first thing she sees, as it must have been for many Indians.

As Tārā becomes part of the lives of Westerners, we are likely to come to see Her in new ways. It is also quite possible She may offer some inspiration to our artists and poets; I point out that while Tārā the Tantric Deity has to be drawn precisely according to the traditional prescriptions that come to us through Tibet, Tārā the Bodhisattva and Tārā the Mother Goddess do not—there is room for experiment, as one can see from Indian Buddhist art.

## THIS BOOK

### *Contents*

This is a collection of source texts on Tārā, with the emphasis on Indian Buddhism, the common origin of the many Buddhist traditions and schools of Tibet, China and elsewhere. All have been translated by myself either directly from the original or, if (as in the case of most of the Indian texts) this is not available, from Tibetan translations. The majority are translated into English for the first time.

I begin, naturally enough, with the canonical texts deemed to be the Word of the Buddha. The longest included here is the complete Tantra of Tārā, *The Origin of All Rites*. This is the main surviving fragment of a once much longer Tantra, *The Origin of Tārā*. Its chief claim to fame is that it includes the Sanskrit text of the most widely used of all songs to Tārā, the *Praise in Twenty-one Homages*. It also includes much else of interest and historical importance, so merited translation despite its feeble literary qualities, which can hardly have gained by its translation into Tibetan. There follow two poetical works, one a sermon supposed to have been taught by Tārā in a heavenly realm, the other presenting Tārā's hundred and eight Names for devotees to chant; this fortunately survives in the original Sanskrit and is noteworthy for its beautiful introduction set on Mount Potala.

In Part Two I make a detailed study of the *Praise in Twenty-one Homages*, based on Indian and Tibetan commentaries, for the benefit of the many Westerners who already recite this regularly and would like to understand it more deeply. Although the earliest Tibetan commentator, Jetsün Dr'ak-pa Gyäl-ts'än, described it as 'easy to understand',[34] his assessment is belied by the many disagreements that have since appeared among the commentators and between them and the Sanskrit text. Some may find this part heavy going and beginners may wish to skip the commentary on first reading.

The Prologue and Part Three contain a single text, a history of Tārā's Tantra in the Indic world written in 1604 by the Tibetan historian Tāranātha, based on tales he heard from his Indian *gurus*. It mostly concerns stories of the lineage-holders of the *Origin of Tārā Tantra*, and their miraculous deeds performed through Tārā's aid. In addition it contains many other stories of Tārā's miracles, arranged by subject rather than chronologically, which are of value in showing how Indians (and Tibetans) thought of Tārā. The history reveals that the transmission of this Tantra did not pass straight from India to Tibet but first went on a long circuit through Thailand, Cambodia and Nepāl. Earlier parts of the history are somewhat confused. I have been at some pains to sort things out by comparison with other sources, wherever possible giving some sort of estimate of the date of each person mentioned; no doubt with a large library and a great deal of spare time these estimates could be improved, but Tantric history is an extremely intricate and uncertain subject.

The heart of the book is the Indian songs in Part Four. I have tried to put them in roughly chronological order and give some biographical information on each author, but often neither the period he lived in nor anything else about him is known with certainty. The outstanding work among them is certainly the famous *Sragdharā* (*Garland-bearing*) *Praise* of Sarvajñamitra. It has an unfair advantage over the others as it is the only one for which I had the Sanskrit text; though philosophical texts may survive translation into Tibetan unscathed, poetry like this loses a great deal—besides the impossibility of transmitting word-play and ambiguities, Tibetan has perhaps a tenth of the vocabulary of Sanskrit, so the most dazzling masterpiece tends to come out sounding rather flat. In addition, whenever one has the opportunity to check, one finds that in this kind of work the Tibetan translators were by no means as infallible as is sometimes thought. Knowing Sanskrit poetry only through its Tibetan translation is like knowing an oil painting only through a black and white engraving of it. If the original texts were available, some of the other songs such as Candragomin's and Nāgārjuna's might run Sarvajñamitra's closer.

It will be seen that the songs are very varied. Some contain scarcely any technical terms, others abound in them, so that to explain their meanings in detail would fill many volumes. But it would have given quite a wrong impression of the literature on Tārā to leave out the latter kind just because some readers will find them hard to understand in places.

Part Five gives a few songs from the Tibetan continuation of Indian Buddhism, demonstrating that the tradition of poetic tribute to the Goddess was still very much alive as recently as the last century; there is of course no reason why it should not continue today. Part Six looks very briefly at the vast field of Tārā's ritual with three short *sādhanas*. An extensive treatment of Tārā's place in Tibetan Buddhism and Her rituals may be found in Stephan Beyer's *The Cult of Tārā*, which even if his translations of verses are not as reliable as they might be provides excellent insight.

Tārā's Chinese counterpart Kuan-yin falls outside the scope of this book, but everyone interested in Tārā should certainly read John Blofeld's exquisite little book *Compassion Yoga*, which shows that Tārā and Kuan-yin still behave much as Tārā did in India, and has some valuable remarks on the manner of their existence.

## *The Translations*

A prose translation of a song to the Goddess is, to my mind, no translation at all. My metre may be loose, but it is there, with a fixed number of stressed syllables in the line (usually the same as in the Tibetan) and either one or two unstressed between each. This way, no loss of accuracy is necessary; those capable of comparing my translations with the originals will find they correspond word for word at least as closely as any non-metrical translation, in the sense that if one translated them back into the original language the original text would be a plausible result. This is quite different from imitating every quirk of Sanskrit or Tibetan syntax and etymology, a practice that leads to numerous errors.

The works translated contain many words that have no close English equivalent. For upwards of a hundred of them I have found it best to retain the Sanskrit term. One class of such terms particularly frequent here is the names of the many kinds of supernatural beings from Indian mythology—*gandharvas, vidyādharas, yakṣas, nāgas, asuras* and numerous others. Even if the correspondences with our native species were agreed on, which is far from the case, it would just sound grotesque to replace them with elves, fairies, dryads, water-sprites, giants and the like—who takes these seriously any more?[35] Likewise there are the names of Indian plants, not least Tārā's own *utpala* flower, most of them a lot shorter and easier to say in Sanskrit than in Latin; and there are Indian musical instruments with their own special sounds, and Indian castes. Apart from such general terms there are the common technical terms of Buddhism already much better known to most Western students in Sanskrit than in any particular translation—words such as *Arhant, Bodhicitta, dhyāna* and *Dharmakāya* (which, with the other *Kāyas,* has attracted some outstandingly unrecognizable translations).

For all the Sanskrit words used, and likewise the translated technical terms, some explanation is given in the notes or the Glossary, but in some cases this can be no more than a first introduction. To understand Buddhist technical terms you have to build up gradually in your mind the concepts they label, through systematic study, just as with scientific terms. For this reason it is useless to expect translators to find a term's one magic translation that the rawest beginner will at once grasp correctly—there is none. Every word has different associations for different readers, and whatever a translator puts is going to mislead someone; but by proper study you can learn to call up appropriate associations, if you recognize the term.

Proper names are normally given in their original language when possible, which means that some Indian names have had to be translated back from Tibetan into Sanskrit. An asterisk in front indicates a speculative reconstruction. Some personal names, however, bear the honorific suffix *-pa,* which is a Tibetan abbreviation of the Sanskrit *-pāda*. This is retained because *Tilli-pa* and *Nāro-pa* are much more familiar than the Indian forms *Tailika-pāda* and *Nāro-pāda*. Some names are variable or of uncertain spelling.

### *Pronouncing Sanskrit*

Some attention to the correct pronunciation of Sanskrit words and names will help in reading the verses. Sanskrit spelling (unlike English) is rigorously phonetic and no harder than that of most European languages, therefore it would be absurd not to use the standard system of romanization, which is understood all over the world. No newspaper anglicizes the spelling of French or Spanish names, or even Polish. Surely my readers can spare a moment to look at the following few points of pronunciation?

The vowels *ā, ī, ū, e, ai, o* and *au* are long, as in f*a*ther, pol*i*ce, r*u*de, pr*ey*, *ai*sle, s*o* and Fr*au*, while *a, i, u* and *ṛ* are short, as in *a*non, p*i*n, p*u*t and p*re*tty. Pronounce *c* as in '*c*ello, *ś* and *ṣ* as in *s*ure, *ṅ* as in si*ng*, *th* and *ph* approximately as in an*th*ill and u*ph*ill. Double consonants, e.g. in Bu*ddh*a, last longer than single ones.

In verse it is also good to know where the stress falls in a Sanskrit word. Any syllable is 'heavy' if its vowel is long or followed by a group of two or more consonants, otherwise it is light. (Note that the aspirated consonants—*kh, gh, ch, jh, ṭh, ḍh, th, dh, ph, bh*—each count as single, being written with one letter in Indian scripts). If the penultimate syllable is heavy, it is stressed, e.g. *dha-rma-KĀ-ya, mai-TRE-ya, ku-ru-KU-llā, mṛ-DAṄ-ga*. If it is light, but the syllable before is heavy, then that is stressed, e.g. *ḌĀ-ki-nī, YO-gi-nī, UT-pa-la, vai-RO-ca-na, a-va-LO-ki-ta, sa-RAS-va-tī*. If both these are light, the third from last syllable is stressed, if there is one, e.g. *BHA-ga-va-tī, MA-dhya-ma-ka*. In any case, the stress is not very strong—in Sanskrit verse it plays no role.

### *Pronouncing Tibetan*

Since Tibetan spelling is very elaborate, Tibetan names are given in the text in an English phonetic transcription. These renderings represent a simplified version of one of many modern pronunciations as it sounds to someone brought up in the South of England; centuries ago the pronunciation would have been quite different and no doubt much closer to the spelling. The correct spellings, indispensable for identification, may be found in the notes or the index.

In the phonetic transcription, apostrophes indicate aspiration,[36] *e* and *o* tend to be longish, *a, i* and *u* are usually short but sometimes long, and the umlaut vowels *ä, ü, ö* are much as in German. Tibetan words are usually stressed noticeably on the first syllable. Names of authors and of Tibetans active in the West are not necessarily written in this system.

*Pronouns*

In view of Tārā's evident feminist leanings and Her perfection as an ideal, I have seen fit to give priority to feminine pronouns, using 'she' in the sense of 'she or he' and so on, in the parts of this book that are of my own composition; in the translations, however, this has sometimes seemed inappropriate. Pronouns referring to Tārā, and often to other Buddhas also, are capitalized.

*Acknowledgments*

I thank the Venerable Lamas and western Saṅgha: Geshe Thubten Lodan, Zasep Tulku, Lama Thubten Yeshe, Geshe Rabten, Gonsar Tulku, Geshe Kayang, Geshe Jampa Tekchok, Nick Ribush, Robina Courtin and Hermes Brandt for their various contributions of teachings, advice, and loan or gift of texts; also Professors Alex Wayman and Lokesh Chandra, and others. My parents and other benefactors have supported me during part of this work or subsidized the facilities I have used at Tharpa Choeling, Nalanda Monastery, the Tibet-Institut, Rikon, and elsewhere. The drawings by Andy Weber were benefacted by my father. Countless other beings have also contributed.

Martin Willson
Nalanda Monastery
Lavaur, France
June 1985

*Note to the Second Edition*

I have taken the opportunity offered by the reprinting of this book to correct whatever errors have come to my notice since the first edition appeared. In particular, the translation of the Sragdharā Praise has been checked against Vidyabhusana's edition of the Sanskrit text and commentary and a number of changes made.

Martin Willson
October 1995

# *Prologue*

From *The Golden Rosary, A History Illuminating the Origin of the Tantra of Tārā*, by Tāranātha.

Homage to the Guru!

> Homage to You, for whom all *dharmas* are simple
> from the start!
> Homage to You who do pervade all things with
> great Compassion!
> Homage to the supreme salvation of all migrating
> beings!
> Homage to You, O Tārā, who are the Mother of the
> Conquerors!

Let us relate here the stories told of the beginning of the teaching of the Tantra of Tārā.

Of yore, in beginningless time, there appeared in the universe called Manifold Light[1] the *Bhagavan Tathāgata* Dundubhi-svara (Drum-Sound). There was a princess called Moon of Wisdom-knowledge[2] who was extremely devoted to his Teaching [5]. For a million million years, she made offering to that Buddha and his countless attendant Saṅgha of *Śrāvakas* and Bodhisattvas, every day setting out offering materials of value equal to the ten directions packed tightly for twelve *yojanas* all around with jewels.

Finally, she produced the Thought of Enlightenment (*Bodhicitta*); this was her first generation of *Bodhicitta*.

At that time some *bhikṣus* urged her, 'Because of these roots of virtue, if you pray in this body that you may become a man and perform the deeds according to the Teachings, then you will be thus transformed. Therefore that is what you should do.' [6]

It is said there was much discussion. Finally, the princess spoke, saying:

> Here there is no man, there is no woman,
> No self, no person, and no consciousness.
> Labelling 'male' or 'female' has no essence,
> But deceives the evil-minded world,

etc. And she made the vow, 'There are many who desire Enlightenment in a man's body, but none who work for the benefit of sentient beings in the body of a woman. Therefore, until *saṃsāra* is empty, I shall work for the benefit of sentient beings in a woman's body.'

Then for a million million years she remained in the royal palace. Behaving skilfully towards objects of the five senses, she practised concentration, and thereby attained the acceptance that *dharmas* are unproduced (*anutpattika-dharma-kṣānti*), and [7] realized the *samādhi* called 'Saving all Sentient Beings'. By the power of this realization, every day in the morning she then freed a million million sentient beings from worldly thoughts, and would not eat until they were established in [that] acceptance. Every evening also, she so established a similar number. Because of this, her previous name was changed and she became Tārā, the Saviouress. Then the *Tathāgata* Dundubhi-svara prophesied, 'As long as you manifest the unsurpassed Enlightenment, you will be known only by the name of Goddess Tārā.'

Then, in the eon called Vibuddha, 'Expanded'[3], she vowed before the *Tathāgata* Amoghasiddhi to protect and guard from all harm the sentient beings of all the infinite realms (*kṣetra*) of the ten directions [8]. Therefore, concentrating in the *samādhi* of Overcoming All Māras, each day for ninety-five eons she established a hundred thousand billion ($10^{17}$) leaders of sentient beings in *dhyāna*, and each evening she subdued a billion ($10^{12}$) Māras, Lords of the Paranirmita-vaśavartin[4] heavens. Thus she received the names of Tārā (Saviouress), Loving Mother,[5] Swift One,[6] and Heroine.[7]

Then, in the eon called Unobstructed,[8] a *bhikṣu* called Glow of Immaculate Light[9] was consecrated with light-rays of Great Compassion by all the *Tathāgatas* of the ten directions, and so became Āryâvalokita. [9] Then again the *Tathāgatas* of the Five Families and all other Buddhas and Bodhisattvas consecrated him with great light-rays of the nature of Omniscient Wisdom-knowledge, so that from the mixing of the earlier and later light-rays as father and mother, there came about the goddess Tārā. Having emerged from Avalokita's heart, She fulfilled the intention of all the Buddhas and protected sentient beings from the eight and the sixteen Great Fears.

Then, in the eon called Mahābhadra (Greatly Fortunate),[10] She taught as appears at the 'Immovable' encouragement stage.[11]

Then, in the eon called Asaṅka, through consecration by all the *Tathāgatas* of the ten directions [10], She became the Mother who produces all the Buddhas.[12] All this was in beginningless past time.

Then, in the present eon, on Mount Potala, amid innumerable, measureless Buddhas, Bodhisattvas, *devas*, *nāgas*, *yakṣas* and others, Āryâvalokita taught ten million [*ślokas* of] Tantras of Tārā. It is said he worked the weal of the sentient beings of the six classes in this way in the Kṛtayuga (Age of Perfection). In the Tretayuga, when these [Tantras] had disappeared, six hundred thousand [*ślokas*] appeared. In the Dvaparayuga, when these too had disappeared, twelve thousand appeared. Then in the Kaliyuga (Age of Conflict) there appeared this collection on Tārā, having a thousand *ślokas*. My Guru[13] has said about this, 'In those ages, such as the Kṛtayuga, [11] there were in fact no books of Tantra. But since they were used extensively in the lands of *devas* and *vidyādharas*, it was intended they would also become of great benefit to other sentient beings.' However, it is not contradictory that even in those Ages there may have been disciples of Mantra. Therefore it is possible that there were also books, and it is clear that we should not hold the extremes [—only disciples or only books—] as certain, [i.e. there could have been both].

In particular, these Tantras were again recited and taught by our Teacher (Buddha Śākyamuni), since it is taught in their Explanatory Tantra, the **Ḍākinī-guhya-bindu*,[14]

> Tantras taught by the Lion of the Śākyas[15]
> On the peak of Potala Mountain.

The traditional story of this, from the lips of my predecessors, is as follows. It is said that after the Teacher [12] had agreed to demonstrate to sentient beings the deeds of Awakening, He sat on the *Bodhimaṇḍa* (the 'seat of Enlightenment' beneath the *bodhi* tree at Bodhgayā) and with a ray of light from the point between His eyebrows He filled all the abodes of the Māras. When, thereupon, the armies of the Māras assembled, Tārā laughed eight times, so that they all fell on the ground in a faint. Then the Teacher transformed Himself into the Fierce, Immovable One (Krodhācala), and subdued the Māras with the *samādhi* that crushes[16] all Māras. Afterwards, when He had become fully Enlightened on the seat of Enlightenment, He became nondual with the *Tathāgata* Akṣobhya, and when the Goddess Tārā worshipped Him, taught Her Tantra at length.

He similarly [13] taught at length the *maṇḍala* of the Conquerors (*Jinas*) of the Six Families. Then, so that the Tantras He had thus explained would not disappear, He wished to show them to sentient beings of the six types of destiny. Going to Potala Mountain with a host of Buddhas and Bodhisattvas, He gave empowerment to countless, innumerable sentient beings, including *devas*, *nāgas*, *yakṣas* and *gandharvas*. When He had explained to them the Mantra Vehicle, He established them in *siddhi*.

Finally, He entrusted the Tantras to Vajrapāṇi. They were practised in Alakāvatī[17] and the other abodes of the *vidyādharas*. So that not all the Tantras would disappear from the world of human beings, Vajrapāṇi became King Indrabhūti,[18] wrote all the Tantras in books, and concealed them as a so-called Dharma Treasury [14]. After that, it is said they were practised by Heroes (*vīra*) and *yoginīs*.

[The text is continued on page 178.]

# Part One
## *Canonical texts*

# 1 *Tārā in the Mañjuśrī-Mūla-Kalpa*

Tārā is not mentioned in the early Mahāyāna Sūtras such as the *Sad-dharma-puṇḍarīka*, or the *Kāraṇḍa-vyūha*, where Avalokiteśvara has an honoured place.[1] She seems to make Her appearance in the canonical literature when the Mahāyāna is starting to turn into Vajrayāna. Thus for example the *Mahāvairocana-sūtra*, which was brought to China by Śubha-kara-siṃha in 716 and forms the basis of Japanese esoteric Buddhism (Shingon),[2] mentions Her as an emanation of Avalokiteśvara.[3]

She appears several times in the *Mañjuśrī-mūla-kalpa*. This is a bulky work, known to us in three versions.[4] An early ninth-century Tibetan translation mentioned in the *Padma thang yig*[5] is lost, and it is not known how many chapters it contained. The Chinese version, translated in the second half of the ninth century, contains thirty-two chapters. The extant Tibetan version, translated c.1040, omits one of these and adds five others to make thirty-six chapters. Further chapters continued to be added over the centuries so that by the sixteenth century, when the surviving Sanskrit manuscript (found in a monastery in South India) was copied, the tally was fifty-five chapters. This pattern is typical of the history of many Mahāyāna Sūtras and Tantras.

The overall title of the work in the Tibetan version is *Ārya-Mañjuśrī-mūla-tantra*, and it is placed in the Tantra section of the Kangyur. However, the chapter colophons, like the Sanskrit MS, call it the *Mañjuśrī-mūla-kalpa*, 'Basic Ritual of Mañjuśrī', and mostly say that it is, or forms part of, a *Bodhisattva-piṭaka-avataṃsaka-mahāyāna-vaipulyasūtra*—there is no mention of *tantra*.

Some editions of the Kangyur also contain a *Tārā-mūla-kalpa*. Almost all the first fourteen chapters are common to that text and the *Mañjuśrī-mūla-kalpa*.

*Chapter 2* of the *Mañjuśrī-mūla-kalpa* describes an extremely elaborate *maṇḍala*, in which Tārā finds a place close to the centre, though not a prominent one.

The central figure is Buddha Śākyamuni, with the Bodhisattva Mañjuśrī below Him, Avalokiteśvara on His right, and Vajrapāṇi on His left. Tārā is the second of six goddesses accompanying Avalokiteśvara, the others being Pāṇḍaravāsinī, Bhrukuṭī (= Bhṛkuṭī), Prajñā-pāramitā, Tathāgata-Locanā and Uṣṇīṣa-rājā.[6]

*Chapter 4*, like Chapter 2 common to all versions of *Mañjuśrī-mūla-kalpa*, gives detailed instructions for the preparation of a painted cloth (*paṭa*), a forerunner of present-day Tibetan *thangkas*. This too is very elaborate, but Tārā is much more conspicuous than in the *maṇḍala* and She is described at some length.

The central figure is again the Lord Śākyamuni, teaching the Dharma. Below Him the two *Nāga* kings, Nanda and Upananda, half-man, half-snake, pay homage, in the middle of a beautiful, wide lake of lotuses. On Śākyamuni's left (in Tantra, the Wisdom side) are eight great Bodhisattvas led by Mañjuśrī, and above them a great palace housing eight Buddhas. On His right (the Compassion side) are eight more Bodhisattvas—Maitreya, Samantabhadra, Avalokiteśvara, Vajrapāṇi, etc. Above them are eight *Pratyekabuddhas* and eight great Disciples—Śāriputra, Mahā-maudgalyāyana, Mahā-kāśyapa, etc.

On either side of the *Nāga*-kings, a mountain of jewels rises from the lake. Atop the left-hand mountain, below Mañjuśrī, is the terrible king Yamāntaka, in an unbearably fierce, blazing, two-armed form. At the foot of this mountain, the practitioner of Mañjuśrī who is having the picture painted should be shown.

The right-hand mountain, beneath Avalokiteśvara, is full of heavenly flowers and very tall, like a staircase of rubies. On its summit of lapis lazuli sits Tārā, as follows.[7]

> Draw resting on this the Goddess Who is the Compassion of Āryâvalokiteśvara, Ārya-Tārā, adorned with all the ornaments, in an upper garment of precious[8] silken cloth and a lower garment of multicoloured silken cloth, Her whole body adorned with a woman's ornaments. In Her left hand is placed a blue *utpala*. She is golden in colour and slender of waist, [though] not too thin, and neither too young nor too old. Her mind in *dhyāna*, She is listening to the teaching. With Her right hand She is granting boons. Her body slightly bent, She is seated in *paryaṅka*, Her gaze turned a little towards Āryâvalokiteśvara. She is encompassed on all sides by a garland of flames.
>
> The mountain peak, of lapis lazuli and jewels, is also clothed in *punnāga* trees, studded with flowers on every branch, abounding with open flowers, sheltering the Lady Tārā. Their bending boughs are very variegated, covered with young shoots[9] and sprouts and ablaze with a multitude of colours, and look as if turned towards the Goddess Tārā.

44 The Goddess destroying all hindrances
is the supreme remover of fears.
For the practitioner's protection
draw Her, righteous,[10] granting boons.

45 The daughter of the ten Powers and Compassion
is the Goddess wearing a woman's form.
Draw Her, the bestower of boons,
for the welfare of all beings.

46 This Goddess is the mother of[11]
Prince Mañjughoṣa, great in splendour.

To destroy all hindrances
of the practitioner completely,

47 [To protect the lords of men
or to gain fortune, draw Her picture!]

Smaller versions of the same painting are described in the following chapters, without additional details of Tārā.

*Chapter 53, The Prophecy of the Kings* (*Rāja-vyākaraṇa*),[12] is one of those added to the *Mañjuśri-mūla-kalpa* between the late ninth and early eleventh centuries. It recounts the dynastic history of several kingdoms of Central and Northeastern India up to about 770 AD, presenting it as a prophecy by the Buddha. Bu-tön and other historians have made extensive use of it, despite its cryptic style.[13]

Hidden away towards the end of this lengthy and tedious chronicle are some verses on Tārā. Like the rest, they make a virtue of being obscure and ambiguous; the following preliminary attempt at a translation is from both the Sanskrit[14] and the Tibetan,[15] adopting at each point whichever seems closer to making sense. The passage refers to the praises of Tārā by Candragomin, and mentions some of the places where Her cult flourished.

820 And where the Blessed One did enter
Peace without remainder, there
These two mantras are to be practised,
the Goddess Tārā with Bhṛkuṭī.

821 The object of practice will thus appear
always on the seashore and
everywhere on the bank of the best
of rivers, the Ganges, lotus-born.

822 Then that very [master of
the ten Stages, the tamer of
Sentient beings, the] Bodhisattva
famous by the name of Candra
Proclaimed that Tārā was the queen
of knowledge, great in magic powers.

823 The Goddess, wearing a woman's form,
wanders everywhere in the world
so as to benefit sentient beings,
with Her mind tender with Compassion,

824 And enduring staying in the world,
lives under a woman's name.

. . .

828 For the increase of everyone's
contentment, [She] dwells in [the East];
Multiplying Herself again
and again in a thousand places,

829 She wanders in the entire earth
surrounded by the four oceans.
Then She is realized in the East,
or afterwards in Vārāṇasī.

830 The eastern country is proclaimed
as the Goddess's own land (*kṣetra*).
There the *yakṣa*-king of great
majesty, Jambhala, succeeds.

. . .

832 [Then the wrathful mantras are
practised in the southern region,
In the lands of thieves and *mlecchas*,
and likewise in the oceans,]

833 And then a mighty *yakṣa*-king
also practises Tārā.
In Harikela, Karmaraṅga,
Kāmarūpa and Kalaśa,[16]

834 [Many female envoys and
*yakṣas* achieve great miracles.]

# 2 *Tārā's Tantra, the Origin of All Rites*

## GENERAL REMARKS

As Tārā became a major Buddhist deity, references to Her in Tantras of other deities were no longer enough. She had to have Tantras of Her own.

Long ago, Tāranātha tells us,[1] Lord Avalokita taught some ten million *ślokas*, or well over a hundred million words, of Tantras of Tārā, but in the course of time most of them have been lost to the human world. In particular, although many of these Tantras were transmitted to Nāro-pa and Atīśa, they were not taught in Tibet, because of feelings that they were liable to misuse. Thus the present Tantra was not translated into Tibetan until the late twelfth century, when this feeling had weakened.[2] K'ä-drup Je, in his *Introduction to the Buddhist Tantric Systems*,[3] describes it as the most important Tantra of Tārā—at least among those extant in Tibetan. Beyer, in his very thorough and readable survey, *The Cult of Tārā*,[4] mentions it as a central text of the cult, 'the closest thing we have to a complete textbook on the practice of Tārā's cult, although it gives every appearance of being late and synthetic'. No doubt it was compiled from sections from a number of works—its component parts are sometimes rather weakly related and vary considerably in atmosphere.

ANALYSIS OF CONTENTS

In its present form, the Tantra is divided into thirty-five chapters, as follows:

[*Opening section*]
1 Introduction (*nidāna*)
2 Offering (*pūjā*)
3 Praise (The *Praise in Twenty-one Homages*)
4 Deities (*devatā*) (The *maṇḍala* of nine Tārās)
5 Empowerment (*abhiṣeka*)
6 Mantras

[*The Rites of the Four Activities*]
7 The Rite for Pacifying (*śānti-karman*)
8 The Rite for Increasing (*puṣ ṭi-karman*)
9 The Rite for Subjugating (*vaśya-karman*)
10 The Fierce Rite (*raudra-karman*)
11 All Activities (*viśva-karma*)

[*The Mothers of the Five Families*]
12 The Mother of the Vajra Family
13 The Mother of the Lotus Family
14 The Mother of All the *Tathāgatas*
15 The Mother of the Jewel Family
16 The Mother of the Action Family

17 Burnt-offering (*homa*) [for any of the rites]

[*Circles: A. Protective Circles* (rakṣā-cakra)]
18 Pacifying Protective Circle
19 Subjugating Protective Circle
20 Increasing Protective Circle
21 Greatly Increasing Protective Circle
22 Protective Magic Circle of Great Pacification

[B. *Circles for the rites of the Four Activities*]
23 Pacifying Circle
24 Great Pacification
25 Increasing Circle
26 Fierce Subjugating Circle
27 Dividing and Subjugating Circle

[C. *Miscellaneous Circles*]
28 Driving-away Circle (*uccāṭana-cakra*)
29 Dividing Circle (*bhedana-cakra*)
30 Killing Circle (*māraṇa-cakra*)
31 Insanity-inducing Circle (*madana-cakra*?)
32 Subduing Circle
33 Enemy-subduing Circle
34 Sorcery-subduing Circle

[*Closing section*]
35 The Teaching of the Pledges and Vows (*samaya-saṃvara-nirdeśa*)
— Conclusion.

The Tantra opens with some relatively long chapters forming a more or less coherent narrative. The place of the Teaching and those present are given; the Goddess appears. Questioned by the Bodhisattva Mañjuśrī, the Lord gives teachings on Her—how She is the Mother of all the Buddhas; how to make offerings to Her; Her praise, the famous *Praise in Twenty-one Homages,* given in the original Sanskrit as a *dhāraṇī* or long mantra; how to visualise Her *maṇḍala*; and how empowerment is given. These chapters contain verses, and explanations in the manner of the *Prajñāpāramitā-sūtras*.

Early in Chapter 6, the Tantra turns into a catalogue of information and instructions, and the original mood does not return until the final chapter. After a list of mantras in Chapter 6, we have five chapters describing the rites for achieving the four main activities and 'all activities'. Having prepared the place—for the first two, the peaceful rites, in a room; for the others, in wilder places such as cemeteries—and set out the requisite offerings on a *maṇḍala,* one visualises Tārā in the colour corresponding to the activity and recites the mantra. These colours—white for pacification, yellow for increasing, red for subjugating, green for fierce activity, and dark blue for 'all activities'—form the dominant colour symbolism of this Tantra, often alluded to in the chapters on the magic circles.

Next, Tārā's aspects as Mother of each of the five Families of Buddhas are described. For an extensive and clear account of the Five Families (*pañca-kula*), Lama Govinda's *Foundations of Tibetan Mysticism* may be consulted. These five apparitions are all four-faced and eight-armed, the colour of the body and principal face corresponding to the Family—white for the Vajra Family, whose Lord is Akṣobhya; red for Amitābha's Lotus Family (to which Tārā is normally assigned); yellow for Vairocana's Tathāgata Family; blue for Ratnasaṃbhava's Jewel Family; and green for Amoghasiddhi's Action Family. (Usually one would expect yellow for the Jewel Family and blue or white for the Tathāgata Family.) The right face is white, the left red, and the rear yellow, unless one of these is the principal colour, in which case dark blue is substituted; except that the rear face of the Action Mother is said to be green. Each holds in Her principal right hand the emblem of Her Family—*vajra*, lotus, wheel, jewel and sword respectively. To each is assigned a bizarre, magical rite, tacked on at the end of the chapter without any discernible logical connection.

Chapter 17 describes (in the form suitable for the rite of Pacification) the Burnt-offering with which the practice of any rite should be concluded.

Then come seventeen very short chapters giving brief instructions for a variety of magic circles based on Tārā's mantra—circles for the devotee to wear as a protection, circles to aid in the rites of the main activities, and finally circles for various purposes of sorcery such as driving away enemies and even for killing them or driving them mad. Small wonder that there was some initial reluctance to propagate this Tantra among the aggressive Tibetans! Such rites as killing, of course, are intended to be used only with pure motivation of *Bodhicitta* and Compassion, to prevent enemies of the Dharma from creating further bad karma and causing more suffering for themselves and others. In order to interpret the Tantra's sketchy instructions correctly and actually perform these rites, one would need extensive training under a qualified teacher. Nevertheless, since even to attempt them with wrong motivation would create strong negative karma, Geshe Rabten thought it best to omit the circles for fierce rites.

Finally, with Chapter 35, to one's relief, the atmosphere switches abruptly back to that of the opening chapters with some verses on the behaviour expected of Tārā's devotees. Not only should they avoid killing, stealing and lying, they should abandon eating meat and should be respectful towards women. The Tantra concludes like any Mahāyāna Sūtra with the rejoicing of all the beings present.

## THE MAGICAL RITES

The rites at the ends of Chapters 12 to 16 are not easy to follow, but some help comes from comparison with the *sādhanas* of Vajra-tārā in the Tängyur. Vajra-tārā, with four faces and eight arms, differs no more from the Goddesses described in these chapters than they do from each other.[5] She is used especially for such sorcery. As Ghosh points out,[6] in Her *sādhanas*, 'The maximum number of magical practices and charms with the help of the Tārā-*mantra* is prescribed for bewitching and overpowering women . . . some . . . extremely crude and even cruel.' Of the mantras of our five rites (forms of four of which are found in these *sādhanas*), three are for subjugating, two of these being aimed specifically at women; one is for driving away enemies, and one apparently for killing.

But someone has been playing a practical joke on Tibetan would-be magicians for the last eight centuries—the mantras have been shuffled. Anyone who thought he was summoning a woman with the rite of Chapter 16 was actually driving her away—the mantra given there should have been in Chapter 12. As the best arrangement of the other mantras is uncertain, I have left them all where they appear. Their uses according to the *Vajra-tārā-sādhanas* will be explained in the notes.

Since the other elements of the rites may well be as mixed up as the mantras, it would be foolhardy in the extreme to try to use them. Even with the correct and complete spell to hand, an attempt to injure another person by magic is liable to rebound, causing one's own death or insanity;[7] if the spell itself contains errors, how could it possibly go right?

What are these degraded and revolting practices doing in Tārā's Tantra? Are they not contrary to the moral injunctions of Chapter 35? Their presence does come as a shock, but in fact it is hard to find a major Tantra that is free of such material. Tārā was an extremely popular deity in India; the great bulk of Her devotees must have been ordinary, far from saintly people who sought worldly benefits from their religion just as most Christians do. And we cannot conclude from the male orientation of some of these rites that Tārā's cult in general was largely confined to men, for many stories testify to the involvement of women at all levels from the most mercenary, self-interested worship to the attainment of the highest realizations.

## THE TRANSLATION

This text is known only in its Tibetan translation in the Kangyur. This was made by the translator Ch'ö-kyi zang-po with the Indian teacher Dharma-śrī-mitra. One might be tempted to identify the former with the learned Ch'ö-kyi zang-po of Rong, or Rong-zom Lotsāwa, who is said to have met Atīśa when he arrived in Tibet in 1042,[8] and the latter with Dharma-śrī the One-eyed, of Kashmir, who went to Tibet with his teacher Vajrapāṇi in about 1066.[9] But according to Beyer,[10] not so: it was the translator Ch'ö-kyi zang-po of Chäl, who worked with Śākya-śrī-bhadra when he was in Tibet (1204–13).[11] Perhaps Dharma-śrī-mitra was the *Mahāpaṇḍita* Dharma-śrī who was an Indian disciple of Ch'ak drachom (1153–1216).[12]

For the present translation, the Kangyur reproduced from a manuscript in the Tog Palace in Ladakh was principally used. This is the edition to which the page numbers in square brackets refer. It has the advantage of being outstandingly legible. However, as work proceeded, it became clear that it was not always possible to deduce the correct readings from this version alone, especially in the mantras and the Sanskrit text of the *Praise in Twenty-one Homages*. In the end, the mantras and Sanskrit were checked in all the editions of the Kangyur available in Europe—Derge, Lhasa, Nart'ang, Peking and Tog. We shall refer to these in the notes by their initials: D, L, N, P, and T. In addition, all the mantras and Sanskrit are copied out in the *Collected Works* of Bu-tön Rinpoche,[13] providing version B. For the short mantras in Chapters 12, 13, 15 and 16, the *Vajra-tārā-sādhana* existing in several versions in the Peking Tängyur was used (V1: P4308. V2: P4309. V3: P4312). The Tibetan text was also checked in its entirety against the Lhasa edition and in part against other editions.

Despite this effort, some of the mantras remain unintelligible. There are also some passages in the Tibetan that are less than clear, although this Tantra is much less obscure than those of the *Anuttarayoga* class. It is unfortunate that despite this Tantra's importance, no-one seems ever to have written a commentary on it, except on the *Twenty-one Homages*, which we shall treat in detail later. I have received teachings on some of it from Geshe Kayang at Tharpa Choeling.

## THE TANTRA CALLED THE ORIGIN OF ALL RITES OF TĀRĀ, MOTHER OF ALL THE TATHĀGATAS
(*Sarva-tathāgata-mātṛ*[14]*-tārā-viśvakarma-bhava-tantra-nāma*)

Homage to Ārya-Mañjuśrī!

### *Chapter 1. Introduction*

Thus have I heard at one time. [196] The Lord was residing in the realm of Tuṣita. Countless Bodhisattvas such as Maitreya and Mañjuśrī, and countless [deities] such as Kurukullā and Parṇa-śabarī, and such as Brahmā and Śakra,[15] holding up countless heavenly flowers such as heavenly lotus, *kumuda* and *mandārava* flowers, countless heavenly musical instruments such as conches, *vīṇās*, drums, *mṛdaṅgas* and *śūrpa-vīṇās*, and countless heavenly parasols, banners and flags, circumambulated the Lord clockwise, and made offering with offering-clouds of all kinds of offerings.

Then the Lord concentrated in the concentration called Adamantine, destroyer of hostile forces. Immediately, the earth shook, the circle of the Māras was vanquished, and He sent forth a great shining of light. It was like this: He sent forth all kinds of light—white, red, yellow, green, blue and mixed—which purified all that had suffering; and Tārā, Mother of all the Buddhas, descended on to Kurukullā's crown. Straightway, masses of offerings rained down. That goddess then became [197] like the unclouded disk of the sun.

Then was She praised with this verse of praise:

1 On the whole realm, completely purified,
Many precious flowers descend, like rain.
Mother producing all the three times' Buddhas,
Mother Tārā! Homage and praise to you!

Then the Bodhisattva Mañjuśrī the Youthful draped his upper garment over one shoulder and, kneeling on the right knee, asked the Lord, 'Lord, all the Buddhas of the three times are deep. How therefore does She produce them? How is She their Mother?'

And the Lord said, 'That is true, Mañjuśrī; but all the Buddhas of the three times are also unproduced and unceasing, not defiled and not immaculate, without decrease or increase, and by nature in *Nirvāṇa*; for this reason: that is the nature of all *dharmas*.'[16]

The Bodhisattva Mañjuśrī the Youthful said: 'Lord, how are the Buddhas of the three times produced, who are unproduced and unceasing, not defiled and not immaculate, without decrease or increase, and by nature in *Nirvāṇa*?'

The Lord said: 'Mañjuśrī, [198] the Ultimate is called *Nirvāṇa*, the Universal Law (*dharmadhātu*) is called *Nirvāṇa*; it is a synonym of the True Goal. It[s cause] is Great Compassion. Conventional nature is a synonym of *saṃsāra*. The Mother who produces the Buddhas of the three times is beyond this; therefore She is beyond *saṃsāra* and affliction.[17] Thus, Mañjuśrī, She is to be regarded as the Mother.'

And the Lord said: 'Therefore, Mañjuśrī, with understanding of the Suchness of *dharmas* should one meditate on Her; one should recite this *dhāraṇī*,[18] practise earnestly, understand Her qualities, and make offerings to Her. One should receive instructions and have no doubts. One should act earnestly in the deeds, remember Her praises, and practise the rites severally.'[19] In these words He taught to the Bodhisattva Mañjuśrī the Youthful.

## *Chapter 2. Offering*

Then the Bodhisattva Mañjuśrī the Youthful asked the Lord: 'How, Lord, should one meditate on Her? How should one earnestly practise Her?'

And the Lord said: 'Mañjuśrī, one should direct one's mind like this. All *dharmas*, Mañjuśrī, are unproduced, all *dharmas* are unceasing. All *dharmas* are undefiled; all *dharmas* [199] are in *Nirvāṇa* and by nature pure: so should one meditate. Therefore, Mañjuśrī, one should say this mantra:

> 'OṂ SVABHĀVA-VIŚUDDHĀḤ SARVA-DHARMĀḤ, SVABHĀVA-VIŚUDDHO 'HAṂ.'[20]
>
> (OṂ All *dharmas* are pure by nature, I am pure by nature.)

And the Lord said also: 'One should cultivate Loving-kindness, considering those born from a womb, those born from an egg, those born from moist heat, and those born miraculously. One should generate Great Compassion with regard to birth, aging, sickness and death. One should cultivate Joy and Equanimity with regard to Emptiness, Signlessness and Wishlessness, and the naturally unconditioned. Therefore, Mañjuśrī, the Four Immeasurables are the cause; *Bodhicitta* is their product. Therefore one should earnestly take them to heart.[21]

'Therefore, Mañjuśrī, one should say this mantra:

> 'OṂ BODHICITTA-UTPĀDAYA AHAṂ.'[22]
> (OṂ May I generate *Bodhicitta*!)

And again the Lord spoke, saying, 'Offering should be made with these offerings:

2 'Magically created by whatever
Buddhas dwell in the worlds of the ten
directions,
All kinds of incense, in powders and in pieces,[23]
We'll offer the Mother, Producer of the
Conqu'rors.

3 'Buddha-locanā, high Mother of whatever
*Tathāgatas* dwell in the worlds of the ten
directions!
All kinds of flowers, singly and in garlands, [200]
We'll offer the Mother, Producer of the
Conqu'rors.[24]

4 'Jewel Supreme Mother of whatever
*Tathāgatas* dwell in the worlds of the ten
directions!
All kinds of precious jewels, lamps and garlands
We'll offer the Mother, Producer of the
Conqu'rors.

5 'Pāṇḍara-vāsinī, high Mother of whatever
*Tathāgatas* dwell in the worlds of the ten
directions!
Pure, sweet-smelling water and rivers of
perfume

We'll offer the Mother, Producer of the
Conqu'rors.

6 'High Mother with Divine Actions of whatever
*Tathāgatas* dwell in the worlds of the ten
directions!
Provisions such as hard food and soft food[25]
We'll offer the Mother, Producer of the
Conqu'rors.

7 'Let songs and the sounds of musical
instruments,
Including cymbals, soothing every suff'ring,
And parasols, banners, pennants, flags and
umbrellas
Gather like clouds from all the ten directions!

8 'Let fragrant leafy boughs
of wish-fulfilling trees,
Flowering and other trees gather
from all the ten directions!

9 'Let rain with perfumed fragrance,
rain with pleasing scents
Of grains and flowers and so forth,
definitely descend!

10 'With tumbling brooks and pools
and springs and lakes and ponds,
Lakes of a hundred flavours,
geese[26] and other birds,

11 'A jewel mansion, [201] hung with beautiful
pearls,[27]
With light in east and west, of Sun and Moon,
And apartments most pleasing to the mind,
We'll offer to the Mother, Producer of
Conqu'rors.

'Therefore, Mañjuśrī, these offering mantras should be said:[28]

'OṂ SARVA-TATHĀGATA-DHŪPA-PŪJA-MEGHA-SAMUDRA-SPHARAṆA-SAMAYE HŪṂ!

(OṂ Incense of all the *Tathāgatas* gathers as a pervading ocean of offering-clouds HŪṂ!)
OṂ SARVA-TATHĀGATA-PUṢPA-PŪJA-MEGHA- etc.
(OṂ Flowers of all the *Tathāgatas* . . .)
OṂ SARVA-TATHĀGATA-ĀLOKA-PŪJA-MEGHA- etc.
(OṂ Light of all the *Tathāgatas* . . .)
OṂ SARVA-TATHĀGATA-GANDHA-PŪJA-MEGHA- etc.
(OṂ Perfumes of all the *Tathāgatas* . . .)
OṂ SARVA-TATHĀGATA-NAIVIDYA-PŪJA-MEGHA- etc.
(OṂ Food-offerings of all the *Tathāgatas* . . .)
OṂ SARVA-TATHĀGATA-ŚABDA-PŪJA-MEGHA- etc.'
(OṂ Sounds of all the *Tathāgatas* . . .)

*Chapter 3. Praise*

Then He spoke again to Mañjuśrī the Youthful, saying 'Mañjuśrī, this Mother is Mother of all the Buddhas of the three times. Therefore, Mañjuśrī, take to heart this praise by all the Buddhas of the three times!'

Then the Lord uttered the *dhāraṇī* of praise:

'NAMAḤ SARVA-TATHĀGATĀNĀM. TAD YATHĀ:
OṂ NAMAḤ SŪKASĀṂ, NAMAḤ TĀRĀYAI TĀRA-MITĀ![29]
(Homage to all the *Tathāgatas*, as follows:
OṂ Homage to the Compassionate(?), homage to Tārā, established as Saviour!)

[Now follows the Sanskrit text of the *Praise in Twenty-one Homages*. A translation and commentary is given in Part Two.][30]

*'namas tāre ture vīre*
*kṣaṇair-dyuti-nibhêkṣaṇe/*
*trailokya-nātha-vaktrâbja-*
*vikasat-keśarôdbhave//1//*

*'namaḥ śata-śarac-candra-*
*saṃpūrṇa-paṭalânane/*
*tārā-sahasra-nikara-*
*prahasat-kira*[202]*ṇôjjvale//2//*

*'namaḥ kanaka-nīlâbja-*
*pāṇi-padma-vibhūṣite/*
*dāna-vīrya-tapaḥ-śānti-*
*titikṣā-dhyāna-gocare//3//*

*'namas tathāgatôṣṇīṣa-*
*vijayânanta-cāriṇi/*
*aśeṣa-pāramitā-prāpta-*
*jina-putra-niṣevite//4//*

*'namas tuttāra-hūṃ-kāra-*
*pūritâśā-dig-antare/*
*sapta-loka-kramâkrānti-*
*aśeṣâkarṣaṇa-kṣame//5//*

*'namaḥ śakrânala-brahma-*
*marud-viśvêśvarârcite/*
*bhūta-vetāla-gandharva-*
*gaṇa-yakṣa-puras-kṛte//6//*

*'namas traḍ iti phaṭ-kāra-*
*para-yantra-pramardani/*
*praty-ālīḍha-pada-nyāse*
*śikhi-jvālâkulêkṣaṇe//7//*

*'namas ture mahā-ghore*
*māra-vīra-vināśani/*
*bhṛkuṭī-kṛta-vaktrâbja-*
*sarva-śatru-niṣūdani//8//*

*'namas tri-ratna-mudrâṅka-*
*hṛdyâṅguli-vibhūṣite/*
*bhūṣitâśeṣa-dik-cakra-*
*nikara-sva-karâkule//9//*

*'namaḥ pramuditâṭopa-*
*mukuṭā-kṣipta-mālini/*
*hasat-prahasat-tuttāre*
*māra-loka-vaśaṃkari//10//*

*'namaḥ samanta-bhū-pāla-*
*paṭalâkarṣaṇa-kṣame//*
*calad-bhṛkuṭi-hūṃ-kāra-*
*sarvâpada-vimocani//11//*

*'namaḥ śikhaṇḍa-khaṇḍêndu-*
*mukuṭâbharaṇôjjvale/*
*amitābha-jaṭā-bhāra-*
*bhāsure kiraṇa-dhruve//12//*

*'namaḥ kalpânta-hutabhug-*
*jvālā-mālântara-sthite/*
*ālīḍha-muditā-bandha-*
*ripu-cakra-vināśani//13//*

*'namaḥ kara-talâghāta-*
*caraṇâhata-bhū-tale/*
*bhṛkuṭī-kṛta-hūṃ-kāra-*
*sapta-pātāla-bhedini//14//*

*'namaḥ śive śubhe śānte*
*śānta-nirvāṇa-gocare/*
*svāhā-praṇava-saṃyukte*
*mahā-pātaka-nāśani//15//*

*'namaḥ pramuditâbandha-*
*ripu-gātra-prabhedini/*
*daśâkṣara-pada-nyāse*
*vidyā-hūṃ-kāra-dīpite//16//*

*'namas ture padâghāta-*
*hūṃ-kārâkāra-bījite/*[203]
*meru-mandara-kailāsa-*
*bhuvana-traya-cālini//17//*

*'namaḥ sura-sarâkāra-*
*hariṇâṅka-kara-sthite/*
*tāra-dvir-ukta-phaṭ-kāra*
*aśeṣa-viṣa-nāśani//18//*

*'namaḥ sura-gaṇâdhyakṣa-*
*sura-kiṃnara-sevite/*
*ābandha-muditâbhoga-*
*kali-duḥsvapna-nāśani//19//*

*'namaś candrârka-saṃpūrṇa-*
*nayana-dyuti-bhāsure/*
*hara-dvir-ukta-tuttāre*
*viṣama-jvara-nāśani//20//*

*'namas tri-tattva-vinyāsa-*
*śiva-śakti-samanvite/*
*graha-vetāla-yakṣâugha-*
*nāśani pravare ture//21//*

*'mantra-mūlam idaṃ stotraṃ*
*namas-kārâika-viṃśakam/*
*yaḥ paṭhet prayato dhīmān*
*devyā bhakti-samanvitaḥ//22//*

*'sāyaṃ vā prātar utthāya*
*smaret sarvâbhaya pradam/*
*sarva-pāpa-praśamanaṃ*
*sarva-durgati-nāśanam//23//*

*'abhiṣikto bhavet tūrṇaṃ*
*saptabhir jina-koṭibhiḥ/*
*asmin mahattvam āsādya*
*so 'nte bauddha-padaṃ vrajet//24//*

*'viṣaṃ tasya mahā-ghauraṃ*
*sthāvaraṃ vâtha jaṅgamam/*
*smaraṇāt pralayaṃ yāti*
*khāditaṃ pītam eva vā//25//*

*'graha-jvara-viṣârtānāṃ*
*param arti-vināśanam/*
*anyeṣāṃ câiva sattvānāṃ*
*dvis-tri-saptâbhivartinam//26//*

*'putra-kāmo labhet putraṃ*
*dhana-kāmo labhed dhanam/*
*sarva-kāmān avāpnoti*
*na vighnaiḥ prati-hanyate//27//*

"TĀRĀ-BHAGAVATĪYAṂ SŪTRAṂ SAMYAK-SAṂBUDDHA-BHĀṢITAṂ[31]
(Sūtra on the Lady Tārā, spoken by the Complete and Perfect Buddha)
SARVA-KARA SAMAYĀ ULAKARAYE,[32]
(Meteor-swift in Your all-performing pledge?)
BUDDHANI CA DHARMAṆI CA SAṂGHANI CA TĀRAYE SVĀHĀ![33]

(Tārā, of the nature of (?) Buddha, Dharma and
Saṅgha: to You, SVĀHĀ!)

'This *dhāraṇī*, Mañjuśrī, is blessed by all the Buddhas of the three times. It praises Tārā, the Mother who produces all the Buddhas of the three times, [204] by destroying what is unsuitable. Its benefits are inconceivable. Therefore, Mañjuśrī, I shall speak of them.

'People[34] who speak this *dhāraṇī* will never be reborn in such states as hell-beings, *pretas* or animals; they will never be reborn in border countries, as barbarians, or with incomplete faculties and so forth. They will be free from all danger of diseases such as plague, smallpox and infectious disease, and the danger of disease will not arise. They will be free of the eight great fears and so on. Mañjuśrī, people who retain this praise by all the Buddhas of the three times will have made offering to all the Buddhas of the three times. People retaining it will become purified of all sins, including the [five] immediate ones. They will see all the Buddhas. Untimely death will not occur, and when they die they will see Tārā, the Mother who produces all the Buddhas of the three times. People retaining it will achieve whatever they mentally intend. They will receive perfect body, perfect complexion and all such. All hindrances of bad dreams, the malicious and spirits will be quelled. [205] They will also see the truths of the three times. They will see directly the form of Mother Tārā.

'NAMAḤ SARVA-TATHĀGATA-SAMYAK-
SAṂBUDDHĀYA TREYATE DHĀRATE TU TĀRA![35]
(Homage to all *Tathāgatas* and Complete and
Perfect Buddhas, saving, preserving,
TUTTĀRA(?)):

this is to be spoken.'

*Chapter 4. Deities*

Then the Bodhisattva Mañjuśrī the Youthful asked the Lord, 'Dependent on what should one earnestly take to heart this *dhāraṇī*?'

And the Lord gave utterance: 'One should earnestly practise

it with the desire to be liberated from suffering and with conviction about the Profound Meaning. Then [one should visualize that] from a TAṂ-letter come light-rays, upwards and downwards and all around, which transform into *vajras*. One should say this mantra, Mañjuśrī:

'OṂ VAJRA JVALA VAJRA TANA HŪṂ PHAṬ!
(OṂ *Vajra*, shine! *Vajra*, thunder! HUṂ PHAṬ!)

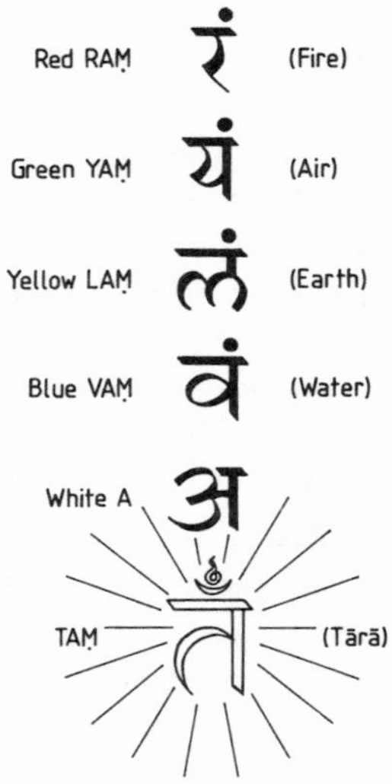


*Seed syllables of the elements at the beginning of the generation of the maṇḍala*

'Then one should visualize coming from the TAṂ a white letter A. Above this one should visualize a blue VAṂ. Above this one should visualize a yellow LAṂ. Above this one should visualize a green YAṂ. Above this one should visualize a red RAṂ. Their light spreads out in rays and comes together.

'OṂ DHARMADHĀTU-VIŚUDDHA HŪṂ.
(OṂ the pure Universal Law HŪṂ!)
OṂ AṂ-DHĀTU-VIŚUDDHA HŪṂ.[36]
(?)

OṂ SAMANTA-VIŚUDDHA HŪṂ.
(OṂ entirely pure HŪṂ!)
OṂ PRAKṢA-VIŚUDDHA HŪṂ![37]
(?)
OṂ KṢATA-BUTHĀNA-VIŚUDDHA HŪṂ.
(?)
OṂ NAMAḤ SARVA-TATHĀGATA-MAṆḌALA-SAMANTA-VIŚUDDHA HŪṂ.[38]
(OṂ Homage O entirely pure *maṇḍala* of all the *Tathagatas* HŪṂ!)

'Thus, Mañjuśrī, by saying these mantras the *maṇḍala*-palace should be generated. [206]

'It is on a multicoloured, four-petalled lotus, surrounded by a *vajra* wall, has four corners, with four gates and eight pillars set in a square, and is beautified with networks of pearls, jewelled tassles hanging down, hibiscus flowers (?)[39] and so forth. Thus such a *maṇḍala*-palace is generated.[40]

'On the anthers in the centre, upon a moon and lotus, is a green TAṂ from which comes an *utpala* with a TAṂ, by whose light of various colours in all world-elements all the world is seen as like an emanation, a magical illusion, a rainbow, a mirage, a moon in water, and a reflected image.[41] From the *utpala* comes a Tārā with green body, one face and two arms. Her right hand is [in the *mudrā* of] granting boons, Her left holds an *utpala*, with its stem. Her beautiful body is adorned with jewel necklaces, earrings, armlets, and all kinds of ornaments. A young maiden, with smiling face, She sits in the *sama-paryaṅka* (?) posture on a lotus and moon.

'In the East, on a moon and lotus, from a TAṂ is produced a blue *utpala* with the seed [syllable TAṂ], from which light of various colours fills all world-elements, so that all world-elements are seen as like emanations, magical illusions, rainbows, mirages, moons in water, and reflected images. From this *utpala* comes a blue Tārā with two arms. Her right hand holds a trident (*triśūla*), [207] in Her left She holds an *utpala* with stem. Her beautiful body is adorned with jewel necklaces, earrings, armlets, and all kinds of ornaments. A young maiden, with smiling face She sits in the *sama-paryaṅka* posture on a moon and lotus.

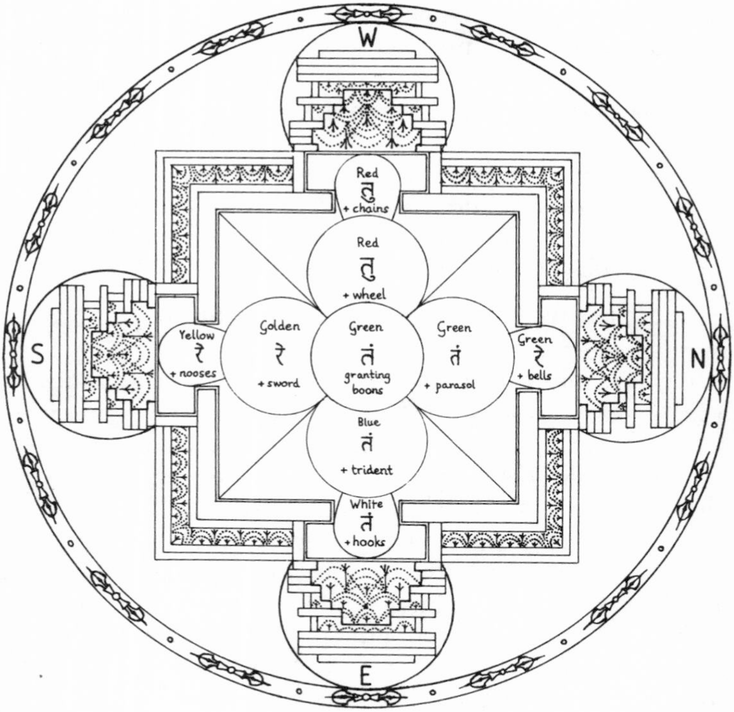


*Principal features of the Maṇḍala of Nine Tārās. The Goddesses are represented by their seed syllables, which after the first spell* TA-RE TU-T-TA-RE TU-RE. *The five central Tārās are peaceful and sit cross-legged, the four outer are wrathful and stand with right leg straight and left bent. Although shown folded down into a plane, the walls and gates should be visualized as three-dimensional.*

'In the South, on a moon and lotus, from a RE is produced a yellow *utpala*, with the Seed, from which light of various colours fills all world-elements, so that all the world is seen as like an emanation, . . . a reflected image. From this *utpala* comes a Tārā with a body like burnt gold in colour and two arms. In Her right hand She holds a sword, in Her left an *utpala* with stem. Her beautiful body is adorned with jewel necklaces, earrings, armlets and all kinds of ornaments. A young maiden, with smiling face She sits in the *sama-paryaṅka* posture on a moon and lotus.

'In the West, on a moon and lotus, from a TU comes a red *utpala*, with the Seed, from which light of various colours fills all world-elements, so that all the world is seen as like an emanation, . . . a reflected image. [208] From this *utpala* comes a red Tārā with two arms. In Her right hand She holds a wheel, in Her left an *utpala* with stem. Her beautiful body is adorned with jewel necklaces, earrings, armlets, and all kinds of ornaments. A young maiden, with smiling face She sits in the *sama-paryaṅka* posture on a moon and lotus.

'In the North, on a moon and lotus, from a TAṂ comes a green *utpala*, with the Seed, from which light of various colours fills all world-elements, so that all the world is seen as like an emanation, . . . a reflected image. From this *utpala* comes a green Tārā with two arms. In Her right hand She holds a parasol, and in Her left an *utpala* with stem. Her beautiful body is adorned with jewel necklaces, earrings, armlets, and all kinds of ornaments. A young maiden, with smiling face She sits in the *sama-paryaṅka* posture on a moon and lotus seat.

'At the Eastern gate, on a moon and lotus, from a TAṂ comes an *utpala*, with the Seed, by whose light of various colours in all world-elements, all world-elements [209] are seen as like emanations, . . . reflected images. From this *utpala* comes Tārā Aṅkuśī, white, Her two hands holding elephant-hooks. Her wrathful body is adorned with jewel necklaces, earrings, armlets, and all kinds of ornaments. A young maiden, with slightly wrathful face She abides[42] in *ālīḍha* posture (right leg stretched, left bent) on a moon and lotus.

'At the Southern gate, on a moon and lotus, from a RE comes an *utpala*, with the Seed, by whose light of various colours in all world-elements, all world-elements are seen as like emanations, . . . reflected images. From this *utpala* comes Tārā Pāśī, yellow, Her two hands holding nooses. Her wrathful body is adorned with jewel necklaces, earrings, armlets, and all kinds of ornaments. A young maiden, with slightly wrathful face She abides in *ālīḍha* posture on a moon and lotus.

'At the Western gate, on a moon and lotus, from a TU comes an *utpala*, with the Seed, by whose light of various colours in all world-elements, all world-[210]elements are seen as like emanations, . . . reflected images. From this *utpala* comes Tārā Sphoṭā, red, Her two hands holding chains. Her wrathful body is adorned with jewel necklaces, earrings, armlets, and all kinds of ornaments. A young maiden, with wrathful face She abides in *ālīḍha* posture on a moon and lotus.

'At the Northern gate, on a moon and lotus, from a RE comes an *utpala*, with the Seed, by whose light of various colours in all world-elements, all world elements are seen as like emanations, magical illusions, rainbows, mirages, moons in water, and reflected images. From this *utpala* comes Tārā Ghaṇṭā, green, Her two hands holding bells. Her wrathful body is adorned with jewel necklaces, earrings, armlets, and all kinds of ornaments. A young maiden, with wrathful face She abides in *ālīḍha* posture on a moon and lotus.

'In this way, Mañjuśrī, one should visualize the circle of deities.'

Mañjuśrī asked, 'How so, Lord, emanations and the rest?'

The Lord said: 'Mañjuśrī, they are elements of those with the defilements of the six destinies. Therefore [211] they are to be understood as like emanations, magical illusions, rainbows, mirages, moons in water, and reflected images.'

## *Chapter 5. Empowerment*

Then Mañjuśrī asked: 'Lord, in what manner are deities to be blessed by these deities?'

The Lord gave utterance: 'Mañjuśrī, in the manner of an emanation, of a magical illusion, of a rainbow, of a mirage, of a moon in water, and of a reflected image.'

Mañjuśrī asked: 'How so, Lord, "an emanation"?'

The Lord said: 'An "emanation" is unreal and mistaken by both [the emanator and the observer of the emanation]. A magical illusion is mistaken by the other [i.e. not by the magician, who knows it is an illusion]. A rainbow is empty. A mirage is a mistaken object and empty. A moon in water is causal.[43] A reflected image is a city of the *gandharvas*.[44] Like that, Mañjuśrī, is the mistaken; like that are the elements of those with defilements. Therefore, Mañjuśrī, the blessing of

ANDY WEBER

not open: what mortal can know all the Names of The Goddess?

## THE BENEFITS

This section leaves no doubt that the recitation of Tārā's Names is a practice intended for ordinary lay people, like the merchants among whom Her cult was so popular from the sixth century on.

## THE TRANSLATION

I have followed principally the Sanskrit text as edited by Godefroy de Blonay (1895) from two manuscripts and a version published in India. Two Tibetan translations have helped the interpretation and allowed some of Blonay's readings to be corrected.

The first Tibetan translation (T1) contains only verses 27–39, the Names. It was made by Garup (or Gorup?) Ch'ö-kyi she-rap[8] with the Kashmiri *paṇḍita* Buddhākara, about the late eleventh century, and may be found in the Tog Palace Kangyur. The second (T2) is essentially complete and present in all Kangyurs examined; the translator is not named in the colophon but is believed to be T'ar-pa Lotsawa Nyi-ma gyäl-ts'än (thirteenth to fourteenth centuries).[9]

In the introduction and benefits, the Sanskrit is more coherent and intelligible than T2. In the Names, when the versions differ it is hard to tell which is correct. In any case, a particular Name can often be translated in many different ways, all justified by tradition and/or reasoning.

Besides these primary sources, the prose translations in French by Godefroy de Blonay and in English by Edward Conze[10] were consulted. Some of the differences in my translation are because I have used the Tibetan texts in addition to the Sanskrit, others are a matter of arbitrary choice.

The original is in *anuṣṭubh* metre, which allows a certain variation of rhythm within the limits of the regular pattern. The rather free metre adopted for this translation is perhaps not too dissimilar in effect.

## THE HUNDRED AND EIGHT NAMES OF THE VENERABLE ĀRYA-TĀRĀ

(*Ārya-tārā-bhaṭṭārikā-nāmâṣṭôttaraśataka-stotra*)[11]

*Spoken by the illustrious Lord Avalokita*

OṂ. Homage to the illustrious Ārya-Tārā!

1 Lovely, delightful Potalaka
glitters with various minerals,
It's covered with diverse trees and creepers,
full of the cries of various birds.

2 'Mid tumult of various waterfalls,
diverse wild animals abound;
Everywhere it is perfumed
with multitudinous kinds of flowers.

3 It's furnished with diverse delicious fruits,
all ahum with the buzzing of bees,
And thronged with excited elephants.[12]
With the sweet songs of *kinnaras*

4 And *gandharvas* it resounds;
by hosts of realized Knowledge-holders,[13]
Sages exempt from attachment,
hosts of Bodhisattvas and others,

5 Masters of the Ten Stages,
and thousands of goddesses and Queens
Of Knowledge, from Ārya-Tārā on,
it is constantly frequented.

6 Hosts of wrathful deities
surround it, Hayagrīva[14] and others.
There there dwelt the illustrious Lord
Avalokita, who labours for

7 The weal of every sentient being,
seated on a lotus seat,
Endowed with great asceticism,
full of friendliness and compassion.

8 He was teaching the Dharma in
that great assembly of deities.
Vajrapāṇi, very mighty,
came to Him as He sat there

9 And, impelled by supreme compassion,
questioned Avalokita: —
'Beset by the dangers of thieves and snakes,
lions, fire, elephants, tigers and

10 'Water, O Sage, these sentient beings
sink in the ocean of *saṃsāra*,
Bound by *saṃsāra*'s nooses, which
come from greed, hate and delusion.

11 'Tell me, great Sage, of that by which
they may be freed from *saṃsāra*!' —
Thus addressed, that Lord of the World,
illustrious Avalokita,

12 Spoke these melodious words unto
the ever-watchful Vajrapāṇi: —
'Listen, High Lord of the *Guhyakas*![15]
By the power of the vow

13 'Of Amitābha, the Protector,
were born to me the Mothers of
The World, wise, having great compassion,
raised up for the world's saving;[16]

14 'Like unto the risen sun,
their faces radiant as full moons,
The Tārās illuminate the trees,[17]
with the gods, men and *asuras*,

15 'They cause the triple world to shake,
and terrify *yakṣas* and *rākṣasas*.
The Goddess holding a blue lotus
in Her hand says, "Fear not, fear not!

16 '"It is to protect the world
that I was produced by the Conquerors.
In the wilderness, in clashes of arms,
where one is troubled by diverse dangers,

17 '"When but my names are remembered, I
protect all beings perpetually.
I, O Lord, shall lead them across[18]
the great flood of their diverse fears;

18 '"Therefore the eminent Seers sing
of me in the world by the name of Tārā,[19]
Raising their hands in supplication,
full of reverence and awe."'—

19 He who dwells blazing in the sky,[20]
[Vajrapāṇi,] spoke this speech:—
'Tell the hundred and eight Names, which
were proclaimed of yore by the Conquerors,

20 'The Lords, the Masters of the Ten Stages,
the Bodhisattvas of great magic power!
Which remove all evil, are meritorious
and propitious, increase renown,

21 'Grant wealth and riches, and also
increase health and prosperity!
Out of your friendliness towards
beings, O Great Sage, declare them!'—

22 Upon this utterance, the Lord
Avalokita, smiling broadly,
Looked about in all directions
with eyes a-sparkle with friendliness,

23 Elevated His right hand
adorned with a propitious sign,
And, great in wisdom,[21] said to him,
'Well said, well said, thou great ascetic!

24 'Listen, most fortunate one, uniquely
dear to all beings, to the Names,
Having recited which correctly
people become lords of wealth,

25 'Liberated from every sickness,
endowed with all virtues of sovereignty,
Their chance of untimely death destroyed,
and having died, go to Sukhāvatī!

26 'These I shall relate in full.
Listen to me, assembled gods!
May you rejoice in the true Dharma,
and may you find tranquillity!

27 'OṂ![22]
Virtuous lady,[23] very majestic,
nurse of the world, of great renown,
Sarasvatī, large-eyed, increaser
of wisdom, grace and intelligence,

28 [24]'Giver of firmness and increase, Svāhā,
OṂ-letter, taking forms at will,
Labouring for all beings' weal,
in battle saviour and victor,

29 'Goddess of the Perfection of Wisdom,
Ārya-Tārā, Who pleases the mind,
She of the drum and conch,[25] complete
Queen of knowledge, speaking kindly,

30 'With moon-like face, intensely brilliant,[26]
unconquered, with a yellow garment,
Great in Illusion,[27] very white,
great in strength and heroism,

31 'Very terrible, very ardent,
slayer of malignant beings,
Pacified, and of peaceful form,
victorious, with blazing splendour,

32 'Lightning-garlanded, standard-bearer,
armed with sword and wheel and bow,
Crushing, petrifying, Kālī,
night of apocalypse,[28] goer by night,

33 'Protector, deluder, peaceful one,
lovely one, mighty[29] and virtuous,
*Brāhmaṇī*,[30] Mother of the Vedas,
hidden one and cave-dweller,

34 'Lucky, auspicious,[31] gentle one,
knowing all kinds, as swift as thought,
Skull-bearer, great in vehemence,[32]
twilight, truth, invincible,[33]

35 'Caravan-leader, Who looks with compassion,[34]
showing the way to those who have lost it,
Granter of boons, instructress, teacher,
measureless valour in woman's form,

36 'Mountain-dweller,[35] *yoginī*, realized,
outcast, deathless and eternal,
Wealthy, of merit, most illustrious,
fortunate, pleasant to behold,

37 'She who terrifies Death, the fearful,
fierce, in great austerities terrible,
Working for only the weal of the world,
fit refuge, kindly to devotees,

38 'Mistress of language, happy, subtle,
constant, companion everywhere,[36]
Gracious, accomplisher of all ends,
concealer, nurse, and prize-winner,

39 'Fearless, Gautamī,[37] meritorious,
glorious daughter of Lokeśvara;
Tārā, with names of infinite virtue,
totally fulfils all hopes.

40 'These one hundred and eight Names
have been proclaimed for your benefit.
They are mysterious, marvellous, secret,
hard to find even for the gods,

41 'They bring good fortune and success,
and destroy all injury,
Allaying every malady,
bringing happiness to all beings.

42 'One who recites them with intelligence
three times, clean from bathing, and
Concentrated, in no great time
attains to royal dignity.

43 'One distressed will be ever happy,
the needy will become wealthy,
The stupid will become very wise
and intelligent, without doubt.

44 'One who is bound is freed from bonds,
in business one will be successful,
Enemies will become friendly,
so will beasts with horns or fangs.

45 'In battles, straits and difficulties
where manifold dangers crowd together,
By mere recollection of these Names
every danger[38] is removed.

46 'One becomes free of untimely death
and gains extensive prosperity;
The human rebirth is very fruitful,
of anyone thus magnanimous.

47 'A human being who, rising early
in the morning, will recite them,
That person will, for a long time, gain
long life and prosperity.

48 '*Devas*, *nāgas* and also *yakṣas*,
*gandharvas*, demons of rotting corpses,
*Piśācas*, *rākṣasas* and spirits,
and the Mothers of savage splendour,

49 'Causers of wasting and convulsions,
injurious *kākhorda* demons,[39]
*Ḍākinīs*, *pretas*, *tārakas*,
*skandas*, *māras* and great evil spirits[40]

50 'Cannot even jump over his shadow,
still less can they take hold of him.
Malignant beings cannot harass him,
and diseases cannot approach.

51 'Of great magic powers, he even perceives
the battles of *devas* and *asuras*.[41]
Endowed with all virtues of sovereignty,
he prospers through children and
grandchildren.

52 'Recalling past lives, he'll be intelligent,
well-born, pleasant to behold,

Affectionate and eloquent,
learned in all the Treatises.

53 'Honouring his spiritual Teacher,
he is adorned with *Bodhicitta*,
And wherever he is reborn,
is never parted from the Buddhas.

54 '[He attains perfection of
every goal desired, through Tārā.]'[42]

The Hundred and Eight Names of the Venerable Ārya-Tārā, spoken by the illustrious Ārya-Avalokiteśvara,[43] is complete.

ŚUBHAM!

*Translated from the Sanskrit.*

# Part Two
## *The Praise in Twenty-one Homages*

# 1 *Introduction*

This 'praise by all the Buddhas of the three times' was presented in the Tantra translated above as a *dhāraṇī,* in Sanskrit. Elsewhere in the Kangyur, however, a Tibetan translation is given, and in this form it became in Tibet the most popular of all hymns to Tārā, or indeed to any deity. Still today, at Tibetan monasteries around the world, it is chanted several times daily by all the monks, and on special occasions and when it is desired to enlist the Venerable Mother's aid for some particular purpose, it is this praise that is recited over and over again by both monks and laity, and in some cases by nuns too.

Now while the Tibetans have made this praise so much their own, their rights over it are by no means exclusive. It belongs to the great tradition of Indian Buddhism. As such, Buddhists anywhere may legitimately examine what it has lost in its passage from Sanskrit into Tibetan. In availing myself of this privilege, I intend no disrespect towards what it gained in the same process – meanings the Sanskrit never had, verbal equivalents of the dog's tooth that became a sacred relic of miraculous efficacity. But loss there must be. Not only is untranslatable word-play characteristic of elegant Sanskrit style, but in a Tantric text a multiplicity of levels of meaning is virtually obligatory. Often the symbolism survives translation, but often too a translator is forced to ignore some aspects of the original in order to express others. A modern translator is not bound to make the same choices as her or his predecessor of centuries ago, any more than she has always to agree with her contemporaries.

One major and inevitable loss is the metre. Tibetan verse, like English, is based on stress, and cannot possibly reproduce the flavour of Sanskrit verse, which is based on *quantity*, i.e. on whether syllables are long or short. The *Praise in Twenty-one Homages* is in the commonest of Sanskrit metres, *anuṣṭubh*, composed of eight-syllable *pādas* or half-lines in the pattern

○ ○ ○ ○ ˘ – – ○ / ○ ○ ○ ○ ˘ – ˘ ○ /,

where ˘ represents a short ('light') syllable, – a long ('heavy') syllable, and ○ a syllable that (subject to certain rules) may be either long or short. (Certain variant forms are also allowed in the first half of the line; one is used in this *Praise* at 2c, 13a and 23c.) Usually this metre is translated into Tibetan as seven-syllable lines. Here, to accommodate the feminine vocative endings conveniently, eight-syllable lines are used; but how crude their unvarying trochaic beat beside the subtler rhythms of the original! In English too, whereas elsewhere in this book verses are translated in more relaxed style, this *Praise* is rendered so that one can chant it with the same rhythm and tunes as the Tibetan version, for the benefit of those who would as soon recite an admittedly inadequate English translation as a no more adequate (though hallowed) Tibetan one.

## SOURCES

### 1. *The Sanskrit text*

We have presented on pages 55 to 58 above the Sanskrit text of the *Praise*, edited from:

(a) Chapter 3 of the Tantra, in five editions of the Kangyur (D: De-ge; L: Lhasa; N: Nar-t'ang; P: Peking; T: Tog) and in Bu-tön Rinpoche's copy from an early edition (B).

(b) Godefroy de Blonay's edition of 1895 in his *Matériaux* (M), prepared from two Sanskrit manuscripts, probably from Nepal. Though too garbled for him to attempt a translation, it was still very useful when I had only the Tog Kangyur text to work from – despite the more than a hundred errors in the latter, I was able to deduce from M and T together very nearly the final text.[1]

(c) A remarkable quadrilingual blockprint (Q), of which Gonsar Rinpoche kindly lent me a photocopy. It gives each of the twenty-one verses of homage in Sanskrit (Lañ-tsha script), Tibetan, Mongolian and Chinese, accompanied by a picture in Chinese style of the corresponding aspect of Tārā in the iconographic system of Sūryagupta (see below).

Another manuscript, in modern Devanāgarī script, of which Gonsar Rinpoche also lent a copy, proved to differ so little from M that it could well have been transcribed from it.

## 2. *The Tibetan translation*

Unfortunately, only one Tibetan translation of the *Praise* appears to have survived. We shall refer to its translator(s), unnamed in the Kangyur, as TT. According to the colophon given in Jetsün Dr'ak-pa gyäl-ts'än's commentary, it is by the translator Nyän (late eleventh century)[2] and was revised by Dr'ak-pa gyäl-ts'än himself, though if this was so it is hard to see why he did not make it consistent with his commentary.[3]

A critical edition of the Tibetan translation, based on a variety of sources, is presented in Appendix 1. The Sanskrit text used by TT clearly differed here and there from ours, but there is no reason to regard it as any more authoritative. There are several places where our Sanskrit text makes good sense while the Tibetan needs unnatural twisting to wring any intelligible meaning out of it.

## 3. *Indian commentaries*

The Tängyur contains Tibetan translations of a set of five texts by the Kashmiri pandit Sūryagupta (probably mid-ninth-century),[4] which are considered to comment on the *Praise in Twenty-one Homages* on the level of *Anuttara-yoga-tantra*. As Je Ge-dün-drup in his commentary and K'ä-drup Je in his *Introduction to the Buddhist Tantric Systems*[5] point out, this is quite consistent with the *Praise* itself being *Kriyā-tantra*, the lowest of the four levels of Tantra.

S1. *Practice of the Twenty-one-fold Praise of Tārā (Tārādevī-*

*stotra-ekaviṃśatika-sādhana-nāma*). P2557, eight pages (i.e. about four leaves). This quotes the twenty-one verses of homage, each one followed by a brief prose description of how to visualize the corresponding aspect of Tārā: colour, seat, posture, number of faces and arms, implements and *mudrās*.

S2. *Summary of the Practice of the Venerable Ārya-Tārā, with the Twenty-one Branches of Ritual* (no Sanskrit title). P2558, thirty-four pages. 26 chapters, describing rituals for the functions associated with each of the twenty-one Tārās, and five other rituals. The ritual for entering the *maṇḍala* (Tārā no. 10) occupies over ten pages.

S3. *Method of instruction on the Accomplishment of Tārā* (*Tārā-sādhanopadeśa-krama*). P2559, three pages. Maps the twenty-one *Tārās*, plus the three Tārās of *Vajra* Body, *Vajra* Speech and *Vajra* Mind, on to the twenty-four parts of the body and the twenty-four places of Jambudvīpa.

S4. *An Approach to the Twentyonefold Praise of the Lady Tārā* (*Bhagavatī-Tārādevy-ekaviṃśati-stotrôpāyika*). P2560, twenty-two pages. After quoting each homage verse from the *Praise in Twenty-one Homages,* this gives a verse of commentary stating that the Tārā concerned is to be meditated on; next comes a concise iconographic description as in S1, and finally a description of the ritual for Her function, more concise than S2 but mostly with what are evidently supposed to be the same mantras.

S5. *Praise of the Twenty-one Tārās, Called the Pure Head-Jewel* (*Devī-tāraikaviṃśati-stotra-viśuddha-cūḍāmaṇi-nāma*). P2561, nine pages. Describes each of the twenty-one Tārās iconographically, as in S1, but in the form of verses of homage, including many remarks on the symbolism, the function of the implements, etc.

Tārā Herself transmitted this cycle to Sūryagupta, when he prayed to Her for three months for a cure for his leprosy (see p. 239). S1 and S2 were translated around 1100 by Mäl-gyo lotsawa and S4 about 1210 by Tr'o-p'u lotsawa J'am-pa päl (see Appendix 3). S3 (like S4) was apparently translated under Śākya-śrī-bhadra while he was in Tibet (1204–13), and S5 is attributed in the Tängyur Index to Tsön-drü seng-g'e of

Gya (d.1041).[6]

Apart from mantras, all the texts are in verse, except S1. Little in them relates perceptibly to the words of the *Praise in Twenty-one Homages* except the commentary verse in S4, which I shall translate below along with the name and iconographic description of each Tārā from these texts.

Since I have no other Indian commentary on the *Praise*, it is appropriate to translate the *Praise* in accordance with Sūryagupta as far as possible.

## 4. *Tibetan commentaries*

Many of the interpretations transmitted in the Tibetan commentaries must have originated in Indian commentaries now lost. Others must be Tibetan developments, at least as regards the details of how individual words are asserted to contribute to the overall meaning.

I shall quote most of the commentary of Je Gedün dr'up-pa (1391–1475), posthumously awarded the title of First Dalai Lama.[7] This is called *The Precious Garland, a Ṭīkā on the Twenty-one Homages to Tārā*.[8] It will be denoted by G.

Many points in G would remain obscure without the oral tradition, which I have received in the form of clear and detailed teachings by the Venerable Geshe Thubten Lodan based on the commentary of Ngül-ch'u Dharmabhadra (1772–1851).[9] This commentary, *The Bunch of Captivating Utpalas, an Explanation of the Praise in Twenty-one Homages to Tārā*,[10] was written at Ngül-ch'u ri-p'uk in 1818. Its explanations will be mentioned occasionally, marked with D.

It is interesting to compare these commentaries from the Gelukpa tradition with those of Jetsün Dr´ak-pa gyäl-ts´än (1147–1216), a celebrated scholar and *yogin* numbered among the 'Five Greats' of the Sakyapa tradition. As lineage-holder of Sūryagupta's Tārā cycle,[11] he wrote as many as thirteen texts on Tārā, including *Outlines of the Praise in Twenty-one Homages*[12] and *Clear Light Explanation of the Praise*,[13] which I shall refer to as J. He is notably silent on the points where later Tibetan interpretations are at odds with the Sanskrit text, as one would expect if these interpretations gradually developed after his time.

## *Translation of the root text*

The translation below is from the Sanskrit text and attempts to follow Sūryagupta where possible. Annotations are held over to the commentary, which follows. Another version, modified to follow the Tibetan translation and accord with Tibetan interpretations, is given in Appendix 2.

# 2 *The Praise in Twenty-one Homages*

THE PRAISE IN TWENTY-ONE HOMAGES TO OUR LADY, THE GODDESS ĀRYA-TĀRĀ, WITH ITS BENEFITS
(*Bhagavaty-ārya-tārā-devyā namaskārâikaviṃśati-stotraṃ guṇa-hita-sahitam*)

1 Homage! Tārā, swift, heroic!
With regard like instant lightning!
Sprung from op'ning stamens from the
Lord of Three Worlds' facial lotus!

2 Homage! She whose face combines a
hundred autumn moons at fullest!
Blazing with light-rays resplendent
as a thousand-star collection!

3 Homage! Golden One, blue lotus,
water-born, in hand adornèd!
Giving, Effort, Calm, Austerities,
Patience, Meditation Her field!

4 Homage! Crown of *Tathāgatas*,
She who goes in endless triumph!
Honoured much by Conqu'rors' Offspring!
having reached ev'ry Perfection!

5 Homage! Filling with TUTTĀRA,
HŪṂ the regions and space-quarters!
Trampling with Her feet the sev'n worlds,
able to draw forth all [beings]!

6 Homage! Worshipped by the All-Lord,
Śakra, Agni, Brahmā, Marut!
Honoured by the hosts of spirits,
corpse-raisers, *gandharvas*, *yakṣas*!

7 Homage! With Her TRAṬ and PHAṬ sounds
crusher of foes' magic diagrams!
Putting Her feet left out, right back,
eyes all full of blazing fire!

8 Homage! TURE, very dreadful!
Destroyer of Māra's champion!
She with frowning lotus visage
who is slayer of all enemies!

9 Homage! She adorned with fingers,
at Her heart, in Three-Jewel *mudrā*!
Wheel of all quarters adornèd,
filled with masses of Her own light!

10 Homage! She of swelling Great Joy,
diadem emitting garlands!
Mirthful, laughing with TUTTĀRE,
subjugating *māras*, *devas*!

11 Homage! She able to summon
all earth-guardians and their trains!
Shaking, frowning, with Her HŪṂ-sign
saving from ev'ry misfortune!

12 Homage! Crowning locks adorned with
crescent diadem, most shining!
In Her hair-mass, Amitābha
shining, with [much] light eternal!

13 Homage! She 'mid wreath of flames like
eon-ending fire abiding!
Right leg outstretched, joy-producing,
destroying the troops of enemies!

14 Homage! She who smites the ground with
Her palm, and with Her foot beats it!
Frowning, with the letter HŪṂ the
seven underworlds She shatters!

15 Homage! Happy, Virtuous, Peaceful!
She whose field is Peace, *Nirvāṇa*!
She endowed with OṂ and SVĀHĀ!
Of the great downfall destroyer!

16 Homage! She bound round with joy, and
tearing foes' bodies asunder!
Luminous with the HŪṂ-mantra,
word-array of the ten syllables!

17 Homage! Swift One! The foot-stamper
with for seed the letter HŪṂ's shape!
She who shakes the triple world and
Meru, Mandara and Kailās!

18 Homage! She in whose hand rests the
deer-marked moon, of *deva*-lake form!
With twice-spoken TĀRĀ and PHAṬ
totally dispelling poison!

19 Homage! She whom god-host rulers,
gods and *kinnaras* do honour!
Joy-producing one, Her fullness
conflict and bad dreams dispelling!

20 Homage! She whose eyes are bright with
radiance of sun or full moon!
With twice HARA and TUTTĀRE
Driver-out of chronic fever!

21 Homage! Full of liberating
power by set of three Realities!
Crushing crowds of spirits, *yakṣas*
and corpse-raisers! Supreme! TURE!

22 This praise, rooted in mantras, a
twenty-one-fold homage — for one
Who recites it, wise and pious,
full of faith towards the Goddess,

23 And remembers it at even
or at dawn on rising, it grants
Ev'ry fearlessness, quells all sins,
and destroys all bad migrations.

24 Quickly he'll be consecrated
by sev'n times ten million Conqu'rors.
Gaining greatness herein, he will
reach at last the rank of Buddha.

25 The most dreadful poison, whether
animal, or plant or min'ral,
Whether he's devoured or drunk it,
meets its end through his rememb'ring.

26 It completely stops the pain of
those whom spirits, fevers, poisons
Afflict – other beings' also.
On performing twice three sevens,

27 One who wants a child will get one,
one desiring wealth will find wealth,
One obtains all one's desires; by
hindrances one's not frustrated.

The Praise in Twenty-one Homages to the Venerable Lady, the Goddess Ārya-Tārā, spoken by the glorious Complete and Perfect Buddha Vairocana, is complete and concluded.[14]

ŚUBHAM!

*Translated from the Sanskrit.*

# 3 *Commentary on the Praise in Twenty-one Homages*

*Abbreviations*

D The commentary of Dharmabhadra (1818)
G The commentary of Gedün-drup (1391–1475)
GL Teachings of Geshe Lodan, July 1978
J The commentaries of Jetsün Dr'ak-pa gyäl-ts'än (1147–1216)
Ln $n^{th}$ left hand, counting from the front
M Blonay, *Matériaux*
Q Quadrilingual blockprint
Rn $n^{th}$ Right hand, counting from the front
RLn $n^{th}$ pair of hands, counting from the front
S1 . . . S5 Sūryagupta's texts on the 21 Tārās (see above: Sources, 3)
S Sūryagupta
Skt Sanskrit
TT Tibetan translator(s) of the *Praise*
Tib Tibetan
W Wayman (1959)
$^{1} \ldots ^{5}$ = S1 to S5
[ ] Translator's comments

*General remarks: iconography*

G prefaces his commentary with a verse of homage:

> Homage to the *Ārya* Triple Gem!
> To Blessed Tārā, Mother of the Conqu'rors,
> Activities of all the three times' Buddhas,
> My body, speech and mind give homage devoutly.

[Thus to pay homage properly, one should use one's three doors of body, speech and mind. Homage of the body is physical prostrations, that of speech is recitation of the *Praise* or mantra, and that of mind includes the attitude of devotion and faith towards the object, Tārā, and the visualization that should accompany the recitation. What then should one visualize when reciting the *Praise*?

As the colophon in M states, this is a Praise in Twenty-one Homages to the Venerable Lady Ārya-Tārā. It is by no means obvious that the author considered each verse as directed to a different aspect of the Goddess, though at least a peaceful and a fierce aspect are involved. Indeed, Chapter 4 of the Tantra describes as the visualization on which the practice of the *Praise* should be based a *maṇḍala* of nine Tārās. One could readily distribute the twenty-one homages symmetrically round this *maṇḍala*. However, the fit could not be perfect, seeing that none of the nine has the *pratyālīḍha* posture mentioned in verse 7, and none holds a moon-disk as in verse 18.

Still, since there is no limit to the forms that Tārā can manifest, there is certainly no bar to supposing a form for each of the twenty-one homages, and the resulting set of twenty-one Tārās has long been popular. According to Beyer[15] there are three iconographic traditions for this set:

1. Sūryagupta school, depicting the twenty-one as differing in all details such as posture, number of heads and hands, colour, implements and gestures.
2. Tradition attributed to Nāgārjuna and Atīśa, in which they are scarcely distinguished except by colour, peaceful or fierce expression, and the colour of the flask that each holds in the right hand.
3. Nyingma tradition, traced to Longchen rapjampa

(1308–1363), depicting them as the same but of different colour and holding individual emblems on top of the lotus in the right hand.

Here we present descriptions according to the Sūryagupta school, illustrated (with occasional discrepancies) from Q and from the Five Hundred Deities of Nar-t'ang (N). However, it should be remembered that this tradition, while more interesting visually, is not at all fashionable at present, and virtually all *sādhanas* based on the twenty-one Tārās use one of the other schemes, which are admittedly more practicable.

In fact, none of the traditions fits the text of the twenty-one homages noticeably better than the nine-fold *maṇḍala*. Several verses suggest a standing Tārā, especially 17, and a scheme in which all the Tārās are seated can hardly fit. Nor can Tārā 18 hold a moon-disk when all the Tārās are limited to an *utpala* and a flask. One would expect S to do better, but though he sometimes matches the text, at other times he seems wilfully to ignore it. Number 5, firmly seated in the *vajra* position, can hardly be said to be 'trampling'; 9 does not have the *mudrā* of the Three Jewels; and as for 'foot-stamping' 17 and moon-holding 18, both are shown seated and it is actually 17 who holds the moon-disk! Can this really be what S meant? The texts seem quite unambiguous. Perhaps it is simply that all these traditions stem from visions received by *yogins*, which are not necessarily neat intellectually.]

### *Plan of commentary*

[I give G's headings, although his identification of Tārās 2 to 7 as peaceful and 8 to 14 as fierce does not agree completely with either the root text or the artistic traditions. J structures this part of the *Praise* quite differently – he recognizes verses 2 to 4, 9 and 10 as on peaceful forms of Tārā, and 5 to 8, 11, 13 and 14 as on fierce forms.

After each root verse I give S's verse of commentary, then some notes on the words, explaining the possible meanings of some of the expressions in the text, pointing out ambiguities, to assist readers not versed in Sanskrit. Significant variations between different versions of the text are also mentioned, especially those between the Sanskrit and Tibetan versions.

Technical terms are mostly explained not here but in the Glossary.

In the names and iconographic descriptions compiled from S1 to S5, we note actual variants among these texts (e.g. 'red[5] or orange[1]'), but not abbreviated forms (e.g. 'Tārā Destroyer of All Attachment[1,2,3,5]' although S1 and S5 actually omit 'All'). The Sanskrit names are taken from Lokesh Chandra's *Tibetan-Sanskrit Dictionary*.

The function of the rites given for that Tārā in S2 and S4 is then stated. In some cases this is clearly secondary to the principal function mentioned in the root text.

Discussion of each verse concludes with the explanations from the Tibetan commentaries, G quoted directly and usually in full, the additional details or alternative explanations from D and J sometimes paraphrased to avoid unnecessary repetition.]

### *Extent of the basic text*

What exactly does the *Praise* include? The couplet

> 22 This praise, rooted in mantra, a
> twenty-one-fold homage

(or, according to TT,

> This praise of (*or* with) the root mantras and
> Twenty-one-fold homage)

has been interpreted by some as implying two separate items, a twenty-one-fold homage which is evidently verses 1 to 21, and a 'praise rooted in mantra' as well. G quotes two such theories, one claiming that the 'praise rooted in mantra' is the mantra immediately preceding the *Praise in Twenty-one Homages* in the Tantra, which he gives as: NAMA SARVA-TATHĀGATĀNĀṂ. TAD-YATHĀ: OṂ NAMO SUKASA NAMA TĀRE PĀRAMITA. The second, that of the translator Pang Lodrö Tänpa,[16] says it is a verse he translated 'from an Indian text', similar to this one, which comes at the beginning of Q and is illustrated there with the picture of ordinary Green Tārā reproduced here:

*Green Tārā, from the Quadrilingual blockprint (Q)*

OṂ! *Namas* TĀRE *ture vīre*
TUTTĀRE *bhaya-nāśane/*
TURE *sarvârtha-dā tāre*
SVĀHĀ-*kāre namo stute//*

OṂ! Homage! O TĀRE, Swift One, Heroine!
TUTTĀRE who eliminates fears!
TURE, the Saviouress granting all benefits!
Sound of SVĀHĀ, worshipped and praised!

[This verse, of which variants are often used in Tārā practices, does not occur in the Tantra, nor in the Tibetan translation of the *Praise in Twenty-one Homages* in the Kangyur.]

G's Gurus, however, teach that the 'praise rooted in mantra' and the 'twenty-one-fold homage' are one and the same. [Indeed, if one examines not just the couplet 22a-b but the whole sentence 22–23, this seems to be the only plausible interpretation.

Furthermore, the Tibetan practice of cutting short the recitation in mid-sentence, half-way through verse 22, should not mislead anyone into supposing that the remainder of the 'benefit verses' is not part of the basic text. It is included in both Sanskrit and Tibetan texts, in the Kangyur and elsewhere, and is required so that the total length of the text should be twenty-seven verses, which is exactly 108 *pādas*, a number we have already found in connection with Tārā in *The Hundred and Eight Names*.]

*Actual commentary*

G: 'We therefore take three divisions:
I. Brief indication (the translators' homage)
II. Extensive explanation (verses 1–21)
III. Teaching of the benefits (22–27).

I. *Brief indication*

'This is
OṂ. JE-TSÜN-MA P'AK-MA DRÖL-MA-LA
CH'AK-TS'ÄL-LO!
(OṂ. Homage to the Venerable Ārya-Tārā!)'

[This phrase is not included in the Sanskrit text, but appears in the Tibetan translation in the Kangyur, without the OṂ, as the translators' homage, which traditionally precedes any Tibetan translation of a sacred text. In recitation, it is made into a mantra by the addition of the OṂ.]

G: 'OṂ means going for Refuge, making offering, or cleansing impurities. (D says that one can consider OṂ as A+U+M, since by the Sanskrit rules for combining sounds (*sandhi*), A+U+M coalesce into OṂ. These three letters represent the Body, Speech and Mind of the object of Refuge.)

'The JE in JE-TSÜN-MA means that of the Mothers who produce all the Buddhas of the three times, She is supreme. The TSÜN means possessing vows: from the outer viewpoint, [*Prāti*]*mokṣa*, from the inner, Bodhisattva, and from the secret, Tantric vows.

'P'AK-MA (*Āryā*, "Superior") means that She is far from non-virtue and what is abandoned by Insight, and above *saṃsāra* and *Nirvāṇa*.

'DRÖL-MA (*Tārā*, "Saviouress") means that She frees from the ocean of suffering. The MA (feminine ending) means that She helps all sentient beings equally, without partiality.

'CH'AK (literally "hand") means "sweeping away (*ch'ak*, but spelt differently) the negativities of karma and defilements", and TS'ÄL means acting devotedly with body, speech and mind.'

II, *Extensive explanation,* has three parts:

A. Praise in terms of Her story (1)
B. Praise in terms of Her aspects, the Buddha *Kāyas* ('Bodies') (2–15)
C. Praise in terms of Her activities (16–21).

A. *Praise in terms of Her story*

*namas tāre ture vīre*
*kṣaṇair-dyuti-nibhêkṣaṇe/*
*trailokya-nātha-vaktrâbja-*
*vikasat-keśarôdbhave//1//*

1 Homage! Tārā, swift, heroic!
With regard like instant lightning!
Sprung from op'ning stamens from the
Lord of Three Worlds' facial lotus!

S4: Compassion of Lord Avalokita,
Tārā who rejoiced to spring
Like lightning coming from a cloud
From stamens from his lotus face–
On Her let us meditate!

[*kṣaṇair-dyuti* (or *kṣaṇa-dyuti*) 'instant lightning': standard phrase for lightning. According to J, it is a simile expressing brightness.

*īkṣaṇe* 'regard' has the senses both of 'look, sight, eye' and of 'caring'.

*vaktrâb-ja* 'facial lotus': literally 'face-water-born', with double meaning: (a) since 'water-born' is a standard expression for 'lotus': 'lotus face', a common honorific term for any deity's countenance; (b) 'born from water from the face', i.e. a lotus born from tears. S4 & TT take (a); J, G and D take (b), D explicitly changing the Tib. translation to fit this choice. The same expression in verse 8 is of meaning (a), without ambiguity.

*vikasat* 'opening': the Tib. *bye ba* is the same as the word for 'ten million', sometimes giving rise to misinterpretation. From the Skt, it is certain that 'opening' is correct.

*Keśara* (or *kesara*) 'stamen', or more strictly, 'filament', can also mean a whole (lotus) flower, and can well be so interpreted here.]

*Tārā Swift and Heroic*

Tārā Swift and Heroic (*Pravīra-tārā*) sits in the midst of space, on a yellow[1,4] or golden[5] lotus seat. She has a red body radiating fiery light, one face with two eyes, and eight arms. RL1 are raised to proclaim the Dharma,[1,4] with the *mudrā* of Great Joy,[1] joining a *vajra* and bell on the crown of Her head.[5] RL2 hold a bow and arrow at Her heart, shooting someone. R3 holds a wheel, R4 thrusts a wisdom-sword; L3 holds a conch at Her heart,[1,5] or a *vajra*[4]; L4 holds a noose. She is adorned with all the ornaments.

Her rite is for turning back the power of others.

*G: '"I pay Homage"* is straightforward. Who to? – to Tārā (the Saviouress from samsaric suffering[J]). What was Her origin? – Ārya-*Lokeś*vara (i.e. Avalokiteśvara[DJ]), *the Lord* and Refuge of the *Three* Realms, Desire, Form, and Formless, which depend on the five or [in the Formless Realm] four aggregates that perish in an instant, saw that however many migrating beings He removed from saṃsāra, they grew no fewer, and He wept. Tārā *sprang from the opening filaments of His face* — of an utpala (blue lotus) that *grew* in the *water* of His tears.

(D explains the *three worlds* as the nāgas' world below the earth, the human world on the earth, and the world of the gods above.)

'She is *swift* in the aid of sentient beings, asking "I shall quickly do them the service of saving them from saṃsāra, so please do not cry!"; and in then turning back the battle of saṃsāra) (D: by destroying without remainder the army of Māra; J: by overcoming defilements), She is a *heroine*. Therefore Her two *eyes* see the three worlds *instant*aneously, *like* a flash of *lightning*.'

[The italicized words are those that appear in the Tibetan translation of the root verse. For clarity, Sanskrit words are not italicized in these extracts.]

B, *Praise in terms of Her aspects*, is twofold:

1. Praise in terms of Her *Saṃbhogakāya* aspects (2–14)
2. Praise in terms of Her *Dharmakāya* aspect (15).

1, *Praise in terms of Her Sambhogakāya aspects*, includes:

a. Praise in terms of peaceful aspects (2–7)
b. Praise in terms of fierce aspects (8–14).

a, *Praise in terms of peaceful aspects*, includes six homages.

i. *Praise in terms of the brightness and luminous radiance of Her countenance*

*namaḥ śata-śarac-candra-*
*saṃpūrṇa-paṭalânane/*
*tārā-sahasra-nikara-*
*prahasat-kiraṇôjjvale//2//*

2 Homage! She whose face combines a
hundred autumn moons at fullest!
Blazing with light-rays resplendent
as a thousand-star collection!

S4: With brightness of face of a hundred autumn
Moons, Her pleasing complexion emits
The bright-shining lustre of thousands of stars,
Dispelling the darkness of ignorance –
On Her let us meditate!

[*pra-hasat* 'resplendent, brightly shining': the principal meaning of HAS is 'to laugh, smile'. It also means 'to open (as a blossom)', as TT translate, which makes no sense here; and 'to excel, surpass', which is quite possible. In the meaning of 'to shine brightly', it carries the implied metaphor of the dazzling whiteness of teeth in a smile.

'Stars' is *tārā*.]

*Tārā White as the Autumn Moon*

Tārā White as the Autumn Moon (*Candra-kānti-tārā*) has three faces, representing the three *Kāyas* [or 'Bodies' of a Buddha – *Saṃbhogakāya, Nirmāṇakāya,* and *Dharmakāya*], and twelve arms, for the links of Dependent Arising. The centre face is white, the right blue, and the left golden[4,5] like gold from the Jambu river (or yellow[1]). Of Her arms, RL1 are in contemplation *mudrā*, R2 holds a *khaṭvāṅga* staff, R3 a (blazing[5]) wheel, R4 a jewel[1,4] or a wisdom-sword[5], R5 a *vajra*, R6 a garland of flowers; L2 a bottle, to wash away defilements and stains, L3 an *utpala*, L4 a bell, proclaiming the sound of Emptiness, L5 a pot of treasure, and L6 a small book, teaching the Dharma to sentient beings. She is bedecked with all the ornaments of a goddess.

Her rite is for calming infectious diseases.

G: *'Autumn moon* unmarred by cloud or mist, *at fullest* being a moon on full moon day when it has finished waxing and has not yet started waning. She has a countenance more luminous than *a hundred* such moons *combined* or heaped together. From this countenance, She is *blazing with light-rays* more *resplendent* than *a collection of a thousand stars.'*

ii. *Praise in terms of Her colour, hand symbols and causes*

*namaḥ kanaka-nīlâbja-*
*pāṇi-padma-vibhūṣite/*
*dāna-vīrya-tapaḥ-śānti-*
*titikṣā-dhyāna-gocare//3//*

3 Homage! Golden One, blue lotus,
water-born, in hand adornèd!
Giving, Effort, Calm, Austerities,
Patience, Meditation Her field!

S4: On Her of Wisdom nature, complete
In five Perfections, the *Āryā*,
We must, according to ritual,
Meditate in the two Stages, recite,
Worship extensively, praise and extol Her.

[The text of the first couplet – word for word, 'Homage! O gold-blue-water-born-hand-lotus-adorned female!' – is ambiguous as to whether 'gold' and 'blue' refer both to Tārā, as Tibetan commentators prefer; both to the lotus (blue with gold stamens), as Wayman and Beyer translate; or one to Tārā and one to the lotus, as translated above. The first choice is bizarre and can only have found favour because in the Tib., 'gold-blue' comes in a single metrical foot, making it hard not to read it as a unit. There is no doubt that for S, this Tārā is golden-coloured, and Her *utpala* lotus is blue by definition. Some lamas, rejecting all S's commentaries, consider that gold and blue makes a shining green. J simply ignores the 'blue'.

S's 'five Perfections' – Giving, Morality, Patience, Joyous Effort, and Meditation – must be completed before the Bodhisattva can attain the sixth, Wisdom. We recall that Tārā is identical with the Perfection of Wisdom since the Tantra describes Her as the Mother of all the Buddhas.]

*Golden-coloured Tārā*

The Golden-coloured Tārā[1,2,3,5] (*Kanaka-varṇa-tārā*), or Tārā of the Perfections[4], sits in the *vajra* cross-legged position (*vajra-paryaṅka*), very beautiful and shining, on a variegated lotus and sun[1,4] or moon[5] seat. She has one face and ten arms, for the ten Perfections: R1 holds a rosary at Her heart, R2 a wisdom-sword, R3 shoots an arrow (piercing defilements), R4 has a *vajra*, R5 a small staff; L1 a silk scarf, L2 a noose, L3 a lotus, L4 rings a bell, L5 holds up the bow (and arrow[5]) of Compassion.

Her rite is for prolonging life.

G: '*Gold* indicates the body colour, and *blue* the lustre colour [a tinge of some of the light radiating from Her]; for She is called the Golden-coloured Tārā. [Following eminent lamas, we here interpret the text as meaning the opposite of what it says – actually it has 'gold' and 'blue' the other way round.] The ring finger of Her left *hand adorns* Her at the heart with a *water-born lotus* or utpala (blue lotus), holding it with the bloom at the level of Her ears. This is a sign of the ten (J: six) pure Perfections.

'Therefore [*She*] is the Perfection of Wisdom, whose *field* is those of *Giving, Joyous Effort, Austerities* (*tapas*) or Morality, *Patience,* [and] *Meditation. Calm* means calming adverse factors such as avarice, laziness, immorality, aversion, distraction and wrong view. All this is Tara's *field of action* (*gocara*), She arose from that cause.' [G is here far from clear, but this is the only intelligible reading I can find and consistent with J. He is taking 'Calm' to be all six Perfections, as the elimination of their opposites. D explains it as Wisdom, the couplet then meaning 'She whose cause is the six Perfections!' Wayman's interpretation, taking 'Calm and Austerities' together as indicating Morality, is as plausible as either, and easier to reconcile with S. J is close to G, saying 'Calm' is the calming of defilements.]

iii. *Praise in terms of the devoted honouring by Conquerors and their Offspring*

*namas tathāgatôṣṇīṣa-*
*vijayânanta-cāriṇi/*
*aśeṣa-pāramitā-prāpta-*
*jina-putra-niṣevite//4//*

4 Homage! Crown of *Tathāgatas,*
She who goes in endless triumph!
Honoured much by Conqu'rors' Offspring,
having reached ev'ry Perfection!

S4: Marked with wish-granting jewel *uṣṇīṣa,*
Triumphant over all noxious foes
And Māras, complete in all the Perfections,

She's therefore worshipped by the Magnanimous –
On Her let us meditate!

[*uṣṇīṣa*, 'crown': the protruberance on the top of a Buddha's head.

'The Magnanimous': Bodhisattvas, = Offspring of the Conquerors.

*aśeṣa-pāramitā-prāpta* 'having reached every Perfection': grammatically, the root text and commentaries are ambiguous as to whether this applies to Tārā or to the Offspring of the Conquerors, but the former makes more sense. *aśeṣa-* makes too many syllables; W writes *'śeṣa-*.]

*Tārā the Victorious Uṣṇīṣa of Tathāgatas*

Tārā the Victorious *Uṣṇīṣa* of Tathāgatas (*Uṣṇīṣa-vijaya-tārā*) sits firmly in *sattva-paryaṅka* on a yellow lotus and moon seat (indicating uncontaminated virtue and non-attachment). She is golden in colour, shining like a golden mountain,[4] beautiful,[4] virtuous,[5] of the nature of Compassion and highest love towards sentient beings,[5] with one face and four arms, with which She has conquered the four Māras. R1 is in the *mudrā* of granting boons (*vara-da*), i.e. granting supreme *siddhis*,[5] R2 holds a rosary, L1 a bottle[1,4] or perfume (*gandha*)[5], L2 a staff[1,4] or a bottle[5].

Her rite is for neutralizing lethal poisons.

G: 'Since She is Mother of all *the Tathāgatas,* they carry Her like a *crowning uṣṇīṣa* on the top of the head. (D: She sits on the top of their *uṣṇīṣa.*) Therefore She is *one who goes in triumph* over *endless* problems of this life, obscurations of defilements (*kleśâvaraṇa*), and obscurations of knowables (*jñeyâvaraṇa*) such as those belonging to the three realms.

'What is honoured by the Conquerors' Offspring is the nature of all the ten Stages. She is *honoured much* with the crown of the head bowed in respect *by the Offspring of the Conquerors,* the Bodhisattvas, *having attained the* ten *Perfections.*'

iv. *Praise in terms of Her suppression of adverse factors*

*namas tuttāra-hūṃ-kāra-*
*pūritâśā-dig-antare/*
*sapta-loka-kramâkrānti*
*aśeṣâkarṣaṇa-kṣame//5//*

5 Homage! Filling with TUTTĀRA,
HŪṂ the regions and space-quarters!
Trampling with Her feet the sev'n worlds,
able to draw forth all [beings]!

S4: With the HŪṂ-sound of Her powerful mantra,
She fills the three realms, and trampling three worlds,
The Lords of All She summons and subjugates.
On the great Ruler let us meditate!

[*āśā-dig-antara* has a double meaning. With *āśā* 'regions' and *dig-antara* 'quarters of space' we get the plain meaning as translated above; but *āśā* can also mean 'wish, desire', hence the Tibetan translation 'desire and direction and space' and the interpretation of these three words as referring to the three realms. This interpretation is somewhat forced – the translation of *antara* ('interior; other') as 'space' is hardly literal, and it is not evident why it should mean the Formless Realm – and in any case it scarcely deepens the meaning.

'three/seven worlds': S4 has 'three worlds' in both root verse and commentary verse, but all other texts have 'seven worlds'.

5c-d: °*krānti aśeṣ*°: Q avoids the hiatus with °*krāntair,* De-ge with *niḥśeṣ*°.]

*Tārā Proclaiming the Sound of* HŪṂ

Tārā Proclaiming the Sound of HŪṂ[1,2,3,5] (*Hūṃ-svara-nādinī Tārā*), or the Tārā Summoning the Three Worlds,[4] sits in *vajra-paryaṅka* on an immaculate moon seat. Yellow[1] or the colour of refined gold[5], She has one face and two arms, R. giving Refuge and L. holding the branch of a golden lotus.

S5: Homage to Tārā Proclaiming HŪṂ,
On a seat of an immaculate moon,
Her colour pure, free of faults and defilements,
With the lustre of refined, rust-free gold!

Homage, O Heroine, wisdom-natured!
With Compassion inwardly pressing *saṃsāra*,
Proclaiming HŪṂ to tame the intractable,
In the three times winning Becoming's battle!

Her rite is subjugating.

G: 'Her speech of *TUTTĀRA HŪṂ* and the HŪṂ-letter at Her heart symbolize Emptiness and Compassion. *With* them *She* [*fills* with] concordant factors the *Desire and direction* or Form Realms *and* the *space* or Formless Realm.

'*The seven worlds* are those of the three ill destinies in the Desire Realm, human beings and devas of the Desire Realm, and the Form and Formless ones. *Trampling* them *with Her feet*, whose essence is Emptiness and Compassion, *She* is *able to draw* them *forth* to bliss *without exception*.' (J: 'She is able to subjugate kings and others.')

v. *Praise by the great worldly devas*

*namaḥ śakrânala-brahma-*
*marud-viśvêśvarârcite/*
*bhūta-vetāla-gandharva-*
*gaṇa-yakṣa-puras-kṛte//6//*

6 Homage! Worshipped by the All-Lord(s),
Śakra, Agni, Brahmā, Marut!
Honoured by the hosts of spirits,
corpse-raisers, *gandharvas*, *yakṣas*!

S4: The Glorious Lady, with mastery over
Lives mundane and supermundane,
Purger of sins and great fears, and granter
Of *siddhis* of *saṃsāra* and *Nirvāṇa* –
On Her the wise do meditate.

[*Śakra*: lord of the *devas* of the Desire Realm, known in Hindu mythology as 'Indra'.

*Viśvêśvara* 'All-Lord', 'Lord of the Universe' or of all the gods: a title applied particularly to Śiva, but also to Brahmā and Viṣṇu. G and D take it generally, as applying to all the gods mentioned, but GL, in agreement with J, taught it as meaning Śiva, and Wayman and Beyer treat it as a single god.]

Tārā Victorious over the Three Worlds[1,2,3] (*Trailokya-vijaya-tārā*), or over sins,[4] sits in *sattva-paryaṅka* on a red lotus and sun seat (because pure of delusion)[5], regarding sentient beings,[5] ruby-red and with one face and four arms. R1 holds a *vajra*, R2 a sword, L1 makes the threatening forefinger gesture (*tarjana*), and L2 holds a noose. (She is also known simply as Victorious Tārā[5] (*Vijaya-tārā*), and is thus likely to be confused with Tārā number 18.)

Her activity is purifying obscurations and negativities.

G: '*Homage*! Who to? – To Tārā *who is worshipped by the*

*Tārā Victorious over the Three Worlds*

*Lords* or chiefs *of the Universe* such as *Śakra,* ruler of the gods; *Agni* (god of fire), *Brahmā,* and *Marut* (god of the wind). In addition, She is *honoured by* Gaṇeśa (D: Īśāna), chief of *the spirits* (*bhūta*), Maheśvara (D: Rakṣas), chief of the *corpse-raising spirits* (*vetāla*), *gandharvas* such as Pañcatīra, and Vaiśravaṇa, chief of the *yakṣas,* together with their numerous *hosts* of attendants.' (D considers the gods mentioned in their role as directional guardians, and the classes of beings as attendants of directional guardians.)

vi. *Praise in terms of Her destroying opponents*

*namas traḍ iti phaṭ-kāra*
*para-yantra-pramardani/*
*pratyālīḍha-pada-nyāsa*
*śikhi-jvālâkulêkṣaṇe//7//*

7 Homage! With Her TRAṬ and PHAṬ sounds
crusher of foes' magic diagrams!
Putting Her feet left out, right back,
eyes all full of blazing fire!

S4: The great Goddess, crushing all adversaries,
Subduing opponents with TRAṬ and PHAṬ,

Beautiful, posture with left leg out
And right back, on yellow lotus and sun.

[*īkṣaṇe* 'eyes, look', but TT follows the reading *uj-jvale*, lit. 'blazing up' but also 'beautiful, glorious', as S, and as glossed by J and G 'looking gracefully (or proudly)' (*'gying bas*).
*ākula* 'full of; confused, raging'.]

*Tārā Crushing Adversaries*

Tārā Crushing Adversaries[1,2,3,4], or Crushing Disputants[5] (*Vādi-pramardaka-tārā*), abides in heroic and graceful *pratyālīḍha* posture – right leg bent and left stretched out – on a yellow[1,4] or orange[5] lotus and sun disk. She is black and fierce, with a wrathful face, and wears a yellow[1,4] or gold[5] dress. She is one-faced and four-armed, the hair of Her head bristling upwards, adorned with snakes, with jewelled tiara raised heavenward, and arms and legs adorned with bangles. R1 holds a wheel, R2 a sword, L1 a noose above the *yoni*, L2 is raised and extends a threatening forefinger.

Her ritual is for upward transference (of the *yogin*'s consciousness to the Akaniṣṭha Pure Land at the time of death).[17]

G: 'Being *She who*, with fierce mantras, *crushes* the hindrances to temporal and ultimate happiness through *the magical diagrams* for spells, curses, etc. which *enemies* create, She is called the Tārā Crushing Adversaries.

'Her posture for this pacification is with *right* foot *drawn back,* symbolizing realization of Emptiness, and *left stretched out,* symbolizing Compassion. *Putting down these feet,* Emptiness and Compassion, on the three samsaric realms, She is *'Beautiful in raging fire-blaze'* – next She does become fierce, but even now She looks gracefully in a rather fierce manner amid a blazing fire.'

D: *'Pressing* below Her *feet* enemies, magically-invoked demons and so forth, *She* burns them so that not even ashes remain, with *blazing, raging* and *greatly blazing fire* of Wisdom-knowledge from Her body.'

b, *Praise in terms of fierce aspects,* includes seven homages.

i. *Her quality of cleansing māras and the two obscurations*

*namas ture mahā-ghore*
*māra-vīra-vināśani/*
*bhṛkuṭī-kṛta-vaktrâbja-*
*sarva-śatru-niṣūdani//8//*

8 Homage! TURE, very dreadful!
Destroyer of Māra's champion!
She with frowning lotus visage
who is slayer of all enemies!'

S4: Great fierce one, protecting from the great fears,
With wrathful appearance slayer of enemies,
Foe of great foes, who gives all empowerments,
Nature of power – meditate on Her!

[*vaktrâbja* 'lotus visage': see note to verse 1.]

The Tārā who Crushes All Māras and Bestows Supreme Powers (*Māra-sūdanā vaśitôttama-da-tārā*) sits in *ardha-paryaṅka* on a red[1] or white[5] lotus, moon[1,4] or sun[5], and crocodile seat (to tame the wicked[5]). She is golden-coloured, with one face and four arms, with wrathful frown and shining complexion. R1 holds a branch of an *aśoka* tree, R2 a jewel,

*Tārā Who Crushes All Māras and Bestows Supreme Powers*

with the *mudrā* of granting boons, L1 a lotus, since She is not enwrapped in defilements and faults, and L2 a pot, bestowing supreme powers on all sentient beings.

Her ritual is the Completion Stage.[2]

G: '*TURE* (Swift One) is Tārā. *Very dreadful*: a fierce goddess. *Māra's champion* (the hardest of the Māras to subdue[D]) being defilements, She is the destroyer of these and (as a by-product[J]) the rest of the four māras. (D takes TURE [part of peaceful Tārā's mantra] to indicate Her speech.)

'Moreover, Her *lotus face* (– Her heroine's face, as pleasing as an open lotus[J] –) *is frowning*, assuming a fierce expression; and with this fierce expression She is *the slayer of the enemies* who obstruct the attainment of Liberation, the obscurations of defilements, and of the enemies who obstruct Omniscience, the obscurations of knowables – of *all* of these, i.e. together with their impressions.' (According to D, She is also slayer of all external enemies.)

[*Khadiravaṇī Tārā*]

Here S5 interpolates a description of KHADIRAVAṆĪ TĀRĀ, Tārā of the Fragrant Forest of *khadira* trees, not corresponding to

*Khadiravaṇī Tārā*

*Her companions, Mārīcī and Ekajaṭā*

any verse of the root text, and not mentioned in S's other texts:

S5: Homage! O Tārā of Khadira Forest!
Goddess born of the syllable TĀṂ!
Beauty with hair-curls bedecked with flowers
As sign of the *Dharmadhātu* Wisdom!

Homage! With left leg clasping the outstretched
Right, insep'rable Wisdom and Method,
Seated upon a lotus and moon,
With peaceful, one-faced, two-armed form!

Homage! Whose right hand grants boons to beings,
Blue lotus in left; complete with all ornaments,
Graceful, with shining blue-green complexion,
Youthful, wide-eyed and full-breasted!

Clearly She is the principal Green Tārā.[18] In the Tibetan tradition, however, She tends to change colour and take over the position of ninth of the Twenty-one Tārās.

ii. *Praise in terms of Her hand symbols, right and left*

*namas tri-ratna-mudrâṅka-*
*hṛdyâṅguli-vibhūṣite/*
*bhūṣitâśeṣa-dik-cakra-*
*nikara-sva-karâkule//9//*

9 Homage! She adorned with fingers,
at Her heart, in Three-Jewel *mudrā*!
Wheel of all quarters adornèd,
filled with masses of Her own light!

S4: She who is Buddha, born of Dharma,
And of all Saṅgha great loving Protector;
With self-produced light produced all around,
Of the nature of the wheel of directions
And secondary points — let us meditate on Her!

[*bhūṣitâśeṣa-dik-cakra* 'Wheel of all quarters adornèd': at least three meanings. (a) (S4:) The wheel of all quarters, i.e. the whole Universe, is adorned (with Tārā's radiance). (b) (TT:) She is adorned with 'wheels of all quarters', i.e. with luminous lines depicting thousand-spoked wheels on the palms of Her hands and the soles of Her feet, the first of the 32 Marks of an Enlightened Being. D seems to say that these are 'wheels of all quarters' because they fill all quarters with their light. (c) All quarters are adorned by Her wheels (because they radiate so much light). (We may note that while the usual Tib. reading implies meaning (b), the omission of the instrumental ending of 'wheel' in blockprint Q transforms the meaning to (a).)

*ākula* 'confused, agitated, disordered; filled with': S4's 'produced all around' (*kun skyes*) appears to be a gloss on this. TT *'khrug pa* 'agitated, disturbed; angry, contending'.]

*Tārā Granter of Boons*

Tārā Granter of Boons[1,2,4] (*Vara-da-tārā*), or Tārā Wheel-governing and Granting All Desires,[3,5] abides (with legs wide apart like a wrestler[5]) on a red lotus and moon, ruby-red, with one face and four arms, and adorned with all the ornaments. RL1 make the gesture of Great Joy, joining *vajra* and bell on Her crown to show the inseparability of Method and Wisdom. R2 makes a dancing gesture and L2 holds a branch of an *aśoka* tree, with fruit, and rains on all beings a torrent of precious things. (Since She accomplishes all activities, an excellent horse adorns the crown of Her head.)[5]

Her ritual is establishment, or consecration (*pratiṣṭhā*).

G: 'Left hand symbol: holding an utpala with the thumb and ring finger, She extends the index, middle and little *fingers at Her heart*: in this manner *She* is *adorned* [with the *gesture symbolizing the Three Jewels*].

'Right hand symbol:' (G being obscure here, we quote D!)

'Filling every part *of all the directions* with mutually *contending masses of Her own light*-rays emitted from the boon-granting palm, *adorned with a wheel*, of Her right hand, She outshines all other light.'

iii. *Praise in terms of Her diadem and laughter*

*namaḥ pramuditâṭopa-*
*mukuṭā-kṣipta-mālini/*
*hasat-prahasat-tuttāre*
*māra-loka-vaśaṃkari//10//*

10 Homage! She of swelling Great Joy,
diadem emitting garlands!
Mirthful, laughing with TUTTĀRE,
subjugating *māras, devas*!

S4: Her mind full of excellent concentration,
Her manner, of playing in joy and delight,
Her diadem of the five deities sparklingly
Laughing with light – meditate on Her!

[*āṭopa* 'swelling; multitude; pride': seems inconsistent with TT 'shining' and S4 'playing'. Could it once have read *āloka*, 'light'?[19]

*hasat-prahasat* (*-prahasa*[Q] scans better) 'mirthful and laughing, sparklingly laughing': with a play on the two senses discussed in the notes to verse 2, S makes this apply both to the light (not mentioned explicitly in the Skt, but introduced by TT) and the mantra. cf. S5: 'Who with loud laughter of TUTTĀRE/Removes all sentient beings' defilements!']

Tārā Dispelling All Sorrow (*Śoka-vinodana-tārā*) abides gracefully on a red lotus (for non-attachment[5]) and moon, beautiful, red as coral[4] or ruby[5], with one face and four arms. RL1 make the gesture of Great Joy[1] – palms joined[5] – on Her crown, R2 makes a sword gesture, L2 holds a branch of an *aśoka* tree ('sorrowless' tree).

[S4 could be read as saying She brandishes an actual sword in R2, as illustration N depicts; Q has merely a gesture.]

Her rite is entering the *maṇḍala*.

*Tārā Dispelling All Sorrow*

G: 'With the Noble Lady's ornaments, having fulfilled the desire of faithful and convinced disciples, *Great Joy*, She *shines*: Her jewelled *diadem emits garlands of light* that outshines other light. (D: 'Generating *Great Joy* by fulfilling the hopes of the faithful, and *shining* since She outshines the unfaithful, Her jewelled *diadem emits* multicoloured *garlands of light*-rays.' J: 'With *Great Joy*, She fulfils the desires of all sentient beings. *Shining*: outshining others. Her *diadem* beautifies [Her] with *garlands* of many jewels.')

'*Laughing* the *mirthful* sound of the Mantra, [*TUT*]*TĀRE*, She *subjugates the māras* and the eight *worldly* devas.'

iv. *Praise in terms of the accomplishment of activities through the ten directional guardians*

> *namaḥ samanta-bhū-pāla-*
> *paṭalâkarṣaṇa-kṣame/*
> *calad-bhṛkuṭi-hūṃ-kāra-*
> *sarvâpada-vimocani//11//*

11 Homage! She able to summon
all earth-guardians and their trains!
Shaking, frowning, with Her HŪṂ-sign
saving from ev'ry misfortune!

S4: Glorious summoner of all earth-guardians
Of the directions and secondary points,
She who with heart-reality, shaking,
Cures all misfortune – meditate on Her!

S5: Homage! Heroic, of wrestler's appearance,
Dark-coloured like a monsoon night,
Most fearful, outshining the army of Māra,
Raining gems and dispelling misfortune!

[The 'heart-reality' in S4 is the syllable HŪṂ in Her heart: see verse 21.

'Shaking': in the root verse it could be either Tārā or Her frown that is shaking, in S4 either Tārā or the HŪṂ, hence for consistency it must be Tārā Herself who quivers with divine rage.]

*Tārā Summoner of All Beings,*
*Dispeller of All Misfortune*

Tārā Summoner of All Beings, Dispeller of All Misfortune (*Jagad-vaśī vipan-nirbarhaṇa-tārā*), abides in graceful posture with right leg extended, on a lotus and sun seat. The colour of darkness, She has one face and two arms, R. summoning the eight great planets from the eight cardinal and secondary points with a hook, L. holding a magic noose[4,5] or magic hook[1].

Her rite is for increasing enjoyments[2].

G: '*Earth-guardians*: the ten directional guardians; *and their trains*: together with their entourages. *She able to summon all* these: She summons them all and induces them to accomplish divine activities. *Frowning, shaking*, i.e. abiding wrathfully, *with* light-rays from the *HŪṂ-syllable* at Her heart, She *liberates* from that suffering, with happiness, *every*one afflicted by *misfortune* or suffering.' (According to D, the light-rays form hooks, which draw forth everything desired.)

v. *Praise in terms of Her crown-ornaments*

*namaḥ śikhaṇḍa-khaṇḍêndu-*
*mukuṭâbharaṇôjjvale/*
*amitābha-jaṭā-bhāra-*
*bhāsure kiraṇa-dhruve//12//*

12 Homage! Crowning locks adorned with
crescent diadem, most shining!
In Her hair-mass, Amitābha
shining, with [much] light eternal!

S4: Adorned with crescent moon, whoever asks,
Increasing prosperity and good fortune;
With light that issues from Amitābha
Making a mass of merit-light shine –
On Her let us meditate!

[*śikhaṇḍa* 'crowning locks or tuft of hair': TT omits, adding in the next line *thams cad* 'all'.

*mukuṭā* 'diadem', normally of crescent shape, Tib. *dbu rgyan* usually altered to *dbu brgyan* which then means 'the crown is adorned'.

*bhāsure* or *bhāsvare* 'shining' (line d): TT has 'making'.

'Much' (line d): absent in Skt but added by TT (*shin tu*).]

Tārā Giver of All Prosperity[1,2,3,4] (*Kalyāna-da-tārā*), or Tārā of Auspicious Light[5] (*Maṃgalâloka-tārā*), sits in *vajra-paryaṅka* on a variegated lotus and moon seat. She is golden-coloured, with one face and eight arms, and adorned with a crescent moon. R1 holds a trident, R2 a hook of Compassion,

*Tārā Giver of All Prosperity*

R3 a *vajra*, crushing the host of Māra,[5] R4 a wisdom-sword; L1 a jewel, at Her heart (to increase enjoyments[5]), L2 a hook, L3 a staff, L4 a pot of money[1,5] or a bottle[4].

Her rite is fire-offering (*homa*).

G: 'Her actual crown-ornament is a *crescent moon*, a moon one day old, *adorning the crown* of Her head. From *all* this moon diadem (D: from this and other *ornaments*) *shine many* (bright[D]) light-rays, which remove sufferings.

'Her second crown-ornament is (the Buddha) *Amitābha*, sitting (as Lord of Her Family[D]) among the (*mass* of black, shiny[D]) hair on the crown of Her head, *eternally* sending forth *much*, or copious, *light* for the benefit of sentient beings.'

vi. *Praise in terms of Her fierce posture*

*namaḥ kalpânta-hutabhug-*
*jvālā-mālântara-sthite/*
*ālīḍha-muditābandha-*
*ripu-cakra-vināśani//13//*

13 Homage! She 'mid wreath of flames like
eon-ending fire abiding!
Right leg outstretched, joy-producing,
destroying the troops of enemies!

S4: The Heroine, ripening and destroying,
Shining 'midst mass of unbearable fire,
Creating joy in Her followers, crushing
Their foes, with fierce form – meditate on Her!

[*jvālā* 'flame, fire, light, blazing': TT 'blazing'.

*muditābandha* or *muditābaddha* 'joy-producing': so interpreted by S. The most literal meaning is 'bound round with joy', which TT translates loosely as 'surrounded with joy'. This phrase is ambiguous in Tib. and has been reinterpreted by Tib. commentators as 'rejoicing in turning', which is not a possible meaning of *muditābandha*. 'Joyous posture', as Beyer translates, is possible, but lacks commentarial support.[20] Note the lack of agreement on the case of *dga'* in the Tib., reflecting the unsettled interpretation.

'Ripening', or 'maturing', is in Skt the same word as 'cooking', and is thus an action of fire, like destroying.]

*Tārā the Ripener*

Tārā the Ripener (*Paripācaka-tārā*) is on a red lotus and radiant sun disk, in erect, striding posture, with right leg stretched and left bent, amid a cosmic fire-blaze. From Her unbearable body, Her ruby-red colour spreads everywhere, burning everything[4]. She has one face and four arms, Her frowning lips and eyebrows shaking[4] up and down[5], very terrible[5]. R1 holds a sword, R2 an arrow, piercing defilements,[5] L1 a wheel, L2 a bow.

Her rite is for subduing hindrances.

G: 'Displaying a fierce posture, amid a *wreath of blazing* flames of wisdom-knowledge, *like the eon-ending fire* which burns up earth and rock with rays hotter than seven suns, with *right* leg *outstretched* and *left bent*, She *destroys the troops of enemies* – the defilements (D: external and internal enemies) – of disciples who *rejoice* with faith in the *turning* of the Wheel of Dharma.'

vii. *Praise in terms of Her radiating light from a HŪṂ-syllable*

*namaḥ kara-talâghāta-*
*caraṇâhata-bhū-tale/*
*bhṛkuṭī-kṛta-hūṃ-kāra-*
*sapta-pātāla-bhedini//14//*

14 Homage! She who smites the ground with
Her palm, and with Her foot beats it!
Frowning, with the letter HŪṂ the
seven underworlds She shatters.'

S4: She who summons, smites and beats,
Holding the supreme syllable
Interrupts twice seven levels.
With devout service to the Goddess
Practise free of hate, and wrathfully!

[*bhedini* 'shattering, splitting': M has *nāśini* 'destroying, conquering', closer to TT *'gems ma*. S4 in the above verse and root verse has *'gegs* 'interrupts, hinders', but later has *'gems*: 'Subduing at once the three realms and sev'n levels.'

'beats' (S4): reading *brdung* for *gdung*.]

Tārā the Wrathful Summoner[1,2,3,4], or Shaking Frowning Tārā[5] (*Bhṛkuṭī-tārā*), abides on a red[5] or orange[1] lotus and sun seat, trampling a human corpse as She dances with outstretched right foot. Her body is black and terrible in form, with three wrathful faces, each with three red eyes staring angrily, frowning with contracted brows and lips, the principal face black,

*Tārā the Wrathful Summoner*

the right white and the left red. She wears a necklace of skulls[1,4] or heads[5], a skull tiara, and a tiger-skin loincloth, is adorned with (eight)[4] snakes, and is devouring human entrails. Her six arms hold: R1 a sword, R2 a hook, R3 a small staff, L1 a skull brimming with blood, L2 a noose, L3 (Brahmā's[4]) head.

Her rite is a protective circle.

J: 'Her left hand strikes the ground and makes the threatening forefinger. Vocally saying HŪṂ, by sending out light from Her right hand, which holds a *vajra,* She fills the places of the seven classes and dispels all their hindrances.' [G seems a little garbled and incomplete, but has the HŪṂ syllable at Her heart.]

D: '*The surface of the Earth,* Mount Sumeru with the continents, *She smites* fiercely *with the palm of Her hand,* with threatening forefinger, and *beats with Her foot. Assuming* a very fierce aspect, face contracted in *a frown,* etc., from blue *HŪṂ-syllables* on the palms of Her hands and the soles of Her feet She emanates a thunderstorm of vajras, thus *destroying* or conquering the harmful beings such as nāgas, asuras and yamas (= pretas?) who dwell in *the seven underworlds* (*pātāla*), Pātāla, Mahātala, Atala, Talātala, Rasātala, Sutala and Vitala.'

2. *Praise in terms of Her Dharmakāya aspect*

*namaḥ śive śubhe śānte*
*śānta-nirvāṇa-gocare/*
*svāhā-praṇava-saṃyukte*
*mahā-pātaka-nāśani//15//*

15 Homage! Happy, Virtuous, Peaceful!
She whose field is Peace, *Nirvāṇa*!
She endowed with OṂ and SVĀHĀ!
Of the great downfall destroyer!

S4: The Goddess, through happiness, grants upper rebirth;
With virtue She gives Liberation,
Likewise with Peace, Perfect Buddhahood.
On the Giver and Downfall-destroyer, meditate!

[*saṃyukte* 'She endowed with': the feminine vocative ending in all versions of the Skt (Tib. *ma*) makes lines c and d into separate phrases. With the perhaps more common Tib. reading *pas* they must be taken together, 'She who destroys . . . *with* that endowed with . . . .

*pātaka* 'downfall, crime' or *pāpaka* 'sin': much the same meaning.]

*Tārā the Great Peaceful One*

Tārā the Great Peaceful One[1,2,3,4] (*Mahā-śānti-tārā*), or Virtuous, Peaceful Tārā,[5] sits in *vajra-paryaṅka* on a white lotus and moon. She is white[1], the colour of the moon[5] or of white jasmine[4], with one face and six arms: R1 holding a rosary, at Her heart, the sphere of the Conquerors; R2 with the *mudrā* of granting boons[1,4], the auspicious *mudrā*[5]; R3 holding a small staff, L1 a lotus, L2 a bottle, and L3, on a broad-petalled *utpala*, a book, teaching the Path to sentient beings.

Her ritual is the external washing ritual.

G: 'Since She is called "Venerable", She is *happy* (reading *bde* for *pad*), endowed with uncontaminated happiness; also *virtuous*, since She is virtuous by separation from the objects of abandonment, the defilements; and *peaceful*, one in whom their result, suffering, has been pacified. She is one who *lives in* (*cara*, part of *go-cara* "field") *Nirvāṇa*, where conceptualizations are *pacified*.

'According to certain scholars, also, She is *happy* because, from cutting projection [of inherent existence] (*samāropa*) by studying and thinking about non-inherent-production, on the Path of Accumulation, She is without unhappiness. She is *virtuous* because by experience arisen from meditation, on the Path of Preparation, She is without signs of coarse conceptualizations or defilements. She is *peaceful* because through separation from their seeds on the Path of Insight, the result, suffering such as birth, aging, sickness and death, has been pacified. On the Path Beyond Learning, She has actualized the Dharmakāya, *Nirvāṇa*, where they are *pacified* with their impressions (*vāsanā*).

'She is the *destroyer, with* Her ten-syllable mantra *which has SVĀHĀ* at the end, *OṂ* at the beginning, and eight [i.e. seven] mantric syllables in between, *of the great downfall*, delusion grasping at true existence.

'This is praise in terms of Her Mind and Speech, which are [of the nature of] the Dharmakāya.'

D: 'She is *happy* because She lacks suffering result, *virtuous* because She does not accumulate its cause, non-virtue, and *peaceful* because the object of abandonment, defilements, has been exhausted. Because She is always concentrated on the sphere of the Supreme *Peace* of *Nirvāṇa*, beyond the two obscurations, *She* is one who has that *field. By* reciting Her ten-syllable mantra ... in accordance with the ritual, *great downfalls* in the reciter's mindstream such as the five immediate [karmas], or abandoning the Dharma, their causes, great defilements such as greed and hatred, and their great suffering results such as the Great [Hot Hells] and Cold [Hells], are *destroyed* without remainder.'

C, *Praise in terms of Her activities,* includes six homages.

1. *Activities of Her peaceful and fierce mantras*

*namaḥ pramuditābandha-*
*ripu-gātra-prabhedini/*
*daśâkṣara-pada-nyāse*
*vidyā-hūṃ-kāra-dīpite//16//*

16 Homage! She bound round with joy, and
tearing foes' bodies asunder!
Luminous with the HŪṂ-mantra,
word-array of the ten syllables!

S4: Bound round with such as acuteness and
mindfulness,
Crushing the hosts of the enemy, ignorance,
With the array of the ten wisdom syllables,
And through HŪṂ, She frees from *saṃsāra*'s
And *Nirvāṇa*'s darkness. Meditate on Her!

S5: Homage! Through HŪṂ endowed with knowledge,
With two arms uniting Method and Wisdom!

[*pramuditābandha*, °*baddha* 'bound round with joy': = *muditābandha*, cf. note to verse 13. The same transformation in the Tib. has occurred here.

*gātra* 'body': S4 reads 'host, army' in both root verse and commentary.

*pada-nyāse* or -*nyāsa*.

*dīpite* 'luminous, illuminated, set on fire; manifested (from)': given that *dīpinī* 'illuminating' can mean a mantra, *dīpite* could mean 'She whose mantras are ...'. The Tib. has no word that corresponds, unless perhaps the gratuitous *nyid ma* 'Herself' was meant to be *nyi ma* 'sun'. Tib. also has *sgrol ma* (= *Tārā*) 'She who Liberates' instead of *kāra* 'syllable' (HŪṂ), for the preceding word. S4's 'frees from darkness' contrives to fit both Skt and Tib. versions!]

*Tārā Destroyer of All Attachment*

Tārā Destroyer of All Attachment[1,2,3,5] (*Rāga-niṣūdana-tārā*), or Destroyer of Enemies,[4] sits in *sattva-paryaṅka* on a red[5] or orange[1] lotus and sun disk. She is coral-red, beautiful and bright,[5] with one three-eyed face and two arms. R. holds a trident at Her heart, piercing an enemy's body, L. holds a tree with fruit at Her heart, with a threatening forefinger gesture.

Her function is mind-increasing:

S5: Through Her ten-syllable essence of Mind,
Source of all needed realizations!

S4: Her essence of Mind, the Supreme Mantra
Of ten syllables, circling, grants
All desired *siddhis*, increases intelligence,
And is abode of all courage.

G: '*The word-array of the ten syllables* is the mantra of the syllables OṂ TĀRE TUTTĀRE TURE SVĀHA! *The* HŪṂ*-mantra* (*vidyā*-HŪṂ-*kāra*) is the fierce mantra, OṂ NAMAS TĀRE NAMO HARE HŪṂ HARE SVĀHĀ! With these two, She *tears asunder the bodies* [*of the*] *foes* of the Liberation of disciples who *rejoice* with faith in the *turning* of the Wheel of Dharma – attachment to the internal as "I" and attachment to the external as "mine".' (D: emitting light rays etc. from these mantras, which surround the syllable TĀṂ (peaceful aspect) or HŪṂ (fierce aspect) respectively in Her heart, She liberates [from] enemies such as hindrances.) (J is silent on this verse apart from identifying the mantras.)[21]

2. *The fierce activity of shaking the three worlds*

*namas ture padâghāta-*
*hūṃ-kārâkāra-bījite/*
*meru-mandara-kailāsa-*
*bhuvana-traya-cālini//17//*

17 Homage! Swift One! The foot-stamper
with for seed the letter HŪṂ's shape!
She who shakes the triple world and
Meru, Mandara and Kailās!

S4: The bliss-endowed Goddess, by stamping Her feet,
Shakes the three worlds, and terrifies.
Protector born from seed-syllable HŪṂ,
She moves and subjugates Meru and all.
On Her let us meditate!

[*padâghāta* 'foot-stamping': *pa*° scans better than *pā*°.
*Kailāsa*: TT replaces this famous Tibetan mountain by Vindhya, the name of a range of low hills stretching across India. Since Kailāsa is often identified with Mount Meru,[22] perhaps the change was thought necessary so as to avoid repetition.]

Tārā Accomplisher of All Bliss[1,2,3,5] (*Sukha-sādhana-tārā*), or Endowed with Bliss,[4] sits in *sattva-paryaṅka* on a shining white lotus, (a moon disk[5]) and a sun seat. She is orange in colour, with one face and two arms, beautiful, and adorned with many jewels. Both hands hold a moon disk at Her heart

*Tārā Accomplisher of All Bliss*

[although the root text demands that the next Tārā should be the one with the moon disk].

Her rite is for binding thieves.

S5: One-faced, two-armed, performing with HŪṂ
The action of subjugating the triple
World and accomplishing every bliss.

G: 'By *stamping Her feet, TURE* (the Swift One), (the Fierce Goddess[DJ]) who is born from a *seed of the form of HŪṂ*, (quells hindrances[J] and) is able to *shake* externally *the three worlds*, Mounts *Meru, Mandara,*[23] *Vindhya* and so on.'

3. *The activity of dispelling poisons, animal and otherwise*

*namaḥ sura-sarâkāra-*
*hariṇâṅka-kara-sthite/*
*tāra-dvir-ukta-phaṭ-kāra*
*aśeṣa-viṣa-nāśani//18//*

18 Homage! She in whose hand rests the
deer-marked moon, of *deva*-lake form!
With twice-spoken TĀRĀ and PHAṬ,
totally dispelling poison!

S4: The *Āryā*, holding the *devas'* clear lake,
Spreads bliss unpolluted and dispels poison.
Pleasing, applying the mantras and substances,
Triumphs o'er poisons. Meditate on Her!

[*hariṇâṅka* 'deer-marked': a standard Indian name for the moon.

*sthite* 'rests': most versions of the Tib. have 'holds'.

*tāra* or *hara*, *phaṭ* or *sphuṭ*[24]: Skt sources evenly divided.

'Pleasing . . .': the second two lines of S's verse refer to the ritual for neutralising poison which he describes. As a preliminary, one must please the Goddess by practising *yoga*; then the actual rite involves five kinds of substances over which corresponding mantras must be recited.]

*Tārā the Victorious*

Tārā the Victorious ([*Sita-*]*vijaya-tārā*, '*Sita*' 'White' to distinguish Her from number 6) sits in *sattva-paryaṅka* upon a white lotus, a moon disk and a goose with fine wings. She is white, one-faced and four-armed. RL1 hold hooks on the crown of Her head, with the *mudrā* of Joy. R2 has the *mudrā* of granting boons, L2 holds a book, on a blue lotus.

Her rite is for curing the *nāga*-disease (leprosy).

S5: Homage! Spreader of unpolluted
Great bliss, white with a conch-like complexion,
One-faced, four-armed, with twice-spoken TĀRĀ
And the sound PHAṬ dispeller of poisons!

G: '*She holding in Her hand the* [*deer-marked* or] hare-marked, a moon-disk, like *the lake of the devas*: this is a sign of dispelling the torment of inanimate poisons, the defilements. In speech, *with twice-spoken TĀRĀ and PHAṬ*, [i.e. with the specially modified mantra OṂ TĀRE TUTTĀRE TURE PHAṬ![D],] *She totally dispels* animal *poisons*.'

['Hare-marked' is another common name for the moon in India and Tibet.

D names the divine lake as Lake Mānasa, i.e. the sacred Mānasa-sarovara at the foot of Mount Kailās, often identified with the legendary Lake Anavatapta, and notoriously round and clear.

Poisons are classified as of animal origin (*jaṃgama*), or inanimate (*sthāvara*), i.e. vegetable or mineral. Here and at verse 25, G adopts an awkward, asymmetrical interpretation, taking the former literally and the latter metaphorically. J and D avoid this by not identifying defilements with either type.

According to GL, to dispel poison for oneself or another one may simply visualize Tārā holding a moon disk, with light coming from the moon disk and the mantra, and recite the above mantra.]

4. *The activity of dispelling conflict and bad dreams*

*namaḥ sura-gaṇâdhyakṣa-*
*sura-kiṃnara-sevite/*
*ābandha-muditâbhoga-*
*kali-duḥsvapna-nāśani//19//*

19 Homage! She whom god-host rulers,
gods and *kinnaras* do honour!
Joy-producing One, Her fullness
conflict and bad dreams dispelling!

S4: Much honoured by rulers of the three worlds,
She generates joy, and with blazing splendour

Drives out bad views and suffering.
At the six times, meditate on Her with effort!

[*ābandha-muditā, ābaddha-* 'Joy-producing One': = *muditā-bandha*, see verse 13. Here the Tib. has 'all [in] armour [of] joy'; maybe TT's text had *ā-varma-muditā*? The meaning of this couplet thus becomes quite different for the Tibetans.

*ābhoga* or *bhoga* 'fullness' in several senses, also 'effort; rule': TT has 'splendour', which S4 seems to confirm – possibly they read *ābhāsa*.

'Six times': see commentary to 26d below.]

*Tārā Consumer of All Suffering*

Tārā Consumer of All Suffering (*Duḥkha-dahana-tārā*) sits in *sattva-paryaṅka* with right leg slightly advanced, on a white lotus and sun[1,4] or moon[5] disk. Her graceful body, one-faced and two-armed, is white like jasmine[4] or a conch[5], and adorned with a garland of variegated, white and red light-rays, eliminating all the defilements of sentient beings. Both hands hold at Her heart a brazier, consuming sufferings.

Her rite is for freeing from prison.

G: '*She whom the rulers of the hosts of devas* – Śakra, of the devas of the Realm of Desire, and Mahābrahmā, of the Realm of Form – *devas, and* the king of the *kinnaras*, Mahādruma (J:

Druma), and others, honour devotedly with the crowns of their heads, is Tārā alone.

'If, *all* devotedly, one takes to heart with one-pointed, *joyful* mind Her *armour* – Her bodies of peaceful and fierce aspects and Her peaceful and fierce mantras – then *with splendour* of inspiration She *dispels conflict* with others (J: with Tīrthikas) *and* also *bad dreams*.'

D: 'For one who in *every* way dons the Goddess's *armour* of meditating on Her form and reciting Her mantra, *with* very *joyful splendour She dispels* all *conflict* with others *and bad dreams*.'

5. *Tārā's activity of dispelling fever*

*namaś candrârka-saṃpūrṇa-*
*nayana-dyuti-bhāsure/*
*hara-dvir-ukta-tuttāre*
*viṣama-jvara-nāśani//20//*

20 Homage! She whose eyes are bright with
radiance of sun or full moon!
With twice HARA and TUTTĀRE
Driver-out of chronic fever!'

S4: The Goddess of gnosis, whose bright wisdom-eyes
See the obscured and the unobscured,
Destroys bad migrations' and *saṃsāra*'s sicknesses,
And the defilements – meditate on Her!

['Full' grammatically covers both 'sun' and 'moon', but by commonsense one can take it with 'moon'.

*viṣama-jvara* is literally 'uneven fever', i.e. a chronic fever that lingers on and on, flaring up again and again – as S explains, the supreme example is samsaric existence itself, a disease that repeatedly flares up in the acute phase of the three bad migrations. TT translates more generally as 'very terrible fever'.]

Tārā Source of All Attainments (*Siddhi-saṃbhava-tārā*) sits in *sattva-paryaṅka* on a red[1,4] or white[5] lotus and moon disk. She is orange[1,5] or coppery golden[4] in colour, (indicating the

*Tārā Source of All Attainments*

Action Family,[5]) with one face and two arms, both holding at Her heart a golden pot, subduing disease and granting all attainments.

Her rite is for making invisible.

S5: Homage! O pot with spices and gems,
Wish-granting cow, great wishing tree,
By thinking of whom all wants arise,
In whom any wish or hope is fulfilled!

J: 'Her right eye is marked with the moon and the left with the sun . . .'

G. 'It may seem to say "right eye like the sun and left eye like the full moon", but it means that fierce [Tārā's] eyes like the full *sun*, and peaceful [Tārā's] *two eyes* like the *full moon* emit *very bright radiance*, (great and cool [respectively][D]). *By* this, and by pronouncing in speech Her mantras – *"twice-uttered HARA"*, i.e. Her fierce mantra, and *"TUTTĀRA"*, i.e. Her peaceful mantra – She is *dispeller of very terrible fevers.*'

6. *The activity of subduing evil spirits and corpse-raisers*

*namas tri-tattva-vinyāsa-*
*śiva-śakti-samanvite/*

*graha-vetāla-yakṣâugha-*
*nāśani pravare ture//21//*

21 Homage! Full of liberating
power by set of three Realities!
Crushing crowds of spirits, *yakṣas*
and corpse-raisers! Supreme! TURE!

S4: The Powerful One, showing the three Realities,
By divinity, mantra, *samādhi*,
In the three places; crusher of harmful
Groups, disyllabic one – meditate on Her!

[*tri-tattva* 'three Realities' (see commentaries). The Tib. and commentaries leave no doubt about the correct reading.[25]

*śiva* 'liberating': the Tib. translation *zhi ba* is valid provided it is interpreted in the special sense of 'Liberation, *Nirvāṇa*'; but its common meaning of 'pacification' in general is not shared by *śiva*.[26]]

*Tārā the Perfecter*

Tārā the Perfecter (*Paripūraṇa-tārā*) sits in *ardha-paryaṅka* on a miraculously born bull on a lotus and moon disk. She is white, beautiful and shining, with one face having three eyes for the three Doors of Deliverance, and two arms, and of a very wrathful appearance, wrapped in a tigerskin loincloth, to purify hatred. With inexhaustible Compassion, She holds R. a string of pearls, L. a three-pronged lance to pierce the three poisons, which are the cause of *saṃsāra*.

Her rite is for 'sky-going', e.g. going to the Akaniṣṭha Pure Land in this very life:

S4: Following one with all rituals, pleasing
The Goddess, habitually off'ring, reciting,
Always remember the three Realities;
One will then realize the perfect sky-going.

G: 'The *set of three Realities* is the set of the Realities of the Body, Speech and Mind: the Reality of the Body [of the deity, symbolised by] the syllable OṂ on the crown (of the practitioner[D]); the Reality of the Speech, ĀḤ at the throat; and the Reality of the Mind, HŪṂ at the heart. She is *fully endowed with* the power of these, and *the power of pacifying* inanimate poison, the defilements. (D: She is *fully endowed with the power of pacifying* all misfortunes of the three doors, *by* meditation on these *three Realities*.)

'She is *crusher* of animal poisons, *the crowds of evil spirits* (*graha*) (of eighteen kinds[D]), *corpse-raising spirits* (*vetāla*) *and yakṣas*; and the *Supreme One* is *TURE*, Tārā.'

(D adopts Tāranātha's rearrangement of the last line to read 'She is the Supreme One quickly crushing the crowds of spirits etc.'. J: '(c) She is liberated from all hindrances. (d) She crushes all adversity by the power of Her ten-syllable mantra.' Neither mentions the two kinds of poisons.)

III, *Teaching of the benefits*, has four parts:

A. Distinction of the thought (22)
B. Distinction of the time (23)
C. Actual explanation of the benefits (24-26c)
D. Condensed statement of the benefits in numerical terms (26d-27).

*mantra-mūlam idaṃ stotraṃ*
*namaskārâika-viṃśakam/*
*yaḥ paṭhet prayato dhīmān*
*devyā bhakti-samanvitaḥ//22//*

*sāyaṃ vā prātar utthāya*
*smaret sarvâbhaya pradam/*
*sarva-pāpa-praśamanaṃ*
*sarva-durgati-nāśanam//23//*

22 This praise, rooted in mantras, a
twenty-one-fold homage – for one
Who recites it, wise and pious,
full of faith towards the Goddess,

23 And remembers it at even
or at dawn on rising, it grants
Ev'ry fearlessness, quells all sins,
and destroys all bad migrations.

[*mantra-mūlam* 'rooted in mantras': TT 'of the root mantra', or in other versions 'with the root mantra'; but the more general sense is used in the first theory quoted by G at the beginning of the commentary, and other mantras and mantric syllables besides the root mantra are mentioned in the verses – HŪṂ, TRAṬ, PHAṬ, OṂ TĀRE TUTTĀRE TURE PHAṬ, OṂ ĀḤ HŪṂ, and the fierce Tārā mantra.

*eka-viṃśakam*[TW] 'twenty-one-fold, consisting of 21 parts': thus *namaskārâika-viṃśakam* means either 'consisting of 21 homages' or 'a homage in 21 parts'.

*prayata* 'pious' implies 'self-subdued, intent on devotion, well-prepared for a solemn rite'. Other readings: *prasanna* 'faith' = Tib. but does not scan; *prayatna* '(with) effort'.

*sāyaṃ* 'in the evening', other texts *śayaṃ* 'at bedtime'.

*vā* 'or' (23a): TT 'and' may come from a simple scribal error, *dang* for *dam*.

*durgati* 'bad migration': in Buddhist texts, usually refers to birth in the three ill destinies, but it can also mean 'distress' in general.]

A. *Distinction of the thought*

G: '*Whoever recites this* twenty-one-fold *praise of* the peaceful and fierce *root mantras and twenty-one-fold* devout *homage* of the three doors, *full of devotion towards the Goddess* Tārā (remembering Her kindness[D]), i.e. not just [reciting] the words with the mouth alone, but *endowed with mind,* i.e. wisdom (distinguishing good and evil[D]), that is one-pointed, and *piously intent,* (mindful of the benefits as described,[D])

B. *Distinction of the time*

'and *remembers* [it] *in the evening and* (i.e. or) *having risen* from his bed *at dawn,* i.e. just by remembering in general the Bodies, mantras and Praise and in particular the fierce Body etc. in the evening and the peaceful in the morning, in this life *it grants* him *every fearlessness* of such hindrances as sickness demons and untimely death, and in the next, since *it quells all sins* which are the cause of bad migrations, *it destroys* the result, *all bad migrations.*'

(D says one should praise in the evening, remembering mainly the fierce aspect, for the fearlessnesses of this life, and in the morning, remembering mainly the peaceful aspect, for those of the next; thus it overcomes the eight great fears, both external and internal.)

C. *Actual explanation of the benefits*

*abhiṣikto bhavet tūrṇaṃ*
*saptabhir jina-koṭibhiḥ/*
*asmin mahattvam āsādya*
*so 'nte bauddha-padaṃ vrajet//24//*

*viṣaṃ tasya mahā-ghauraṃ*
*sthāvaraṃ vâtha jaṅgamam/*
*smaraṇāt pralayaṃ yāti*
*khāditaṃ pītam eva vā//25//*

*graha-jvara-viṣârtānāṃ*
*param arti-vināśanam/*
*anyeṣāṃ câiva sattvānāṃ*

24 Quickly he'll be consecrated
by sev'n times ten million Conqu'rors.
Gaining greatness herein, he will
reach at last the rank of Buddha.

25 The most dreadful poison, whether
animal, or plant or min'ral,
Whether he's devoured or drunk it,
meets its end through his rememb'ring.

26 It completely stops the pain of
those whom spirits, fevers, poisons
Afflict – other beings' also.

[*asmin* (24c) 'herein' = 'in this [life]' (J, G). Tib. *'di la*[GJ] is more accurate than the usual *'di las* that has sadly misled D, '(greater) than this [present state]', unless the meaning is 'thereby'.

*bauddha-padaṃ* or *bauddhaṃ padaṃ* (24d): no difference.

*saḥ* (24d) 'he' (nominative singular) should be *de* in Tib. but has somehow got changed to *der*. It corresponds to the *yaḥ* 'one who' at 22c.

*tasya* (25a) 'he, that' (genitive singular) can be straightforwardly identified with this *saḥ*, meaning that the whole verse is to be taken 'in relation to him'. But in the Tib., the alteration in the previous line tends to make this pronoun refer to 'the rank of Buddha', as G interprets.

*sthāvaraṃ* (25b) 'plant or mineral, inanimate': cf. verse 18. I translate the plain meaning, in accordance with D, but G interprets it metaphorically using the literal meaning 'stationary, stable'.

*ārtānāṃ* (26a) is genitive *plural*: 'of those afflicted'. TT obscures the sentence considerably by failing to make this point. All three lines 26a-c must concern the benefit of others. *anyeṣāṃ sattvānāṃ* 'of other beings' can be read as extending the meaning to beings afflicted by other sorts of pain, or else simply taken in apposition to *ārtānāṃ*: 'It also completely stops the pain/even of other beings afflicted/By spirits, fevers or poisons.']

G: '*Quickly*, in this life, *by seven times ten million Conquerors he will* gradually *be consecrated* (or empowered) (with light-rays or streams of nectar[D]). *Gaining in this* life the common *great* attainments such as subjugating human beings and ghosts, *he finally reaches* the supreme attainment, *the rank of Buddha*. (D: 'By the power of this, temporally *he gains* perfect abode, body, enjoyments and entourage, *greater* and more excellent *than this* present state, and traversing quickly the Stages and Paths, he reaches the *Final* Result, *the rank of Buddha*.')

'*The most dreadful poison* which is a hindrance *of that* rank of Buddha is just perverse view. What makes it extreme, *fixedly abiding* (*sthāvaraṃ*), is denial of the mode of existence of dharmas through the dharma of delusion, and destruction of [positive] karmas by hatred towards the Dharma and its proponents, through violent hatred: such are the inanimate poisons. These are eliminated. (For D, *the most dreadful poisons* are the defilements, such as the well-known 'three poisons' of greed, hate and delusion; for J, just 'thieves etc.' *Inanimate* poisons are those that exist in the physical environment.[D])

'*Or else* animal poison – [when one is] seized by *sentient beings*, a venomous dog or a venomous snake – and *whether devoured or drunk*, poison of food and drink *indeed, meets its end* just *through* (reciting the Praise[D]) *remembering* the form etc. of the Goddess (J: remembering the Praise, the mantra and the Goddess). 'This is elimination of causes of suffering. As to the elimination of violent suffering result: *it completely stops the pain of those afflicted by*, i.e. [that] produced by, *evil spirits, fevers and poisons.*

'This is one's own benefit. As to others' benefit, as is said, "*of other sentient beings also,*" when for others' sake also one endowed with devotion recites in the evening and on rising at dawn, remembering Her Bodies etc., benefits are received as above.'

D. *Condensed statement of the benefits in numerical terms*

*dvis-tri-saptâbhivartinam//26//*

*putra-kāmo labhet putraṃ*
*dhana-kāmo labhed dhanam/*
*sarva-kāmān avāpnoti*
*na vighnaiḥ pratihanyate//27//*

26d On performing twice three sevens,

27 One who wants a child will get one,
one desiring wealth will find wealth,
One obtains all one's desires; by
hindrances one's not frustrated.

[*abhivartinam* 'performing': TT suggests the reading *abhivādinam* 'saying'.

*putra* 'child' or (perhaps more likely) 'son'.

*dhanam* 'wealth' is sing. but TT adds a plural particle just for the metre.

27d is perfectly clear and unambiguous in the original but the Tibetan translation is very loose, reversing the sense of the existing verb, ignoring the endings, and expanding the 'not' into another verb: 'hindrances do not exist and will be subdued'.]

G: 'As to the meaning of 26d, some smooth-talkers say that on reciting *twice, one desiring a child will get a child,* on reciting *three* times, *one desiring wealth will find wealth,* and on reciting *seven* times, *one obtains all one's desires.*

'The translator Pang[27] says that the *two* refers to distinctions of the person who is the basis, the practitioner: "*who . . . wise*" (22) indicates one of sharp faculties, the Dharma-follower (*dharmânusārin*); and "*pious*" indicates one of dull faculties, the Faith-follower (*śraddhânusārin*). [These terms come from a standard classification of the types of Ārya beings.] *Three* indicates distinction of time: "*at even Or at dawn, on rising* (= having risen)", i.e. from daybreak to the evening watch. "*On reciting in sevens*" indicates the distinction of the number; on reciting seven times at each of the three times, i.e. 7 × 3 = 21 times, *it grants every fearlessness,* etc., and *one obtains all one's desires,* for it is impossible to obstruct this attaining: *hindrances not existing,* objects of abandonment *will be subdued* by their respective antidotes.

'Butön Rinpoche teaches as follows. *On reciting in two* – the daytime and nighttime halves of the day – *three,* the morning, midday and afternoon watches of the daytime and the evening, midnight and dawn watches of the night, making six watches – and *seven,* seven times in each of these six, or 42 times per day in all – these benefits will come.'

(D follows Butön. He says that '*one desiring a child*' includes someone holding a spiritual lineage who desires a disciple to continue the lineage. '*All one's desires*' are one's desires both temporal and ultimate. *Hindrances* do *not* newly arise, and those already arisen *will each be subdued.*)

'The analysis of the Praise to the Venerable Ārya-Tārā by the complete and perfect Buddha Vairocana is completed.'

# Part Three
## *History*

# 1 *Tāranātha's Golden Rosary*

## THE AUTHOR[1]

Tāranātha, or Kün-ga nying-po, born in 1575, was the most prominent scholar of the Jo-nang-pas, a small school noted for their unorthodox views on the nature of Reality.[2] He was a disciple of the widely-travelled Indian master Buddhagupta, who must have supplied much of the material for the present work. His many writings include histories and Tantric commentaries, particularly on Tārā and one of the main preoccupations of the Jo-nang-pa school, Kālacakra. The most famous is his great *History of Buddhism in India* (*rGya gar chos 'byung*), written in 1608, four years after *The Golden Rosary*, and similar in style. It is available in an English translation by Lama Chimpa and Alaka Chattopadhyaya. Another such historical work is his *Precious, Amazing, Marvellous Biographies of the Lineage-holders of the Sevenfold Descent of the Word*[3] (1600), of which an English abstract of Grünwedel's German translation exists under the title of *Mystic Tales of Lāma Tāranātha*. These works complement the present one and will be referred to by the initials *HBI* and *MT*.

About 1615 he built the monastery of Tak-tän,[4] where the blocks of his works were kept. Afterwards he was invited to Mongolia, where he founded several more monasteries and eventually died. Soon after his death, the Jo-nang-pa school was suppressed, probably for political reasons. His line of incarnations has continued in northern Mongolia until modern times.

## SYNOPSIS

*The Golden Rosary* recounts the history of the Tantras of Tārā, particularly the *Origin of Tārā Tantra* (*Tārā-bhava-tantra*), of which the *Sarva-tathāgata-mātṛ-tārā-viśvakarma-bhava-tantra* translated above is the main surviving fragment.[5]

We have already given as our Prologue the opening section, from the ultimate origin when, inconceivable eons ago, the woman who was to become Ārya-Tārā first took the Bodhisattva Vow, through Her Enlightenment, to the teaching of Her Tantras. What follows is the remainder of the text, set in historical time and describing the transmission of this Tantra through Buddhist India, with numerous stories of its successive lineage-holders. At intervals, the chronological sequence is interrupted by sets of further anecdotes of Tārā's practitioners and Her miraculous interventions on their behalf. These tales are arranged mainly around the ever-popular theme of Tārā's saving from the eight (or sixteen) fears.

## TĀRANĀTHA'S CHRONOLOGY

The earlier Tibetan historian, Gö Lotsawa (1392–1481), went to much trouble to calculate dates with respect to the Tibetan calender of sixty-year cycles. Within his chosen field, the introduction of the Buddha-dharma to Tibet and its transmission there, he succeeded remarkably well. Tāranātha's main interest as a historian was Indian Buddhism, all the way back to its origins. He had no hope of extending Gö's system of absolute dating over this terrain, but in *HBI* he nevertheless did his best to set up a frame of reference in the form of a list of kings prominent in North India, with (wherever possible) the supposed durations of their reigns. It is not his fault that the Indian records available to him were so sparse and unreliable that he must often have had to guess (or press his Indian teachers to guess) which king came after which. Unfortunately, the wrong assumptions involved in his analysis mean that his statements about dates and contemporaneity must often be in error or hard to interpret.

In *The Golden Rosary*, he had not yet developed his king-lists, but the same problem arises. He divides the history of the Tārā Tantra into three main periods:

(a) The period of earlier dissemination, subdivided into
  (i) before Master Nāgārjuna,
  (ii) during Nāgārjuna's life, and
  (iii) from the passing of Ārya-Nāgārjuna to the coming of King Dharmapāla.

(b) A period of decline, following Dharmapāla's suppression of the Tantra.

(c) The period of later dissemination, beginning with Tilli-pa.

In each of the three parts of (a), he says, some five thousand people attained *siddhi* through this Tantra.

The accession of King Dharmapāla of Magadha and Bengal, an important patron of Buddhism, is dated by modern historians at c.783 AD,[6] while Tilli-pa is given dates of 928 to 1009 (see below). But Tāranātha's Nāgārjuna is not a simple historical figure. He is supposed to have been born 400 years after the Buddha's *Nirvāṇa*, as stated in the Sūtras, and have lived either 529 or 571 years—the first 200 years in the Madhyadeśa and the rest in the South, in particular at Śrī-Parvata, a rocky crag overhanging the River Kṛṣṇa near Dhānyakaṭaka and Amarāvatī.[7] This 'chronological Nāgārjuna', then, despite his extraordinary longevity, must be supposed to have passed away at least three centuries before Dharmapāla came. (Archaeological evidence bears out the tales of the historical Nāgārjuna's presence in that region early in our era;[8] he had certainly passed away long before Hiuan-tsang visited there in 639.)

The trouble is that Tāranātha assumes the *Siddha* Nāgārjuna who is important in the history of Tārā Tantra to have been the same person. Since this Nāgārjuna probably flourished around 800 AD,[9] this error is enough to make the account of the earlier dissemination thoroughly distorted. To span the fictitious centuries from Nāgārjuna to the advent of Dharmapāla, Tāranātha has worked out a list of eleven names (Chart 1), many of them unrecorded elsewhere and so readily assignable to any

Guhya-śīla
|
Tripiṭaka Hayapāla
|
Haya-ghoṣa
|
Ārya-Nāgārjuna (c.800)
|
Āryadeva
|
Rāhulabhadra the Younger
|
Jvalaśeṣpa
|
Dharmabhadra-pāla of Kashmir
|
Nāgamitra
|
Sūryagupta
|
Sarvajña-mitra (c.700)
|
Dhana-mitra
|
Tathāgata-mitra
|
Dharmamitra of Siṃhala-dvīpa
|
Śīla-rakṣita
↓

*Chart 1. Lineage of the earlier dissemination of the* Tārā-bhava-tantra, *according to* The Golden Rosary.

period. With the equally obscure predecessors of Nāgārjuna, the lineage purports to go back to about the fourth century, far earlier than any other known Tantric lineage and long before Tārā images took recognisable form. This is absurd.

Tāranātha surely did not invent the names. What he must have done is put in one linear sequence what should really be several parallel branches, rather like the lineage of the later dissemination (Chart 3). The earliest name in the list could well be Sarvajña-mitra's.

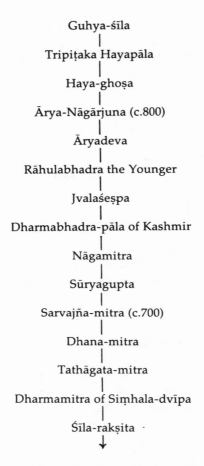

## THE DATES OF NĀRO-PA

Nāro-pa's biography says he passed away at Phullahari in the Iron-male-dragon year in his eighty-fifth year.[10] Guenther has claimed that because Marpa met Nāro-pa and told him of Milaräpa, who was only born in 1040, this Iron-male-dragon year could not have been 1040 and must have been the next one, 1100.[11]

This theory, however, is unacceptable. It implies, for example, that Nāro-pa was thirty-four years younger than Atīśa, though the present Tārā lineage makes him two spiritual generations older, and the lineage of the Guhyasamāja Tantra (*BA* 361) places him no less than three spiritual generations before Atīśa's *guru* Ser-ling-pa. More ludicrous still, it makes Nāro-pa four years younger than his disciple Marpa (1012–97),[12] whereas the biographies make it clear that when they first met, Marpa was a young man, in his early twenties at the most,[13] while Nāro-pa had already spent many years in study with numerous teachers, become a great *paṇḍita* at Nālandā university, and then followed Tilli-pa for many years more. Besides, the story of Nāro-pa, just before he died, conferring responsibility for the order on Atīśa at Vikramaśīla, after which Atīśa took his relics to Tibet, where they remained at Nye-t'ang,[14] shows that his death could not possibly have been later than 1040.

Thus if it is true that Nāro-pa passed away in an Iron-male-dragon year, that year must have been 1040 and not 1100. Marpa's later meetings with him must have been in the nature of apparitions after Nāro-pa's physical passing, as indeed their position in his biography (just after the account of his death) suggests. We can take it that Nāro-pa probably lived from 956 to 1040.

The dates of his *guru*, Tilli-pa, become accordingly Earth-male-mouse year 928 to Earth-female-hen year 1009.[15]

## THE LATER DISSEMINATION

The later lineage, unlike the earlier one, was a live lineage that Tāranātha had himself received. We can therefore have more confidence in its accuracy.

It reached him by two main routes (see Chart 3), a long

transmission via Atīśa, taking eighteen steps to pass from Tilli-pa to Tāranātha, and a short one in only eight steps via Asitaghana. Tāranātha had already given the stories of the *yogins* involved in the short transmission in *MT*, and does not repeat them here. Asitaghana, he says, was nearly two hundred years old when he met Jñāna-mitra, and the latter spread the Doctrine for a hundred years, Śānti-gupta being a later disciple of his. If we can believe this—and such long lives are reported for some Indian *yogins* even today—we can accept the short transmission as quite possibly true.

Fortunately for anyone trying to make sense of Tantric history, such extreme longevity is exceptional even among Tantric practitioners—though plenty of them live to eighty or ninety, few go much beyond that. Thus few will pass on a lineage more than sixty years after receiving it. Often the interval will be much less, so the average length of a spiritual generation is of the order of thirty-five years.

*Tantra* in Sanskrit means a warp thread. Chart 2 shows just a few threads of the thousands in the tangled skein of Buddhist Tantra, some lineages that intersect the long transmission recorded by Tāranātha. By combining different lineages in this way, positioning them in relation to the time scale so that the intervals are plausible, we can share out the few established dates and get a reasonable idea of when each person lived. Of course there are problems—the chart includes two Buddha-śrī-bhadras who are surely not the same person, and two Ratna-rakṣitas who might possibly be; the source is ambiguous as to whether Muni-śrī-bhadra and Karuṇā-śrī-bhadra occupy successive positions or share the same one; and names are often mis-spelt and elements of them dropped or added. Even so, someone spending a few years sorting out all the known lineages with a computer could surely clarify the subject a great deal.

The chart reveals an excessive gap between Nāyaka-śrī and Dharma-śrī. Perhaps the 'Nayaka-śrī' of the Tārā lineage is not the same person as the 'Nāyaka' and 'Nāyaka-pāda' of S and V and the abbot Nayaka-pa-śrī; or perhaps he has simply slipped two places down the list from where he should have been. Such a switch is quite possible, for Tāranātha admits knowing nothing of the people concerned. Either correction

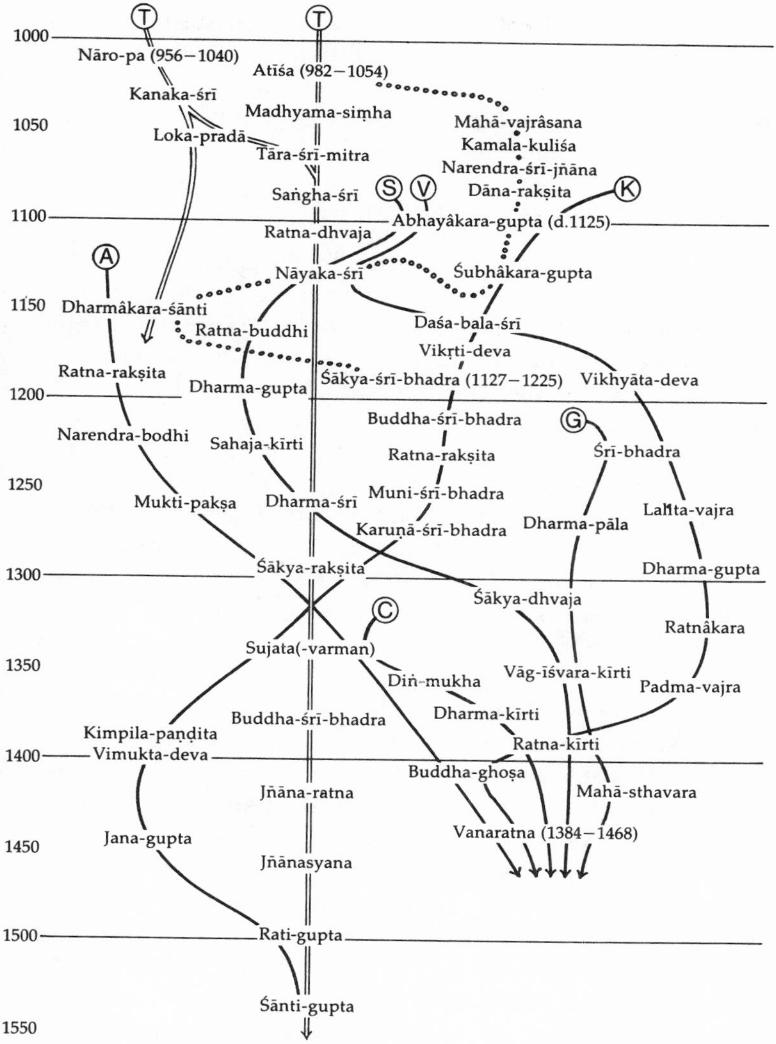


*Chart 2. Part of Tāranātha's lineage for the Tārā Tantra (T); with relevant segments of other Tantric lineages (solid lines) and the succession of abbots of Vikramaśīla (circles). A: Anupama-rakṣita's Ṣaḍ-aṅga-yoga* (BA *800*). *C: a Cakrasaṃvara practice* (BA *803*). *G: Guhyasamāja Ṣaḍ-aṅga-yoga (Wayman,* Yoga of the Guhyasamāja-tantra, *36*). *K: Kālacakra texts* (MT *63–68*). *S:* Śrī-saṃpuṭa-tantra *commentary* (BA *801*). *V:*Vajrāvalī *after Abhaya* (BA *801*).

would allow Tāra-śrī-mitra, and thus Loka-pradā, to be later, reducing the interval of nearly a hundred years between Loka-pradā and Dharmâkara-śānti; but when you have read Loka-pradā's extraordinary life-story below, you will probably not be too worried about this.

## THE INDOCHINESE CONNECTION

The most interesting feature of the long transmission is that when Buddhism finally collapsed in India in the early thirteenth century, this lineage went east to Haripuñjaya (now Lam-phun, Thailand) and then Cambodia, before returning west to Nepāl in the mid-fifteenth century and eventually reaching Tibet with Tāranātha's gurus about 1600.

Haripuñjaya was a colony founded by Mòn people from Lop-buri under their queen Cama-devī in the eighth century.[16] The Mòns were Buddhist, predominantly Theravādin, but on Haripuñjaya's southern border was Sukhodaya, until 1260 a province of the Mahāyānist/Śaivite Khmer empire. In 1260, Sukhodaya was taken over by local Thais in a coup, while at the same time a leader of the Thai Lao tribe named Mangrai set up his head-quarters at Chieng-rai in what is now the far north of Thailand. Mangrai extended his influence south-west and in about twenty years managed to take control of Haripuñjaya. It would seem to be during this turbulent time that Śākya-rakṣita was in Haripuñjaya, and Tāranātha's 'Caṅgala-rāja' must surely be 'Chieng-rai-rāja', i.e. this Mangrai.

In the new Thai kingdoms, Sinhalese Theravāda Buddhism rapidly gained ground, while the Indianized Khmer social order broke up and the Mahāyāna declined. It would have been natural for the remaining Mahāyāna teachers, Śākya-rakṣita or Sujata among them, to retreat to the Khmer heartland, Cambodia. There too, after the fall of Angkor in 1431, Mahāyāna Buddhism died out in the second half of the fifteenth century[17] and there was nothing left for Jñānasyana to do but move to Nepāl.

As Chart 2 shows, the Tārā lineage was not the only one to be transmitted through Śākya-rakṣita and Sujata. No doubt some of the other masters appearing in that part of the figure also lived in Cambodia. According to Tāranātha, the great *paṇḍita* Vanaratna came from that part of the world, but this conflicts with the account in *BA*.[18]

This story of almost constant decline of Mahāyāna Buddhism finds no mention in Tāranātha's pages, as one would expect of an author who has managed to present Indian Buddhism, during its disintegration under the Muslim onslaught, as going from strength to strength.

## THE STORIES

The many tales of miracles performed with Tārā's aid are what most people will read this text for, and mostly provide welcome relief from the rather controversial history. Some may have grown in the telling, but the plausible background details of many confirm that they are undoubtedly of Indian origin. Other versions of several of these anecdotes are to be found in Beyer's book.

Such stories are an inseparable part of Tārā's cult, and John Blofeld has beautifully retold some more modern examples from Tibet and China in his *Compassion Yoga*.

## THE TRANSLATION

I first encountered this text in a translation by an American, Vajranātha, which conveyed much of its charm but on comparison with the original proved to be often wildly inaccurate. Recently another purported translation has been published in India, whose perpetrator has hardly understood a single sentence correctly. He not only distorts many of the stories out of all recognition, but conveys the grossly misleading impression that Tāranātha (and very likely all Tāntrikas) were virtually incapable of rational thought. To correct this, I feel obliged to publish my own translation here.

# THE GOLDEN ROSARY: A HISTORY ILLUMINATING THE ORIGIN OF THE TANTRA OF TĀRĀ

*(sGrol ma'i rgyud kyi byung khungs gsal bar byed pa'i lo rgyus gSer gyi phreng ba zhes bya ba)*

*By Tāranātha*

(Continued from the Prologue)

As to the teaching of the Mantrayāna in general in six 'encouragements', it is taught that the present is [the period of] the teaching of Heruka. The arrangement of the six 'encouragements' is made clear in the [Heruka] Tantra itself.[19]

As to this teaching in particular:

## HOW THE TĀRĀ TANTRA APPEARED IN JAMBUDVĪPA

Three hundred years after the *Nirvāṇa* of the Conqueror, sometime after the Śrāvakas held their third Council,[20] most of the Sūtras of the Great Vehicle,[21] which had been in the abodes of the *devas, nāgas, yakṣas, gandharvas* and *rākṣasas,* arrived in various places in India. [15] Spontaneously-arisen books also appeared and spread at the same time. The ascetics and Dharma-preachers who taught them attained the acceptance that *dharmas* are unproduced and saw the faces of Mañjuśrī, Avalokita, Maitreya and others; the five hundred masters (*ācārya*) of the Yogācāra, the eight *mahātmas* of the Niḥsvabhāva-vādins (= Mādhyamikas) and others appeared.[22] At the same time as them, the *Kriyā-*, *Caryā-* and *Yoga-tantras* also spread, together with all kinds of Method and Wisdom Tantras of the *Anuttara* Vehicle. Those who saw the faces of Vajrasattva and Guhyapati (= Vajrapāṇi) taught fortunate beings, so that at that time, it is said, not one of all those who listened to the Mantrayāna [16] failed to attain realizations (*siddhi*).

In the east, in Bhaṅgala (Bengal), King Haricandra and his court of a thousand realized the Body of Unification, and in Oḍiviśa (Orissa), King Muñja and his court of a thousand attained the state of *vidyādhara*. In the west, in Mālava (Malwa, central India), King Bhojadeva and his court of a thousand became invisible. In the south, in Koṅkaṇa, King Haribhadra and his innumerable retinue attained the *siddhi* of pills.[23] Thus, for one or two hundred years, over one hundred thousand people attained *siddhi*. It is said, however, that because secrecy was always kept, no-one else would know they were practising Mantra practices until they gained *siddhi*. [17]

## [STORIES OF TĀRĀ'S ASSISTANCE]

In those days, Venerable Ārya-Tārā would, out of Her Compassion, show Her face even to the unrealized. Let us relate in brief some stories of Her assistance, found in oral tradition.

### 1. *Protection from the fear of enemies*

It is said that a certain *kṣatriya*, having fallen asleep in a park in Oḍiviśa, was surrounded by an enemy army, a thousand strong, bearing weapons. He had no other refuge, but he had heard there was someone called Tārā who protected from the sixteen fears, and thinking 'I take refuge in Her alone,' he called on the name of Tārā. The moment he cried out, the Venerable Lady appeared in the sky before him. From beneath Her foot [18] arose a mighty wind, by which the soldiers were carried to the ten directions and reached their own country.

### 2. *Protection from the fear of lions*

A wood-gatherer went to the forest, and met a hungry lioness who set about eating him. Carrying him in her jaws, she returned near her den. Frightened and terrified, he implored Tārā, and there appeared before him a woman clad in leaves,[24] who took him out of the lioness's mouth and set him down in the marketplace of the town.

### 3. *Protection from the fear of elephants*

A twelve-year-old country girl, who had gone to a dense forest to gather flowers, [19] met a fierce elephant called Khuni ('Wantonly-sportive'). He caught her in his trunk and began to crush her against his tusks. When she remembered the name of Tārā, and begged Her aid right from the heart, the elephant was brought under control. He set her down on a high ledge of rock, saluted her with his trunk, and took her up again. Then he did the same thing in the marketplace of the town, then at the council chamber, at the temple, and at the gate of the king's palace. Thinking 'This girl is one of great merit', the king made her his queen.

### 4. *Protection from the fear of fire*

A certain family was involved in a feud. One night their enemy set fire to their house. [20] When they tried to escape and could not get out, they called out by name, 'O Tārā, O Tārā, alas!' Thereupon there appeared above the house a beautiful, very blue cloud, and a torrent of rain fell only on the house, to the measure of an ox-yoke (four cubits, or about two metres), putting out the fire.

### 5. *Protection from the fear of poisonous snakes*

A certain prostitute in a city once met a merchant, who gave her a necklace of five hundred pearls. Wishing to go to the merchant's house at midnight, she left her own house, and on the way took hold of a branch of a *śirīṣa* tree (*Acacia sirissa*). a poisonous snake coiled in the tree wound itself round her body and held her. By her merely remembering Venerable Tārā, the poisonous snake [21] was transformed into a garland of flowers. It is said that it remained on her body for seven days, then the snake became white and non-poisonous and went into the river.

### 6. *Protection from the fear of bandits*

In a part of Gujiratha (Gujarat) called Bharukaccha (Broach) was an extremely wealthy merchant. Loading his baggage on some thousand camels and five hundred bulls, he set out for the country of Maru (Mārwar). On the way, he came to a wilderness where there lived as many as a thousand bandits. The whole place was full of the flesh, blood and bones of all the merchants who had come before and been killed. A hundred thousand of them had been impaled on stakes. These bandits were like *rākṣasas* (ogres), even eating human flesh. [22] So the merchant was very afraid, and as he had no other protector, prayed to Tārā. Thereupon appeared a measureless army of heroes, wielding weapons, who were emanations of Tārā, and drove the bandits a long way away, but without killing any. Thus the bandits were dispersed, while the merchant went his way easily and got back to Bharukaccha.

7. *Rescuing from prison*

The leader of some thieves pierced a way into a king's treasury. When he went in, he found a pot of wine, which he drank, and so became drunk and fell asleep. Perceived by the king's men, he was seized and thrown into prison. He was tied up with ropes and experienced manifold sufferings. [23] Then, lacking any other protector, he prayed to Tārā, and a five-coloured bird descended from the sky and loosed his bonds. The prison door opened of itself, and he was free to go as he wished.

When he had returned to his own country, there came to him in a dream a woman adorned with all the ornaments. She said, 'If you remember my kindness, you and your followers should abandon your thieves' work!' Therefore that thief and his five hundred followers gave up thieving and performed a great many virtuous deeds.

8. *Protection from the fear of ocean waves*

Some five thousand merchants set out on the way south. They took three big ships, [24] boarded the biggest, and went to the Island of Jewels.[25] There they filled one ship with jewels. Leaving there again, they came to an island of white sandalwood, and filled the second ship with white sandalwood. Then they wished to go home, but the lords of wealth (*dhanapati*) of the ocean were angry and sent a great wind, which carried them far away. After they had crossed seas of many different colours, they met violently agitated waves. Although the merchants on board prayed day and night to Brahmā, Viṣṇu, Śiva, Soma, Sūrya, Kuvera and other gods, they did not help. The ships' cables parted and the ships of jewels and sandalwood were lost, while the biggest ship was about to sink, [25] when a Buddhist layman on board thought of Tārā and recited in a loud voice Her ten-syllable mantra. Immediately, a favourable wind sprang up, and the ship came back again and in one night reached India. The ships of jewels and sandalwood were also driven home by the wind, and they came together.

### 9. *Protection from the fear of* piśāca *demons*

There was a monastery in the east inhabited solely by Saindhava Śrāvakas (monks of the Saṃmatīya school).[26] At one time there, each evening every *bhikṣu* who went for a walk in the grounds outside the monastery died. Thus the monastery's congregation dwindled. One evening a certain novice went to the walking [26] area, and a black, ugly *piśāca* demon appeared, baring its fangs, and grabbed him by the head. Thinking 'They say that according to the Mahāyānists, there is someone who protects from the eight fears, called Tārā. I take Refuge in Her,' he called on the name of Tārā. A black goddess brandishing a sword appeared there, and threatened the demon. The demon begged the novice's pardon and gave him an iron pot he extracted from under the ground, full of pearls. From then on, the harm to the monastery stopped.

### 10. *Protection from the fear of leprosy*

In the country of Kumārakṣetra,[27] by the power of karma a brahman teacher caught leprosy. [27] By contagion from one to another, five hundred brahmans were infected with the virulent disease. Rejected even by relatives and doctors, they violated the brahmans' rules of purity and subsisted on refuse. While living as beggars, they saw by the road a stone image of Venerable Ārya-Tārā. Faith was born in them, and the five hundred brahmans prayed to Her. Then from Tārā's hand came forth a stream of medicine, and just bathing in it cured their leprosy. It is said their bodies became extremely beautiful, like those of gods.

### 11. *Protection from the messengers of Indra*

Indra is the directional guardian of the east [28], and his messengers are the evil spirits that are *gandharvas*. They are very rough and fast-moving and a great hindrance to the Dharma. Here is a story of protection from them.

In a grove in Mathurā were five hundred Śrāvaka *bhikṣus*, practitioners of *dhyāna* meditation, who lived striving after virtuous qualities. At one time, some messengers of Indra came, some in the semblance of brahmans, some of women, and some of *bhikṣus*; sometimes many appeared with the fierce aspect of *yakṣas* and the faces of terrifying animals such as lions, elephants or *śarabhas*;[28] sometimes they beguiled them with threats and sometimes with flattery and the like. Some of the monks [29] lost their memory, some went crazy, and some became mentally deranged and spent their time only in singing and dancing.

One *bhikṣu* there understood that they were being harmed by interferences from spirits. Since it was well-known that the Goddess Tārā saves from all fears, he thought She would help in this case, so he wrote 'This grove belongs to the Goddess Tārā' and fixed it to a tree. Just through this, the danger subsided of itself, and with conviction towards the Goddess Tārā they all entered the Great Vehicle.

12. *Protection from the fear of poverty*

It is said that a certain very poor brahman, greatly afflicted, related to a stone image of Tārā, which was in a lane, [30] the story of how his sufferings came about. She then pointed to a place near a *stūpa*, and said 'Dig[29] there, and you will find treasure!' By digging,[29] he found many things such as a golden jar full of pearls and a silver jar full of all sorts of jewels, which eliminated the suffering of poverty down to the seventh generation.

It is also said that a poor farmer made request to Venerable Tārā, calling upon Her name, and a woman in a dress of leaves[30] appeared, and instructed him, 'Go to the east!' He went to the east, and as he slept on a sandy surface, he was awakened by the sound of bells. [31] There was a green horse, with bells as ornaments, digging the sand with its hoof. Then, in a moment, the horse went away somewhere else. He dug[29] in the mark of the horse's hoof. First there was a silver door, then a golden one, then crystal, then lapis lazuli, and so on—doors of the seven precious things, which opened in turn. In a country under the ground, he became the chief of many *nāgas* and *asuras*, and enjoyed many sensual pleasures. One day he returned through a hole in the earth to his own country, and by then three successive kings had passed away.

13. *Protection from the fear of separation from kinsfolk*

There was a brahman who had many relatives [32] and much wealth. It happened once that a great pestilence came, through which his children, wife, brothers, brothers-in-law, maternal uncles and other relatives all died. His mind oppressed by sorrow, he went to Vārāṇasī.

Then he came to a place where some Buddhist lay-followers were holding a great festival for Tārā. Thus he heard of the greatness of Tārā. Scattering some handfuls of flowers, he prayed to Her. When he returned home, he won as a bride the daughter of King Jayacandra,[31] and became a ruler of the land. He built a hundred and eight temples to Tārā and instituted in all of them a great Buddhist festival.

14. *Protection from the fear of punishment by the king*

In the country known as Ayodhyā, [33] there was a householder great in fortune and wealth. At one time, for some reason the king of the country became displeased with him, and began to criticize him. He in turn seduced and led away many of the king's men and went to Tirāhuti (Tirhut). Another time, he went to the country of Campārṇa (Champāran), and the king of Ayodhyā sent four strong men, who bound the householder and led him to Ayodhyā. Remembering Venerable Tārā, he prayed to Her, and by Her divine inspiring power, the threshold turned to gold when he set his foot on it, and when he was put into the prison, a rain of pearl necklaces fell there. When they set about impaling him on a stake, the stake became a mango tree adorned with flowers and fruit. The king [34] was amazed, as was everyone else, and saying 'This man is greatly endowed with merit. How can he deserve to be killed in punishment?' assigned him the rank of a royal minister.

15. *Protection from the fear of falling thunderbolts*

A certain lay follower in the country of Bhaṅgala (Bengal) was going along watching the field-work. On the road was a *yakṣa's* shrine. The layman stepped over it and went on, which made the *yakṣa* angry. In the night, twentyone blazing skybolts hurtled down from the sky at the layman as he rested in his house. At this, he thought of Ārya-Tārā, and simply by this the flames of the skybolts all turned into flowers, while the layman himself and his children, wife, possessions and so forth were completely unharmed. The skybolts [35] remained on the house and he gave them all to some five hundred *vidyā-mantra-dharas* (Tantric practitioners). It is said they came in useful as materials for their practice.

16. *Protection from the fear of failure in one's aims*

A householder went to another country, bearing goods. He wished to receive some land from the king. He entrusted his property to a friend and embarked in a big ship on the sea. For many years he travelled to islands in the sea, but attained no kind of wealth. Eventually, the ship was driven fortunately by the wind and reached the island of Malakha (Malacca?). On this island there were coral and white sandalwood that one could take at will, so he took a lot, filled his ship and left.

Before the journey was complete, his ship was broken, holed by a blow from the snout of a sea monster of the fish family, called Macchi ('Fishy'). Grasping a plank of wood, [36] he was driven by the waves and reached India. When he inquired after his friend again, he learned that he too had gone travelling and was dead, having been eaten by a tiger. Since he had realized no profit in this, he suffered from weariness and was mentally unhappy.

At this time, urged by a friend, he developed faith in Tārā and made request to Her. She told him in a dream, 'Go to the bank of the River Sindhu (Indus)! The aims you desire will be accomplished.' He did so, and found in the River Sindhu all the wealth that had previously been in his ship and been lost in the sea. Then he went to his late friend's land and dug[29] in the ground, and his possessions that he had entrusted to him emerged.

Then he returned to his own country. He offered the king a piece of white sandalwood trunk as a present, [37] and the king gave him five fine towns.

In addition, there are very many marvellous legends of later times, such as Her inciting Master Nāgārjuna to practise, twice protecting Candragomin from the fear of water,[32] protecting Sarvajñamitra from the fear of fire,[33] protecting the *upāsaka* Bhadanta Asvabhāva from the fear of poisonous snakes,[34] and showing Her face to Master Sthiramati.[35]

## [MIRACULOUS IMAGES OF TĀRĀ AT BODHGAYĀ]

A Saindhava Śrāvaka living at Vajrāsana (Bodhgayā) was going in the rainy season to Māyā.[36] The River Nairañjanā, known in the common speech as the Phalgu,[37] [38] was newly in flood. When he crossed it, he could not reach the bottom of the ford, and was swept away by the waters. He thought 'They say the Mahāyānists have a protector from the fear of water, called Tārā,' and shouted out 'Tārā!'. Because of this, a wooden statue of Tārā that was in the outer courtyard at Vajrāsana actually came there, and said 'You never think of me—how is it right that you call me now?' But he got out of the water. That image is known as the Tārā of the River.[38]

Another time, an old woman erected a temple to Tārā at Vajrāsana, showing the face outwards. When it was finished, the old woman felt regret, thinking 'She has Her back to the Mahābodhi [temple]—that is not right.' Then speech came from the image [39] itself, saying 'If you are not pleased, I shall look towards the Mahābodhi.' And the door of the temple and the image both turned to face the Mahābodhi. So it is known as the Tārā of the Turned Face.

In the time of King Dharmapāla,[39] near a spring northeast of Vajrāsana where the *bhikṣus* drew their water, there was a stone image of Tārā. At that time, some Sinhalese Saindhava Śrāvakas burnt many Tantras in a fire, destroyed a large statue of Heruka made of silver, for the sake of gain, and also did great damage to the *Dharma-cakra* of Master Buddha-śrī-jñāna.[40] Therefore royal punishment was imposed on the Śrāvakas from Ceylon.

A certain Saindhava *Bhikṣu* [40] went before the image of Tārā and made request, 'Please protect me from the fear of the king's punishment!' [The statue] said 'So you don't think of me when things are easy, but you think of me now?' And again it spoke: 'Get into that conduit!' Although the conduit for the stream was very small, there was room for his whole body in it, and the king's men searched but could not find him. Then at night he escaped and reached eastern India, a long way away.

At the time of a festival, the door below the balcony of the upper room at Vajrāsana would not open. Again the same Sinhalese *bhikṣu* was summoned, and when he opened it the door opened on its own. Even the king was pleased with him, and offered him many necessary things.

It is said that prior to Master Nāgārjuna there were some five thousand who attained *siddhi* by relying on Tārā's mantra [41], and during Nāgārjuna's life there were another five thousand.[41]

## STORIES CONNECTED WITH THIS TANTRA IN PARTICULAR: [THE LINEAGE-HOLDERS OF THE EARLIER DISSEMINATION]

In Bengal in the east, a *bhikṣu* called TRIPIṬAKA HAYAPĀLA, gone forth from the brahman caste,[42] had great conviction towards the Mahāyāna of the first dissemination.[43] Having listened well to the masters, he understood wisely. Then from a brahman called Guhya-śīla, 'Secret Conduct', who had seen the face of Vajrapāṇi, he received the empowerment of the Origin of Tārā (*Tārā-bhava*) and obtained all the instructions and additional instructions.

At that time, apart from someone who taught bits and pieces of this Tantra in the oral tradition in the places of the *vidyā-mantra-dharas*, there was no complete version of its words [42] and it did not exist in writing.

Then, by meditating single-pointedly, that Master attained

magical powers (*ṛddhi*). He went to the *vajra* place of Oḍḍiyāna (Swat) and procured from the *ḍākinīs* the root and explanatory tantras of the *Tārā-bhava*, the root text and explanation of the *Caṇḍa-mahā-roṣaṇa-tantra*, the **Vajrapāṇi-parama-guhya-tantra*,[44] and the **Herukotpāda-nāma-tantra*.[45]

He built a temple in a dense forest in the country of Tipura (Tripurā) and lived there. To ordinary beings he taught the condensed Perfection of Wisdom [sūtras].[46] Relying on Tārā's mantra he subjugated five kings in the east and made them all have faith in the [Three] Jewels, and he subjugated the goddess Umā and the king of the gods called Pramodita[47] and thus made [them] provide him with everything he needed. [43] Relying on the mantra of Acala (a wrathful deity), he realized magical powers, and manifested in an area twelve *yojanas* across jewel trees, walls, mansions, gods, goddesses and so forth. Relying on the mantra of Vajrapāṇi, he put an end to five hundred who were hostile to the Doctrine.

After he had taught the Dharma of the Perfection [of Wisdom] for many years, through the power of the mantra of Heruka he went obliquely into the sky, departing for Alakāvatī in this very body.

The sole disciple to whom he taught Secret Mantra was Master HAYAGHOṢA. He too was similar in his deeds to the earlier Master, for example he realized the wrathful king Hayagrīva [44] and departed for the world of the *rākṣasas* without abandoning this body. Both these Masters were contemporary with the brahman Saraha.[48]

*Ārya* NĀGĀRJUNA requested those four Tantras from that Master [i.e. Hayaghoṣa], and through him realized all those mantras. He explained [them] to ĀRYADEVA,[49] and he instructed RĀHULABHADRA THE YOUNGER.

This Master was of the *śūdra* caste before he took ordination. He was skilled in the five Sciences and learned in all the *piṭakas* of both Vehicles. It is said that he wrote a treatise called *Asmagarbha*,[50] teaching the texts of Ārya Nāgārjuna rolled up into a single body of the Path. He refuted the *tīrthika* Cakravarman in debate [45], and established him in the Buddha's Doctrine. He defeated many Śrāvakas in debate and introduced them to the Great Vehicle. It is said that relying on his own Tārā mantra, he coerced a *yakṣī* and extracted treasure from underground, and was able to provide sustenance for a thousand *bhikṣus* even in barren forests. In the end, he passed away in the country of Dhiṅkoṭa (Dhānya-kaṭaka?).

The assertion that the Rāhulabhadra mentioned in *Prasannapadā*—'Besides Nāgārjuna from Rāhulabhadra, Āryadeva also taught, and . . .'—is the same one, and thus that he is the Great Brahman [Saraha], is an emanation of darkness.[51]

It is taught that from then on these tantras were but a single volume, and the lineage itself [46] has not split into two.

He instructed Master JVALAŚEṢPA (sic). He instructed the Kashmiri DHARMABHADRAPĀLA, and he instructed NĀGAMITRA. Their stories are not taught. [Nāgamitra] instructed Sūryagupta and others.

SŪRYAGUPTA[52] was born in Kashmir. It is reported that he had been a practitioner of Tārā for seven lives. In this life his intellect was very sharp and he was skilled in all the Sciences from when he was little. He went to the Madhyadeśa and took ordination, and relying on the method of Nāgārjuna made himself learned in all the Mahāyāna *sūtras*. He requested the empowerment of Tārā from Master Nāgamitra. He is generally reported to have known a hundred and eight tantras of Tārā. It is said that this Master [47] composed as many as thirteen texts based on the *Tārā-bhava-tantra*, including *sādhanas* and a *maṇḍala-vidhi*.[53] This Master was approximately contemporary with Master Sthiramati's disciple Candragomin. Therefore the work now known as *Praise of the Protector from the Eight Fears, with Blessing*, must be by another Sūryagupta, and it should be understood that it is not by this Master.[54]

His principal disciple was SARVAJÑAMITRA.[55] Countless Masters accomplished (*siddha*) in Mantra of Tārā arose as well. Sarvajñamitra instructed DHANAMITRA, he instructed TATHĀGATAMITRA, [48] he instructed DHARMAMITRA of Siṃhaladvīpa (Ceylon), and he instructed ŚĪLA-RAKṢITA, who was contemporary with Lalitavajra.[56] It is taught that thereafter the lineage was unbroken, as appears in the Verses on the Succession and Sayings of Former Masters.[57]

## STORIES OF EIGHT MASTERS BEING SAVED FROM THE EIGHT FEARS

### [1. *Digvarman saved from fire*]

Master Digvarman, in the south of India, was a great ascetic and *piṭakadhara* (scriptural expert), accomplished in Mantra relying on Yamāntaka and on the *Tārā-bhava-tantra*. In the country of Vidarbha, in the south, he debated with the non-Buddhist (*tīrthika*) Master Gapurīla, a brahman, and because he defeated him, [49] all the *tīrthika*'s associates were received by the Buddhists. Then, when this Master requested Dharma teaching at the monastery (*vihāra*) together with the *bhikṣus*, the *tīrthikas* set fire to the monastery. Master [Digvarman] prayed to the Venerable Lady, and She appeared in the sky and a stream of water actually fell from the sky and put out the fire.

### [2. *Amarasiṃha saved from water*]

Master Amarasiṃha[58] was a royal scribe who took ordination, a propounder of the Abhidharma of the Great and Small Vehicles. He took Ārya-Tārā as his tutelary deity, relying on the *Tārā-bhava-tantra*. He made his home in the country of Mālava (Malwa), in the west, and lived there teaching Abhidharma to some five hundred Abhidharma students. It is said he stayed in the same place for twenty-four years, [50] surrounded throughout by an entourage of five hundred, training their minds in the Abhidharma.

Once during this period, an evil *nāga*-king called Lalita was in that region, and suddenly sent violent and severe rain. From the rainwater arose a stream the size of the Yamunā River. When it was on the verge of carrying away the Master's home and several towns, the Master, by praying to Venerable Tārā, made the flood circle many times clockwise[59] round his home and the city of Ujjayinī (Ujjain), then finally flow into another great river and carry away the *nāga*'s own home and a small town of the Turks.

Because Tārā revealed to him, 'Write a dictionary!', [51] he composed the *Amara-koṣa*, which to this day is very widespread in India among Buddhists and non-Buddhists alike.

The king whose scribe he was is reported to have been Vikramāditya.[60]

[3. *Devasiṃha saved from prison*]

Master *Devasiṃha[61] lived as an *upāsaka* (lay follower). Very learned in the Sūtras and Abhidharma of both Vehicles, he became Guru to King Śrī-Harṣa-deva[62] of Kashmir. He was a preacher of the Dharma, and having generated faith in kings, householders and all kinds of brahmans in Kashmir, Lahore and Maru (Marwar, Rajasthan), built some five hundred Buddhist temples.

In the countries near Kashmir, such as Ghazni, he taught the Dharma so much that the religion of the Turks and Persians[63] [52] generally declined. A Persian king held him in prison, saying 'If you give up your refuge in the Jewels and practise the Muslim religion you will be all right, but if not you will be killed.' Since the Master replied that though it put his life at risk, he had no other Refuge than the Jewels, he was put in chains and thrown into a terrible dungeon. The Master prayed to his personal deity, Tārā, and the iron chains turned into chains of flowers, while goddesses showered flowers and sandalwood powder abundantly in the prison and music resounded. When the Muslim king came to investigate, he saw [the prisoner] had no chains, and when he was put into more chains [53] these too became flower garlands. When seven sets of chains had been turned into flower garlands in this way, amazement grew in the king, and he took [the Master] as an object of veneration. However, since he could not spread the Doctrine there, [Devasiṃha] was depressed and returned to Kashmir.

[4. *Saṅghamitra saved from bandits*]

To the great Master of the Vaibhāṣika school, Saṅghamitra, there appeared in dream a green goddess, in front of the Great Sage (Śākyamuni) and his entourage. She said, 'Train well in the Great Vehicle!' He went to Kashmir and studied extensively the systems of Sūtra and Tantra of the Great Vehicle. He took Venerable Tārā as his tutelary deity.

Not finding a place to study the Perfection of Wisdom, he

set out for the Madhyadeśa, [54] having heard there was a teacher of the Perfection of Wisdom there called Master [Vi]muktisena.[64] On the way he was captured by bandits, who said 'We have to make offering to the goddess Durgā with the warm blood of a slain man, so we are leaving to do that.' When they reached the goddess Durgā's abode, like a charnel ground, he prayed to the Venerable Tārā and the image of the goddess spontaneously split into many fragments. At this, the bandits were frightened and ran away, and the Master was freed.

[5. *Subhāṣā-kīrti saving from elephants*]

Master Subhāṣā-kīrti was a great expert on Vinaya (monastic discipline), who inwardly relying on the *Tārā-bhava-tantra*, took [Tārā] as his tutelary deity. Once he went from the Madhyadeśa for a look at the western ranges, [55] and finally on a mountain top set up a *vihāra* (monastic school). Because of his teaching the Dharma, a large group of monks settled there. Then many chiefs of the Qarluq (Turkish Muslim invaders) who were there, saying 'These red-robed shave-pates have come to harm us. We must destroy them all,' came in an army three hundred elephants strong. When [the Master] prayed to Tārā, She said 'Throw water in the direction the army is coming from!' All the elephants were most frightened and terrified by their doing this, and no-one could control them but were all carried home.

[6. *Buddhadāsa saving from tigers*]

There was a Master Buddhadāsa, who was made abbot of Dhanapuri.[65] When he went on a journey, in an empty town there were many tigers' dens. When the Master enquired, [56] he was told 'Every day the tigers eat many even of the human beings of the town. What need to mention the other, small creatures?' Therefore great compassion arose in him. As the Master walked along the road, all the tigers came towards him. He prayed to Tārā and sprinkled some water over which he had recited mantras. Through this, the tigers became of peaceful mind; thereafter they did no harm to living creatures, but stopped eating and passed away. A great rain of flowers fell, as a sign that they had thus been reborn as *devas*.

[7. *Triratnadāsa saving from a snake*]

Master Triratnadāsa[66] was a disciple of Master Diṅnāga.[67] Once, when he was living and teaching the Dharma in the country of Oḍiviśa (Orissa), in the east, [57] a huge poisonous snake came out of the ocean and devoured many human beings and elephants. When it approached the town of Utkala,[68] [the Master,] seeing harm coming to countless beings, prayed fervently to Tārā. Scattering white mustard seed over which he had recited Tārā's mantra, he said:

> Though you are lord of the snakes of this earth,
> This is the word of him who has
> Benevolence: arise and go
> To your delightful nether realm!

As soon as he had said this, the snake turned round and went back to the ocean, by way of the Ganges.[69]

[8. *Jñānadeva saving from an evil spirit*]

Master *Jñānadeva[70] was a disciple of Śāntideva.[71] For a long time he engaged in study and teaching in the country of Trimala[72] in South India. [58] Finally he was told 'Now you should meditate in the Himālaya,' and went north. In the country of Tirāhuti he did whatever was necessary for the benefit of sentient beings.

Then in a region of that country, in a small town of the Tharu tribe (Western Nepal), appeared an evil spirit, a *brahma-rākṣasa*, and everyone from the district chief to the foremen of the farm-work died at the same time. The Master arrived that day. A terrible *vetāla* (risen corpse, animated by an evil spirit) came running, and he threw his ritual dagger, on which he had recited Tārā's mantra. It sank into the top of the *vetāla*'s head, so that [the *vetāla*] collapsed as it was going along. He went into the town, and through his request to Tārā there fell a great rain of nectar with the power of curing death. Most of the dead townspeople [59] revived.

## TALES OF THE ATTAINMENT OF THE EIGHT SIDDHIS NOT YET ATTAINED[73]

[1. *Siddhi of pills*]

A *bhikṣu* who took Tārā as his special deity went for alms in order to build a *vihāra*. A brahman gave him a measure of cow-bile orpiment (*go-rocana*), which he took and made into pills at a temple of Tārā. A remaining portion he put in the sun, so that the wind, bearing dust of such pill ingredients as gold and herbs, struck it; of this too he made a pill. While he was reciting a session of mantras, fire blazed up from the centre of the pill. He kept it fixed to his body, and once when he thought of the city of the gods of the Thirty-three, [60] he went to the Heaven of the Thirty-three (*Trayastriṃśa*) and stayed there for twelve human years.

[2. *Siddhi of dominion over the underworld*]

It is said that a farmer who took Tārā as his tutelary deity dug the earth, panting, and a door to the subterranean world opened. He reached the abode of the *nāgas* and drank nectar, so that his body was transformed into a rainbow body.

[3. *Siddhi of invisibility*]

A *yoginī* for twenty-nine nights burnt many human corpses in a cremation ground, reciting the mantra of Tārā. From amidst the ashes produced, there was light emanating. By smearing them on her eyes, she became invisible where she was, among her companions.

[4. *Siddhi of sky-going*]

A lay follower who took Tārā as his tutelary deity went with his companions to a cremation ground. When a terrible *vetāla* appeared, [61] with fire blazing from its mouth, his companions were frightened and ran away, but this lay follower thought of Tārā and climbed onto its neck. It thereupon changed shape, to be three-armed, three-legged and three-headed, and displayed the miraculous power of roaming the seas with one arm and leg, the interior of the earth and mountains with another, and the heavens with the other. Each of its three faces said, 'Great hero, what should I do? By way of the heavens, I can go to the abodes of the gods. By way of the underworld, I can go to the abodes of the *asuras*. By way of the seas, I can go to the abodes of the *nāgas*.'

Whichever of these the practitioner said he wanted would have been accomplished, but being of feeble intellect he said 'These are not what I want. [62] Give me a treasure of jewels!'

It replied, 'Then you want to go to the blue mountain,' and instantly they arrived there and it pointed out a great treasure of jewels.

It is said that as long as he lived he was wealthier than a great king.

[5. *Siddhi of life*]

Another adept (*sādhaka*) of Tārā sat reciting Her mantra at the root of a *bimpala* tree. One morning he saw in front of him a road that had not been there before. He entered it and walked along. After a while, he saw in the middle of a pleasant grove a golden house. When he went in, the *yakṣī* Kālikā, maidservant to the *yakṣa* Naḍa-kūbara,[74] was there. She was adorned with all the ornaments and [63] her body was of an indefinite [i.e. variable] colour. She said 'O adept who hast come hither! Partake of this elixir!' and gave him a flask full of elixir. By drinking it for one month, he became of birthless and deathless body.

[6. *Siddhi of the magic sword*]

A faithful lay follower who took Tārā as his special deity found a magnetic sword as he was travelling. When he walked on, reciting Tārā's mantra, smoke rose from the sword; when he recited some more, fire blazed forth. After that, he became able to go to places just as he wished. Every day he used to go to the various abodes of *devas*, *nāgas* and spirits, take every variety of their enjoyments, and offer them to the Saṅgha. [64] After many years, he went to the land of the *vidyādharas*.

[7. *Siddhi of the elixir of youth*]

A certain *bhikṣu* circumambulated a temple of Tārā for three years. Because of this, from the boon-granting [right] hand [of the Tārā image] flowed elixir, like a stream of milk. By drinking it, he became free of old age: it is said he lived for three hundred years, remaining as youthful as if he was sixteen.

[8. *Siddhi of enjoyments*]

A lay follower lived in a temple of Tārā, praying [to Her]. One morning, when he prostrated to the feet of the Tārā image, a stone pot emerged from beneath Her feet. Whatever enjoyments (i.e. food) he desired came out of the pot inexhaustibly. With this, he provided sustenance for five hundred *bhikṣus* for thirty years.

[HISTORY, Continued]

[65] From the passing away of *Ārya* Nāgārjuna to the coming of King Dharmapāla,[75] there were again some five thousand who attained *siddhi* by relying on Tārā. It is taught that many of these attained *siddhi* just relying on the *Tārā-bhava-tantra*.

The above is the manner of the earlier dissemination of this Tantra of Tārā.

## HOW THE TANTRA DECLINED SOMEWHAT FOR A WHILE

Some say it was in the latter part of the life of King Dharmapāla, on the instigation of some *bhikṣus* learned in the [Hīnayāna] scriptures; some that it was just after he assumed the throne. But since it is clear that it was after the passing of Buddhajñāna,[76] the former is correct. How ever it was, when he had visited every place in East India[77] where there were books and oral explanations of the secret mantras, and after investigating very precisely, [66] knew all about the manner of functioning of the various tantric oral teachings, then it appeared that because of the peculiarities of the time, the 'secret mantras' were not being practised secretly as before (see p. 16). Study, explanation and meditation on the *Mahā-yoga-tantras,* in full public view, were very widespread. Therefore he proclaimed 'Let those sealed with *vajra* words, such as the *Tattva-saṃgraha,*[78] be explained extensively. Let the very secret ones that have contradictory words not be explained henceforth!'

There were a great many Tantras—several Tantras of Śrī Heruka, some great Tantras including the *Mahākāla, Tārā-bhava, Caṇḍa-mahā-roṣaṇa* and **Catuḥ-pīṭha-karmâvalī,*[79] and some five hundred or, some say, thousand small fragments of Tantras procured by *siddhas* [67]—whose books were all collected and placed in vessels of the seven precious things, being put in eight great gold boxes, which were put in silver vessels, and so on, and hidden in the Śītavana cremation ground.[80]

It is said that at this time the study and teaching of these Tantras were interrupted for a while.

## THE MANNER OF THE LATER DISSEMINATION

When Master TILLI-PA (or Tilopa) was staying at a monastery in the east,[81] before he attained *siddhi,* there was a statue of the King of Sages, from beneath whose throne light emerged repeatedly. From time to time, he heard sounds of music coming forth. When he dug in the ground and looked, this Tantra of Tārā came to light. At this time he did not find a person to request [empowerment] from.

Subsequently, after he had attained *siddhi,* [68] he went to the country of Oḍḍiyāna (Swat) in the west. There was a dark green[82] woman with the marks of a *ḍākinī;* he showed her the signs explained in the Tantra, and she gave the answering signs.[83] When he made request to her, she transformed herself into the Goddess Tārā, bestowed Her inspiring grace on his mental continuum, and gave him empowerment.

From him, the teaching was transmitted as shown in Chart 3. [69.11] Thus it was disseminated for a time in many different lineages. Later it rested only with the *mahā-siddha* Śānti[gupta], so now it spreads widely from him.

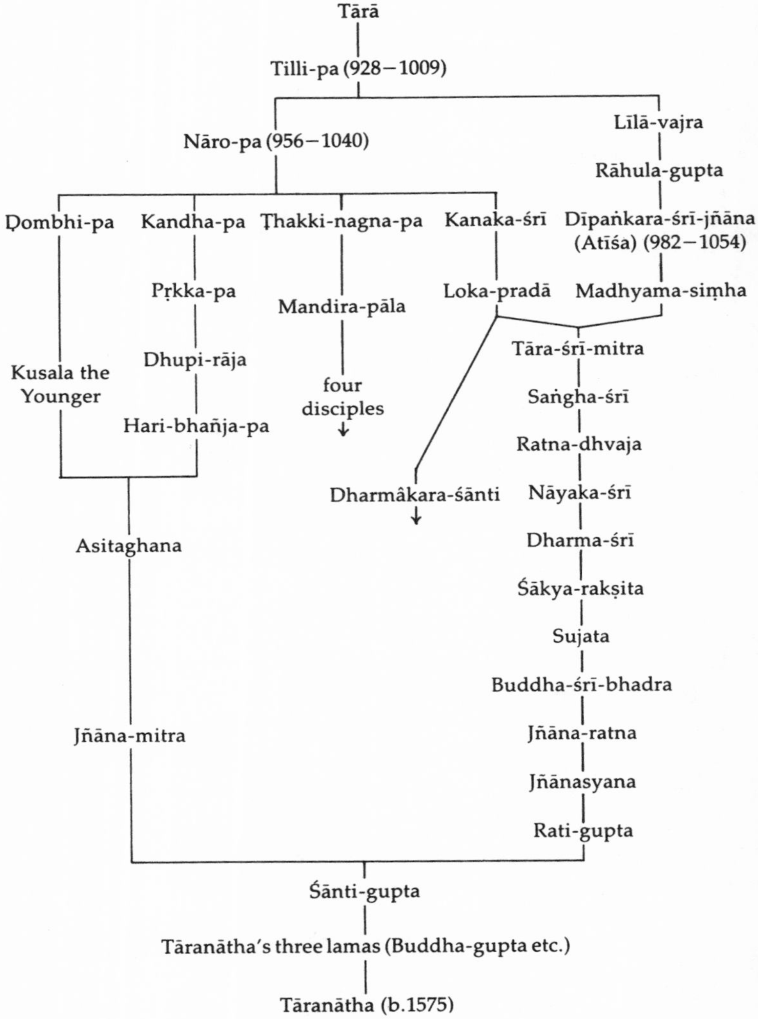


*Chart 3. Lineage of the later dissemination of the* Tārā-bhava-tantra, *according to* The Golden Rosary.

## [STORIES OF THE LINEAGE-HOLDERS OF THE LATER DISSEMINATION]

Stories of some of these I have already set down elsewhere, and they may be known in those places.[84] [70] Let me explain some not set down there.

This KANAKA-ŚRĪ was not the Nepalese Ka[naka]-śrī,[85] but was born in Magadha. He took ordination from a follower of Kurukullā. At the monastery of Vikramaśīla[86] he trained skilfully in the sūtras, the tantras and all the sciences. In Bengal he received the empowerment of Guhyasamāja from a *paṇḍita* called Dharmamitra. Although he meditated and recited the mantra for seven years, not one auspicious sign appeared; he broke off his meditation and lived as he pleased.

Then one night, in a dream, a woman revealed to him that he should go before *Śrī* Nāro-pa. From Nāro-pa he then requested the empowerment of Cakrasaṃvara, because of which good concentration developed spontaneously in him.[87] When he had meditated for six months, he saw the face of Cakrasaṃvara. [71] Again he adhered to the great Nāro-pa for seven years, listening to countless Tantras. In particular, it is reported that he was learned in the *Cakra-śaṃvara*,[88] the *Catuḥ-pīṭha* and the *Tārā-bhava Tantras*.

In Magadha, in the time of King Neyapāla,[89] he competed in [magical] powers with a follower of Īśvara called Khasamadeva ('Divine being equal to the sky'). The *tīrthika* drew a magic circle (*maṇḍala*) in the air, a fathom high (1.8 m), and stood a pot on it; but by throwing white mustardseed, the Master broke the magic circle, and the pot fell down. The Master stood an image of Tārā one palmyra-tree high in the air; until the Master himself collected it, it could not be made to fall by any means, including non-Buddhist mantras and burning arrows, so the Master won.

[72] The king invited him to Vikramaśīla as a master expert in Mother-tantra. It is said that he saw the face of Tārā, and that by applying the rite of mutual subjugation based on Her mantra, he eight times reconciled fierce disputes.

KANDHA-PA was a Buddhist *yogin* who seemed as if he was

of very dull intellect. From Lord Nāro-pa he requested the empowerment and blessing of the *Tārā-bhava*. By practising for twelve years, meditating on the nine deities appearing in this Tantra as Heruka, he saw the faces of Heruka and Tārā. He attained *siddhis* and covered a road of a hundred leagues (*yojana*) in an instant.

At that time there was a Mongol king in Delhi. When he was rebuilding his great palace, this Master stayed nearby, sewing a patched garment.[90] [73] When the palace was finished, he ripped the garment to pieces, and the palace was destroyed from the foundations. This happened three times. The king, hearing rumours about it, summoned the Master and prostrated at his feet. It is said the Master made him take four vows, which he dictated, namely: (a) Not to harm any Buddhist temple; (b) That those living in the palace would abandon taking life; (c) To make offerings to monks; and (d) To make homage each day, pronouncing the name of the Buddha.

The name for a patched garment being *kandhari*, the *siddha* was known thereafter as Kandha-pa. For a long time he worked the weal of sentient beings. In the end he went in this very body [74] to a Sky-soarers' realm (pure land).

Now, ṬHAKKI-NAGNA-PA. *Ṭhakki* means someone who makes a living by various deceitful actions. It is taught that it is a low, barbarian caste. *Nagna* means 'great man', or 'strong one'.[91] Since those of the Ṭhakki caste have very strong bodies, they also bear this name.

He acted as a *yogin*. Having requested [the empowerment and teaching of] Hevajra from a disciple of Durjayacandra,[92] he meditated one-pointedly for fifteen years at a mountain in the south called Nīla ('Blue'),[93] but no sign [of success] appeared. Therefore, praying to succeed in another rebirth, he leapt into a great abyss. Yet his body was unharmed, and a voice came from the sky, 'You will be received by Nāro-pa.' [75]

After that he adhered to Nāro-pa. When he requested the empowerment of Hevajra, [Nāro-pa] told him 'You will not realize Hevajra. You ought to practise Cakra-śaṃvara, so you need the empowerment of Śaṃvara.'

He then petitioned Lord Nāro-pa, 'It is very hard to request

Cakraśaṃvara—you need eight times more things than for other *maṇḍalas,* and at the moment I do not have any things. And since I am of feeble intellect, I lack the ability to study anew an extensive Tantra.'

So [Nāro-pa] gave him the empowerment and Tantra of Tārā, and also gave him completely all the instructions for Śaṃvara in union reversed.[94] By meditating one-pointedly, he gained supreme *siddhis.* Coming to prostrate before Nāro-pa, who was sitting at the head of the rows at a great ritual feast (*gaṇa-[cakra-] pūjā*) [76], he displayed several miraculous powers, such as making fire blaze from his body and shaking the earth, [then] became invisible. Since on that occasion he was not acting for the benefit of sentient beings, he is not counted among the four *siddha* disciples of Nāro-pa.

But later there was a disciple of Abhayākara[95] called MANDIRA-PĀLA, a very good *yogin.* For the space of one month, [Ṭhakki-nagna-pa] revealed himself bodily to him, and gave him the empowerment of Tārā and the explanation and oral instructions on the Tantra. [Mandira-pāla] then meditated assiduously, and in six months attained *siddhi.* It is said that in the end he went to the abode of the *nāgas.*

He too had some four disciples. Although there were also two or three lineage-holders to whom the transmission, explanation and so forth of this Tantra came, [my Gurus] say they have not heard their stories at length. [77]

LĪLĀVAJRA[96] was a *kṣatriya.* When going to Magadha for his work, on the way he saw a *yogin* sitting by a tree. He felt extraordinary faith and made prostration at his feet. When he had returned to his country again, his heart was broken by his woman being involved with another man and that sort of thing, so he went back to Magadha for the Dharma. By the tree, he met the same *siddha* as before. This *siddha* was the great Tilli-pa.

Tilli-pa thereupon bestowed his inspiring grace on his mindstream, then gave him empowerment and taught him the instructions. With no great delay, he attained realization. It is said he was one who worked the weal of sentient beings by blowing on a flute and crazy behaviour [which would explain his name, 'Playful Vajra']; I have not been taught this story at length. [78]

Since the story of DĪPAṂKARA [ŚRĪ-JÑĀNA] (Atīśa) is very well known, one can learn it elsewhere.[97]

MADHYAMA-SIṂHA was a disciple of Jowo (Atīśa), skilled in language, logic and the sūtra systems. He did not know the other Tantras, but was learned in this Tantra of Tārā alone. His powers too were evident: even when he went to the Ganges River in East India, it offered no obstruction to him, as if he was walking on a plain; and he was someone able to command poisonous snakes, tigers and the like.

TĀRA-ŚRĪ[-MITRA] was a bull among debaters. It is said that in Magadha he was three times victorious over *tīrthika* debaters, in countries of the South he rebutted the debates of the Śrāvakas, and in the country of Kashmir he overcame in debate all the Buddhist and non-Buddhist *paṇḍitas*. He became *guru* to the king of Kashmir. He subjugated the king of the country of Ghazni with the mantra of Tārā [79] and converted him to Buddhism.

The stories of those from SAṄGHA-ŚRĪ to DHARMA-ŚRĪ have not been taught [me].

ŚĀKYA-RAKṢITA was born in Ceylon. At first he was a Saindhava Śrāvaka, very skilled in their system. In Haripuñja[ya], 'the golden city', which is included in part of the land of Arakan,[98] he listened to many doctrines of the Perfection of Wisdom and of Mantra from Master Dharma-śrī. In particular, he was learned in most of the *Hevajra, Cakra-śaṃvara, Tārābhava* and *Mahākāla Tantras*. It is said that he saw the face of Heruka, and relying on the mantra of Tārā he subjugated Mahākāla, [through whom] in the form of a black lay follower (*upāsaka*) [80] he used to summon whatever things he needed from beyond a hundred leagues.

When a certain king called Caṅgala-rāja ('Chieng-rai rāja')[99] set about calling up an army to destroy the town and temples of Haripuñja[ya], [Śākya-rakṣita] threw a trident (*triśula*), an emblem carried by Mahākāla, and although it was more than a month's journey away, the trident reached its mark on top of the king's palace and destroyed it. In this way he was reputed to possess magical powers.

SUJATA was abbot of the Daṇḍapuri *vihāra* in Kamboja (Cambodia).[100] Before his ordination, he was a *kṣatriya*.

BUDDHA-ŚRĪ-BHADRA and JÑĀNA-RATNA also went to that country.

JÑĀNASYANA was born in that country and took ordination from the preceptor Jñāna-ratna. [81] He was learned in many tantras of the outer and inner[101] Secret Mantra. In particular, he was skilled in the Tantra of Tārā, and attained [magical] powers. In the latter part of his life he lived in Nepāl and practised the conduct of a *yogin*. Through a *padminī*[102] consort (*mudrā*), he attained *siddhi*. He was one endowed with many remarkable signs, such as making one measure of rice and one jar of wine suffice most abundantly for a ritual feast ([*gaṇa*-] *cakra-pūjā*) for some two thousand tantric monks.

Master RATI-GUPTA came to Nepāl to seek the empowerments and lineages of several Tantras, including the Tantra of Tārā, the *Mahākāla-tantra*, the *Śaṃvarôdaya* and the [*Tārā*-] *kurukulle-kalpa*. Besides hearing many Tantras from Jñānasyana, Jīvasyana, Śrī-tanupāla and Gittipāla [82], he heard this Tantra from Master Jñānasyana.[103]

The *siddha* PṚKKA-PA obtained from the *siddha* Kandha-pa all the empowerments and oral instructions, and practised for a long time. Finally he set up a *maṇḍala* in a garden of *spṛkkā* (or *pṛkkā*) flowers (*Trigonella corniculata*) and did the practice [there], because of which one flower did not wither during twelve months. In the end, one night fire blazed on the flower. Just by wearing it, he attained ordinary *siddhis*, and could travel unobstructed under the ground.

It is taught that DHUPI-RĀJA was someone of the washermen's (Hindī: *dhobi*) caste who attained *siddhi*.

I have not been taught the history of HARI-BHAÑJA-PA.

LOKA-PRADĀ-PA[104] was a *paṇḍita* of the *kṣatriya* caste. He took Kanaka-śrī as his root *guru*. In the doctrine of Secret Mantra, he trained well just in the *Tārā-bhava* division of the Teachings [83]. Making his home in a deserted park in the country of Gujiratha (Gujarat), for six years he was assisted in the practice by a female practitioner of Mantra. Through meditating only on the Developing and Completing Stages of Tārā, he achieved prediction by a *ḍākinī*, then by six months of *vidyā*-practice with twelve *vidyās* (consorts) obtained the *siddhis* he wanted.

Once, while [the Master] was living in the same place, when the Qarluq king of that country came to inspect the districts of his land he saw that the Master's abode was agreeable, and asked who lived there. The king's servants said 'There is a respectable Buddhist householder here.'

Then, [84] when the king set about appropriating the place, it all instantly burst into flames, inside and out. The king and his retinue were stopped short in their speech. Realizing that the Master had attained *siddhi*, they made request to him, and the fire went out.

Then the Master said, 'O King, it were well that you pay respect to Buddhists. If you do not, you will be destroyed now.' [The king] took an oath that he and his descendants would pay respect to the Buddhists. And from that day to this, the kings of that country, though of Qarluq extraction, have paid respect principally to Buddhists.

Before that, there had been but few Buddhists in that country, but this king set up eight *vihāras*. From then on [85], the Buddhist doctrine has been progressively spreading, until now.

When that king developed faith in the Buddha, the Muslim teachers, the Kazis,[105] set fire to the Master's house. By directing a (magical) gaze upon them, the Master petrified them all and they became unconscious.[106] When in three days they had not recovered, on the request of their relatives he revived them by the sound of ringing a bell. Afraid of punishment by the king, they fled and went to their own country, a long way to the west.[107] The Master destroyed every place of the Muslims, or mosque,[108] just by scattering white mustard seed, and in the place of each [86] he erected a Buddhist *stūpa*. He [also] built a hundred temples to Tārā. He initiated the king into the *maṇḍala* of * Āśvāsana Padma-nartêśvara ('The Encouraging Lotus Lord of the Dance'),[109] and built a temple of Secret Mantra too.

Previously, there were many brahmans and *tīrthikas* under the sway of that king, while as the king made his main place of worship that of the Qarluq Kazis, there were a thousand or so holders of Muslim tenets. There were no more than about twenty Buddhist monks, but it is said that during the life of that Master all the Muslims disappeared, while as a result of the king's inviting many Buddhist Masters, our *bhikṣus* increased to as many as two thousand.

Once, when a great famine occurred in that country [87], the Master extracted from underground a vast hoard of grain, from which everyone in the country was given a hundred *khāri* each.[110] Taking them from the *nāgas* and *yakṣas*, he gave to every poor person a pearl necklace each, and a *tola's* worth of food every day for three years.[111]

Finally, since there was a suitable body of a dead child on an island near Drāviḍa (South India), he performed the transference of his consciousness (*grong 'jug*) into it.[112] His former body, because of his supernatural control, did not putrefy, and was contained in a *stūpa* with a door. In Drāviḍa too he was a busy practitioner; eight women disciples of his became unaging and immortal of body. Since they had been worshipping his former body, [88] after sixty years he re-entered that body and in it benefited some fortunate sentient beings for another ten years. After he had again exchanged bodies every three human years some six times, both bodies became invisible, along with his attendant host of *vidyās* (consorts).

From this Master, both Tāra-śrī-mitra and DHARMÂKARA-ŚĀNTI[113] heard this Tantra. Although Sūrya-śrī[114] said that Dharmâkara-śānti was famous as an Omniscient One of the Age of Conflict (*Kali-yuga*), he did not teach his story. Saṅgha-śrī asked him, but he had taught enough.[115]

The accomplished Master Loka-pradā wrote *sādhanas*, the condensed meaning of the Tantras, [89] rituals for the Completing Stage and empowerment, and rites of burnt-offering (*homa*). The commentary by Narâditya [116] also follows him.

Later, when the transmission and explanation of this Tantra were very rare, the *mahāsiddha* ŚĀNTI-PĀDA (i.e. Śānti-gupta) disseminated it widely. I too, being fortunate in my own previous merit, have received it on this side of the Himâlaya, by properly receiving[117] Śanti-pāda's unerring oral teachings, which have become exclusive instructions from the mouth of my Guru, and his two commentaries and eight short texts.

> This Origin of that king[118] of Mother-Tantras,
> Of uttermost depth–the *Tārā-bhava-tantra*–
> Set down according to his Guru's teachings,
> Was written by the Wanderer[119] [90] Tāranātha.

Spoken at Ch'ö-dr'a Ser-dok-chän ('The Golden-coloured Dharma School') in my thirtieth year.

May good fortune increase! Good luck!

*Translated from the Tibetan.*

# Part Four
## *Songs by Indian Devotees*

# 1 *Praises Attributed to Mātṛceṭa*

Tibetan tradition has it that Mātṛceṭa was a *Brāhmaṇa* who defeated many Buddhists in debate until he himself was defeated and converted by Āryadeva. The story of this conversion, with the aid of a cat, a jar of oil and a shameless *upāsaka*, is a favourite with Tibetan lamas and need hardly be retold here.[1] Tāranātha[2] says that when he had become learned in the Buddhist scriptures, Ārya-Tārā told him in a dream to compose many praises to the Buddha, to atone for his past deeds against the Buddhist Doctrine.

Whatever truth there is in this, his two great praises of the Buddha, the *Varṇanârha-varṇana* (*Praise of him Worthy of Praise*) in four hundred verses and the *Śata-pañcāśatka* (*The Hundred and Fifty* [*Verses*]), were indeed among the most widely studied works of all Buddhist literature. I-tsing, the Chinese traveller who visited India around 674, tells us that everyone in India who became a monk, whether Mahāyānist or Hīnayānist, had to learn them as soon as he could recite the five and ten precepts.[3]

Tāranātha[4] confusingly identifies Mātṛceṭa with Aśvaghoṣa, celebrated author of the *Buddha-carita*, and Śūra, or Ārya-śūra, whose *Jātaka-mālā* was likewise as popular as Mātṛceṭa's praises.[5] The Tängyur, too, attributes Mātṛceṭa's *Śata-pañcāśatka* to Aśvaghoṣa. But earlier writers such as I-tsing distinguish clearly between them, and it appears that

Mātṛceṭa was a disciple of Aśvaghoṣa.[6]

Aśvaghoṣa was a contemporary of King Kaniṣka (c.128–151).[7] Mātṛceṭa himself addressed a letter to King Kaniṣka, which survives in Tibetan and Chinese translation, but according to Lamotte[8] this would have been Kaniṣka II, c.270.

Besides the second-century Indian Aśvaghoṣa, who probably belonged to the Sarvāstivāda school of the Hīnayāna, we now know that there was a fifth-century Chinese Yogācārin of the same name, who wrote *The Awakening of Faith in the Mahāyāna*, and later still an Aśvaghoṣa who composed various Tantric commentaries. I have not seen it suggested that Mātṛceṭa too is multiple, but the two hymns to Tārā below stand out among the works attributed to him[9] as the only ones of a Tantric nature. Otherwise he is considered a Hīnayānist.[10] Since verse 20 of the longer praise hails Tārā as saving from the eight great fears, it can hardly be earlier than the seventh century, when Tārā took over this role from Avalokiteśvara.[11] Verses 30 to 33 describe the standard form of eight-armed Vajra-Tārā and Her entourage, surely later still. Thus it seems impossible to accept the attribution of this work to the third-century Mātṛceṭa. Perhaps the author(s) of these hymns felt the *nom-de-plume* of Mātṛceṭa was appropriate, or perhaps all knowledge of their authorship was lost and they were ascribed to Mātṛceṭa simply because he was famous for writing hymns.

## THE WORKS

The shorter hymn is a straightforward eulogy of Tārā, built on an explanation of Her iconography (1–7) and the etymology of Her name (8). The bow and arrow (6) are attributes of certain many-armed forms of Tārā such as Kurukullā and Vajra-Tārā.

The longer praise is more elaborate and, whatever one may think of its literary qualities, offers some interesting material for study. The opening ten verses of praise could with a few changes of details be addressed to almost any deity. Verses 11 to 14 are of a polemical nature, describing Tārā's superiority to Brahmanical deities and practitioners. In the remaining verses of eulogy, up to 24, a more personal note enters with the mention of Tārā's role as Saviouress in 19–20. Verse 21 lists some of the worldly benefits that practice of Tārā can bring, including even victory in battle, mentioned again in verse 43.

Verses 25 to 38 are homage; the rhythms of the Tibetan version give the strong impression that while reciting these the practitioner, her or his devotional fervour aroused by the preceding praises, would make physical prostrations. These could be prolonged indefinitely by repeating some of the verses. Then she would sit and recite the mantra, and at the end of the session perhaps conclude with the benefits section (39–45), which is in a different metre.

The homages are not all addressed to Tārā—many invoke related deities and Bodhisattvas, some of them quite obscure. Avalokiteśvara, under a variety of names, is particularly prominent.

*The translations* are from the anonymous Tibetan versions in the Peking Tängyur. A few words are illegible and have had to be guessed.

## PRAISE OF ĀRYA-TĀRĀ
(*Ārya-tārā-stotra*)

*Attributed to Mātṛceṭa*

Homage to the *Bhagavan* Lord of Speech![12]

1 You sit on a lotus seat of strong effort,
Its lotus roots of aspiration firm
In the ground of faith fully developed,
Venerable Tārā—homage to You!

2 You sit on a moon seat, cooling with compassion
Migrating beings scorched by the heat of
defilements.
Goddess, Saviouress of tormented beings,
Venerable Tārā—homage to You!

3 With the two accumulations as chariot-wheels
You've conquered the two veils;[13] established in
the Ten Stages,
You stay as a Goddess until *saṃsāra* is empty,
Venerable Tārā—homage to You!

4 Your body, unmoved by defilements, is firm like
a mountain,
Well-grown, since nourished by Your perfect
virtues,
Full-breasted, since loving-kindness moves
Your heart,
Venerable Tārā—homage to You!

5 Graceful, Your complexion unstained by
*saṃsāra*;
Of charming apparel, with jewel ornaments,
Your hair blue-green,[14] with a diadem of the five
Families,
Venerable Tārā—homage to You!

6 Your smiling face spreads uncontaminate bliss;
Born of Vairocana,[15] You have compassion and
deeds.

With Wisdom's and Means' bow and arrow
subduing the Māras,
Venerable Tārā—homage to You!

7 Right hand giving Refuge, You save from fears;
In the form of a maid of sixteen, You captivate
beings;
Your blue *utpala* is for the Action Family,
Venerable Tārā—homage to You!

8 You are the skilful boatman who carries us over
(*tāraṇa*)
The rivers of rebirth, aging, sickness and death
[To] the harbour (*potalaka*) of loving-kindness,
with oars of compassion,
Venerable Tārā—homage to You!

9 Now that I have praised the Goddess so,
In eight stanzas, with faith in Her, through this
May every migrating sentient being
Quickly win the rank of Buddhahood!

The Praise of the Venerable Lady by Masteṛ Matrici ṭa (sic) is complete.

*Translated from the Tibetan.*

## THE KING OF PRAISES CALLED THE FULFILLER OF ALL AIMS, A PRAISE OF THE ĀRYA GODDESS TĀRĀ

(*Ārya-tārādevī-stotra-sarvârtha-sādhana-nāma-stotra-rāja*)

*Attributed to Mātṛceṭa*

Homage to the Lord endowed with Great Compassion, Āryâvalokitêśvara!

1 [As] the moon is fair 'midst the sky and constellations,
The Protector, surrounded by '*sattvas*,[16] is fair 'midst migrators.
As the immaculate moon dispels distress,
Free of all ignorance You dispel migrators' sorrows.

2 Endowed with the thirty-seven Aids to *Bodhi*,
*Dhyānas*, and many *samādhis* and Liberations,
You are adorned with the thirty-two Marks [of Great Beings]
And further adorned with the eighty excellent Signs.

3 You've found the three points needing no guard, three Special Awareness[17]
And four Fearlessnesses, and have the four Purities.[18]
Skilled in the ten Powers, You've great Compassion for beings.
All imprints destroyed, You've overcome all kinds of lack.

4 Five *kleśa* o'ercome are five Wisdoms of the five Families;
Five Bodies, five Enlightenments[19] You have gained;
You've trained in five Paths and have Bodies of the five Buddhas,
Five *skandhas* abandoned, no outflows,[20] and five superknowledges.

5 Essence of all the Conquerors of the three times,
You are the source and supreme cause of all virtues.
Free of greed and hatred, for the sake
Of migrating beings You take diverse appearances.

6 You have a Body that's green, for all activities.
On Your crown You're adorned with Amitābha,
With the look of a universal ruler,
Tārā, captain of beings, [such] is Your Body.

7 Your lovely locks are beautified with a crown,
Diadem, ribbons, crescent and double *vajra*.
Earrings, adornments of neck and shoulders, bracelets,
Girdle, anklets and lower-leg wrappings adorn You.

8 Richly adorned with necklaces beset
With precious jewels, shoulder-gems, strings of pearls,
You are clad in raiment of coloured cloth,
Variegated silk, and heavenly satin.

9 Of lotus birth, in the Lotus Family,
You sit on a seat of a supreme all [-coloured] lotus,
Pure like to a red lotus, untainted with
Such [defilements] as greed, hate and delusion.

10 Your Body moves for migrators all guards of directions—
Indra, Yama, Varuṇa and Yakṣa,
Bhūta, Agni, Vāyu, Rākṣasa,
Lords of the soil, and the host of upper gods.[21]

11 Tārā, You are the god of gods, triumphant
Over such as Brahmā, Viṣṇu, Īśvara,
Mahādeva, Rudra, Śiva and Umā;
You are renowned as sovereign of all the three Realms.

12 You don't hold a skull, but have the skull of Compassion;
No matted hair, but You're lovely with intense Joy;
You've no skin mat, but the Marks and Signs adorn You;
Though not smeared with ashes, Your nature's full of Love.

13 No three staves[22] for You, but You have the threefold Training;
Rejecting charnel-grounds, You dwell(?) in *Dharmadhātu*.
You've given up sounds like the slim-waisted *ḍamaru*'s,
But proclaim all Dharmas with Voice of sixty qualities.

14 Your Body, of one in *Nirvāṇa*, wears no sacred thread;
You've left off going by night, and go equally all times(?).[23]
You've cast off(?) wrong cravings, rejected the bent ascesis,[24]
And are fully endowed with every holy practice.

15 Rejecting sharp weapons, You wield the sword of Wisdom.
Hatred abandoned, You cut off buried[25] roots.
Having no bias, You've mastered every tenet.
Having no greed, like space You go everywhere.

16 Your Mind is free of limits, just like space.
Your Body is the entire sphere of knowables.
Your Speech is every sound or appearance of speech.
Tārā, You have the essence combining all *dharmas*.

17 You have the rites of all the three times' Conqu'rors,
Like calming, increasing, subjugating, bewitching,

Summoning, driving away, expelling mobs(?),
Silencing, robbing of speech, transforming,
protecting.

18 You have the eight Masteries—those of Body and
Speech,
Masteries of Mind and of Sense Objects,
[Likewise too the Masteries of Place,][26]
Magical Powers, Omnipresence and Qualities.

19 You've realized insep'rably space-like
*Dharmakāya*,
But show Form-bodies, like rainbows, to
migrators.
Always, supreme chief of all the *maṇḍalas*,
Tārā, You save migrators from *saṃsāra*'s straits.

20 If one thinks of You, You save from the fears of
realms
Of woe, the fears of kings, thieves, fire and water,
The fears of lions, tigers, *rākṣasas*, snakes.
From every kind of disease that robs of life,
Produced by disturbance of elements or by
spirits,
And from all *ṛṣis*' and *ḍākinīs*' curses You save.

21 For sentient beings, like those who want to get
jewels,
Mantras or medicines, to those who think of You
with
Conviction You grant all supermundane *siddhis*.
Those who want power [You make] triumphant
in battle;
Those who want wealth or fame, or wish to be
free
Of stains of slander, You bring [this] about.

22 Whoever praises You praises all the *Sugatas*—
Mother producing all Buddhas of the three times,
Your Body is all the Buddhas and their Offspring,
Ven'rable Tārā, endowed with a heap of virtues!

23 Impeller and leash of Brahmā, Viṣṇu and
Īśvara and their sort, of such as Rudra,
Umā, Sitā and Śama(?)![27] And Bhṛkuṭī,
Māmakī, Locanā, Pāṇḍara-vāsinī![28]

24 For the benefit of migrators who cultivate [You],
Your Body shows in infinite ways the method,
How one may have the appearance of supernal splendour.
Most Ven'rable Tārā, migrators' supreme Refuge,
On whose crown sits Amitābha—homage to You!

25 I bow to the Body of Tārā who saves from eight fears.
I bow to the Body of Tārā of infinite fame.
I bow to the Body of Tārā, the world's benefactor.
I bow to the Body of Tārā, sure curer of sorrow.

26 I bow to the Body of Tārā
of thousand hands and eyes.
I bow to the Body of Tārā
infinite as space.
I bow to the Body of Tārā
adorned with the Marks and Signs.
I bow to the Body of Tārā
whose limbs are like the moon.
I bow to the Body of Tārā
who is as bright as the sun.
I bow to the Body of Tārā
unchanging in the three times.

27 I bow to the Body of Tārā supporting like earth.
I bow to the Body of Tārā cohering like water.
I bow to the Body of Tārā ripening like fire.
I bow to the Body of Tārā expanding like air.[29]

28 I bow to the Body of Tārā
who is the Sovereign of Doctors.
I bow to the Body of Tārā
subduing disease like medicine.

I bow to the Body of Tārā,
the river of compassion.
I bow to the Body of Tārā
skilled in means of taming.
I bow to the Body of Tārā
lovely but free of desire.
I bow to the Body of Tārā
who teaches the way to Freedom.

29 Great Lion, who by truly proclaiming to all
Migrators the sound of the Dharma of Emptiness
Like space, terrifies beast-like *tīrthikas*—
Ven'rable Tārā, homage to Your Body![30]

30 You hold a changeless *vajra* and a noose,
A conch proclaiming the Dharma, a wisdom
arrow,
A driving hook, a pleasant *utpala*,
A bow of compassion, raised forefinger of
view.[31]

31 Your eight hands are adorned with the eight
tokens,
*Vajra* and so forth, which are blessed as signs
In the manner of symbols of purity of mind—
Ven'rable Tārā, homage to Your Body!

32 Surrounded by an entourage of twelve—
Vajra-tārā, Ratna-tārā and
Padma-tārā, Karma-tārā and
Dhūpa-tārā, Puṣpa-tārā and

33 Dīpa-tārā, Gandha-tārā,[32] then
Aṅkuśa-tārā, Pāśa-tārā and
Sphoṭa-tārā and Ghaṇṭā-tārā[33]—
Venerable Tārā, homage to You!

34 Homage to Protector Amitābha!
Homage to you [also], Padmapāṇi!
Homage to Lord Avalokita!
Homage to You, O Lord of the World![34]

35 Homage to You, O Amoghapāśa!
Homage to *Krodha-rāja* Hayagrīva!
Homage to You who protect from the eight
fears![35]
Homage to You of a thousand hands and eyes!

36 Homage to eleven-faced Compassion!
Homage to You, Great in Mastery![36]
Homage to You, O Great *Vajra* Dharma![37]
Homage to You, Supreme Meaning of Truth![38]

37 Homage to You, O World's Highest Ruler![39]
Homage to You, *Vajra* Large-eyed One![40]
Homage to You, [Goddess] Ekajaṭā!
Homage to You, Goddess Bhṛkuṭī!

38 Homage to You, Great Compassionate One!
Homage to You, apparition as a woman![41]
Homage to You, [Goddess] Kurukullā!
Homage to You, Pāṇḍara-vāsinī!

OṂ TĀRE TUTTĀRE TURE SVĀHĀ!

[*Benefits*]

39 Should anyone have taken vows
and before an image of Tārā
Bathed, praised [Her] one-pointedly
with faith with this king of praises,

40 And done this mantra recitation,
Ven'rable Tārā then will show
Her face, eliminate all distress,
and inspire with every *siddhi*.

41 If on the eighth of the waxing moon,
amidst a weighty *maṇḍala*
One worships Venerable Tārā,
praises, and recites this secret mantra,

42 One will become like the Protector
in nature, free of obscurations,
And pure of any foul slander, achieve
all qualities of the triple continuum.[42]

43 If a king, when entering battle,
wears this essence on his crown
And recites this praise and mantra,
he will subjugate foes at will.

44 Any woman who desires
to be free of womanly things,
Or wants to achieve the supreme worldly
purpose, or the supermundane,

45 If she bathes, puts on white raiment
and on the eighth of the waxing moon,
Fasting,[43] worships, makes praise and recites,
she will achieve it without doubt.

The King of Praises called the Fulfiller of All Aims, a Praise of the *Ārya* Goddess Tārā, is complete. It is a praise by Master Mātriciṭa.

*Translated from the Tibetan.*

# 2 *Praises by Candragomin*

We continue our selection of praises by Indian devotees with some by Candragomin (mid-seventh century—he was still alive when I-tsing visited India in 673–685). The following notes on his life are drawn from Tāranātha's and Bu-tön's Histories.[1]

He was born the son of a *kṣatriya paṇḍita* in the small kingdom of Varendra, in Bengal.[2] It is said that in his previous life he was a *paṇḍita,* who deliberately died and took rebirth with certain marks in order to prove the existence of rebirth to a materialist (Lokāyata) opponent.

At the age of seven, completely untaught, he defeated a *tīrthika* in debate. He learnt the Sūtras and Abhidharma from Sthiramati and received Tantric instruction from Master Aśoka, seeing visions of Avalokiteśvara and Tārā. He soon became a famous scholar and married the king's daughter, whose name was Tārā. After a while he realized it was improper to have as his wife someone with the same name as his tutelary deity, and left her. This angered the king, who had him sealed in a box and thrown into the Ganges. But when Candragomin prayed to Tārā, She miraculously created an island in the middle of the river to save him. Tāranātha reports, 'It is said that the island still exists and is large enough to have seven thousand villages'. This 'Candra's Isle' (*Candra-dvīpa*) may be one of the islands near Bakarganj, Bangla Desh.

At Nālandā University, he engaged in a legendary debate with Candrakīrti, for no less than seven years. Candrakīrti defended *Ārya* Nāgārjuna's Madhyamaka philosophy, of which he is still considered the most authoritative exponent, while Candragomin argued very subtly for the Cittamātra view, with the help of Avalokiteśvara, who every night gave him answers to Candrakīrti's arguments of that day.

He wrote a commentary on Pāṇini's Sanskrit grammar, known as the *Cāndra-vyākaraṇa*, in which he criticized the earlier commentary by Patañjali, whom the Tibetans consider to have been the *nāga*-king Śeṣa. When he saw that Candrakīrti's commentary, *Samantabhadra-vyākaraṇa*, was better written than his own, he threw his into a well, but (according to Tāranātha) Tārā or (according to Bu-tön) Avalokiteśvara told him to take it out, as he had written it with the intention of benefiting sentient beings and it would thus be more beneficial than Candrakīrti's work, which had been written with pride in the author's scholarship.

The *nāga* Śeṣa, however, did not forget the slight, and when Candragomin was on a sea voyage to Potala, almost wrecked his ship. On Candragomin's prayer, Tārā came with Her attendants and frightened the *nāgas* away. He is said to be still living at Potala.

Another story tells how a poverty-stricken old woman once came to him begging for alms to enable her daughter's marriage. Candragomin had nothing but his clothes and a sūtra, but weeping with compassion, prayed to a painting of Tārā on the wall. The Tārā came to life and took off Her jewels to give to the old woman, who was overjoyed; thereafter the picture was known as the Tārā without ornaments. Ch'ak Lotsawa was still able to see it in 1234–6.

Candragomin wrote prolifically on both secular and religious subjects, until Tārā pointed out to him that he would do better to concentrate on teaching the great Mahāyāna sūtras. Praises to various deities formed a large part of his output—one is supposed to have made an image of Mañjughoṣa turn its head to listen—but as we have seen, his principal deities were Tārā and Avalokiteśvara.

## THE PRESENT WORKS

Four of his praises to Tārā that have come down to us in Tibetan versions are translated here, from the Peking Tängyur (P4869–71 and 4873). Though two of them are built on the stock theme of the eight great fears, altogether they are remarkably varied and unrepetitive, bearing witness to the closeness of the author's acquaintance with the *Āryā* Goddess.

The first praise, much the longest, has a noteworthy place in the history of Tārā's cult in Tibet: it was translated at the great Buddhist university of Vikramaśīla by the translator Nak-ts'o with the *paṇḍita* Dīpaṃkara-Śrījñāna, commonly known as Atīśa. That is, it would have been translated between probably 1036, when Nak-ts'o came to invite Atīśa to Tibet, and 1040, when they set out,[3] after which it was principally Atīśa's enthusiasm for Tārā that led to Her great popularity in Tibet. The title, 'Pearl Garland', is apt enough—each of the thirty-six homage verses is complete in its own beauty, independent of the others but of the same size and shape and strung together with them in a linear sequence so that they enhance one another's brilliance by mutual diffuse reflections. The first verse, prostration and promise of composition, and the last, dedication of the merits of composition, we can consider to make up the clasp, while the verses on the benefits of reciting it (38–42) form a kind of pendant.

The second praise deals straightforwardly with the usual eight great dangers, plus two more, leprosy and poverty. The third is a concise praise mainly in iconographic terms, followed by some brief but powerful prayers. No information is given on the translators of either.

The fourth, again on the eight great dangers, is also of historical interest; it is one of only three texts on Tārā listed in a catalogue of translations from the time of King Tr'i-song detsen (755–797).[4] The Tibetan translation is rather clumsy, being inconsistent in metre and a little obscure in places. Though Beyer has already published an English rendition, no apologies are needed for presenting a new one, for alas, he frequently misinterprets words and grammar alike. To portray the compassionate Goddess as slaughtering elephants and trampling lions and robbers beneath Her feet is a libel, which his graceful language serves only to make the more offensive. As numerous other accounts in this volume and elsewhere make plain, Tārā's power to subdue dangerous sentient beings is utterly non-violent. The Tārās saving from the eight great dangers are among Her peaceful forms.

We cannot judge Candragomin's style adequately from translations. It may be that if he had lived up as well as Candrakīrti to the complex style then fashionable, his work would be less readable to us now. As it is, some of his poetic images seem to owe more to literary convention than to observation or the writer's imagination (assuming it was not Candragomin himself who originated the convention). For example, if a lion had gorged itself on an elephant so recently that it still had blood on its paws, would it be likely to attack a mere human passer-by? But this is what the convention demands.

## THE PEARL GARLAND, A PRAISE OF THE GODDESS ĀRYA-TĀRĀ

(*Ārya-tārā-devī-stotra-muktikā-mālā-nāma*)

*By Candragomin*

Homage to Venerable Ārya-Tārā!

1 I bow with my crown at the feet of beings'
Protector, who's granted me the Truth (*tattva*).
To remove obscurations, defilements and stains,
I shall give praise to the supreme Goddess.

2 Your Body born from the syllable TĀṂ,
with light of a hundred thousand suns
Of compassion You dry up *saṃsāra*'s ocean,
emptying it of suffering—homage!

3 You burn our fuel of karmic results
on a bonfire of wisdom-knowledge,
And make us realize supreme *siddhis*,
cleanser of *kleśa* of six classes—homage!

4 With magical body of space, unobstructed,
You cross with compassion *saṃsāra*'s great ocean
And conduct migrators to the land
of Liberation, great Captain—homage!

5 Even by making request to Your painted
form, the eight great *siddhis*[5] are won.
Granter to any of *siddhis* they want,
source of all we need—homage to You!

6 Subduing with mantras hostile gods,[6]
taking Your image upon one's crown
Becomes a cause to achieve the four rites,
You of power unimpeded—homage!

7 Adorned with the *Saṃbhogakāya* adornments—
earrings, throat-jewel, necklace of many
Gems, with armlets and strings of pearls,
You with magnificent light-rays—homage!

8 In those who've developed supreme devotion
towards You, even if not one word
Of a *guru's* instructions has reached their ears,
You produce the even heat of the Bliss-void
experience, supreme Wisdom—homage!

9 In Your supreme Speech, past description,
come playful sounds of vowels and
consonants.
You proclaim[7] the *Ārya* Path
with thunder of TUTTĀRA—homage!

10 Tārā of wealth (*Dhana-tārā*), with PHAṬ
irresistible
subduer of Māra's tribe and forces!
Invincible one of great terrible power,
O Sorceress—homage to You!

11 Subduer of others' magic, such as
curses and maledictions of *devas*,
*Nāgas*, *gandharvas*, *yakṣas*, *ṛṣis*
and *ḍākinīs*[8]—homage to You!

12 With SVĀHĀ destroyer of birth from heat,
closing womb-doors with HŪLU-HŪLU,
With OṂ overcoming birth from eggs,
with TĀRE miraculous birth stopping—
homage![9]

13 In Your nature of Emptiness and Compassion
aglow with Your inner thought outwardly
seen,
Blazing with glorious wisdom light-rays,
dispeller of unknowing's darkness—homage!

14 Burning the hindering *māras'* five arrows
with light of the blazing bonfire of Gnosis,
You don't forsake practice in face of misfortune,
dispeller of foes of the *Bodhi*-path—homage!

15 You whose nature's the Buddhas' activities!
You with [their] Body, Speech, Mind, magic
powers,

Omnipresence, ten powers, all Perfections!
You of eight Masteries[10]—homage to You!

16 Your Bodies' nature, the sphere of knowables:[11]
*Dharmakāya* of space nature, free
Of elaboration; and two Form-bodies
You emanate many and varied—homage!

17 Your voice of the sixty melodious aspects,
a Dharma bell[12] of vowels and consonants,
Proclaims to objects of six classes[13] Voidness
of non-inherent existence—homage!

18 One who, devoid of wealth, begs food
and drink in potsherds at others' doors,
If she should recite Your praises,
You grant a kingdom—homage to You!

19 Through Your pictorial image, a book of
true meaning, adorned with the alphabet,
Is of the Perfection of Wisdom's nature—
Ārya-tārā, homage to You!

20 With sword of wisdom that frees from delusion
You rout defiled ignorance, *saṃsāra*'s force.
Lamp that dispels the dense darkness of
bewildered unknowing—homage to You!

21 You, on lotus and moon seat,
extend Your right leg and fold the left,
Having a thousand lotus petals
[beneath] Your soles—homage to You!

22 You have a large *utpala*, showing that You
are Mother of all the three times' Conqu'rors;
On Your hands You bear the supreme Marks
of wheels with full thousand spokes—homage
to You!

23 Your perfect *dhyāna*, which abandons
the three Realms, cuts all binding ropes;
Unstained by mud of the three becomings
You save from *saṃsāra*—homage to You!

24 Bedecked with many kinds of jewels
like garb of a universal monarch,
Your hair, dark blue[14] and coiled in braids,
is adorned with Akṣobhya—homage to You!

25 In whoever sees the image of
Tārā's form, conviction grows;
The thought alone dispels all suff'rings
of realms of woe—homage to You!

26 Encircled by garland of SVĀHĀ and OṂ,
full of mantric power, jewels and medicines,
Source of the rites that make arise
diverse conditions—homage to You!

27 Complete in virtues of body, speech, mind,
You've perfected wish and engaging:[15] Your energy's
Swift as lightning to benefit beings,
Ender of laziness—homage to You!

28 Freed from impressions and karma, You've cut
the four doors of birth, and lack rebirth;
So unmistaken, transcendent in virtues,
You're in *Nirvāṇa* by past training—homage!

29 If to a woman whose name is Tārā
one develops respect and pays devout homage,
The merits of this will be cause of Buddhahood—
to You worthwhile to see and hear, homage!

30 Like white sandalwood growing among
castor-oil plants (*eraṇḍa*) in a forest,
Among the deities aiding migrators
You are superior—homage to You!

31 You've found the four kinds of Fearlessness,[16] and
with lion's roar proclaiming Selflessness
Subdue the sixty-two wrong views
of the personality[17]—homage to You!

32 As the sun and moon stand out
like Mount Meru by their greatness
Midst the constellations, You
are without rival—homage to You!

33 When, Fair-faced, one sets out on a journey,
if she goes making request to You,
No harm from foes or robbers arises—
Excellent Refuge, homage to You!

34 A moment's conviction becomes the cause
to achieve whatever result one wishes;
You who fulfil [all] hopes desired
like a wish-granting jewel—homage to You!

35 When a migrator is leaving this life's
formations, to hear the supreme name,
TĀRĀ, tears her becoming[18] in pieces,
You who purify *saṃsāra*—homage!

36 A person with refuge in You, the Protector
of beings, although her friends may desert her,
Is taken in charge by superior people,
O shedder of light—homage to You!

37 Simply by uttering the words,
'*Hulu-hulu*[19] Tārā!', one
Will be reborn in a land of sky-soarers,[20]
Highest of Marvels—homage to You!

[*Benefits*]

38 Reciting this Pearl-garland Praise
has inconceivable qualities.
Poison and other contrivances cannot
affect one; one's saved from every danger.

39 The merits of hearing it even with
an animal's ears win a happy-realm body.
Emperors hear one's orders like servants.
One always accomplishes what one wishes.

40 If one recites it twenty-one times,
untimely death and disease are abolished.

It is a medicine subduing the body (?).
It will free one from royal punishment.

41 Manifold virtues arise in one;
their practice runs into no danger.
From the way of Awakening one's aim's not diverted;
one will arrive at the end of its practice.

42 Recitation makes grow in one
the supreme, essential, immaculate meaning,
And eighty thousand *samādhi*-doors opening,
destroys becoming's net—one Awakens.

[*Dedication*]

43 May the merit of praising You, Goddess,
with [this] Pearl Garland, like a full moon
Dispel the darkness in beings' hearts
and make light of wisdom-knowledge shine!

The *Pearl Garland Praise*, a praise of Ārya-Tārā by the great master Candragomin, also called the Immortal Moon, who was undeluded[21] about the five sciences and like the crown jewel of poets, is complete.

It was translated, revised and finalized under the eyes of the Indian *upādhyāya* Dīpaṃkara-Śrījñāna by the venerable Tibetan translator Lotsawa Nakts'o Ts'ültr'im Gyälwa, at the Vikramaśīla *vihāra*.

*Translated from the Tibetan.*

## PRAISE OF THE NOBLE GODDESS TĀRĀ

(*Ārya-devī-tārā-stotra*)[22]

*By Candragomin*

Homage to the Goddess Tārā![23]

1 *Saṃsāra*'s darkness, hard to repel,
You overcome like light of the sun.
To You with mind moist with compassion,
Tārā, I forever bow.

2 Through You, Goddess, angry lions,
who can slay great elephants
Endowed with mind exceeding sharp,[24]
are scared and run away on sight.[25]

3 With the tip of his spear-point tusks
he can split rocks or uproot trees;
But when Your mantra is recited
the elephant runs away, afraid.

4 Hard to bear, it fills all space
and quarters, overpoweringly,[26]
Burning one's couch[27] with its blaze; and yet
the rain of Your praise puts out the fire.

5 Emitting hisses, which arise
from its whole[28] hood, venomous,[29]
A snake is frightened by Your praise,
Goddess, as by a *garuḍa*'s might.

6 Though they cut travellers[30] with swords
and their limbs are stained with blood,
Just because they hear Your name[31]
robbers will become powerless.

7 When seized by the hair and bound in chains
by servants of an angry king,
One who praises You, O Goddess
Who saves from prison, will have no fear.

8 When masses of waves fill up the ten
directions and even the sky,

Your servant,[32] in the ocean after
shipwreck, reaches the other side.

9 Smeared with a slime of blood and brains,
which they are fond of devouring,
*Piśācas*, Goddess, are scared off
by recitation of Your mantra.[33]

10 Lepers with torn limbs, noses adrip
with stinking blood and bodily ooze,
Just by gathering before You[34]
become like gods of the Realm of Desire.

11 Beggars resembling hungry ghosts,[35]
naked, tortured[36] with hunger and thirst,
Just by bowing down to You[37]
are transformed into emperors.

12 By the virtue I've amassed
through thus praising You, Pure One,[38]
Frightener-off[39] of the Great Fears,
may the world gain happiness![40]

The praise of the Goddess Tārā by Master Candragomin is complete.

It is said that with [this] Praise, the Master made a wooden image of Tārā raise Her forefinger. When he asked, 'Why do You do that?', She replied, 'This praise of yours is well-spoken.' She was known as the Tārā of the Raised Forefinger.[41]

*Translated from the Tibetan.*

## A PRAISE OF ĀRYA-TĀRĀ, CALLED THE ACCOMPLISHER OF VOWS

(*Ārya-tārā-stotra-praṇidhāna-*[*siddhi-*]*nāma*)[42]

*By Candragomin*

Homage to the Venerable Ārya-Tārā!

1 Appearing from an *utpala* and green syllable,
Green of body, with one face and two arms,
Body and arms bedecked with many jewels,
To You, special deity[43] Tārā, homage and praise!

2 Five *Jinas*, like Amoghasiddhi, adorn Your crown.
Sixteen years old, You have a smiling face.
Your dazzling radiance ever subdues hosts of foes.
To You, special deity Tārā, homage and praise!

3 Your right hand grants boons; Your left holds an *utpala*.
On variegated lotus and sun[44] disk
You sit with right leg out and left leg folded.
[To You, special deity Tārā, homage and praise!]

4 Forever You look on beings with eyes of compassion.
Your body emanates Tārās who save from th'eight fears.
Rescuing from all *saṃsāra*'s sorrows,
To You, special deity Tārā, homage and praise!

5 Making the Calming, Increasing, Subjugating,
Fierce rites and All Rites[45] be accomplished fast,
You carry out swiftly the ocean of [Buddha-] activities;
To You, special deity Tārā, homage and praise!

6 Saving completely from all the eight fears—
Lions, elephants, fire, serpents and robbers,
Fetters, the ocean, and *piśāca* demons—
To You, special deity Tārā, homage and praise!

7 [You pacify fully every suffering, such as
Demons of sickness, plagues, insanity,
*Yakṣas* and other fears of untimely death;
To You, special deity Tārā, I pay homage.]

8 Karma amassed in past lives, and defilements;
Whatever unbearable evil acts I've done,
Such as the five immediate and ten
unwholesome—
Let all these be purified without remainder!

9 In this my present rebirth also, let
Bad dreams, ill omens, and untimely death,
Foes and all ill fortune be cleared away,
While lifetime, merits and enjoyments grow!

10 In all rebirths yet to come, may I
Recollect my special deity, Tārā,
Realize all supreme and common *siddhis*
And all my wishes, just as I desire,
And govern each and every divine activity!

11 By the merits I've amassed through praising
With intensely striving, longing mind
Tārā, the compassionate special deity,
Let me, O Worshipful Tārā, not part from You!

The Praise of the Venerable Tārā called the Accomplisher of All Vows is by the great Master Candragomin.

*Translated from the Tibetan.*

## PRAISE OF ĀRYA-TĀRĀ WHO SAVES FROM THE EIGHT GREAT FEARS

(*Ārya-tārā-mahā-aṣṭabhayôttārā-stava*)[46]

*By Candragomin*

Homage to the Venerable Ārya-Tārā!

1 All gods and *asuras* pay homage at Your feet.
You look with compassion on beings in ill migrations.
Tārā, Who's left off [all] that is unfitting!
I, Candragupta,[47] shall write a praise to You.

2 Paws red with blood of elephants it's slain,
The lion sees the traveller and advances.[48]
If on the way one thinks of You, it enters
A forest extremely dense and hard to cross.

3 Spurred by the noise of swarms of millions of bees
Circling his cheeks, which rut-fluid stains all over,
Not pausing a moment, on his way to kill—
If one salutes You, Tārā, he's[49] subdued.

4 Kindled by fierce wind as of the Age of Destruction,
Fire is blazing up as vast as the sky;
Should some citizen[50] call upon Your name,
Then immediately it is extinguished.

5 In a constricted, tortuous, cave-like[51] valley,
The mighty serpent spots the traveller and
Darts up the path; but to remember Tārā
Puts down its pride[52] and turns it back again.

6 Robbers brandishing various sharp weapons
See the traveller and advance upon her;
But by the power of thinking of Ven'rable Tārā,
In no great time she safely reaches home.

7 A lord of the earth,[53] who's skilled at making
wishes
Daily fulfilled, has one bound in prison;
But think of Worshipful Tārā, and in a moment
Th'unbearable shackles will be in a hundred
pieces.

8 One's ship is broken amidst an ocean whose
Commotion towers up high as the Brahmā
heavens,
[By] fish and sea-monsters of terrifying forms;[54]
But thinking of Tārā, one finds security.

9 Tawny-haired *vetāla* demons, their bodies like
kohl,
Lean[55] and hungry, held together by prominent
Sinews, delighting in slaying human beings,
Will be subdued if one remembers You.

10 Through the merit that I have gained here
Thinking of Her victorious over the Māras
Who in this way saves from the eight fears,
May She be known to all the entire world!

The Praise of Ārya-Tārā Who Saves from the Eight Great Fears, by the Venerable Master Śrī-Candragomin,[56] is complete.

*Translated from the Tibetan.*

# 3 *Praise by Sūryagupta*

## THE AUTHOR

### *Sūryagupta or Ravigupta?*

The Tibetan, *Nyi ma sbas pa,* can correspond to either. Occasionally the name is given in Sanskrit, but unfortunately both alternatives are found. The colophon of his *Praise of the Twenty-one Tārās* (referred to above as S5) gives *Sūryaguptapāda;* Bu-tön's version of the lineage of the seventeen-deity Tārā, given as a prayer in Sanskrit,[1] also has *Sūryagupta.* On the other hand, the lineage of Vajra-tārā quoted by P'ak-pa[2] gives *Ravigupta,* and the Buddhist logician of the same Tibetan name—conceivably the same person—is referred to as Ravigupta in a work by a Naiyāyika opponent.[3]

For the sake of consistency, I have translated *Nyi ma sbas pa* as Sūryagupta throughout, but it may turn out that this form was no more than Bu-tön's reconstruction from the Tibetan.

### *Tāranātha's Sūryagupta*

According to Tāranātha,[4] Sūryagupta the Tārā-*siddha* was contemporary with Candrakīrti, Candragomin, Śāntideva, *Ācārya* Dharmapāla and others, and Sarvajñamitra was his disciple. The last is known from an Indian source, the *Rājataraṅgiṇī,* to have lived around 700 AD.[5] Thus Tāranātha places Sūryagupta firmly in the middle to late seventh century. Beyond this he gives very little information on Sūryagupta's life, except that he built twelve large Dharma centres in Kashmir (his birthplace) and Magadha, with the aid of the *yakṣas*. The cycle on the twenty-one Tārās is attributed to this Sūryagupta, but the Praise P2562, which mentions Candragomin and Sarvajña[mitra] and hails Nāgārjuna as the author's *guru*, 'must be by another Sūryagupta'. The first Sūryagupta's *guru* is said to have been Nāgamitra, but this can hardly be the fifth-century Nāgamitra mentioned in *HBI*.

### *Sūryagupta in other sources*

Other sources give Sūryagupta great prominence in the history of Tārā practice. He is the origin (the first living human holder) of several important lineages (see Appendix 3). Only Bu-tön's lineage (1) gives him a human *guru*—Nāgārjuna. This name is absent in P'ak-pa's earlier version of the same lineage (2). In lineage (1), the eleventh-century scholar Dānaśrī, known as 'the great Dā', appears as Sūryagupta's direct disciple, but the lineages (2) to (4) show that (1) is seriously incomplete. They suggest that Sūryagupta (or Ravigupta) lived around the mid-ninth-century; he could hardly have lived in the seventh century unless these lineages are incomplete as well.

It appears, then, that the important Sūryagupta, the only one known to authors apart from Tāranātha, is Tāranātha's 'other Sūryagupta', the disciple of Nāgārjuna. This Sūryagupta, according to *BA* 1050–1, received *siddhi* from Tārā when he contracted leprosy and meditated in a hut for three months to seek a cure. Tārā healed him except for a small sore on his forehead, which She said was the last vestige of a *karma* of killing animals—he had been a hunter and set fire to a forest—for which he had just endured five hundred existences in hell. This also sounds like a different person from Tāranātha's Sūryagupta, who had been practising Tārā for seven lives.

The logician Ravigupta, by my calculation, flourished in the mid-tenth-century and so is unlikely to have been the same person as either 'Sūryagupta'.[6]

## THE WORK

If the seventh-century Sūryagupta existed, this Praise could well be by him. It is evidently the work of a monk-scholar who has spent many years studying the treatises of such Masters as Asaṅga and thinks in terms of their doctrines. That its content is pure ordinary *Mahāyāna* with scarcely a trace of Tantra suggests an early date.

For the author and his intended readers, one word can suffice to conjure up a whole network of doctrinal ideas—ideas more refined and subtle than everyday concepts, and so expressing more of the *Āryā* Goddess's mysterious splendour. By going a little beyond ordinary thoughts, they give an intimation of that which transcends them utterly. For us, of course, many of the allusions are lost altogether, while even if the reference is to some theory we have studied, the lack of agreed English equivalents for the technical terms may make it difficult for us to recognize it. Some of this praise is therefore obscure, but most is reasonably clear.

The heart of the work is thirty-two Names of the Goddess. While they are not unlike those in the *Hundred and Eight Names*, in the present work the Names are not simply listed, but explained each in its own verse. I have put each Name at the beginning of its verse, for clarity; in the Tibetan and probably in the original Sanskrit it came at the end, with a feminine ending, which usually cannot be expressed in English without sounding grotesque.

One small puzzle is why there should be thirty-three verses with apparently one name in each, when both text and title announce but thirty-two Names. It does not seem likely that an extra verse has been interpolated (although verses 35 and 38 partially duplicate each other), since in view of Indian authors' preference for round numbers the Praise's present length of just fifty stanzas is probably the same as the original length. Conceivably verse 38 is not counted, on the grounds that the thirty-two have to be titles different from *Tārā*; but the Sanskrit there was more likely *Tārikā* or *Tāriṇī* than *Tārā*. The most plausible solution is that verses 32 and 33 are counted as giving the same name, 'Life-giver' (*jīvikā*).

The last twelve verses describe the beneficial results to be gained from reciting the Names of Tārā—a practice more akin to Pure Land Buddhism than to Tantra. The emphasis is all on creating good conditions for practice and progressing efficiently along the *Mahāyāna* Path. Worldly benefits are little stressed, and the *siddhis* that tend to be all-important for many Tantric authors are not mentioned explicitly. This may well be the Sūryagupta who 'held that the views of *Ācārya* Nāgārjuna were the same as those of Asaṅga,'[7] but it does not seem like the one who compiled the series of rituals in S2 and S4.

## PRAISE OF THE THIRTY-TWO NAMES OF THE VENERABLE ĀRYA-TĀRĀ CALLED THE JEWEL-ORNAMENT-LIKE FULFILLER OF ALL AIMS

([*Ārya-tārā-bhaṭṭārikā-nāma-dvātriṃśatka-stotra Sarvârtha-sādhaka-ratnâlaṃkāra-saṃnibha-nāma*])

*By Sūryagupta*

Homage to the Venerable Ārya-Tārā!

[*Introduction*]

1 Of boundless nature, a pleasant, delightful place,
Potala's charming, high in properties
Of pure Great Bliss and spontaneous virtues. In
This land provided with precious
sense-enjoyments,

2 Amitābha's jewel-like Compassion,
Though he stirs not from the brilliant non-dual
sphere,[8]
Appears to others as Woman with Marks and
Signs
To benefit people of our world,[9] great in
attachment.

3 This Fortunate She, with friendly Masters of
The Ten Stages, Knowledge-holders, fierce
deities[10] such as
Hayagrīva, hosts of gods, *asuras*,
*Yakṣas*, *gandharvas*, Queens of Knowledge and
others,

4 Parts never in the three times[11] from the realized
meaning
Of the space-like gem-store of the ocean of
Doctrine,
The vast, profound essence, fulfilling hopes,
hard to fathom,
Useful to speak of, pure in its start, end and
middle,

5 Released from fears, defilements and sufferings.
At wanted occasions and times She appears to migrators.
Her thirty-two supreme Names, which purify evil,
I'll tell to others, that they may be saved through hearing.

[*The thirty-two Names*]

6 *Buddhā*! knowing all the three times as one,
You pierce the Deep Meaning, Great Bliss and the simple True Nature,
Non-dual, with nothing to accept or reject,
Released from conceptions of signs, in the unborn sphere![12]

7 Emanator! appearing in manners indefinite,
Taming all by means of Deeds for the good
Of other sentient beings with loving compassion,
Though unmoved from Sameness as to th' intended aim![13]

8 Chief Guide![14] You dispel *saṃsāra*'s fears,
Such as the eight fears, by magic, intelligently,
Without pride, in those evil spirits oppress,
In places of exceeding measureless terror!

9 You of noble morals! In youthful body, You're used
To the scent of morality, not clad in immoral faults
But in secret robes of consideration and conscience;
The beautiful ornament, pure contentment, adorns You.

10 Superior One! Unstained by Saṃsāric faults,
With the cord of kindly compassionate Means[15] You fish out
Migrators of six realms, their consciousness sunk in the ocean
Of sorrow, onto the dry land of Awakening.

11 Sole Mother producing the Buddhas of the three
times!
Through *samādhi* applying united intuitive
knowledge
Of th' sphere of non-dual appearance[16] and Void
to its object,
The Mode of Existence, You generate blissful
Gnosis.

12 Saviouress! ferrying over the river of suff'ring
The five lines,[17] who wander in agony of
unvirtue
In hard-to-cross floods of birth, aging, sickness
and death
With Your boat of *Bodhicitta* and Compassion!

13 Leader! Who guides to Liberation's city
The caravan of migrators on *saṃsāra*'s roads,
Bereft of the wealth of uncontaminate Bliss,
By the land of gold and jewels of Omniscience!

14 Doctor! removing the pain of suffering from
The patients gripped by that chronic disease, the
three poisons,
In triple-realmed *saṃsāra*'s house of sorrow,
With streams of healing nectar of True Dharma!

15 Jewel! fulfilling hopes, desires and needs
Of greedy beings tormented with desire,
A storehouse of riches, the *Āryas'* seven
Treasures
And uncontaminate virtues at disciples' will!

16 Bearer of Knowledge![18] of no change or decay
In the three times, perceiving there's no birth or
passing away
In the sudden untimely death of beings by
sickness,
Weapons or famine in this degenerate eon!

17 Heroine! victorious over *saṃsāra*;
Wearing the armour of Patience, with Wisdom's
sword

You overcome the troops of perverse defilements
In those overpowered by the faults in their own
mind.

18 Turner of the wheel of healthy Dharma!
Uninterruptedly satisfying migrators,
Thirsty because of the faults of Becoming in all
Migrations, with water of nectar of
non-attachment!

19 Sun![19] that shines on everyone, high or lowly!
The light of Your splendour outshines the
seven[20] planets;
The rays of Your knowledge open the lotus of
mind;
Your light of Compassion dries up the stream of
Becoming.

20 Full Moon! pleasant since bearing the hare of
virtues![21]
With full-moon face 'midst constellations of
servitors,[22]
Free of bad planets, You clear obscurations' poor
vision,
Your rays of Morality cool for those scorched by
defilements.

21 Lotus! Your stem of mind grown in the pool of
*dhyāna*,
You're unstained by mud of agitation and fading.
Your petals of Heat-signs[23] and stamens of bliss
have developed.
Open, Your sweet scent satisfies swarms of
bees.[24]

22 Fearless One![25] since You outshine the
Hīnayānists,
Perfect in skill by Your power in snow
mountains of Purity,
Conqu'ring with reasoning's teeth and claws[26]
*tīrthika* beasts,
Frightening the *śrāvaka* fox-pack with roar of
Non-self.

23 Very firm one![27] ent'ring the sea of conviction,
Perfect in *Bodhi*'s strength in the garden of Joy,
An elephant drunk by the power of the wine of *samādhi*,
Conquering recklessness with the sword of mindfulness!

24 Thoroughbred! perfect in wisdom and vow, You take
The wanderers in the desert of *saṃsāra*
On *Mahāyāna*'s swift mount over the way
Of *Mahāyāna*, on feet of psychic power.[28]

25 Peahen![29] producing wonderful beauty, unharmed
Though You eat the poison of the defilements, of lovely
Colour, unstained by faults and hosts of defects;
You see undisturbed profound True Nature's splendour.

26 *Kalaviṅkā*! with sweet Brahmic voice!
Flapping wings of View cut Emptiness[30] like the sky,
You have no fear of the cliff of the realms of woe;
Bill and claw of practice subdue *nāga*-kings of conceptions.[31]

27 Lamp! removing the darkness of ignorance—
For the aim sought by those who've lost their jewel minds
In dust-clouds of faults in the black dark of this eon
You make a lamp with the oil of Quietude and Insight.

28 Clear revealer of beauty![32] of th' Mode of Existence's nature—
In the *ālaya*'s mirror, free of the rust of imprints,
The stains of conceptless obscurations cleared,
Its stable image arises in [Your] clear mind.[33]

29 Liberator! You free from the bondage of suff'ring
The prisoner mind in the prison of the five heaps,
Bound in the chains of defilements that grasp a self,
With the key of realizing Emptiness-deliverance.[34]

30 Great-voiced One! proclaiming for clear understanding
With thunder of Dharma and lightning of Joyous Effort
To those weighed down by sleep and idle laziness
In the darkness of sin, in the lair(?)[35] of signs.

31 *Amṛta*! healing without birth or cessation
With nectar of *Bodhi*, deathless and ageless, View's life,
Dead in th' extremes of permanence and destruction
In the cemetery of Personality's filthy heaps![36]

32 Guarding Life-giver! sentinel of alertness
In case the watchman of mindfulness breaks instructions
When foes of misdeeds all rob the wealth of virtues
In merit's stockade of laziness and distraction!

33 Life-giver healing the world! since when the sprouts
Of virtue are scorched by the drought of perverse view,
From Your cloud-mass of Love the downpour of Compassion
Soaks Faith's field and ripens the leaves of *Bodhi*.

34 Sole Friend in the three becomings! for when the life
Faculty ceases, and we are led by Yama,
Bereft of life and friends, and scream aloud
With roars of pain, You rescue us from fear.

35 *Ḍākinī*! swiftly killing foes when beings
Of five hundred Ages of Strife,[37] with the five gross poisons
Abuse Buddha's Word and plague wise people's bodies,
And by perverse view obstruct Enlightenment!

36 Way-shower! When, the film of ignorance blinding
Our wisdom eye, we fall down the cliff of unfreedom,[38]
You grasp us with the hook of Your [Means of] Attraction
And put us unerringly straight on the perfect Path.

37 Friendly-minded one! tireless in Your promise
To work for beings until *saṃsāra*'s empty,
By power of *Bodhicitta* and growth of vow
Of undelayed Mercy, not tarrying in the three times!

38 Savioureess! swiftly killing enemies
Who make obstruction to the Buddha's Doctrine
When, though You move in the space of realized True Nature,
You emanate in fierce forms to subdue the vicious!

[*Benefits*]

39 Such praise of the fruit of the [thir]ty-two[39] flowers of Marks
And eighty exemplary Signs is beautiful as
A jewel adornment accomplishing every aim,
The supreme monarch of praises of all the Conquerors.

40 Through hearing the Names, for a thousand eons you'll not
Take woeful rebirth; bad karma, sins, obscurations

Are spent; you're freed from all accidental perils;
It makes you intelligent, fortunate and
well-born.

41 Should you first take purity in the morning[40]
Then proclaim them, reciting aloud or reading
With undistracted concentration, in joy
And devotion, three, seven, twenty-one [times]
or more,

42 'Twill consume[41] bad karma and imprints from
previous lives,
Cleanse defilements, non-virtues, sins,
obscurations,
And purify every strong evil, such as the five
Immediate and the five approaching them.

43 It will cut the bonds of the suff'ring of realms of
woe
And free from all the sufferings of *saṃsāra*.
Supreme and ordinary virtues will be perfected.
You're consecrated as heir of all the Conquerors.

44 The Friendly-minded, *ḍākinīs* and the eight
classes
Of spirits[42] befriend you and see you in
honoured place.[43]
Predispositions and obscurations of knowables
Are purified and you quickly attain
Buddhahood.

45 As to fears of this life, remembering clears away
Fear of harm by greedy and rough beings, such
as
Polluting demons and hosts of many *yakṣas*,
*Rākṣasas*, spirits, *vetālas* and *piśācas*.

46 Hostile armies, wild beasts, savages,
The eight fears—robbers, venomous serpents,
royal
Punishment, lions, elephants, tigers, fire,
Water—and other [means of] untimely death:

47 Remembering and reciting these Names with
conviction
Pacifies suff'ring and liberates from evil.
It quells and removes the suffering of such harms
As leprosy, epidemics and poisoning.

48 Prosperity, fame and merits will increase;
Talents, lifetime and nature will develop;
Wealth, enjoyments and family will increase;
Wisdom will grow and you'll understand the
treatises.

49 Versed in the sciences, you will conquer
conventions.
Dependence clear, virtues and signs of Heat
arise.[44]
Superknowledges come; you remember [past]
rebirths;
You will be radiant, pleasant and bright to
behold.

50 Your voice will be sweet, resembling the tones of
Brahmā;
Your true words clear, your body and mind will
be strong.
Everywhere, wherever you are reborn,
You'll never be abandoned by all the Buddhas.
Relying insep'rably on your Spiritual Friend,
You will accomplish all the aims you desire.

The Praise of the Thirty-two Names of the Venerable Ārya-Tārā called the Jewel-ornament-like Fulfiller of All Aims, by Sūryagupta of Kashmir, is complete.

*Translated from the Tibetan.*

# 4 *Sarvajñamitra's Sragdharā Praise*

## INTRODUCTION

### *The author*

The *bhikṣu* Sarvajñamitra of Kashmir was a contemporary of Śāntideva, author of the *Bodhisattva-caryāvatāra*, living in the late 7th and early 8th centuries.[1] The two had much in common. Both are said to have been of royal birth, both received visions of Ārya-Tārā and are credited with various miracles, and their literary works are alike remarkable for their beauty and the intensity of devotional feeling they convey.

According to Tāranātha's *History of Buddhism in India*,[2] Sarvajñamitra was the son of a king of Kashmir, but as a baby was carried away by a vulture and set down at a temple at Nālandā, where he was brought up by the pandits. We preface the translation with his story as told by the *bhikṣu* Śṛī-Jinarakṣita of Vikramaśīla,[3] in introduction to his commentary on the *Sragdharā-stotra*. Tāranātha also tells the same story, his much later version differing in such details as the name of the king and the manner of the sacrifice.[4]

*The title*

This is a *sragdharā* praise in that the verses are composed in the metre called *sragdharā*, 'garland-bearing'. This is appropriate in that *Sragdharā* is an epithet of Ārya-Tārā, 'She who wears a garland'.[5] Furthermore, the author regards his verses of praise themselves as garlands which he offers to the Goddess, thus the work is a 'Praise Bearing Garlands to Ārya-Tārā'.

*The work*

A verse in *sragdharā* metre consists of four *pādas*, each of the following form:

– – – – ᴗ – –/ᴗ ᴗ ᴗ ᴗ ᴗ ᴗ –/
(Bā lār kā lo ka-tām ra-pra va ra-su ra-śi raś-

– ᴗ – – ᴗ – –/
cā ru-cū ḍā ma ṇi-śrī-)

Here, each such four-line stanza is a single sentence, which must be read as a whole. Sarvajñamitra writes in this complicated rhythm with notable ease and skill, making full use of the immense resources of the Sanskrit language to create intriguing patterns of words and sounds while conveying the meaning with grace and subtlety. He can juxtapose related or similar-sounding words with different meanings, e.g. *vetālôt-tāla-tāla* '*vetāla* demons' violent hand-clapping', or let the alternative meanings of words provide a counterpoint; for example, to look no further than the first word, *bālârka* 'rising sun' also means 'new praise', foreshadowing the explicit occurrence of that meaning later in the verse. There are fine echoic phrases such as *uḍḍamara-ḍamarukôḍḍāmara* 'tumultuous like the tumult of a *ḍamaru*', or the succession of nine Ls in ten syllables for the rolling billows in verse 10, which then break with heavy thuds of multiple consonants and a spattering of -Ṭ-sounds.

Just as its Subject's ornaments, although of unimaginable splendour, must harmonize perfectly naturally with the matchless beauty of their Wearer, this very Indian poetry's richness in literary devices in no way mars its delicacy and refinement. Translating it into a European language is like trying to play *rāgas* on a Western piano—doubtless certain aspects could be transmitted in the alien medium but too much must disappear. To extend the analogy, the Tibetan language would perhaps be more like a piano with only the black keys working.

The plan of the *Praise* has certain features in common with the Tibetan 'Songs of Longing' in Part Five. The first verse, as always, is one of prostration to the feet of the Goddess. Here it also includes a promise of composition.Then come some verses (2—8) bewailing the author's unhappy state and calling upon the *Āryā* Mother to fulfil Her duty by helping him. The corresponding section in Lodr'ö Gyats'o's and Lozang Tänpä Gyälts'än's hymns, similar in spirit, is their most interesting part, full of conviction and feeling. It is here that one sees vividly the reality of the Mother as a person with whom the devotee can relate. In verse 9 Sarvajñamitra explains his object in composing the praises, then the actual Praises begin, when he is no longer talking about himself.

Ten verses (10—19) describe how Tārā saves from suffering and danger; they deal with the eight great fears, plus the dangers of battle and of sickness. The next ten praise Her as the cause of all fortunate rebirths in *saṃsāra*, in the human state (20—23), as a Universal Monarch (24), or as a god in the heavens of the Desire Realm (25—29), culminating in the state of Indra himself, their ruler (29). The author dwells lovingly and much longer than a Tibetan lama would on the worldly pleasures of wealth, sex, honour and power in some very sensuous poetry, before a cursory glance at higher things in his praises of the Enlightened Mother's forms (30—33) and infinitude of qualities (34).

In the short concluding section, Sarvajñamitra says he addresses Tārā only for his own peace of mind (35), makes request (36)—in the Tibetan hymns, this section is greatly expanded—and dedicates the merits of composing the *Praise* (37).

*The translation* is from the Sanskrit text edited from six manuscripts by Godefroy de Blonay (1895). These praises must have been very popular, for even at that date de Blonay was able to locate another six copies, which he did not use. The interpretation largely follows de Blonay's French translation, which was based on the commentary of Jinarakṣita and another, anonymous, commentary. The story from Jinarakṣita's commentary is also translated from the Sanskrit text published by de Blonay.[6]

Three Tibetan translations of the Praise are found in the Tängyur. Gaining access to them two years after my translation was complete, I have made a few corrections in their light.

Translations A and B are academic and literal, written in ponderous nineteen-syllable lines and sometimes hard to understand. B is by Pa-ts'ap Nyi-ma-dr'ak (eleventh century),[7] who also translated Candrakīrti's great texts on Madhyamaka philosophy, with the *paṇḍita* from Kashmir whom he invited to Tibet, Kanaka-varman. It was later corrected by Ch'ak Lotsawa with Maṇika-śrī-jñāna. A bears no translator's name, but is obviously another state of the Pa-ts'ap translation, perhaps before Ch'ak revised it. (If so, not all Ch'ak's changes were for the better.) Both versions are very drab compared with the scintillating original. The colophon of B says Sarvajña-mitra 'practised one-pointedly the conduct of a Bodhisattva'.

Translation C is the only example I know of a Tibetan translation that does not set out to be literal. Significantly, it is by '*paṇḍita* Candrakumāra himself'—no Tibetan would have dared. We can visualize him, evidently an Indian in Tibet, sorrowing that his students could not experience the magic of this work. Poetry for them was something you could sing and follow the meaning of as it went along—these stanzas that needed hours of poring over with a dictionary were not recognizably of the same art form. So he wrote a paraphrase quite like indigenous Tibetan songs, all in short, straightforward sentences that fitted exactly into the seven-syllable lines. Passages that did not come over too well in Tibetan he shortened. When a sentence did not fit the lines he either left a word or two out or made something up to fill out a line. This may not startle us, but for Tibet it must have been outrageous. The effect is a bit like jazzed-up Bach—something gets through, though much subtlety is necessarily lost. Generally his line length is similar to mine, about a third of the original; the length of the stanzas in his version varies from six lines (verse 14) to fifteen (verse 32), with an average of 10.6.

Here is just one stanza from Candra-kumāra's version, chosen more or less at random. Sometimes he departs much more from the original, but this stanza (verse 4) is typical.

> I, of ill fortune, have no luck.
> Though the sun rises, it's dark and black.
>
> The Gaṅgā's water is very cool,
> so, though on the bank I sit
> thirsty, I find nothing to drink.
>
> I am broke, although I live
> in a house that's full of gems
> in the isle where there're many jewels.
>
> Thus, though I want You, my Lady,
> as Protector, I've no protector,
> Unique Mother of all the world!

Just after the first edition of this book had gone to press, I came across another edition of the Sanskrit text, by Satis Chandra Vidyabhusana, published by the Asiatic Society of Bengal in Calcutta in 1908. I shall refer to it as V and to Jinarakṣita's commentary, accompanying it, as J. In a number of places it gives better readings than de Blonay (Y), which has made possible some improvements to the translation. Note that the Tibetan translations I have called A, B and C – which Vidyabhusana also edits, in a volume of over 300 pages – are referred to by him as C, D and E respectively.

## THE STORY OF SARVAJÑAMITRA

*By Jinarakṣita*

In the land of Kashmir there lived a *bhikṣu* resembling a Bodhisattva, full of the water of Compassion of the Teachings of the King of Sages, his heart and mind nourished with Great Compassion, Sarvajña-mitra (Omniscient Friend) by name. Since he accomplished the wishes of those in want like a wish-fulfilling gem, he was celebrated in the world for his generosity.

Having renounced all his goods to the needy so that his sole property was his robes and bowl, he was travelling abroad, when he came to the country of King Vajra-mukuṭa (Diamond Crown). There he saw on the road a brahman, worn out with old age, and lacking attendants. In the course of conversation, this [brahman] said he was going to see the *bhikṣu* Sarvajña-mitra to beg. The latter said, 'That *bhikṣu* has distributed all his possessions to the poor and gone to another country. Hadn't you heard?'

Hearing this, the old hermit sighed for a long time and stood motionless and dejected for a while. Then, as he grieved in such a pitiable manner, [Sarvajñamitra] said comfortingly, 'I am Sarvajñamitra. Do not be so lacking in courage, I shall accomplish all you desire!' Taking him into the presence of King Vajramukuṭa, he sold his own body for its weight in gold, and gave him the proceeds. Then he sent him away and remained before the king.

At that time the king had been advised that if he bathed upon the severed heads of a hundred men endowed with various characteristics as described, his desire would be fulfilled; so he had commanded accordingly, and after a diligent search for a long time, ninety-nine men had been purchased for their weight in gold. With the one standing there, the hundred was complete. 'Now we shall perform our bath upon severed heads. Lead [him] among them!' he ordered the guard.

When the servant given this order had carried it out, all the condemned men saw this one. Crying out loudly, 'Tomorrow morning we shall be dead,' they said, 'This shaveling who's arrived is our peril of imminent death!'

The Bodhisattva said to them, 'Why such lack of fortitude? Did you not know before, when you sold yourselves?' Then, having comforted them in their utter despair, and looked upon them with eyes moist with Great Compassion, convinced that apart from the Mother there was no-one else who would rescue them, the great devotee Sarvajñamitra began to praise the Venerable Ārya-Tārā.

Thereupon, just after a certain number of verses, the Venerable Lady Herself made Her appearance, thought what was to be done and gave instructions, ascended and disappeared. Sarvajñamitra, having thus received every favour, announced: 'Tomorrow morning, you must all bathe at the same time.'

When morning came, the condemned men were conducted by the king's men to the bank of a lake. They said to them, 'We must all bathe at the same time, why delay for long?', and plunged into the lake. By the power of the Venerable Lady, each one arrived at his own country. A couple of minutes afterwards, the [guards] searched for them diligently but could not find them present; but they perceived on the bank of the lake their price in gold, arranged in heaps according to each one. Then, their minds bewildered with amazement and dread, the king's men informed the king.

When he heard it, the king was overcome with amazement, and said 'It is just by the power of that one *bhikṣu* I bought.' An extreme serene faith was born in him, and he had [Sarvajñamitra] sought out and became his disciple.

This is the beginning of the story, but it is well known, so we shall not tell it.

Homage to the Glorious Goddess!

*Translated from the Sanskrit.*

## SRAGDHARĀ PRAISE OF ĀRYA-TĀRĀ
(*Ārya-tārā-sragdharā-stotra*)

*By Sarvajñamitra*

OṂ. Homage to the Venerable Ārya-Tārā!

1 Your feet, O *Āryā*, Saviouress, Giver
of Refuge from misfortune,
that are worshipped by highest gods
And adorned with red lac tint
freshly put on by contact
with the splendid perfection of the
Lovely jewels on their heads,
red like the rising sun's light,
I too, head bowed in adoration
By pressure of hands joined in a crest,[8]
celebrate in devotion
with flower garlands of new praises.

2 In the fire of suffering, hard to
escape, my body has fallen.
Unlucky, I flee in all directions,
Perplexed—whatever am I doing?—
weary of uselessness
of efforts repeatedly undertaken.
Like one with damaged eyes, who has
heard much from others of
the sun and moon's beauty in the sky,
I am bound by the wish to see,
and guided by others, come
for protection to You, the destroyer of evil!

3 On every path of sentient beings,
surely, Your Compassion
operates without distinction;

By grasping them, it certainly
manages to grasp,
amidst them, even one like me.

Your power without match is the disk
of a sun for the darkness of
the evils of the entire world.

Even so, I am afflicted:
indeed, alas! for shame!
wrong-headed, evil action torments me.

4 Woe, O woe! unhappy me!
Whose dark is not dispelled
even by the light of the sun!

Thirsty upon the chilly bank,
rocky and snow-flecked, of
the daughter of the Himālaya![9]

A pauper, in his house where is
a cache of abundant gems
from the broad way of the Isle of Jewels!

Without protector, Blessed One,
although I have chosen Your Ladyship,
sole Nurse[10] of all worlds, as protection![11]

5 Even a mother can become
dejected, when her baby
cries for milk repeatedly;

Even a father can get angry
when pestered every day
with impossible requests;

But You, beṣt creeper[12] on the great
wish-granting tree whose fruit
is abundance of the three worlds' desires,

Grant to everyone the things
they asked for; nor is there
in You any failing whatsoever.

6 'Whoever's body is burned in the fire
of the swarm of afflictions,
I it is who am his Saviouress.'—

Now I am plunged in the underworld
of suffering, fulfil
this promise that You have revealed!

Great as injuries, abuse
and floods of suffering
of living beings grow, at last,

So does the compassion of those
whose thoughts are fixed on the vow
of the Vehicle of the Perfect Buddhas.[13]

7 If one thus cries aloud, arms raised
a howl of lamentation
in the semblance of words of praise,

No other is entitled to be
indifferent; how much less,
O Mother! such a one as You?

Seeing that, thanks to You, requests
of others for wealth are allowed,
and wishing mine to be fulfilled,

I am consumed anew by continuous
internal fever, born of
discontent, and unendurable.

8 If I am wicked, then how is it
that this great devotion
I have towards You is increasing?

Just by the hearing and recalling
of Your name, You alone
snatch away evil forcibly.

How can You abandon this task,
Your function, in my case?
Let this be explained, Truth-teller!

When a sick person is going to die,
does a physician with much
compassion withhold what would help?

9 Like the monastery's camel,
  shares of which are owned
in common by several, I am driven,[14]

At the same time or in succession,
  by my worst faults, such as
pretension, avarice and pride:

To venerate Your lotus feet
  I find not even a moment.
Particularly with that object,

I have composed these lines of syllables,
  sad and pitiful—
through this may my wishes not be vain!

10 Whirling wind like the end of the world
  whisks the water around
in frivolous billows, rolling and heaving,

Which with a violent shock are tossed,
  huge, on the shore to break,
crashing, crushing, in roars of mirth.

From this, let those shipwrecked and sinking,
  paralyzed in misery,
cry out in pitiful lamentation,

They, Goddess! for whom Your praise[15] is
    supreme—
  at once, spontaneously,
they are thrown out on the ocean's shore.

11 Out of swirling clouds of smoke
  rises in the sky[16]
a mansion; in it billows up,

With crackle of sparks, a terrible blaze
  of swift flames, entering
the house, where lie at ease in bed

Some who, joining their hollowed palms
  on their heads in rev'rence to You,
stammer out their songs of entreaty.

In a moment they are covered
  by fast water-giving clouds
arising, lit by the play of flashes.

12 When from the mountainsides of both
an elephant's temples, filled
with rut-fluid, hang festoons of bees,

So that he's inflamed with anger
towards rival elephants
summoned by his trumpeting;

And with the tip of his tusks, he lifts
one's body up from beneath,
as on a high swing, remembering You

Death is averted, and thrilled with delight
one sits as if in the fortress
of the peak of his broad-topped head.

13 In the lonely forest, whose festive
creepers[17] are stakes that bear
the heads of men killed with violent blows

From missiles, the bandits are all puffed up
with arrogance, like boils;
with their finger-tips, they hold

Glittering swords; they scowl, their eyes
dart sidelong glances, 'neath crooked
brows. But one the pen of whose thoughts

Tires not of writing clear words upon
the splendour and majesty of
Your Name, can bind them in servitude.

14 With a ferocious, lightning-like stroke
of his harsh claws, he gouges
the temporal bumps of a ruttish elephant,

Sending a trickle of viscous blood
to wash his monstrous expanse
of dense mane, parted on the shoulders.

Angry, close and ready to pounce
on one, the foe of beasts,
the lion, whose jaws are full of sharp teeth,

Turns around trembling and goes away,
if one's speech is anointed with meaning
through praises composed for Your delight.

15 In forms of darkness, like coils of smoke,
hideous serpents fill
[the air] with violent hissing sounds.

Busily their extended tongues
dart from their open mouths.
They are the ropes of Yama's nooses

Met with because of sin. But if
one's supreme concern is You,
if one's great aim is to reckon Your virtues,

Then he wears magnificent ornaments—
garlands of water-lilies,
girdled by swarms of delighted bees.

16 Frightened by the frown of their chief,
impassioned royal soldiers
drag one by one's ill-attached hair.

Agitated, talkative servants,
yelling in fury, bind one
round with bitter knotted cords.

One's throat and lips are dry with hunger
and thirst. But one's free at once
of this infinite misfortune,

If one goes for Refuge to
the feet of Ārya-Tārā,
though abandoned by friends and kinsfolk.

17 Terrifying *rākṣasa* demons,
creating by series of works
of magical transformation, many
Changes of attire, false forms
and dazzling, noisy weapons[18]
suited to their undertakings,[19]

And who wear garlands composed of piles
of spun entrails from corpses,
bestow inviolable protection

On one who eliminates difficulties
by remembering
mantras extracted from Your Tantra.

18 When darkness of pent-up streams[20] of rivers
of rut-fluid from elephants,
which are like thundering clouds made solid,

Is lit in flashes by the glint
of weapons, and a rain
of arrows falls—in time of battle,

When he is obstructed by
enemies full of hatred,
mighty in the strength of their arms,

With the increase in power given by You
the single hero crushes
violently the field of foes.

19 Those full of sickness caused by evil
conduct—their wasted limbs
devoured by worms that ooze through the
mouths

Of the pits of fistular ulcers fixed
in putrid flesh and skin
exuding stinking pus and blood—

If intent on devotional practice
of worship at Your feet,
a remedy like the choicest pills,

Become quite beautiful in form,
similar to gold,
their eyes extended and lotus-like.

20 One in the begging-bowl of whose ears
the alms of sacred instructions
offered by *gurus* do not repose,

And who is reduced to silence
in learned conversations
because he is lacking in wealth of knowledge,

By the power of devotion to You
gains mastery of speech,
is furnished with all the ornaments,

Decorations and high rank,
and at the royal court
wins the thrones of the eloquent.[21]

21 One whose limbs are exposed by the torn
   rags about his hips,
dust-dark from sleeping on the ground,

Who crushes lice alive to beg
   in front of others' houses
for a scrap in a sherd to eat;[22]

If he undertakes Your worship,
   receives a wide land, with
its one royal parasol raised above him,

Strong with the tusks of ruttish elephants
   beautiful with the smiles
of lovely young women bearing chowries.

22 Those who, wearied of the succession
   of means—solicitation,
service, trading, crafts and farming–

Do not meet with property as
   the happy result of heaps
of merit acquired in former lives,

Once they have requested wealth
   of You who transcend fortune,[23]
Mother of miserable people,

Then these poor folk encounter hoards,
   vomited from the earth,
of golden treasure [in abundance].

23 One who, deprived of livelihood,
   knows not what to do,
reviled by his wife in tattered garments,

And avoided at great distance,
   since they are selfish, by
his kindred, children, friends and relatives,

Having informed You of his sorrow
   is master of a house
whose bounds are roughened by horses' hooves,

Where he is woken from his slumbers
   just by the jingling of bangles
of the women of his harem.

24 That the wheel may touch the horizon,[24]
that the wife be adornèd
with the marks and of far-shining radiance,

That the best elephant have six tusks,
that the finest of horses
have brilliant blue coat like a peacock's neck,

That the jewel be of spotless qualities,
shining with sun-like rays,
that the treasurer be rich in treasure,

The general lead an army of heroes,
comes about, O Lady,
by a small share of Your favour.

25 At will, the king of the *vidyādharas*
goes to the pleasure grove[25]
of Malaya, where his lovers give him

Assignations on rocks of gemstone,
fragrant with sandal water,
out of fondness for play with their dear one

Treating him with true hospitality
constantly renewed;
for by Your mantras he has gained *siddhi*.

Bracelets glitter on the bar[26]
of his noble, muscular arm,
darkened[27] by the rays of his sword.

26 Pearl necklaces press between their breasts,
blue lotuses in their ears
vie with their elongated eyes;

Noble *mandāra* flowers in their tresses
distil a fresh perfume
whose scent intoxicates black bees.

The constant tinkle of [bells on] their girdles
is magnified by the musical
ornaments upon their feet.

The heavenly maidens, devoted and
delighting in amorous raptures,
long for him who takes Refuge in You.

27 By a pond with gem-covered banks,
garlanded with golden
lotus plants with diamond filaments,

And coral trees coming into bloom,
throwing off an awning
of sweet pollen from their flowers,[28]

While charming girls from the town of
'immortals',[29]
skilled on flute and *vīṇā*,
give a concert of exquisite beauty,

One who has engaged in Your worship
experiences long
the festival in Nandana garden.[30]

28 In the River Mandākinī,[31]
whose water is scented with powder
of spikenard, aloewood, cinnamon,

Camphor, cloves and cardamom,
whose ripples abate in eddies
in hollows between their darlings'[32] breasts

Swelling with amorous elation:
in sport in the surging river
splashing quite unsluggishly,[33]

Those who by setting their heart on You
have developed a glowing force
of merits dally with beautiful women.

29 Heads bowed beneath the burden of discipline,
chiefs among the gods
venerate his authority

In the lap of heaven; he's mounted
on the celestial elephant,
whose limbs are splendid with sounding
ornaments.

Wantonly encircled close
by the swinging garland of Śacī's
arms, the hairs of his body thrill.[34]

Purified by Your glances' alighting,
he governs the land of the gods,
distinctive *vajras* [35] on his forearms.

30 Your form, crowned with a jewel crest
of *Sugatas* on their seats,
is canopied with the heavens' splendour;[36]
The triple world is pervaded by
its radiance, more intense
than ten million newly risen suns.
Beneath the weight of one leg's stride
of its bold *ālīḍha* stance
bend Brahmā, Rudra, Indra and Viṣṇu.
When meditated on, for those
liable to rebirth
it is the destruction of fears of Becoming.

31 Some perceive You full of anger,
raising shimmering weapons
with arms like tree-trunks of which a fragment
Would fill the interior of space;[37]
with conduct none can frustrate,
snakes with terrible hoods as armlets;
Dispersing foes with tumultuous laughter,
like the tumult caused
at the moment of striking a *ḍamaru*,
Or the mighty uproar of *vetāla* demons
in madly excited loud play
violently clapping their hands.

32 Others, in every single hair
of Your body see the expanse
of space, those on and in the earth,[38]
Brahmā, Indra, Rudra and so on
at ease, the Maruts, humans,
*siddhas*, *gandharvas* and *nāgas*;
And the manifold emanations
of infinite hundred *Sugatas*,
on light-rays invading the Universe,

Excellent One whom the three worlds should
praise,
of the nature of all existence
composed of the animate and the fixed.

33 Some see Your form as red like the sun,
with rays that are redder still
than the red of minium or red lac;

Others, as beautiful intense blue
like a powder of splintered fragments
of the precious stone, sapphire;

Others again as shining like gold,
or dazzling white, surpassing
the milk when the Ocean of Milk is churned.

It is a universal form,
varied like crystal, since
it changes according to circumstance.

34 Unique observer of the reality
of all that is to be known,
clear by the light of Omniscient Knowledge,

The Omniscient or His Offspring
perceives directly the tally
of Your multitude of qualities;

But what one like me can croak, when he
has opened wide his mouth,
is as the cawing of a crow.

This failure is cause of ridicule of
my mind, in which it occasions
pain as of fever, with horrible suffering.

35 What I wish to tell You about,
You already understand
before, in detail; but to make

The extra effort of speaking it
is, for my own foolish
heart, a cause of satisfaction,

Just as, vomiting any sorrow
like a poison, by speaking
before an affectionate relative

Although his meaning was already known,
through lightening his heart
an afflicted person finds well-being.

36 Moon crescent, manifest in an ocean
of joy in what is right!
Grant us Your refreshing vision![39]

Make us develop by teachings on
Your knowledge, You who are all
Compassion, scatter our inner darkness!

When my mind has been purified
in the water of Your praises,
I'll be in the supreme state of bliss:

This I know, because the praise
of Your virtues is alone
unfailing in the world of beings.[40]

37 In praising a fraction of Your abundance
of qualities, I have gained
an undetermined amount of merit,

To be enjoyed until Liberation,
tasting the sweet juice of
the fruit of a propitious wish;

Through this, may the world progress
to a speedy arrival at
that land of *Sugatas'* Offspring that bears

The auspicious Swastika mark of the soles
of the noble Lord of the World,[41]
and is known by the name of Sukhāvatī!

The Sragdharā Praise of Ārya-Tārā is complete. It is the work of Ven. Sarvajñamitra of Kashmir, grey with the dust of Tārā's feet.[42]

*Translated from the Sanskrit.*

# 5 *Praises by Akṣobhya-vajra and Dīpaṃkara-bhadra*

## AKṢOBHYA-VAJRA

According to Lalou's *Répertoire du Tanjur*, Akṣobhya-vajra is an alias of Buddha-jñāna-pāda; presumably it is his Tantric name. This eminent master, also known as Jñāna-pāda, Buddha-jñāna, or Buddha-śrī-jñāna, is mentioned by all the historians.[1]

Buddha-jñāna, a contemporary of King Tr'i-song de-tsen of Tibet (reigned 755–97(?)[2]), was born in Takṣaśīla. He became a monk at Nālandā. With the great expert on *Prajñā-pāramitā*, Haribhadra,[3] he studied the *Perfection of Wisdom* texts, on which he composed his own commentaries. Then he went to Oḍḍiyāna for tantric teachings, which he received from Master Lalita-vajra (sGeg pa'i rdo rje) and the *yoginī* Guṇeru. He practised for eight months with a *caṇḍāla* girl called Jaṭijālā (Dza thig dza la) and attained *siddhi*. Then he practised for some years in forests in South India and north of Bodhgayā.

Probably at this point, he met his principal Guru, Mañjuśrī-mitra, an emanation of Mañjuśrī and first holder of the Dzok-chen tradition after its origination by the seemingly mythical Garap Dorje. It is implied that the teachings Mañjuśrī-mitra gave him included Dzok-chen—some time before its introduction to Tibet—but that he did not transmit it to anyone else. However, his direct disciples included the Nyingma masters Sang-gyä sang-wa and Sang-gyä zhi-wa.

Eventually he settled in Vajrāsana (Bodhgayā), where he built a temple and made extensive offerings. He wrote many tantric texts, especially commentaries on Guhyasamāja, and is credited with various miracles such as appearing in several places at the same time.

He lived more than eighty years and died, as we have seen,[4] during the reign of King Dharmapāla, so his dates will be roughly 705 to 790.

## DĪPAṂKARA-BHADRA

Buddha-jñāna had eighteen 'excellent' disciples, of whom Dīpaṃkara-bhadra is placed first. The latter[5] was born in West India, and studied the Vedas before becoming a Buddhist monk. He met Buddha-jñāna at Nālandā. He is said to have procured by magic the death of a *Vaiṣṇava* king of Mālava who had been destroying Buddhist temples; and a *tīrthika* adept who tried to kill him by similar means died himself.

He succeeded Buddha-jñāna as *tantra-ācārya* at Vikramaśīla. Thirty-nine works on Tantra are attributed to him in the Tängyur. He is supposed to have met his end at the hands of a king in Sindhu.

## THE WORKS

The praise by Akṣobhya-vajra stands out for its single-minded emphasis on Wisdom and its clear-cut structure. Built of five groups of three verses and one of five, with the form of the verses constant within each group, it is easy to memorize. Its stark, almost skeletal elegance contrasts sharply with the opulence of praises such as Sarvajñamitra's or Nāgārjuna's. If there is one hymn in this book by a Dzok-chen master who has realized the meaning of the *Perfection of Wisdom* Sūtras, this is it.

The first three verses praise Tārā as the three 'Bodies' (*kāya*) of a Buddha. It is well to try and understand these on the comparatively concrete and straightforward level of ordinary *Mahāyāna* before delving into advanced tantric explanations. Briefly, the *Dharmakāya* is the Buddha's Omniscient Mind, evidently beyond our comprehension. If the term must be translated, Govinda's 'Universal Body'[6] is better than most attempts. The *Saṃbhoga-kāya*, literally 'Enjoyment Body', and *Nirmāṇa-kāya*, 'Emanation Body', are the forms that a Buddha displays to *Ārya-Bodhisattvas* and to lesser beings respectively. Tārā's characteristic iconographic features—Her green colour and so forth—belong to Her *Saṃbhoga-kāya* aspect; the *Nirmāṇa-kāyas* She constantly emanates are of any form, to suit the circumstances.

Verses 4 to 6 hail Tārā as the Three Jewels; 7 to 9 as simultaneously desirous, free of desire, and neither, depending how the words are interpreted; and 10 to 14 as embodying the five Buddha-families. 15 to 17 praise Her *Vajra* Body, Speech and Mind in terms of their lack of inherent existence, with similes familiar from the *Perfection of Wisdom* Sūtras; then the author pays homage with his own body, speech and mind, making sure that each of these actions is 'pure in the three spheres' (*tri-maṇḍala-pariśuddha*), i.e. that he is acting from realization of Emptiness, perceiving neither the action, its agent nor its object as inherently existent.

Dīpaṃkara-bhadra gives us four stanzas of homage, mostly in the standard iconographic terms, and three of dedication and request; a workmanlike effort that could have come from any competent scholar who had made some study of Tārā.

## PRAISE OF ĀRYA-TĀRĀ
(*Ārya-tārā-stotra*)

*By Akṣobhya-vajra*

Homage to the Venerable Ārya-Tārā!

1 Homage to Tārā, the *Dharmakāya*,
resting in the Realm[7] born of Knowledge,[8]
Great Bliss, simple[9] and free of concepts,
quite pure, Ultimate *Bodhicitta*![10]

2 Homage to Tārā, the *Saṃbhoga-kāya*,
the beautiful Body with youthful manner
And radiant face of the finest colour
resting amidst a circle (*maṇḍala*) of goddesses!

3 Homage to Tārā, the *Nirmāṇa-kāya*,
sending out, from Her secret heart
*Maṇḍala*, forms of perfect Knowledge,
saving beings from the six destinies!

4 Homage to Tārā Who is Buddha!
Whose supreme Mind, free of wrong concepts
And sleep of unknowing, pervades all
knowables!
Who receives honour of perfect Buddhas!

5 Homage to Tārā Who is true Dharma,
showing Great Bliss, *Nirvāṇa*'s Peace,
The highest of holy *Dharmas*, the ten
Wisdom-knowledges,[11] and ten Perfections!

6 Homage to Tārā Who is Saṅgha,
Who's realized the Body, Speech and Mind
Of all *Sugatas* of the three times,
the *Ḍākinī* of the combined Wisdom-
knowledges!

7 Homage to Tārā the Desirous,
Who, wanting to calm migrators' sorrows,
Devotes Herself to the three realms in
the form of a Goddess Who loves like a mother!

8 Homage to Tārā free of desire,
Who, knowing *saṃsāra*'s nature is pure,
Has no attachment to the three realms—
the form of the Mother, Producer of
Conquerors!

9 Homage to Tārā the Non-abiding,
Who by uniting Method and Wisdom
Abides in neither *saṃsāra* nor Peace,
neither desirous nor free of desire!

10 Homage to You, Sugata-Tārā,
Body of all the Buddhas' Gnosis,
Dispeller of darkness of ignorance
from sentient beings delusion has blinded!

11 Homage to You, O Jewel Tārā,
collection of all the Buddhas' virtues,
Subduer of the mountain of pride
of sentient beings o'erpowered by arrogance!

12 Homage to You, O Lotus Tārā,
immaculate Speech of all the Buddhas,
Dispeller of *saṃsāra*'s torments[12]
for sentient beings pained by desire!

13 Homage to You, O Karma-Tārā,
supreme Deeds of all the Buddhas,
Extractor of the thorn of envy
from sentient beings smitten with envy!

14 Homage to You, O Vajra-Tārā,
*Vajra*-body of all the Buddhas,
Annihilator of weapons of hate
in sentient beings oppressed by anger!

15 Homage and praise to Your *Vajra* Body,
You Who bear a form like a reflection,
Free of gross or subtle matter
and furnished with the Marks and Signs!

16 Homage and praise to Your *Vajra* Speech,
You Who utter speech like an echo,

Abandoning syllables and phrases,
transcending the ways of words and
language![13]

17 Homage and praise to Your *Vajra* Mind,
You Who have a mind like a dream,
Not seeing real, unreal or other,[14]
not knowing eternity or destruction!

18 To Tārā dustless and space-pervading
I bow with formless *vajra* body,
Without limbs and without frame,
observing no homage nor object of homage.

19 To Tārā simple and without conceptions
I give praise with speechless *vajra* words,
Free of sounds and utterance,
observing no praise nor object praised.

20 To Tārā free of feeling or object[15]
I make obeisance with *vajra* mind,
without apprehender or cognizing,
observing no thinking nor object of thought.

By Master Akṣobhya-vajra.

*Translated from the Tibetan.*

## PRAISE OF ĀRYA-TĀRĀ
(*Ārya-tārā-stotra*)

*By Dīpaṃkara-bhadra*

Homage to the Venerable Ārya-Tārā!

1 Wide-eyed Mother, Protector of the three
worlds!
Mother producing all the three times' Buddhas!
Though You move not from the state of non-dual
Gnosis,
Your power of Compassion works diverse good
for migrators.
I bow in homage to You, O kindly Mother!

2 Your Body green, You perform all
Buddha-activities.
Like a sixteen-year-old, mature in qualities,
Gladdening sentient beings, with smiling face
And peaceful eyes You look on the three worlds.
I bow in homage to You of abundant
Compassion!

3 A moon of *Bodhi*-mind nature is spread as Your
seat;
In *vajra*-position, undisturbed by the
defilements,
You sit on a lotus seat, all obscurations
abandoned,
Your backdrop a full moon of bliss
uncontaminated.
Homage to You of great uncontaminate bliss!

4 Arrayed in superb clothing and numerous gems,
With right hand, boon-granting, You give
practitioners *siddhis*;
In th' left, a faultless *utpala*, sign of purity.[16]
Your two hands are Method and Wisdom united.
Homage
To You of the Union Body, free of extremes!

5 Because of my homage with body, speech and
mind,
Pray pardon my low views, my inferior practice
And worship, and damage to pledges controlled
by defilements!
Please will You support me with Compassion.

6 Your Body's adorned with Marks of infinite
virtues.
Through my praising but an atom with joy in
You,
Grant me the everlasting view of Your face
And the supreme Path to high rebirth and
Liberation
By showing advice on the supreme, perfect Path!

7 Thinking of us, O Mother of loving-kindness,
Guard and protect us and our entourage,
Turn aside [bad] conditions in this life,
Cut off the entrance to realms of woe in the next,
And make a wholesome mind develop in us!

The Praise of Ārya-Tārā by Master Dīpaṃkara-bhadra[17] is complete.

It was translated and revised by the Kashmiri *upādhyāya* Buddhākara-varman and the translator Gelong Ch'ökyi Yeshe.[18]

*Translated from the Tibetan.*

# 6 *Praises by Nāgārjuna and Candrakīrti*

## NĀGĀRJUNA, THE MAHĀSIDDHA

But for his name, biographical information on a master as prominent as the *Siddha* Nāgārjuna would no doubt be readily available. As it is, the first Nāgārjuna, founder of the Madhyamaka system if not of the very Mahāyāna, has been glorified to such an extent that Tibetan historians have identified with him everyone named after him. No doubt there exists, mingled with the great mass of legends that grew up around this towering figure, some information that in fact relates to the *Siddha* Nāgārjuna; but how is one to recognize it?

Our most useful sources are tantric lineages and the ninety-odd tantric texts attributed to Nāgārjuna in the Tängyur. It is generally accepted that Nāgārjuna's principal Guru was Saraha, alias Rāhulabhadra; certainly it is recorded in the respective lineages that he received the transmissions of Guhyasamāja and the *Mahāmudrā* from him. On analysis, the lineages establish that Nāgārjuna must have flourished around 800 AD. For example, the *Mahāmudrā* lineage descends from Nāgārjuna to Tilli-pa (928–1009) in just four steps;[1] this shows Nāgārjuna could not have been much earlier than 800. On the other hand, the lineage of the Saṃvara cycle takes nine steps to pass from Saraha to Tilli-pa,[2] which indicates Nāgārjuna is unlikely to have been much later than 800 either. Other evidence also bears out this dating of the *Siddha* Nāgārjuna in the late eighth and early ninth centuries.[3]

Among his works, his commentary on the *Guhyasamāja-tantra* is important; it is the origin of a commentarial tradition distinct from that of Buddha-jñāna.[4]

Some biographies of Nāgārjuna indicate connections with Tārā, which may well be interpreted as referring to Nāgārjuna the *Siddha*. Sum-pa k'än-po[5] says he received *siddhi* of Tārā when staying at Kahora, in Kāñcī (near Madras), and later beheld Her countenance when practising at Nālandā. Tāranātha[6] mentions his wishing to make a Tārā statue of sandalwood from the land of the *nāgas*. Besides the *Praise of Khadiravaṇī Tārā* translated below, the Tängyur contains an untitled praise of Tārā in eight stanzas, and four or five *sādhanas* of Tārā, attributed to Nāgārjuna.[7] Two of the *sādhanas* survive in the original Sanskrit. In addition, some traditions of Tārā practice are ascribed to him without textual support, in particular a system of iconography for the twenty-one Tārās.[8]

## CANDRAKĪRTI

The tantric Candrakīrti was a disciple of Nāgārjuna,[9] and must have flourished in the early ninth century. Since hardly two centuries separate him from his famous namesake, the author of the *Madhyamakâvatāra*, *Prasanna-padā* and other important works, there is little hope of disentangling from the Tibetan histories the details that refer to him.

He composed a commentary on the *Guhyasamāja-tantra* in the tradition of Nāgārjuna, still extant in Sanskrit.[10]

## THE WORKS

If it be true that Sūryagupta was later than Nāgārjuna, then this praise of Khadiravaṇī Tārā must be the earliest known reference to Her and could well mark the very origin of Her cult. According to Ghosh,[11] the conception of this Tārā, characterized by the presence of Her two companions Mārīcī (also known as Aśoka-kāntā) and Ekajaṭā, is not prior to the ninth century; no image of Her earlier then the tenth century has been found, but the form became enormously popular in the eleventh century. In Nāgārjuna's praise we have a marvellously full description of Her no later than the early ninth century.

The praise implies clearly that Khadira-vaṇa was an actual forest where Nāgārjuna meditated and presumably beheld Tārā in this form. Verse 6 refers to it as a 'supreme place' or place of pilgrimage (*gnas mchog*). Ghosh[12] has proposed an identification of the site with Koṅgoda, which comprised parts of the Ganjam and Puri Districts in Orissa. A miniature in a manuscript dated 1015 depicts a particularly revered image of Khadiravaṇī Tārā there, whose existence is confirmed by a copper plate dated 1024 found in Puri District. A large stone statue of Khadiravaṇī Tārā, of the eleventh century, has also been unearthed there.

The hymn appears to have been written mostly in long nominal compounds. The effect of this is to pack the words very closely together with few endings or particles between, creating a rich, kaleidoscopic sequence of images, which like the unfathomably complex sound sequences of Indian classical music, overwhelm and intoxicate the reader or listener although she cannot clearly discern the whole. Since the relationships between the words are not explicitly defined, long compounds generally have several possible meanings, so it is necessary to read a verse several times to work out just what the author most probably meant; even then, one cannot always be certain.

The Candrakīrti praise, by contrast, is plain and immediately intelligible. It too regards Khadira-vaṇa as Tārā's home, from which She sends out emanations in other forms, notably that of Vajra-vārāhī, 'the Adamantine Sow'.

## PRAISE OF KHADIRAVAṆĪ TĀRĀ
(*Khadiravaṇī-tārā-stotra*)

*By Nāgārjuna*

Homage to Ārya-Khadiravaṇī-Tārā!

1. High Ārya-Tārā's palace is in the Khadira Forest,
A grove of glomerous figs,[13] *khadiras*, jujube trees,
Banyans, sandal, three thousand fruits, nutmeg and cloves,
A pleasant leafy place of flowers open and closed.

2 Among the close-packed[14] trees and fruit, ripe and unripe,
There sweetly trickles water with the eight qualities;*
Sweet, joyous cries of peacocks, parrots and cuckoos resound;
Tigers and leopards run, stags frolic and bears leap.[15]

3 Jackals sing, monkeys play and antelope[16] calves suck;
Youthful heavenly maidens play music in the woods.
*Bhikṣu* Nāgārjuna acts as a *mahāsiddha*
In Khadira Wood; to the land Tārā comes from, homage and praise!

4 On the flower of an emerald lotus from unborn Compassion's lake,
And moon, fair woman beautified with the finest of jewels,
Going with gait like a goose and looking with elephant's pride,
Tender with a *Sugata's* Pity, You show forms at will.

5 With golden lotus earrings, and ribbons of *utpalas*,

On the jewel crown on Your head sits
Amoghasiddhi as crest.
Hanging strings of fused pearls and coral adorn
Your neck,[17]
Beauty with anklets, bracelets, armlets and silken
sash!

6 Compassionate Saviouress from *saṃsāra*!
Goddess born
From the tears of Him with Lotus in Hand,[18] by
the power of the vow
Of Amitābha; most loving, striving for others'
good,
Young maiden of the pure supreme place,
Khadira Forest!

7 Your lotus face is pleasing, a face like the full
moon;
Your lovely lotus eyes are long, clear white and
black.
Your hair is adorned with golden pores and black
as bees,
And smooth as the lord of mice(?);[19] Your *ūrṇā*[20]
curls like a conch.

8 In Your hands—the two Truths—open *utpalas*
dispel delusion's darkness
In self and others: at Your heart's budding lotus,
the *utpala*
Held in Your left [hand] increases
Wisdom-knowledge; the right
Opens its blue flower to the bees of migrating
beings.

9 To benefit sentient beings, who've fallen into
*saṃsāra*
In sorrow and lamentation, You rise and leave
Khadira Forest,
O youthful maiden possessing breasts swollen
with milk,[21]
Who by all means stirs and moves [us in] *saṃsāra*
and *Nirvāṇa*!

10 One with bull's eye[lashes],[22] graceful, Whose
navel bears a lotus,[23]
Endowed with the excellent fragrance of
nutmeg,[24] cloves and magnolia,[25]
Hands and feet red like a lotus, unstained by
faults of *saṃsāra*,
Adorned above and below with divine silks and
*pañcalika*!

11 Your Body's non-local, pervading, a Body of
Deeds of Compassion,
A perfect boat[26] for the sea of the Sage's
Teachings, in essence
Seen in the forest,[27] slowly bearing the great load
of beings,
Ferrying them to Peace from *saṃsāra*'s
impervious thickets.

12 Old woman of youthful appearance, following[28]
all the Buddhas,
You the mere recollection of Whose name
delivers from fears!
Unwearied by long in *saṃsāra*, not resting in
*Nirvāṇa*,
Compassion of Conquerors' Offspring with
mastery of the Ten Stages!

13 Ven'rable One! I cannot describe Your infinite
virtues.
*Dharmakāya*, free of imag'ning, possessed of
Gnosis!
Unshakeable Body[29] going about in Khadira
Forest!
Forest maid free by nature[30] of *saṃsāra*! Homage
and praise!

14 On right and left come yellow Mārīcī and blue
Ekajaṭā,
Peaceful and fierce; their two hands hold *vajra*,
*aśoka* and *kartṛ*.[31]
Going before and after, with unmatched
devotion they honour You.

Beauty Mārīcī and Ekjaṭā wait on! Homage and
praise!

15 Worshipped and followed by parasol-bearers
and maids, queens of knowledge,[32]
Who satiate with chowries, cymbals, shawms,
*vīṇās*, songs and dances!
Fifteen daughters of gods with adornments and
beautiful dresses
In manifold forms hold off'rings: to this display,
homage and praise!

16 By the excellent, inexhaustible[33] merits of my
giving praise
To the beautiful, virtuous Forest Goddess and
Her attendants,
May all migrators, their *kleśa* cleansed by the
water of Mercy,
Go from *saṃsāra*'s thicket to the grove of Peace!

The Praise in sixteen stanzas to the youthful Khadiravaṇī-Tārā, by Master Ārya-Nāgārjuna, is complete.

SARVA-MAṆGALAM!

*Translated from the Tibetan.*

## PRAISE OF VAJRAVĀRĀHĪ TĀRĀ

(*Vajravārāhī-tārā-stotra*)

*By Candrakīrti*

Homage to the Venerable Tārā!

1 Homage to the Body of Tārā,
great Sow (*Vārāhī*) of Emptiness and
Compassion!
Homage to the Speech of Tārā,
Perfection[34] without words, thought or
speaking!
Homage to the Mind of Tārā,
the mind of immaculate Moon of Gnosis![35]

2 Moonlight dispelling *saṃsāra*'s darkness
like an o'erpowering solar disk!
To Tārā, endowed with the qualities of
Method and Wisdom, I bow forever.

3 You always love migrators like Your children,
and fix the three realms in the three
Liberations.[36]
Living in the Khadira Forest,
You save us strongly from the eight fears.

4 Tārā, I pay homage to You.
In the Pure Land Abhirati[37]
You show the form of Vajra-ḍākinī,[38]
Tārā, homage and praise to You!

5 In the Pure Land Glorious[39]
You show the form of Ratna-ḍākinī,
Dispeller of migrators' sickness of sorrow,
Tārā, homage and praise to You!

6 In the Pure Land Sukhāvatī
You show the form of Padma-ḍākinī,
Living in the state of Great Bliss,
Tārā, homage and praise to You!

7 In the Pure Land of Viśuddhi
You show the form of Karma-ḍākinī,
Helping migrators with the four rites,
Tārā, homage and praise to You!

8 In the Pure Land An-anta-madhya
You show the form of Pāramitā,[40]
With th' assembly of Buddhas of ten directions,
Tārā, homage and praise to You!

9 In the Pure Land of the eight charnel grounds
You show the form of Vajra-vārāhī,
Amidst a blazing mass of fire,
Tārā, homage and praise to You!

The praise by the *paṇḍita* Candrakīrti is complete.

*Translated from the Tibetan.*

# 7 *Praise by Atīśa*

## THE AUTHOR[1]

He was born in 982 as Prince Candragarbha, second son of King Kalyāṇaśrī and Queen Śrī-Prabhāvatī, in Vikramapura, Bengal.[2] The accounts of his childhood and youth vary wildly and give mainly the impression of pious invention. Very likely he was already beautiful in appearance, as he is said to have been in later life; very likely too, he showed early signs of intellectual ability and progressed rapidly in his academic studies, which must have included Sanskrit grammar and some sort of grounding in Buddhist ideas—even if he did not actually deliver a sermon at the age of eighteen months.[3] Likewise, there is no reason to doubt the assertion of Gö Lotsawa that the young Candragarbha experienced visions of Ārya-Tārā, his tutelary deity from previous lives, and that it was through Her influence that he renounced royal power and went to another country to seek a *guru*.

It is agreed that from the *yogin* Rāhula-guhya-vajra (or Rāhulagupta) of the Black Mountain (thought to be one of the seven hills of Rājagṛha), the prince received his first tantric empowerment, and with it his tantric name of Jñāna-guhya-vajra. For some years he practised the Tantras, including it is said three years with the *ḍākinīs* in Oḍḍiyāna. But then he abandoned the life of a *yogin* for that of a monk. A dream in which Buddha Śākyamuni asked why he was not a monk is supposed to have prompted this decision; some say Tārā, Hevajra and his early *guru* Rāhulagupta also gave similar hints. At his ordination as a *bhikṣu,* he received the name by which he is generally known, Dīpaṃkara-śrī-jñāna.[4] According to Gö Lotsawa, he was then in his twenty-ninth year (1010).

Now for two years he studied the *Mahāvibhāṣā* and other treatises of Hīnayāna and Mahāyāna schools, until various portents indicated that he should go to the island of Suvarṇa-dvīpa to study with Master Dharmakīrti (not to be confused with the famous logician of nearly four centuries earlier). Suvarṇa-dvīpa seems to have included a number of islands of Indonesia, but evidence in the Tängyur connects Dharmakīrti with the capital, Śrī-Vijaya (near modern Palembang, Sumatra) —for some centuries a great centre of Buddhist learning—and even suggests that he was a member of the royal family, the Śailendras. Dīpaṃkara was there from about 1013 to 1025; his departure may well have been linked with the fall of the Śailendra empire in 1025, when it was conquered by the Colas of South India.[5] It was evidently through Dharmakīrti of Suvarṇa-dvīpa that he became a master of the non-tantric Mahāyāna teachings, by then largely superseded by Vajrayāna in India itself.

Back in India, Dīpaṃkara lived and taught at the great monasteries of Nālandā, Odantapurī, Somapurī and, above all, Vikramaśīla. He became famous as a *paṇḍita* and acquired the reverential sobriquet of Atīśa, 'great lord'; it is by this and its approximate Tibetan equivalent Jowo Je that Tibetans most commonly refer to him.

At this time in Tibet, certain corrupt practices alleged by their followers to be Buddhist Tantra had become prevalent. For example, we are told,[6] there was a doctrine called *sbyor sgrol,* literally 'Union [and] Liberation', which gangs of 'robber-monks' interpreted as teaching rape and human sacrifice. In the wake of the persecutions by King Lang-dar-ma (838–42 according to Tucci), true Buddhist teachings were hard to find.

A king of G'u-g'e in Western Tibet, Lha-la-ma Ye-she-ö, devoted much wealth and energy to remedying this situation by sending young Tibetans to study in India, building a monastery at T'o-ling, and inviting Indian *paṇḍitas* to teach. According to *The Blue Annals*, he was eventually captured by the Qarluq; his officials collected most of the ransom demanded, but he ordered that it should be used instead to promote the Dharma and invite the most eminent *paṇḍita*, Atīśa, to Tibet. His great-nephew J'ang-ch'up-ö carried out this wish, sending the monk Nak-ts'o Ts'ül-tr'im gyäl-wa, who had just been to India, back to invite Atīśa. With another Tibetan, Tsön-drü seng-g'e of Gya, who was already at Vikramaśīla translating texts with Atīśa and other *paṇḍitas*, Nak-ts'o transmitted the invitation.

Atīśa consulted his tutelary deity Tārā and a *yoginī* at Vajrāsana (Bodhgayā): both told him that his going to Tibet would greatly benefit the Doctrine, although it would shorten his life by twenty years. He therefore accepted, but remained still a few more years in India, teaching and helping Tsön-drü seng-g'e and Nak-ts'o translate texts.

In 1040 the party left for Tibet. Tsön-drü seng-g'e died on the way, in Nepāl, but Atīśa and Nak-ts'o arrived in Ngari (Western Tibet) in 1042. Atīśa taught in Ngari for three years, and composed there his best-known work, the *Bodhi-patha-pradīpa*, a summary of the stages of practice one should complete before undertaking Tantra.[7] After this Nak-ts'o was supposed to have taken him back to Vikramaśīla, but the road through Nepāl was closed because of fighting. Instead, Atīśa met his chief Tibetan disciple, Drom-tön-pa (1005–64),[8] and went with him to Central Tibet. In the end he remained in Tibet until his death at Nye-t'ang, near Lhasa, in 1054.

The influence of Atīśa on the development of the Buddha-Dharma in Tibet was enormous, far exceeding that of any other Indian *paṇḍita* who taught there. From him stems the earliest of the 'new' schools of Tibetan Buddhism (as opposed to the 'old' school, the Nyingmapa), the Kadampa. This was founded by his disciple Drom-tön-pa. It continues today as the Gelukpa or 'New Kadampa' tradition, which dominated Tibet for its last three centuries of independence.

Atīśa's contribution to Tibet included the cult of Tārā, his tutelary deity. He wrote little about Her, but it would seem that Her name was constantly on his lips and that She frequently helped him. There is hardly a significant event in his life that one or other of his biographers fails to connect with the Goddess. Thanks to his devotion, Tārā became one of the two most popular deities of Tibet.

## THE WORK

Atīśa's works on Tārā that survive in Tibetan translation comprise the following *Praise* and three *sādhanas* or methods of practice, two of which will appear in Part Six below. The *Praise* is short and mostly straight-forward. Except for verses 8 and 9, the Tibetan translation is in standard seven-syllable metre—the Sanskrit must have been in *anuṣṭubh* metre, whose very name means 'praise'.

The first verse is extremely well known and appears in rituals of Tārā about as frequently as the *Twenty-one Homages*. Contrary to Beyer's remark (p. 11) that this hymn 'is inserted somewhere in almost every one of [Tārā's] rituals', the same cannot be said of the rest.

## THE TRANSLATOR

Ts'ül-tr'im gyäl-wa (Skt.: Jayaśīla), or Nak-ts'o Lotsawa, was born in 1011 in G'ung-t'ang, the region of Kyirong.[9] He became a monk and went to India to study. When he returned to G'ung-t'ang, J'ang-ch'up-ö asked him to go back to Vikramaśīla and invite Atīśa, the greatest *paṇḍita* of the time, as described above. After that, he was with Atīśa until shortly before the latter's death, when the Master, promising that Nak-ts'o could be reborn in his presence in the Tuṣita Pure Land, sent him to meet the *paṇḍita* Jñānākara of Kashmir.[10] Altogether, he spent nineteen years (by Tibetan reckoning) in attendance on the great Master, a longer association than that enjoyed by any other Tibetan, 'and obtained from him most of the secret precepts.'[11]

He was a prolific translator—over a hundred of his translations, made with the assistance of Atīśa and other *paṇḍitas*, are to be found in the Tängyur, while yet other major translations of his, such as the *Ratna-gotra-vibhāga*,[12] are omitted, having been superseded by later versions.

Unkind remarks have been made about him, from the animosity of later Kadampas on the pretext of his absence from Atīśa's deathbed[13] to Chattopadhyaya's (p. 360) jibe that he cared more for the quantity of his translations than for their quality. In fact, his work can hardly be called careless compared with much of what passes for translation in our own day, and Tsong-k'a-pa, for example, often quotes with approval his pioneering translation of Candrakīrti's *Madhyamakāvatāra*. Bearing in mind that many of the works he translated (like the present one) are very short and that he did not have to spend three-quarters of his time compiling carefully-researched introductions, glossaries, indices and all the rest of the scholarly trappings required of modern translators, his output was probably not excessive for a working life of thirty years or more. His critics would do well to note that after this productive life he was reborn as K'ön-p'u-wa (1069–1144), brother and constant companion of the renowned manifestation of Ārya-Tārā, Ma-chik Lap-drön-ma (1062–1149), and his teacher Ma Lotsawa (1044–89) prophesied that this would be his last rebirth.[14]

## PRAISE OF ĀRYA-TĀRĀ
(*Ārya-tārā-stotra*)

*By Atīśa*

Homage to the Venerable Ārya-Tārā!

1 Gods and *asuras* with their crowns
bow down to Your lotus feet;
Liberator from all problems,
[Mother] Tārā—homage to You!

2 On those Avīci's fire torments,
filling them with a blazing net,
Your compassion rains down nectar—
Tārā, further homage to You!

3 To those tired of circling long,
again and again, among the six
Destinies, You grant the rest,
supremely pleasant, of Great Bliss.

4 Goddess who works the weal of others!
Just to think of You dispels problems!
You, endowed with love and compassion,
liberate from *saṃsāra*'s bonds.

5 Goddess who at all times is
impartial towards sentient beings,
On the whole crop of migrators
You rain incessantly—homage to You!

6 Like the sun and moon, dispeller
of distress of darkness for
All migrating sentient beings,
Supreme Goddess—homage to You!

7 On a lotus and moon seat
immaculate as an *utpala*,
Your body blue-green coloured, graceful,
You hold an *utpala*—homage to You!

8 Three countless eons You've gathered Merits and
Wisdom,
Cast off all the hindering obscurations,
And with the four Means of Attraction attracted
migrators,
O compassionate Mother—homage to You!

9 Bodily faults gone, You have the Marks and
Signs;
Faults of speech gone, like the *kalaviṅka*'s strains;
Faults of mind gone, You know all knowable
things.
Blaze of fortune and glory—homage to You!

10 Like the water-clearing gem,
Goddess, You forever clear
The mud of sentient beings' minds
and strive for their welfare—homage to You!

11 Those who do retain Your name,
praise You, and do practise You,
Always do You make fruitful,
Unforgetful One—homage to You!

The Praise of the Venerable Tārā by Dīpaṃkara-śrī-jñāna is complete.

Translated by that Indian *upādhyāya* himself and the Tibetan translator Ts'ül-tr'im gyäl-wa.

*Translated from the Tibetan.*

# Part Five
## *Songs by Tibetan Devotees*

# 1 *Song by Gedün-dr'up*

## THE AUTHOR[1]

Gedün-dr'up is famous as the first Dalai Lama of Tibet, although he did not receive this title until long after his death.

He was born in 1391 in a small farm in the upper Shap valley in the Nyang district of Tsang, whose chief town is Gyantse. He was given the name Päma-dorje. On the night of his birth some robbers came and his mother had to hide him between some stones. When she went to look the next day, she saw a raven standing guard over him; it was later considered this was a manifestation of Mahākāla.

In his seventh year, when his father died, he took *upāsaka* vows and began his education at Nart'ang monastery. He learnt Indian and Tibetan writing from the Indian teacher Candra-pa. In his fifteenth year, 1405, he took novice ordination, receiving the name Gedün dr'up-pa päl (*dGe 'dun grub pa dpal*, 'Glorious Realized Sangha'), to which he was allowed to add Zang-po (*bZang po*, 'good'). He learnt Sanskrit from *Mahāpaṇḍita* Saṅgha-śrī and logic from Abhayakīrti, began various deity practices such as Hevajra and the Medicine Buddha (Vaidyarāja), and studied various Dharma texts.

In 1410, his twentieth year, he took the full *bhikṣu* ordination.

Then he went to Central Tibet, where he spent twelve years

studying with many famous lamas. Foremost among these was the great Tsongk'a-pa.[2] From him and his chief disciple Gyäl-ts'ap Je, Gedün-dr'up heard numerous teachings.

When he returned to Tsang, he began to compose texts, some of which are still among the most widely used in their field. They include commentaries on the *Madhyamakâvatāra* of Candrakīrti and on the monks' disciplinary code. In this period, too, he received from the great *paṇḍita* of B'o-d'ong, Jik-me dr'a-pa or Ch'ok-lä nam-gyäl, teachings on many forms of Tārā. This teacher asked him many questions and was so pleased with his replies that he praised him as 'omniscient'.

He spent much time in meditation; many deities and Dharma-protectors, including White Tārā, Yamāntaka and Mahākāla, appeared to him.

Then in 1447, following various prophecies, he began building his monastery of Trashi-lhünpo. Tsongk'a-pa had died in 1419 and the leadership of his followers, the Gelukpas, passed in turn to Gyäl-ts'ap Je (d.1432) and K'ä-dr'up Je.

After the latter's death in 1438, no-one was regarded as head of the Gelukpas until Gedün-dr'up came to the fore. He was invited in 1450 to assume the throne of Ganden, but declined and went on completing Trashi-lhünpo until 1453. He was accepted as the Gelukpas' leading scholar and spokesman until he passed away amid many miraculous manifestations in January 1475. Soon after, a child was born near Trashi-lhünpo, who eventually came to be recognized as his incarnation.

Gedün-dr'up was noted for his devotion to Tārā. In a set of t'angka paintings of the Dalai Lamas and other incarnations of Avalokiteśvara,[3] his picture is the only one that includes Green Tārā. It is said he always consulted Her before undertaking anything. Besides the song to Green Tārā below, his writings on Tārā include a commentary on the *Praise in Twenty-one Homages*, most of which we presented above, and a praise of White Tārā.[4]

## THE WORK

The first part of the song is a praise of Khadiravaṇī Tārā, to be compared with Nāgārjuna's of six centuries earlier. The iconography is the same except that the Lord of the Family, on Her crown, is now Amitābha instead of Amoghasiddhi; several verses are quite similar. However, although Gedün-dr'up's style is strongly influenced by Indian models—he uses many literary phrases taken over from Sanskrit, some rather obscure—he does not simply describe Tārā but explains clearly the meanings of Her various features.

The second part introduces a theme absent from Nāgārjuna's Praise but familiar to us from many others, that of Tārā saving from the eight great fears. Here again Gedün-dr'up's approach is illuminating. He brings out the twofold nature of the fears, their outer aspect of lions, elephants and so on and their inner aspect, the mental defilements they represent.

The concluding verses dedicate the merits, like Nāgārjuna's final verse.

## THE COMMENTARY

This song is so popular as to boast a commentary, composed in 1837 by Ngül-ch'u Dharmabhadra (1772–1851). This author, whose commentary on the *Praise in Twenty-one Homages* we have quoted above, was one of the most revered Gelukpa lamas of Central Tibet in the first half of the nineteenth century. He lived at the Ngül-ch'u Ch'ö-dzong hermitage in Zhä.[5]

According to him, the principal divisions of Gedün-dr'up's song are as follows.

- I. Praise
  - A. Brief teaching 1–2
  - B. Extensive explanation
    - 1. Praise of Her Body
      - a. Praise of the actual Body 3–7
      - b. Praise of the Body's ornaments and clothing 8–10
      - c. Praise of the Body's entourage 11–13
    - 2. Praise of Her Speech 14
    - 3. Praise of Her Mind 15–18

- II. Requests
  - A. Brief Teaching 19
  - B. Extensive explanation 20–27
  - C. Summary 28
- III. Prayers
  - A. Prayers for the fulfilment of others' aims 29
  - B. Prayers for the fulfilment of one's own aims 30–32

My translation was based on teachings of the Ven. Geshe Thubten Lodan, who used this commentary, and subsequently revised with reference to the commentary itself. Explanations and quotations from Dharmabhadra in the notes will be indicated with a D.

## PRAISE OF THE VENERABLE LADY KHADIRAVAṆĪ TĀRĀ CALLED THE CROWN JEWEL OF THE WISE
(commonly known as LEk-Dr'I-MA[6])

*By Gedün-dr'up, First Dalai Lama*

Homage to Ārya-Avalokiteśvara, the treasure of Compassion!

[*Praise*]

1 *Devas*,[7] Lakṣmī's husband, gold-hatched
Brahmā,
Bṛhaspati, Gaṇeśa and Śiva,
Sūrya and more—crown-jewels of hundreds of
gods
Revere Her foot-lotus[8]—at Tārā's feet I bow!

2 By compassion magic of the Greatly
Compassionate,[9]
The three times' Conquerors' Wisdom, Mercy
and Power
Appear in the lovely form of the Goddess of
Action,
Who saves from all want—at Tārā's feet I bow!

3 On a lotus seat, for pure understanding of
Emptiness,
Emerald-coloured, one-faced, two-armed girl,
In full bloom of youth, right leg out, left drawn in,
Uniting Method and Wisdom[10]—homage to You!

4 Prominent, full breasts, treasures of undefiled
bliss,
Face with a brilliant smile like the full moon,
Mother with calm-mannered, wide,
compassionate eyes,
Beauty of Khadira Forest—to You I bow!

5 Like the outstretched branch of a heavenly tree of
turquoise,
Your supple right hand, in the gesture of
Granting Boons,
Invites the wise to a feast of supreme *siddhis*
As if to an entertainment—homage to You!

6 Your left hand gives Refuge, showing the Three
Jewels;[11]
'You people who see perils of hundreds of kinds!
Do not be frightened, I shall quickly save you,'
It clearly signifies—homage to You!

7 Both hands signal with blue *utpala* flowers,
'Saṃsāric beings! Cling not to worldly pleasures,
Enter the city of the Great Liberation!'
Like prods with a stick for Energy—to You I bow!

8 Ruby-coloured Amitābha holds
In meditation an alms-bowl full of nectar
And, granting the deathless *siddhi*, adorns Your
crown,
Subduing the lord of my death—to You I bow!

9 Formed by the builder of heaven[12]—Merits and
Wisdom—
Inestimable celestial wish-granting gems[13]
Most beautiful, combined in captivating
Ornaments, fully adorn You—homage to You!

10 Like an emerald mountain clothed in rainbows,
Your upper body is draped in heavenly silks;[14]
Your lovely, supple, slender waist supports
A skirt of *pañcalika*[15]—to You I bow!

11 On Your right, Mārīcī of the *aśoka*,
Peaceful, golden, radiating sunlight.
On Your left, Ekajaṭā, sky-blue,[16] wrathful
But loving and bright, O Beauty—to You I bow!

12 Skilled in musical songs[17] and gorgeous dances,
Holding white parasols, chowries, *vīṇās*, flutes
And endless such offering-objects, hosts of
goddesses,
Filling space, make offering—homage to You!

13 Lakṣmī, Śacī, Pārvatī and thousands
Of other attractive daughters of the gods
Hardly come up to maid-servants before You—
In goddess's form so lovely, homage to You!

*Tārā of the Khadira Forest (Khadiravaṇī Tārā) (top) and Her attendants Mārīcī (shown here with needle and thread) and Ekajaṭā.*

14 From the vast expanse of clouds of Your Compassion,
Whose thunder is Your sweet voice of Brahmic tones,
On the earth of disciples You're skilled in letting fall
The eightfold rain of Dharma[18]—homage to You!

15 Ocean-like treasure of virtues, seeing all knowables!
Who could describe You fully as You are?
Your mind has the ten Powers of unobstructed perception—
Mother perfect in Wisdom, homage to You!

16 You have found Peace; yet governed by Compassion,
You swiftly draw out with compassionate hand
Sentient beings sunk in a sea of suff'rings—
Mother perfect in Mercy, homage to You!

17 Your Calming, Increasing, Subduing and Fierce Activities,
Like the tides[19] of the ocean, never late,
You enter without effort or interruption,
Mother perfect in Action—homage to You!

18 The eight dread calamities,[20] harm by evil spirits,
Obscurations of defilements and knowables—
From these dangers You save us as soon as we think of You,[21]
Mother perfect in Power—homage to You!

[*Requests*]

19 Refuge thus worthy! From all dangers such
As evil spirits, demons, sickness and plague,
Untimely death, bad dreams and evil signs,
Please protect embodied beings swiftly!

20 He dwells between the mountains of wrong views
Of selfhood,[22] puffed up with holding himself superior,

With long claws of contempt for other beings,
The Lion of Pride—please save us from this
fear![23]

21 Untamed by sharp hooks of mindfulness and
awareness,
And dulled by the maddening liquor of sensual
pleasures,
He enters wrong paths and shows his tusks of
harming,
Delusion's Elephant—save us from this fear!

22 Driven by the wind of wrong attention,
Amidst a tumult of smoke-clouds of misconduct,
It has the power to burn down forests of merits,
The Fire of Anger—save us from this fear!

23 Attached to its dark hole of ignorance,
It cannot bear seeing the wealth and excellence of
others,
But quickly fills them with its vicious poison,
The Snake of Envy—save us from this fear!

24 Roaming the fearful wild of inferior practice[24]
And ghastly desert plains of the two extremes,[25]
They sack the towns and retreats of ease and
bliss,
The Thieves of Wrong Views—save us from this
fear!

25 In the unbearable prison of *saṃsāra*
It binds embodied beings, with no freedom,
Clasped by the lock of Craving, hard to open—
The Chain of Avarice—save us from this fear!

26 It sweeps us towards the stream of Becoming, so
hard
To cross, and, conditioned by karma's stormy
blast,
Waves of birth, age, sickness and death convulse
it,
Attachment's Flood—please save us from this
fear!

27 They wander in space of darkest ignorance,
Sorely tormenting those who strive for Truth,
Of lethal danger to Liberation, the Fell
Demons[26] of Doubt—please save us from this
fear!

28 Through these praises and requests to You,
Quell conditions bad for Dharma practice
And let us achieve life, merits, wealth and plenty
And other helpful conditions as we wish!

[*Prayers*]

29 In Sukhāvatī Pure Land, let all beings
Be received by Amitābha, Guide;
And though not practising hundreds of arduous
things,[27]
Let them quickly reach the Buddha Stage!

30 May I always remember previous lives,
Never be parted from the *Bodhi*-mind,
And maintain Energy like the flow of a river
In pursuing the Buddha-child's powerful
conduct!

31 Never hoping to benefit myself,
Devoted only to benefiting others,
Let me have all that's needed for helping others—
The Eyes, Superknowledges,[28] Eloquence,
Patience and so forth!

32 So that in infinite worlds I may spread all
The Conquerors' True Dharma, never dismayed,
And always work the weal of all sentient beings,
Let me swiftly gain a Conqueror's rank!

This Praise of the Venerable Lady Khadiravaṇī Tārā, called the Crown Jewel of the Wise, was composed by the Buddhist monk Gẹdün-dr'up-pa Päl-zang-po after long practice at the Great Enlightenment retreat at T'ek-ch'en P'o-dr'ang.[29]

*Translated from the Tibetan.*

# 2 *Songs by Lodr'ö Gyats'o (Matisāra)*

Information on Lodr'ö Gyats'o is hard to come by. The brief entry in Khetsun Sangpo's *Biographical Dictionary*[1] says he lived from 1664 to 1740 and was a monk of Gomang College of Dräpung Monastery (just outside Lhasa).

Two songs of his are translated here. The first, signed with the Sanskrit form of his name, Matisāra, is addressed to the twenty-one forms of Tārā connected with the *Praise in Twenty-one Homages* (see Part Two). It begins with homage to the principal Tārā (verse 0), then to the twenty-one aspects in turn (1–21). These praises, except in verse 14, entirely ignore the appearance of the Tārās and just describe their functions. The function given sometimes differs from that of the rite for that Tārā in Sūryagupta's system, but is reasonably consistent with that allotted in the system ascribed to Nāgārjuna.[2]

The second half of this song is a 'Song of Longing' (*gdung 'bod*), an impassioned plea for the Goddess's attention and assistance, followed by requests. So passionate is it that the regular structure of four-line stanzas collapses—I have had to divide the verses rather arbitrarily to correspond with the sentences, and have grouped them in 'paragraphs'. The fashion of appealing to Tārā in such a way no doubt stems from Sarvajñamitra's verses 2 to 9, though there the rhythm did not falter an instant. With the requests, the song soon settles down to a four-line rhythm again. From verse 35, the requests run quickly through the meditation scheme known as *Lam rim*, the Orderly Arrangement of the Path to Enlightenment,[3] to conclude with some general prayers for good qualities.

Lodr'ö Gyats'o's second song is simply a Song of Longing, with only one verse of Homage. The requests again follow an orderly sequence of practice, from verse 12 to verse 18, with slightly more emphasis on the Tantric stages than in the first song.

## PRAISES AND REQUESTS TO THE ASSEMBLY OF DEITIES OF THE VENERABLE MOTHER OF THE TWENTY-ONE HOMAGES

*By Matisāra (Lo-dr'ö Gyats'o)*

Homage to Ārya-Tārā!

*Praises*

0 Well-born of the holy Actions of all universal
Conquerors! Supreme Refuge of all the three
Realms'
Beings! Ven'rable Treasure of Compassion!—
I bow at Your lotus feet, Tārā, Mother of
Conqu'rors![4]

1 With divine actions quick as instant lightning,
You make the foes of the Conqu'rors or objects of
practice,
And Ganesh and others, all as obedient as
slaves—
Devout, I prostrate at Your feet, Tārā, Mother of
Conqu'rors!

2 Demons of sickness and plague and evil spirits,
Untimely death, bad dreams and obscurations—
All such dark adversity You quell!—
Devout, I prostrate at Your feet, Tārā, Mother of
Conqu'rors!

3 All qualities, good collections, merits and power,
Glory, excellence, and two kinds of realizations,[5]
And th' *Āryas'* seven Treasures, You fully
develop—
Devout, I prostrate at Your feet, Tārā, Mother of
Conqu'rors!

4 Of beings and world You increase all the
splendour and majesty,
Granting the special, deathless, supreme *siddhi*,[6]
And You conquer in battle the Lord of Death!—
Devout, I prostrate at Your feet, Tārā, Mother of
Conqu'rors!

5 As requisites for practitioners travelling to Freedom,
You quickly summon each and every pleasing
And longed-for collection, and do conducive actions—
Devout, I prostrate at Your feet, Tārā, Mother of Conqu'rors!

6 By the mere mental thought of You, You make
All assemblies of spirits, such as the ten
Directional Guardians, gather with servile devotion—
Devout, I prostrate at Your feet, Tārā, Mother of Conqu'rors!

7 Should evil ones, thinking and acting to injure others,
Bring down on us magic spells, curses, imprecations
And so on, You turn all their power back upon themselves—
Devout, I prostrate at Your feet, Tārā, Mother of Conqu'rors!

8 From noxious beings, who injure the Conqueror's Doctrine,
Perversely rebelling against right Dharma-conduct,
You quickly separate the life and body—
Devout, I prostrate at Your feet, Tārā, Mother of Conqu'rors!

9 From outer and inner adversities and harm
Through producers of suffering physical and mental,
You guard and protect us in this and all future lives—
Devout, I prostrate at Your feet, Tārā, Mother of Conqu'rors!

10 If one seeks Refuge in You, You quell his injurious

*Māras*, and perverse thought of *tīrthika* conduct,
And then apply him to the perfect Path—
Devout, I prostrate at Your feet, Tārā, Mother of Conqu'rors!

11 With torrents of rain of all desired precious things,
Such as food and wealth and stores of enjoyments and beasts,
You eliminate every poverty, hunger and thirst—
Devout, I prostrate at Your feet, Tārā, Mother of Conqu'rors!

12 You let us achieve ev'ry aim we intend, as we wish;
With mundane and supermundane auspiciousness and
Goodness, You fill the directions all the time—
Devout, I prostrate at Your feet, Tārā, Mother of Conqu'rors!

13 For hindering demons, obstructions and evil signs,
Just by one's mentally recollecting Your form,
You put him in a *vajra* tent, without fear—
Devout, I prostrate at Your feet, Tārā, Mother of Conqu'rors!

14 With frowning, very active, open eyes,
You smash as if into atoms all bearers in mind
Of cruelty, Gaṇeśa and his hindering demons—
Devout, I prostrate at Your feet, Tārā, Mother of Conqu'rors!

15 All sins and obscurations of karma and *kleśa*
Which throw one into the realms of woe, You cleanse
And purify, Mother, just through recalling Your face—
Devout, I prostrate at Your feet, Tārā, Mother of Conqu'rors!

16 Deep Wisdom which realizes True Nature's meaning; explaining,
Debating and writing; the wisdoms of listening, thinking
And meditation—all these You increase and develop!—
Devout, I prostrate at Your feet, Tārā, Mother of Conqu'rors!

17 With power that shakes all the three worlds in an instant,
Every enemy, robber and thief, without
Exception, Victorious Mother, You bind and subdue—
Devout, I prostrate at Your feet, Tārā, Mother of Conqu'rors!

18 Harm from poison and contagion, and all
Poisoning by noxious *nāgas* and earth-owning spirits,
You quickly allay till the very name does not exist—
Devout, I prostrate at Your feet, Tārā, Mother of Conqu'rors!

19 Mutual conflict, torment by the law
Through fear of the king, and bad dreams—on all such things
You perform the action of rapidly pacifying—
Devout, I prostrate at Your feet, Tārā, Mother of Conqu'rors!

20 Most violent and unbearable sickness and plagues
And every adverse and injurious group—
All these You protect from, and totally pacify!—
Devout, I prostrate at Your feet, Tārā, Mother of Conqu'rors!

21 Your universal actions, like calming spirits,
Corpse-raisers, *yakṣas* and fears; increasing, subduing

And fierceness; and all aims, You accomplish at will—
Devout, I prostrate at Your feet, Tārā, Mother of Conqu'rors!

*Song of Longing, and making requests*

22 Alas! Lady *Āryā*, listen a little to me!
All qualities of Your Body, Speech and Mind
Are manifested for sentient beings' sake.

23 You understand well the thoughts of Your disciples,
And in all the universal Conquerors' holy
Actions, O Goddess, You directly appear!

24 So, as soon as this name of Her Who Quickly Liberates
From the Samsaric Ocean falls on my ears,
Like the beloved in the heart of a lover,
Again and again, Your moon-like Body's reflection
Appears in the dancing lake of my mental devotion.

25 Since, in my previous lives without beginning,
I've gathered unwholesome karma through defilements,
Again and again I have fallen to realms of woe,
And experienced endless, unbearable, violent suff'ring.

26 Of the bodies I've taken in human migrations alone,
The blood and pus would, collected, exceed a great ocean;
The flesh and bones, heaped up, would be taller than Meru.[7]

27 But though I have thus experienced violent suffering,
If, Supreme Refuge, You don't seize me with Your Compassion,

Still I shall have to wander much more than that.
Alas! O, rescue me from the fears of *saṃsārā*!

28 Of yore, in the perfect deity land of Tuṣita,
The Supreme Holy Teacher gave utterance to
The Conquerors' Son Mañjuśrī, pronouncing that those
Who praised with the supreme Praises[8] that are taught
In the King of Tantras would win immeas'rable virtues.

29 If, although with my effort I've praised with these Praises,
Recited and practised, made offerings and requested,
You see the foul conduct of beings of times of decline
And, *Āryā* Mother, act with indifference towards us,
Then what is the use of Your names of 'Specially Loving
Towards Inferior Beings', 'Swift One', and 'Saviour'?

30 However, since Your loving Compassion is free
Of near and far, it applies to everyone;
Therefore, although, with inferior fortune, I suffer
From my karmic obscurations, at present
I've not found another Refuge superior to You;

31 So in all future lives, Superior Deity, will You
Look after me without parting for even an instant,
And manifest Your supreme face as visual nectar!

32 Rescuing from the eight fears, outer and inner;[9]
Your twenty-one ways of action, and all such
Universal actions—just by thinking,
Make all these quickly spontaneously arise!

33 All that hinder my practice of the Dharma—
Assemblies of human beings, ghosts and spirits,
And all interruptions such as the eight fears—
Please will You pacify without exception!

34 Especially, Supreme Refuge, from Your
Compassion,
In my mindstream let not perverse thoughts
Be born for even an instant, but let only
Wholesome minds arise—inspire me thus!

35 Especially, on the sole base of all good
collections'
Arising, a qualified, supreme, holy *Guru*,
Let me rely correctly with thoughts and actions
And follow him as he wishes—inspire me thus!

36 The base with which Buddhahood can be
achieved in one life,
This opportune, fortunate rebirth, found but
once,
Perishes fast as lightning. Let me produce
This thought, and grasp its essence—inspire me
thus!

37 Driven by fear of woeful rebirth after death,
Let me abandon unvirtue and practise virtue,
Confess with regret all the sins I've created
before,
And be able to stop them henceforth—inspire me
thus!

38 Like seeing filthy sewage as *amṛta*,
Let me not see *saṃsāra*'s perfections as bliss,
But produce the mind that wants to be free of it
quickly,
And train in the Conqueror's Doctrine—inspire
me thus!

39 Since they are tortured by suff'ring and poor in
happiness,
Let me produce well the thought of Supreme
Awak'ning,

Which sets in Buddhahood sentient beings, my mothers,
And train in the Powerful Conduct[10]—inspire me thus!

40 Especially, let the Path uniting Calm
And Insight—the Middle View, excellent and profound—
Be born within my mindstream well and truly,
And grasping at extremes uprooted—inspire me thus!

41 Then let me enter the Supreme Vehicle teaching
And ripen my mind with the rivers of pure empowerments,
Protecting the vows and pledges that I've taken
As the apple of my eye—inspire me thus!

42 Let me understand right the two Stages, heart of the various
Tantras, then quickly, by good meditation, produce
In my mindstream the state of Union of the Four *Kāyas*,
A wish-fulfilling jewel—inspire me thus!

43 Showing before each mother sentient being
Countless emanations, when I'm Buddha earlier,
Let me transfer them to Buddhahood, through the abandonment
Of all their two obscurations—inspire me thus!

44 Let the realm where I accomplish a Conqueror's Deeds,
My entourage, the measure of my incarnation,
And so on, all far surpass even *Sugata* All-Seeing's[11]—
To gain these excellent qualities, please inspire me!

45 From now till I reach the supreme point of Enlightenment,[12]

Let me know well that the root of all good
collections,
Samsaric and beyond, is only the Conqueror's
Doctrine,
And strive to support and enact it—inspire me
thus!

46 Wealth, respect, fame, desires, entertainments,
diversions?—
Let me not enter such actions blamed by the holy,
But sticking to solitude, think well on meanings
I've learned,
And do the essential practice—inspire me thus!

47 Let me realize easily and correctly
The subtlest intentions of the Conqueror!
May all qualities, such as the *Āryas'* Treasures,
Completely fill my mindstream—inspire me
thus!

48 Through the infinite virtues arisen from this,
May I and all other beings without exception
Be well upheld by the Holy Protector's
Compassion,
Never becoming separate from the pure Path!

One overcome by obscurations, called Matisāra, made this request for his own wishes in the Nyima Ding (Sun Plateau) retreat.

Translated from the Tibetan at Nalanda Monastery in France, on the 15th day of the 7th month of the Iron Bird year (14 September 1981), and subsequently revised with advice from the Venerable Geshe Rabten.

May it be auspicious!

## THE GARLAND OF JEWELS, A SONG OF LONGING FOR VENERABLE ĀRYA-TĀRĀ

(*Dung-bö ratnä tr'eng-wa*)

*By Lo-dr'ö gyats'o*

Homage to Guru Mañjughoṣa![13]

1 Dispelling the eight fears of whoever remembers You,
Treasure of Love, never tired of helping others,
Constant Protector, Venerable Tārā—
I touch my head to the lotus of Your feet.
Listen a little, while I lament my sorrows!

2 While in the endless dense forest of *saṃsāra*
I wander, careless, drenched in both kinds of defilements,[14]
*Āryā* Mother, where is Your hook of Compassion?

3 Ah me! Alas! O loving, kind-natured Mother!
All the Conquerors of the ten directions
Ordained and appointed You a Refuge for beings.

4 Unattached to enjoying Your own Nirvanic bliss,
You help migrators, I've long heard it said.
So, turning my mind in Your direction, I
Renounce other refuge and seek Refuge in You.

5 If now, *Āryā* Mother, without a glance
You abandon me amid my mass of sins,
Where has Your loving Mother's Compassion gone?
If You damp down Your surging *Bodhicitta*,
In Your sacred office, is this quite the thing?

6 Of yore, You've shown Your face and cared for people
Times past counting, here in Tibet, I've heard.
*Āryā*, is this a lie, or have You favourites?

7 Well, if You're specially kind to inferior beings,
Then, this minute, come and show Your face!
With the nectar of Your voice, give me
refreshment,
Wash off all my stains of evil actions!

8 Next, as soon as I leave this life's formations,
In His wonderful Pure Land, Sukhāvatī,
Near the Protector, Amitābha Buddha,
May I taste His Speech's nectar—inspire me thus!

9 From that most excellent Realm, to other Pure
Lands
Let me be able to travel through magical powers,
And saving migrating beings by my emanations,
Let me become like Lord Avalokita!

10 Throughout all my lifetimes yet to come,
Let me meet the Venerable Lady,
Tārā, hear Her Speech, be cared for by Her,
And carry out Her orders—inspire me thus!

11 With rank, wealth, fortune, wisdom, great
compassion,
Faith, renunciation and firm intention,
Let me always strive to achieve Enlightenment,
While ev'ry hindrance is quelled—inspire me
thus!

12 From my ordination, as long as I live,
Contrary to my *Prātimokṣa* vows
Let me not perform the slightest action,
But practise the common Path—inspire me thus!

13 The best of *saṃsāra*'s a razor-edge sticking up;
This life's appearances just a play of illusion—
This knowledge born in my mind, let me strive in
the means
Of reaching Omniscience—please inspire me
thus!

14 In the six Perfections which ripen one's own mindstream,
And four Attractions whose purpose is helping others,
Let me train with the force of continuous effort,
Growing them right in my mindstream—inspire me thus!

15 Then, let me enter swiftly the Profound
Uncommon Path, the Path of the *Vajra* Vehicle,
And from a fully qualified Spiritual Friend
Receive the four pure empowerments—inspire me thus!

16 Through practising well the path of the First Tantric Stage,
May I purify all the stains of birth, death and *bardo*,
And seeing the circle of deities of Great Bliss,
Train in the Second Stage—inspire me thus!

17 On the Second Stage also, as taught in the Tantras,
Let me gain the full experience of each level,
And having perfected the Learning Union, gain
The Union Beyond Learning[15]—inspire me thus!

18 After that, to many impure lands
Let me send out many emanations,
And by the Mantra Path linked with the view of Emptiness
Guide ev'ry sentient being—inspire me thus!

19 Through Your Compassion, Venerable Lady,
May my sincere words, just as I've expressed them,
Be fulfilled! In short, may all my wishes
Without exception easily come to pass!

This is a Song of Longing, the Garland of Jewels.
When a faithful disciple strongly urged
That an exhortation to the Venerable

Supreme Mother of Conquerors of the three
times
Would have immeas'rable blessings, and in that
way
One should strive devotedly with the three
doors,
The Buddhist monk, Lo-dr'ö gyats'o, composed
it, having
With unchanging faith in the Mañjughoṣa Guru
Tsongk'a-pa, long revered as his Special Deity
Venerable Tārā, so that by
These merits, all beings may gain Omniscience.

*Translated from the Tibetan.*

# 3 *Song by Lozang Tänpä Gyälts'än*

Lozang Tänpä Gyälts'än was a Rinpoche, or incarnate lama, who wrote this remarkable song, the colophon says, in 1852 at the age of eighteen. His year of birth would thus have been 1834–5. According to Khetsun Sangpo's *Biographical Dictionary*,[1] he was born in Ch'ö-ts'ä O-rung in 1836, his father's name being Lu-bum and his mother's Lhamo-gyäl. He was recognized as the incarnation of Gom-gän of Hor-mo, who came from Me-kyä Hor-mo. We can assume that as a Rinpoche he did not have to devote as much of his time as an ordinary novice would to the rigorous intellectual training characteristic of the Gelukpa school, but was encouraged to exercise his talent for meditation. Certainly this Song of Longing is no mere rehearsal of stock ideas and phrases.

The first verse praises Tārā as the combination of all the Three Jewels—Buddha, Dharma and Saṅgha. This is orthodox in that any Buddha is also Dharma and Saṅgha, but is surprisingly rarely applied to Tārā, though Akṣobhyavajra's Praise uses the idea.

The next few verses, however, have no parallel in the other praises. They deal with three groups of beings who are a kind of Tantric manifestation of the Three Jewels—the *Guru*, from whom one receives inspiration, or 'blessings'; the *Yidam* or main personal deity, from whom one receives *siddhis* (realizations and magical powers); and the Dharma-protectors, who enable one to accomplish the Tantric rites. (The *ḍākinīs,* though often included in this group, are here not mentioned.) The author goes beyond conventional teachings on Tārā and boldly hails Her as uniquely competent to fill all these roles. Normally such ideas are applied only to one's *guru,* but the author is taking Tārā Herself as his personal *guru.*

Not only is Tārā all these Holy Beings, She is his wealth, his best friend and everything he needs.

The requests for inspiration (verses 14 to 18) do not, like Lodr'ö Gyats'o's, follow the *Lam rim* step by step, but start on the Mahāyāna level with Great Compassion, as befits a writer who has taken his present rebirth deliberately in order to benefit sentient beings. They skilfully present the most essential points of all three Vehicles—Hīnayāna, Mahāyāna and Vajrayāna—as something to be practised simultaneously in a unified whole.

In the concluding prayers also (verses 19 to 23), the author seems to be very close to the Venerable Mother.

The whole song is most profound and the author's advice in the colophon worth heeding. He was surely no ordinary eighteen-year-old.

Though Beyer has already published a translation,[2] no apologies are needed for presenting a more accurate one.

## A SONG OF LONGING FOR TĀRĀ, THE INFALLIBLE
(*Dung-bö lu-me-ma*)

*By Lozang tänpä gyälts'än*

Homage to Guru Ārya-Tārā!

1 Three infallible Jewels of Refuge combined
In one, Divine Mother Whose nature is Compassion,
I bow to You from my heart! Till I'm enlightened,
Support me, I pray, with the hook of Your Compassion!

2 I call the Jewels as witness—from not just my mouth,
But the depth of my inmost heart and bones, I pray—
Think of me somewhat! Show me Your smiling face!
Loving One, grant me the nectar of Your Speech!

3 Others cheat us with their made-up teachings,
Selling Dharma for money that's marked by impermanence,[3]
Proclaiming ignorance knowledge, puffed up with pride
Through the eight worldly *dharmas*,[4] *gurus* great and small.

4 Since I cannot trust such Friends[5] of degenerate times,
The principal Guru of mine is You Yourself.
Inspire me, Mother of the nature of love!
Arouse Your great power of Compassion! Think of me!

5 Relied on as Refuge, none of them will deceive us;
But, seeing the ways of this degenerate age,
Most Buddhas sink down into the bliss of *Nirvāṇa*;
Some, though compassionate, have weak karmic connection.[6]

6 Since I have no other *Yidam* Deity,
My principal Deity is You Yourself.
Grant me *siddhis*, Mother of loving nature!
Arouse Your great power of Compassion! Think of me!

7 Most protectors[7] don't show their powers and skills—
Disgusted with their practitioners, they do not act.
Others, proud of worldly fame, may be
Good for a while, but cheat us in the end.

8 Since I cannot trust protectors such as these,
My principal Protector is You Yourself.
Fulfil the Activities, Mother of loving nature!
Arouse Your great power of Compassion! Think of me!

9 Common worldly riches, the meaning like the name,[8]
Arouse defilements and bind one in *saṃsāra*.
What jewels,[9] except the *Āryas'*, though they grant wishes,
Can let me take even a sesame seed when I die?

10 Since I cannot trust illusory riches,
The principal wealth I have is You Yourself.
Grant my desires, O Mother of loving nature!
Arouse Your great power of Compassion! Think of me!

11 Not fit to be trusted even for one day,
Their thoughts determinedly set on misbehaviour,
Just acting friendly, these friends of no virtue
Play the friend when they wish, the enemy when they don't.

12 Since I cannot trust these friends of degenerate times,
The principal friend of mine is You Yourself.

Be close to me, O Mother of loving nature!
Arouse Your great power of Compassion! Think of me!

13 In short, my Guru, my Deity and Protector,
My Refuge, dwelling, food, wealth, friends and all—
Everything whatsoever I wish, You are;
So make me accomplish everything easily!

14 Let me stop also my present stubborn mind,
And rouse the Compassion that even on coming to give
A billion times for every being's sake
My body and life, tires not—inspire me thus!

15 The uprooter of *saṃsāra*'s maker, self-grasping,
The deep Middle Way, so hard to understand,
Avoiding all errors of the two extremes,[10]
Pure Right View—please inspire me to realize it!

16 Wishing, for sentient beings' sake, to win Buddhahood,
Let me not think for a moment of my own pleasure,
But dedicating all virtues to beings and Doctrine,
Perfect my renounced *Bodhi*-mind—inspire me thus!

17 Rich in the *Āryas'* Treasures, faith and the rest,
Let me become the best of Buddha-sons, able
To keep the smallest precept taught by the Conquerors,
Never contemptuous of it—inspire me thus!

18 In outward behaviour keeping the Hearer's conduct,[11]
Let me, in inward belief, revere the Profound
*Vajrayāna*, and practise the Two-Stage Path,
So winning Enlightenment swiftly—inspire me thus!

19 Whether I'm happy or troubled, whether things
Go well or badly for me, whatever I do
You know about it, Ven'rable Tārā, so
Think of me lovingly, my only Mother!

20 Myself and all the beings with hopes of me
I offer to You, Venerable Tārā!
Make us Your own, and to the highest Pure Land
Make us go quickly, with no births intervening!

21 My mothers, who do not follow the Conquerors'
Teachings,
All mother sentient beings, whoever they are—
With Your hook of compassionate skilful Means
Please transform their minds into the Dharma!

22 Reciting this at morning, noon and night,
And bearing in mind Venerable Tārā,
Let all sentient beings with hopes of me
Be born in whatever Pure Land they desire!

23 May every member of the Three Precious Jewels,
Especially the Ven'rable Mother, compassionate-
natured,
Look after me till I reach the point of
Enlightenment,
Letting me conquer quickly the four Māras'
hosts!

If you recite this morning, noon and night as long as you live, not just from your mouth, but from the depths of your innermost heart and bones, with your consciousness penetrating its inner meaning each time you recite it, Venerable Tārā will care for you and you will see Her face. No hindrance can harm you, and your intentions will be fulfilled. The Buddhas and their Offspring also will be pleased and will take care of you. Making effort in the *Twenty-one Homages* and this practice, realize Venerable Tara! This is my heartfelt speech and quite certain.

This prayer to the Venerable Tārā, in heartfelt words making his own requests and also non-deceptive to others, was composed by the Buddhist monk Lozang tänpä gyälts'än, in his nineteenth year, the Water Mouse year (1852), on the third day of the Miracle month,[12] at B'än-gar nam-gyäl ling. It is sure to have great benefits.

Translated from the Tibetan in accordance with teachings of the Venerable Lama Thubten Yeshe.[13]

May auspiciousness prevail!

'So now we finish, yes, this incredible isn't it? Blow your minds, I think so. . . . So simple . . . anyway, don't worry, they just words you know.'

*Lama Yeshe*

# Part Six
# *Sādhanas*

# 1 *Sādhanas*

## INTRODUCTION

Reciting praises of Ārya-Tārā is a simple and beneficial practice that anyone can do. The only qualification needed is some degree of faith in the Goddess. As one recites, one visualizes Her either in front of oneself or above one's head, with the attributes described in texts and taught by *gurus*, and perhaps others one has deduced. She is not flat like a painting, but with as many dimensions as one can visualize; not static and opaque like a statue, but intensely alive and made entirely of light, brilliant and with every detail sharp yet all transparent. Even far off, one senses Her presence through the waves of calm radiated by Her perfect inner peace, making our worldly troubles seem insignificant. Closer, one sees She is not withdrawn into trance but is looking at oneself with total understanding. Though fully aware of one's faults and inadequacies, She accepts one as one is, with good humour. Not only this, but if one looks to see what She is doing for other sentient beings, one observes countless emanations all the time going out from Her, helping them, and when their work is done, reabsorbing into the principal Tārā Body. In response to one's requests, streams of light and nectar from the seed syllable at Her heart fill every part of one's body—generally either white light, for pacifying hindrances, purifying one's faults and evil actions and removing all sorts of problems, or yellow light, for granting realizations, wealth and so forth. The light and nectar also fill all other sentient beings, whom we can if we like visualize around us.

But all this, although it may develop our faith in Tārā to the point where She can do remarkable things to help us, does not amount to Tantric practice. The Tantric practitioner is not content to pray to Tārā as an external person—she or he wants actually to become Tārā, to realize the Tārā nature within herself. To do this, she must first receive the empowerment of Tārā from a *guru*, then engage in the appropriate *sādhana*, or 'means of accomplishment', in a retreat of several months or years.

For a deity as popular as Tārā, innumerable *sādhana* texts are available. Some are very short, some lengthy; some straightforward, some elaborate; some general, some for special purposes. There is no space here to accommodate all tastes and schools; I confine myself to three classical examples from India, to illustrate the principal features.

### *The texts presented*

One *sādhana* by Candragomin and two by Atīśa are translated below. All are quite short but reasonably complete.

Atīśa's *Protecting from the Eight Fears* presents the essential elements of a Tārā *sādhana* about as briefly as it could be done. The *sādhana* by Candragomin is very slightly more elaborate; the text is longer mainly because it is more explicit about some of the details and includes some literary flourishes. It is written entirely in verse, although only some of it is meant to be recited during the practice. Apart from trivial differences of style and typography, this *sādhana* of thirteen centuries ago is closely similar to modern ones. Like the same author's *Pearl Garland Praise*, it was translated into Tibetan by Nak-ts'o Lotsawa with Atīśa. However, Mäl-gyo Lotsawa (whom we have encountered as the translator of some of Sūryagupta's texts) found it necessary to revise the translation some decades later.

The longer *sādhana* by Atīśa, though nothing in the title suggests it, turns out to be devoted to a form of White Tārā.

However, apart from the colour of the Deity and Her seed syllable, Her cross-legged posture, and the wheel at Her heart, it could probably all be applied to Green Tārā also, with appropriate changes of the colour of the light-rays. I include it because it deals in helpful detail with several points passed over in the other two texts.

### *Analysis*

We note first of all that the short Atīśa text contains no words to be recited, except the mantras. While many *sādhanas* involve reciting a great many words, this is secondary; what is important is the practice done with the mind, notably visualization. Even the recitation of the root mantra, as both authors explicitly state, is only to be entered upon when one tires of holding the principal visualization.

The heart of the *sādhana*, then, is visualizing oneself as the deity. Still, one does not plunge directly into this; a number of preparatory practices lead up to it.[1]

To start with, as already mentioned in the Tantra (Chapters 7 to 11), one must prepare the room and set up an altar with an image of the Goddess and suitable offerings. To serve as the palace of the Deity, the room should at least be clean, tidy and sweetly scented.[2] One also prepares one's body, washing it respectfully as the actual body of the Deity.

The external preparations complete, one sits down and does whatever exercises one finds helpful for getting into a relaxed state of mind comparatively free of everyday thoughts and emotions. Generating suitable motivation, one visualizes an array of holy beings as the Field of Accumulation of Merit before which the remaining preparatory practices are to be performed. As the texts describe it, the central figure in the Field of Merit is Tārā, seen as being of one nature with the Root Guru (from whom one received the empowerment). Hosts of other Gurus surround Her—those of the lineage of the empowerment, those of the Wisdom and Method lineages, and all one's own Gurus. Also present are all the other *Ārya* beings, the Saṅgha of the three Vehicles, generally arranged in descending tiers from other Deities, through Buddhas, Bodhisattvas, Arhants, Heroes and *Ḍākinīs* down to the Dharma

Protectors; one's Guru will explain the details. All the beings in the Field are of the same nature as Tārā and the Root Guru.

The indispensable practices to be done before this Field of Merit are taking Refuge and generating *Bodhicitta*. For example, in a very short daily practice of Vasudhārā ('Stream of Wealth'), the wealth-granting form of Tārā, by His Holiness Dudjom Rinpoche, the preparatory practices are condensed into a single stanza expressing these two thoughts:

> NAMO!
> To Guru, Three Jewels and Ven'rable Lady
> Devotedly I go for Refuge. To free
> Migrators throughout space from sorrow
> and want,
> I'll practise the Goddess Stream of Wealth.

Of course, just saying 'I go for Refuge' is not enough—one must have clear in one's mind the reasons that give meaning to the words. Lamas can teach for weeks on this topic alone, which is the very foundation of Buddhist practice.[3] *Bodhicitta* means basically the resolve to practise in order to release all beings from suffering; this too can be expounded *ad infinitum*, indeed 'the Vast' is a common synonym for it. As the practitioner has meditated extensively on these subjects before (else she could not have received the empowerment properly), the words of the prayer will quickly recall the necessary attitudes to mind.

Other preparatory practices often included are the Four Immeasurables, the Seven Limbs, and the *Maṇḍala* Offering. Their order varies.

The four Immeasurable thoughts, or Divine States of mind (*brahma-vihāra*), are a way of increasing the power of one's *Bodhicitta* by concentrating in turn on Loving-kindness, wishing 'May all beings be happy!'; Compassion, 'May all be free of suffering!'; Joy, 'May all never be separated from the supreme bliss of Liberation!'; and Equanimity, 'May we all abandon attachment and aversion and see each other as equal!' There are various ways of meditating on these; often, as in the present *sādhanas*, the practitioner is left free to choose whichever she prefers.[4]

The Seven Limbs are means of accumulating merits and

purifying negativity. Candragomin's *sādhana*, which inserts Going for Refuge and Generating *Bodhicitta* among them to make nine, expresses them clearly. Atīśa mentions or alludes to most of them, his intention no doubt being that the practitioner should here insert suitable verses, such as Candragomin's. The second Limb, offering, can be developed at great length—the series of six offerings described in the longer *sādhana* by Atīśa would not usually be considered sufficient.[5]

The *Maṇḍala* Offering, a symbolic offering in visualization of an entire universe full of precious things, may be included in the Limb of Offering or placed after the Seven Limbs. Atīśa's 'offering of the body' may be done in the manner of a *maṇḍala*.[6]

Having completed the preparatory rites, the practitioner dissolves the Field of Merit, herself and the entire environment into Emptiness. From this she emerges as the seed-syllable TĀṂ (in Indian or Tibetan script), becoming Tārā surrounded perhaps by Her attendants. These visualized deities are known as the Symbolic Beings (*samaya-sattva*). One may then go on to invoke the actual deities from wherever they are—the Wisdom-knowledge Beings (*jñāna-sattva*)—and make them absorb into the Symbolic Beings. Oneself is thus one with Tārā. This unity is usually confirmed with a rite of empowerment with the Body, Speech and Mind of the Deity, by the Buddhas of the Five Families.

Now follows the period of one-pointed concentration on oneself as Tārā. When weary of this, the practitioner recites the ten-syllable mantra, counting with a rosary, until it is time to end the session.

Before leaving her seat, she dedicates the merits created to the Enlightenment of herself and all sentient beings. The standard prayer for this, common to all Tibetan schools, is:

> Through these merits, may I quickly
> Realize Ārya-Tārāhood,
> And transfer each sentient being
> Into Her [Enlightened] State!

If it is the last session of the day, she also offers to the spirits the 'offering-cake' on the altar, with mantra and *mudrā* as Candragomin describes. The flat Indian offering-cake (*bali*) developed in Tibet into the tall, conical torma (*gtor ma*), assuming a multitude of forms depending on the purpose. Tormas may also be offered to the Deity and to the *Ḍākinīs* and Dharma-Protectors.[7]

*The Translation*

The only copy of the text available was a photocopy from the small-scale reproduction of the Peking edition, which is sometimes less than legible. I apologize if my guesses have occasionally gone astray.

To assist cross-comparison of the three *sādhanas*, I have added headings such as are often included in *sādhana* texts of the present day.

Finally, I emphasize that you should definitely not attempt to practise any of these *sādhanas* unless you have received an empowerment of Tārā, and even then you should consult a lama first.

## SĀDHANA OF ĀRYA-TĀRĀ CALLED PROTECTION FROM THE EIGHT FEARS
(*Ārya-tārā-aṣṭabhaya-trāta-nāma-sādhana*)

*By Candragomin*

[*Translators' homage*]

Homage to the Venerable Tārā!

[*Author's homage*]

Homage to the Omniscient Ruler of Conquerors
with the innate *Dharmakāya* and
*Saṃbhogakāya* and *Nirmāṇakāya*,
Whose eyes are broad like petals of a lotus,
Whose Body, Speech and Mind appear in *saṃsāra*
and out of it, purely liberated by
Practice; Who is non-dual Method and Wisdom,
worshipped by gods, *asuras* and human beings!

[*Promise of composition*]

Since You've abandoned birth and destruction,[8]
really
You are insep'rable from the unchanging True
Nature (*dharmatā*);
But for the sake of deluded migrators, You emanate
manifold Goddess forms, acting with Body,
Speech
And Mind, in particular quickly subduing veils[9]
of the Secret Mantra Path. Mother producing
all Buddhas,
Saving from the eight dangers! I shall now
write in faith for [those who] delight in Your
practice.

[PREPARATORY PRACTICES]

[*Preparation*]

You who delight to practise the Goddess,
faithful, diligent, keeping your pledges (*samaya*),
Without violence, set out
in a pleasant, lonely place

An image as source of *siddhis* and
various offerings. On a comfortable
Seat sit in the Buddha's manner,
purified outside and in by ablutions.

[*Visualization*]

Then, at your heart, from the first vowel (A)
appears a moonstone;[10] at its centre
Is the first letter of the fourth series (TA),
adorned with the dot of the last of the fifth (Ṃ).[11]
This invokes with its light-rays
the Goddess and the host of *Āryas*.

[*The Seven Limbs, with Refuge and Bodhicitta*]

[1. *Prostration*]

Wisdom-body of all the Buddhas,
dispelling the darkness of ignorance
Of delusion-blinded sentient beings!
*Sugata* Tārā, homage to You!

[2. *Offering*]

All kinds of sweet-scented flowers;
incense such as aloe-wood (*agaru*);
Lamps, eliminating darkness;
camphor and other finest perfumes,
Pure and mixed; foodstuffs; also
melodious sounds—hosts of all such
Offerings I offer [You],
augmented with mantras and *mudrās*.

[3. *Confession*]

Every evil I have done
in beginningless *saṃsāra*
At this moment I confess;
henceforth I shall never do it.

[4. *Rejoicing in virtue*]

Thinking of the virtue done,
with and without contamination,
By perfect Buddhas, other *Āryas*
and all migrators, I rejoice.

[5. *Requesting Teachings*]
Sentient beings' Protectors, like
the full, unclouded disk of the sun,
I exhort to turn the wheel of Dharma
so as to aid[12] migrating beings.

[6. *Asking to remain*]
Conqu'rors who wish to receive *Nirvāṇa*
in the uncontaminate sphere:
As long as *saṃsāra* remains,
please stay, not entering *Nirvāṇa*!

[7. *Going for Refuge*]
To You, beings' Protectors, taking
in the signless, ultimate Nature,
The non-conceptual *Dharmakāya*,
the aspect of Form Bodies, I go for Refuge.

[8. *Generating Bodhicitta*]
Just as Protectors in the three times
produce the thought of supreme Awakening,
I too, to save migrating beings,
produce the thought of supreme Awakening.

[9. *Dedication of merits*]
Through the merit I've received
from prostration and the rest,
May sentient beings without exception
quickly attain Buddhahood!

[*The Four Immeasurables*]
Meditate too on the four Measureless—
may beings meet happiness, and so forth.

[*Dissolution of the Field of Accumulation of Merit*]
Then let the *Āryas* leave, and reflect
on all *dharmas*, fixed and moving, as Empty.

OṂ ŚŪNYATĀ-JÑĀNA-VAJRA-SVABHĀVÂTMAKO 'HAM.
(OṂ, I have the nature of the *vajra* essence that is
Wisdom-knowledge of Emptiness.)

[THE MAIN PRACTICE]

[*Visualization*]

Now, a lotus, upon which
a moonstone, and on that the seed (TĀṂ).
This turns into an *utpala*,
marked with the same seed syllable.

This cleanses all beings with its light,
then transforms into the Lady,
One-faced, two-armed, the colour of grass (*dūrvā*),
sixteen years old, with full adornments.
Note Her right and left [hands] have
boon-granting and *utpala*.
Half-cross-legged; smiling face;
on a lake, in a jewel cavern.

Visualize the attendants She emanates[13]
and supporters. On right and left
First, Goddesses from MAṂ and PRAṂ—
Mārīcī and Pratisarā,[14]
Golden-coloured, one-faced, two-armed,
lovely with ornaments, in their left [hands]
Holding *aśoka* tree and *vajra*,
right in the manner of wish-[granting].[15]

At lower right, the Pig-faced Goddess,
*palāśa*-coloured,[16] lovely with ornaments,
With *mudrā* of explaining the Dharma.
At lower left is Bhṛkuṭī,
The colour of kohl, of wrathful mien,
holding a knife[17] and bloody skull.

To eight intermediate points
between these, emanate eight Tārās
Who protect from the eight dangers—
hindering demons, enemies,
Elephants, fire and serpents, robbers,
being bound in chains, and water.

Thus should the *yogin* visualize.

[*Invocation of the Wisdom-knowledge Beings*]

Now, from the seed at the heart spreads
light
Invoking Wisdom-knowledge Beings
who have the manner as above.
Make offerings, then with the four syllables[18]
let them absorb non-dually.

[*Empowerment*]

With the three letters in the three
places, do blessing. After that
You are empowered. The Lord of the Family,
Amoghasiddhi, adorns your crown.

[*Concentrating on oneself as Tārā*]

Then for a while let light from the seed
radiate and come together.

[*Recitation of mantra*]

When tired of this, recite the mantra:
that of ten syllables is to be counted,

OṂ TĀRE TUTTĀRE TURE SVĀHĀ!

The rites are accomplished from [four][19] or six
hundred thousand, or else a million.

[CONCLUSION]

[*Offering-cake*]

If you are giving an off'ring-cake
to spirits, put in a clean vessel[20]
Food, and bless it ritually.

With the palms of both hands joined,
separate well both forefingers
And middle fingers, in the *mudrā*
of the opening *utpala*.

Touching this to the three places,
offer the offering-cake to the spirits.

OṂ A-KĀRO MUKHAṂ SARVA-DHARMĀṆĀM
ĀDY-ANUTPANNATVĀT

(OṂ The letter A is a door [to insight] because all
*dharmas* are unproduced from the very
beginning)[21]
OṂ ĀḤ HŪṂ PHAṬ SVĀHĀ!

[*Concluding remarks*]

Since all branches of the rites
are taught extensively in the Tantra,
Here they're not set out—look there.

A *yogin* who practises this meaning
[Has] excellent food, actual and non-actual,
peace without beginning or end,
Abandons rebirth and contaminations,
and finds the Glorious Mother Herself,
Not to mention accomplishing
such *siddhis* as the vase of fortune,
Or rites of killing, expelling, dividing,
summoning, calming and increasing.

[*Author's dedication of merits*]

Through the immaculate merits I've received
from thus presenting according to the Tantra
The *sādhana* of Our Lady, Mother of all
whose nature is Samantabhadra's conduct,
The *Kāya* Whose subject and object are non-dual,
Her of nature of Emptiness and Compassion,
Whose rebirths in the three realms are truly
exhausted,
may all beings find *Nirvāṇa*'s eternal bliss!

The *sādhana* of Ārya-Tārā called Protection from the Eight Fears, by the great Master Candragomin, is complete.

It was translated by the Indian *upādhyāya* Dīpaṃkara-śrī-jñāna and the Tibetan translator Ts'ül-tr'im Gyäl-wa, and subsequently corrected and finalized by the Indian *upādhyāya* Bodhisattva Dāna-śrī and the Tibetan translator Mäl-gy'i Lo-dr'ö dr'a-pa.

*Translated from the Tibetan.*

## PROTECTING FROM THE EIGHT FEARS
([*Asṭạbhaya-trāṇa*])

*By Atīśa*

Homage to *Bhagavatī* Tārā!

### [PREPARATORY PRACTICES]

The adept of *yoga* enters the meditation chamber and, sitting on a comfortable seat, makes the promise, 'With great Compassion I shall raise up all migrating beings.' Then she or he should meditate on the Goddess Tārā.

#### [*Visualization; Seven Limbs; Refuge*]

This is done according to the following procedure. At your own heart, visualize coming from an A a moon disk, with the syllable TĀṂ on it. From this spread hook-like light-rays [drawing] to the space before you the Goddess, your own Guru and the Complete and Perfect Buddhas; behold these clearly. To them prostrate, confess your sins, go for Refuge to the Three [Jewels], dedicate your roots of virtue, offer your body, and make prayers.

#### [*Emptiness*]

Next, meditate on Emptiness, thinking 'Ultimately, I, the Deity and all are without inherent nature and have been unproduced from the very beginning,'[22] and saying

> OṂ ŚŪNYATĀ-JÑĀNA-VAJRA-SVABHĀVÂTMAKO 'HAM,

to make it firm.

### [THE MAIN PRACTICE]

#### [*Visualization*]

Now [visualize coming] from PAṂ an eight-petalled lotus, in the centre of which your own mind [appears] by the power of your previous vows as a syllable TĀṂ, from which the Goddess Tārā is produced. She is green in colour, with one face and two arms, with Her right hand resting in the *mudrā* of granting boons (*vara-da*) and the left holding an *utpala*. She has Amoghasiddhi as head ornament and is in *ardha-paryaṅka*.

[*Concentration on oneself as Tārā*]

Meditate on this until tired.

[*Recitation of mantra*]

When tired, begin the recitation. The mantra-string,

> OṂ TĀRE TUTTĀRE TURE SVĀHĀ,

is sent out from your heart and in stages either enters your mouth or emerges from your heart. Visualizing the mantra as white in colour and slowly rotating, recite it.

[CONCLUSION]

When you are tired even of reciting, make offerings and give the offering-cake, and make prayers.

In all your postures you should remain in the pride of the Goddess [i.e. feeling that you are Her]. When you go to sleep, do so entering Emptiness. When you wake up, arise instantaneously [as the Goddess].

Protecting from the Eight Fears, by the wise Master Śrī-Dīpaṃkara-jñāna, is complete.

(Catalogued as having been translated by the author and Lotsawa Ts'ül-tr'im gyäl-wa.)

*Translated from the Tibetan.*

## SĀDHANA OF THE VENERABLE TĀRĀ
([*Tārā-bhaṭṭārikā-sādhana*])

*By Atīśa*

[*Translators' homage*]

Homage to the Venerable Tārā!

### [PREPARATORY PRACTICES]
[*Preparation*]

First the mantric practitioner washes her or his face, and so forth. In a clean, agreeable place of meditation, she sprinkles perfume, and sits cross-legged on a clean, comfortable seat.[23] She blesses the offering-cake with the mantra for offering-cakes for all spirits (*bhūta*).

Reciting ten times the mantra

> OṂ ĀḤ VIGHNÂNTAKṚT HŪṂ PHAṬ!
> (OṂ ĀḤ Putting an end to hindrances HŪṂ PHAṬ!),[24]

she should expel all the hindrances that are in the ten directions.

[*Visualization*]

Then she visualizes at her heart white light-rays radiating, their whiteness like the autumn moon indicating that all *dharmas* are of the nature of the *Dharmadhātu*, lacking production; they radiate strongly, lighting up her body. This she visualizes transforming into a dot of white light, like a pure piece of crystal, which gradually grows into the form of a moon disk. Upon this she visualizes the syllable TĀṂ, emitting a mass of light-rays like a white Jewel Tārā.

Then she should visualize that the TĀṂ-syllable illuminates the entire universe with masses of exceedingly white light-rays, whereupon the Goddess Tārā and other Buddhas, Bodhisattvas and Gurus are exhorted and invoked to the region of space in front of her.[25]

[*Offering*]

In addition, she should make offerings, of mental nature. The method for the offering ritual is as follows.

(a) Reciting the mantra OṂ VAJRA-PUṢPE HŪṂ! (OṂ *Vajra* Flower-Goddess HŪṂ!), make offering with masses of offerings of flowers that come from the TĀṂ-syllable.

(b) Then recite the mantra OṂ VAJRA-DHŪPE HŪṂ! (OṂ *Vajra* Incense-Goddess HŪṂ!) and make offering with masses of offerings of incense[26] sent out from the same TĀṂ-syllable.

(c) After that, recite the mantra OṂ VAJRA-DĪPE HŪṂ! (OṂ *Vajra* Lamp-Goddess HŪṂ!) and make offering with precious lamps sent out from the TĀṂ-syllable.

(d) Next, recite the mantra OṂ VAJRA-GANDHE HŪṂ! (OṂ *Vajra* Scent-Goddess HŪṂ!) and make offering by sending out offering-clouds [of perfume] that come from the TĀṂ-syllable.

(e) Then recite the mantra OṂ VAJRA-NAIVEDYĀ HŪṂ! (OṂ *Vajra* Food-offering-Goddess HŪṂ!) and make offering by sending out from the TĀṂ-syllable diverse offering-clouds of heavenly foodstuffs, of the finest tastes, served in all kinds of jewel [vessels].

(f) Then recite the mantra OṂ SARVA-VIŚIṢṬA-PŪJA-MEGHA-PRASARA-SAMUDRA ĀḤ HŪṂ! (OṂ Ocean of a multitude of clouds of every distinguished offering HŪṂ!) and make offering with parasols, banners, bells, pennants, canopies and so forth of the seven precious things, and the seven precious possessions of a universal monarch,[27] all from the TĀṂ-syllable.

[*Remaining limbs*]

Having made offering in this way, she should in front of those [holy beings] confess her sins, rejoice in merits, urge [them to give teachings], request [them to stay until *saṃsāra* ends], dedicate her merits, and go for Refuge to the Three [Jewels].

[*Four Immeasurables and Bodhicitta*]

Then she should meditate on the four Divine States of mind (*brahma-vihāra*), namely Loving-kindness, Compassion, Joy and Equanimity, and so make firm her Awakening Attitude (*Bodhicitta*).

[*Emptiness*]

Next, she should recite three times the mantra

OṂ SVABHĀVA-ŚUDDHĀḤ SARVA-DHARMĀḤ,
SVABHĀVA-ŚUDDHO 'HAM

(OṂ All *dharmas* are pure of own-being, I am pure of own-being),

and perceive all sentient beings as of the nature of Emptiness, like dreams, illusions or mirages.

[THE MAIN PRACTICE]

[*Visualization: self-generation as Tārā*]

Now she visualizes a letter A, transforming into a moon disk. Upon this is visualized the white syllable TĀṂ, as a collection of white light-rays. This transforms into a blue *utpala*, at whose centre is visualized on a moon-disk the white syllable TĀṂ. From this, white light-rays spread to the ten directions. They purify all sentient beings so that they become of the form of Tārā. The same light-rays draw them back so that they absorb into the *utpala* and TĀṂ-syllable. Because of this,

In the centre of a white lotus
is a seat of lunar form
Where I sit cross-legged in *vajra*,
granting boons,[28] holding an *utpala*,
Resting my back upon a moon
of colour like the autumn moon.
Complete with all the ornaments,
I have a sixteen-year-old's body.
Mother of all the Perfect Buddhas
and their Offspring, I end all desires.[29]

By transforming the white TĀṂ on the moon-disk at the heart of this Ārya-Tārā,

Visualize a wheel of white
light. On its eight spokes are eight
Syllables, while at the hub
that they surround are OṂ and TĀ
With the name of the object of practice between.[30]
For six months' service,[31] with certainty
meditate with one-pointed mind.

Recite in the mind, until you're tired,
this mantra of ten syllables.
First we place an OṂ, and then
after that we add TĀRE,
After that TURE and TUTTĀRE,
finally SVĀHĀ—this does all rites.

[*Invocation of the Wisdom-knowledge Being*]

From the wheel at the heart, white light-rays spread, exhorting and invoking the naturally-existing Wisdom-knowledge Being similar to the Symbolic Being; She is visualized in space in front. Offerings are made, as before.

Then [the practitioner] should assume the *samaya-mudrā* ('Pledge Gesture'). Joining the palms with a hollow inside, she joins the forefingers to the backs of the middle fingers and bends the thumbs inside: this is the *utpala-mudrā*. In the middle of it she visualizes a white syllable TĀṂ, radiating white light-rays, which surround the Wisdom-knowledge Being. Then with the four syllables JAḤ HŪṂ BAṂ HOḤ, she invokes Her, makes Her enter herself, the Symbolic Being, binds [Her there] and rejoices.[32] She expresses her self-consciousness [of being the Deity] with

OṂ DHARMA-DHĀTU-JÑĀNA-VAJRA-
SVABHĀVÂTMAKO 'HAM
(OṂ I have the nature of the *vajra* essence that is the
*Dharmadhātu* Wisdom-knowledge).

[*Empowerment*]

After that, she visualizes that light-rays spread from the wheel and the syllables, so that the five Tathāgatas [come] in space before her. She seeks empowerment with this stanza:

Just as Bodhivajra made
request for the most high to the Buddhas,
Now do I request the *vajra*
of space for the sake of my protection.

Then she visualizes that from the bodies of the Tathāgatas come Locanā, Māmakī, Pāṇḍaravāsinī and Tārā, holding in their hands precious flasks full of nectar of Wisdom-knowledge; saying

> The empowerment of the Great *Vajra*,
> which the three Realms pay homage to,
> Will be bestowed by all the Buddhas
> come from the places of the Three Secrets,[33]

they give empowerment.

As soon as the empowerment is complete, she visualizes on her jewel crown the Tathāgata Amitābha, his body white in colour, with one face and two arms, in the *mudrā* of concentration.

### [*Recitation of mantra*]

For the blessing of her body, speech and mind, she sets at her crown a white OṂ, resting on a moon-disk; at her throat a red ĀḤ, resting on a moon-disk; and at her heart a dark blue HŪṂ, resting on a moon-disk.

Visualizing clearly that white light-rays spreading from the ten syllables purify all sentient beings, so that they realize Buddhahood and are then drawn back and absorb into the wheel and syllables, she should say the recitation.

## [CONCLUSION]

When she has meditated and recited until she is tired, and wants to finish, she recites the heart mantra of Vajrasattva, known as the hundred-syllable [mantra], to make up for faults in the ritual. Then she makes proper offering to the Wisdom-knowledge Being, dedicates the merits, and asks Her to leave. The verse for asking the Wisdom-knowledge Being to leave is:

> OṂ!
> You do all that's good for sentient beings;
> grant [me] favourable *siddhis*!
> I request, when You've departed
> to Your Buddha Land, come again!
> MUḤ!

The mantra recited is OṂ TĀRE TUTTĀRE TURE SVĀHĀ!

The hundred-syllable heart mantra of Vajrasattva is:

OṂ VAJRASATTVA SAMAYAM ANUPĀLAYA, VAJRASATTVA TENÔPATIṢṬHA, DṚḌHO ME BHAVA, SUTOṢYO ME BHAVA, SUPOṢYO ME BHAVA, ANURAKTO ME BHAVA. SARVA-SIDDHIM ME PRAYACCHA, SARVA-KARMA-SŪCA ME CITTAṂ ŚREYAḤ KURU HŪṂ! HA HA HA HA HOḤ! BHAGAVĀN SARVA-TATHĀGATA-VAJRA MĀ ME MUÑCA. VAJRĪ-BHAVA MAHĀ-SAMAYA-SATTVA ĀḤ!

[*Dedication*]

Through these merits, may all migrators
be like Venerable Tārā!
May I too realize this meditation
and become Buddha for beings' sake!

The *Sādhana* of the Venerable Tārā, by the great Master Śrī-Dīpaṃkara-jñāna, is complete.

It was translated, revised and finalized by the Indian *upādhyāya* Dīpaṃkara-śrī-jñāna and the Tibetan translator Gelong Ge-wäi lo-dr'ö.

*Translated from the Tibetan.*

*Appendices*
*List of Abbreviations*
*Notes*
*Glossary*
*Bibliography*
*Index*

# *Appendix 1*
# *Tibetan Translation of the Praise in Twenty-one Homages*

By putting together many copies of a text, from different sources, one can derive a more accurate version free of many mere misprints, and in addition find where there is significant disagreement as to the correct wording. The critical edition below is drawn from ten sources, as follows:

A Small lithographed pe-cha, entitled *rJe btsun sgrol ma la bstod pa phyag 'tshal nyer gcig pa zhes bya ba*. Last pages absent in my copy, so no publication details.

D Quoted in the commentary of Ngül-ch'u Dharmabhadra (his *Collected Works*, Vol. *2*).

G Quoted in the commentary of Gedün drup-pa (his *Collected Works*, Vol. *6*).

J Quoted in the commentary of Je-tsün Dr'ak-pa gyäl-ts'än (*Sa skya pa'i bka' 'bum*, Vol. *4*, 92-94).

K Type-set pe-cha, 10 leaves, *sGrol ma dkar sngon gyi bstod pa dang gzungs bcas*. Mani Printing Works, Kalimpong.

L Lhasa Kangyur, *rGyud 'bum*, NGA.

Q Tibetan text in the Quadrilingual blockprint (see p. 109).

S1, S4 Quoted in the commentaries of Sūryagupta, Peking Tängyur, P2557 and P2560.

T Tog Palace Kangyur, *rGyud 'bum*, NGA.

Three sources (Q, S1, S4) give only verses 1 to 21; the other seven are complete apart from a few words in G.

༄༅། །ཨོཾ་རྗེ་བཙུན་མ་འཕགས་མ་སྒྲོལ་མ་ལ་ཕྱག་འཚལ་ལོ། །

ཕྱག་འཚལ་སྒྲོལ་མ་མྱུར་མ་དཔའ་མོ། །སྤྱན་ནི་སྐད་ཅིག་གློག་དང་འདྲ་མ། །
འཇིག་རྟེན་གསུམ་མགོན་ཆུ་སྐྱེས་ཞལ་གྱི། །གེ་སར་བྱེ་བ་ལས་ནི་བྱུང་མ། །༡། །

ཕྱག་འཚལ་སྟོན་ཀའི་ཟླ་བ་ཀུན་ཏུ། །གང་བ་བརྒྱ་ནི་བརྩེགས་པའི་ཞལ་མ། །
སྐར་མ་སྟོང་ཕྲག་ཚོགས་པ་རྣམས་ཀྱིས། །རབ་ཏུ་ཕྱེ་བའི་འོད་རབ་འབར་མ། །༢། །

ཕྱག་འཚལ་གསེར་སྔོ་ཆུ་ནས་སྐྱེས་ཀྱི། །པདྨས་ཕྱག་ནི་རྣམ་པར་བརྒྱན་མ། །
སྦྱིན་པ་བརྩོན་འགྲུས་དཀའ་ཐུབ་ཞི་བ། །བཟོད་པ་བསམ་གཏན་སྤྱོད་ཡུལ་ཉིད་མ། །༣། །

ཕྱག་འཚལ་དེ་བཞིན་གཤེགས་པའི་གཙུག་ཏོར། །མཐའ་ཡས་རྣམ་པར་རྒྱལ་བར་སྤྱོད་མ། །
མ་ལུས་ཕ་རོལ་ཕྱིན་པ་ཐོབ་པའི། །རྒྱལ་བའི་སྲས་ཀྱིས་ཤིན་ཏུ་བསྟེན་མ། །༤། །

ཕྱག་འཚལ་ཏུཏྟཱ་ར་ཧཱུྃ་ཡི་གེས། །འདོད་དང་ཕྱོགས་དང་ནམ་མཁའ་གང་མ། །
འཇིག་རྟེན་བདུན་པོ་ཞབས་ཀྱིས་མནན་ཏེ། །ལུས་པ་མེད་པར་འགུགས་པར་ནུས་མ། །༥། །

ཕྱག་འཚལ་བརྒྱ་བྱིན་མེ་ལྷ་ཚངས་པ། །རླུང་ལྷ་སྣ་ཚོགས་དབང་ཕྱུག་མཆོད་མ། །
འབྱུང་པོ་རོ་ལངས་དྲི་ཟ་རྣམས་དང་། །གནོད་སྦྱིན་ཚོགས་ཀྱིས་མདུན་ནས་བསྟོད་མ། །༦། །

ཕྱག་འཚལ་ཏྲཊ་ཅེས་བྱ་དང་ཕཊ་ཀྱིས། །ཕ་རོལ་འཁྲུལ་འཁོར་རབ་ཏུ་འཇོམས་མ། །
གཡས་བསྐུམ་གཡོན་བརྐྱང་ཞབས་ཀྱིས་མནན་ཏེ། །མེ་འབར་འཁྲུག་པ་ཤིན་ཏུ་འབར་མ། །༧། །

ཕྱག་འཚལ་ཏུ་རེ་འཇིགས་པ་ཆེན་མོ། །བདུད་ཀྱི་དཔའ་བོ་རྣམ་པར་འཇོམས་མ། །
ཆུ་སྐྱེས་ཞལ་ནི་ཁྲོ་གཉེར་ལྡན་མཛད། །དགྲ་བོ་ཐམས་ཅད་མ་ལུས་གསོད་མ། །༨། །

ཕྱག་འཚལ་དཀོན་མཆོག་གསུམ་མཚོན་ཕྱག་རྒྱའི། །སོར་མོས་ཐུགས་ཀར་རྣམ་པར་བརྒྱན་མ། །
མ་ལུས་ཕྱོགས་ཀྱི་འཁོར་ལོས་བརྒྱན་པའི། །རང་གི་འོད་ཀྱི་ཚོགས་རྣམས་འཁྲུག་མ། །༩། །

ཕྱག་འཚལ་རབ་ཏུ་དགའ་བ་བརྗིད་པའི། །དབུ་རྒྱན་འོད་ཀྱི་ཕྲེང་བ་སྤེལ་མ། །
བཞད་པ་རབ་བཞད་ཏུཏྟཱ་ར་ཡིས། །བདུད་དང་འཇིག་རྟེན་དབང་དུ་མཛད་མ། །༡༠། །

ཕྱག་འཚལ་ས་གཞི་སྐྱོང་བའི་ཚོགས་རྣམས། །ཐམས་ཅད་འགུགས་པར་ནུས་པ་ཉིད་མ། །
ཁྲོ་གཉེར་གཡོ་བའི་ཡི་གེ་ཧཱུྃ་གིས། །ཕོངས་པ་ཐམས་ཅད་རྣམ་པར་སྒྲོལ་མ། །༡༡། །

ཕྱག་འཚལ་ཟླ་བའི་དུམ་བུས་དབུ་བརྒྱན། །བརྒྱན་པ་ཐམས་ཅད་ཤིན་ཏུ་འབར་མ། །
རལ་པའི་ཁྲོད་ན་འོད་དཔག་མེད་ལས། །རྟག་པར་ཤིན་ཏུ་འོད་ནི་མཛད་མ། །༡༢། །

ཕྱག་འཚལ་བསྐལ་པའི་ཐ་མའི་མེ་ལྟར། །འབར་བའི་ཕྲེང་བའི་དབུས་ན་གནས་མ། །
གཡས་བརྐྱང་གཡོན་བསྐུམ་ཀུན་ནས་བསྐོར་དགའ། །དགྲ་ཡི་དཔུང་ནི་རྣམ་པར་འཇོམས་མ། །༡༣། །

ཕྱག་ཚལ་ས་གཞིའི་ངོས་ལ་ཕྱག་གི། །མཐིལ་གྱིས་བརྡུང་ཞིང་ཞབས་ཀྱིས་བརྡུང་མ། །
ཁྲོ་གཉེར་ཅན་མཛད་ཡི་གེ་ཧཱུྃ་གིས། །རིམ་པ་བདུན་པོ་རྣམས་ནི་འགེམས་མ། །༡༤། །

ཕྱག་འཚལ་བདེ་མ་དགེ་མ་ཞི་མ། །མྱ་ངན་འདས་ཞི་སྤྱོད་ཡུལ་ཉིད་མ། །
སྭཱ་ཧཱ་ཨོཾ་དང་ཡང་དག་ལྡན་པས། །སྡིག་པ་ཆེན་པོ་འཇོམས་པ་ཉིད་མ། །༡༥། །

ཕྱག་འཚལ་ཀུན་ནས་བསྐོར་རབ་དགའ་བའི། །དགྲ་ཡི་ལུས་ནི་རབ་ཏུ་འགེམས་མ། །
ཡི་གེ་བཅུ་པའི་ངག་ནི་བཀོད་པའི། །རིག་པ་ཧཱུྃ་ལས་སྒྲོལ་མ་ཉིད་མ། །༡༦། །

ཕྱག་འཚལ་ཏུ་རེ་ཞབས་ནི་བརྡབས་པས། །ཧཱུྃ་གི་རྣམ་པའི་ས་བོན་ཉིད་མ། །
རི་རབ་མན་ད་ར་དང་འབིགས་བྱེད། །འཇིག་རྟེན་གསུམ་རྣམས་གཡོ་བ་ཉིད་མ། །༡༧། །

ཕྱག་འཚལ་ལྷ་ཡི་མཚོ་ཡི་རྣམ་པའི། །རི་དྭགས་རྟགས་ཅན་ཕྱག་ན་བསྣམས་མ། །
ཏཱ་ར་གཉིས་བརྗོད་ཕཊ་ཀྱི་ཡི་གེས། །དུག་རྣམས་མ་ལུས་པར་ནི་སེལ་མ། །༡༨། །

ཕྱག་འཚལ་ལྷ་ཡི་ཚོགས་རྣམས་རྒྱལ་པོ། །ལྷ་དང་མི་འམ་ཅི་ཡིས་བསྟེན་མ། །
ཀུན་ནས་གོ་ཆ་དགའ་བའི་བརྗིད་ཀྱིས། །རྩོད་དང་རྨི་ལམ་ངན་པ་སེལ་མ། །༡༩། །

ཕྱག་འཚལ་ཉི་མ་ཟླ་བ་རྒྱས་པའི། །སྤྱན་གཉིས་པོ་ལ་འོད་རབ་གསལ་མ། །
ཧ་ར་གཉིས་བརྗོད་ཏུཏྟཱ་ར་ཡིས། །ཤིན་ཏུ་དྲག་པོའི་རིམས་ནད་སེལ་མ། །༢༠། །

ཕྱག་འཚལ་དེ་ཉིད་གསུམ་རྣམས་བཀོད་པས། །ཞི་བའི་མཐུ་དང་ཡང་དག་ལྡན་མ། །
གདོན་དང་རོ་ལངས་གནོད་སྦྱིན་ཚོགས་རྣམས། །འཇོམས་པ་ཏུ་རེ་རབ་མཆོག་ཉིད་མ། །༢༡། །

རྩ་བའི་སྔགས་ཀྱི་བསྟོད་པ་འདི་དང་། །ཕྱག་འཚལ་བ་ནི་ཉི་ཤུ་རྩ་གཅིག །
ལྷ་མོ་ལ་གུས་ཡང་དག་ལྡན་པའི། །བློ་ལྡན་གང་གིས་རབ་དད་བརྗོད་དེ། །༢༢། །

སྲོད་དང་ཐོ་རངས་ལངས་པར་བྱས་ནས། །དྲན་པས་མི་འཇིགས་ཐམས་ཅད་རབ་སྦྱིར། །
སྡིག་པ་ཐམས་ཅད་རབ་ཏུ་ཞི་བ། །ངན་འགྲོ་ཐམས་ཅད་འཇོམས་པ་ཉིད་དོ། །༢༣། །

རྒྱལ་བ་བྱེ་བ་ཕྲག་བདུན་རྣམས་ཀྱིས། །མྱུར་དུ་དབང་ནི་བསྐུར་བར་འགྱུར་ལ། །
འདི་ལས་ཆེ་བ་ཉིད་ནི་ཐོབ་ཅིང་། །སངས་རྒྱས་གོ་འཕང་མཐར་ཐུག་དེར་འགྲོ། །༢༤། །

དེ་ཡི་དུག་ནི་དྲག་པོ་ཆེན་པོ། །བརྟན་གནས་པ་འམ་གཞན་ཡང་འགྲོ་བ། །
ཟོས་པ་དང་ནི་འཐུངས་པ་ཉིད་ཀྱང་། །དྲན་པས་རབ་ཏུ་སེལ་བ་ཉིད་ཐོབ། །༢༥། །

གདོན་དང་རིམས་དང་དུག་གིས་གཟིར་བའི། །སྡུག་བསྔལ་ཚོགས་ནི་རྣམ་པར་སྤོང་སྟེ། །
སེམས་ཅན་གཞན་པ་རྣམས་ལ་ཡང་ངོ་། །གཉིས་གསུམ་བདུན་དུ་མངོན་པར་བརྗོད་ན། །༢༦། །

བུ་འདོད་པས་ནི་བུ་ཐོབ་འགྱུར་ཞིང་། །ནོར་འདོད་པས་ནི་ནོར་རྣམས་ཉིད་ཐོབ། །
འདོད་པ་ཐམས་ཅད་ཐོབ་པར་འགྱུར་ཏེ། །བགེགས་རྣམས་མེད་ཅིང་སོ་སོར་འཇོམས་འགྱུར། །༢༧། །

། །སངས་རྒྱས་དང་བྱང་ཆུབ་སེམས་དཔའ་ཐམས་ཅད་ཀྱིས་གསུངས་པ་བཅོམ་ལྡན་འདས་མ་
འཕགས་མ་ལྷ་མོ་སྒྲོལ་མ་ལ་ཡང་དག་པར་རྫོགས་པའི་སངས་རྒྱས་ཀྱིས་
བསྟོད་པ་ཕྱག་འཚལ་བ་ཉི་ཤུ་རྩ་གཅིག་གིས་བསྟོད་པ་སྒྲོལ་མ་ལས་སྣ་
ཚོགས་བསྟན་པའི་རྒྱུད་ལས་བྱུང་བ་རྫོགས་སོ། ། ། །

In the edited text, syllables that have an alternative reading worth considering are underlined. Many of these are simply different spellings or different tenses of verbs (at 26b, past, present and future are all found, and all make sense!).

In the list of variants, '6d *kyis* (*kyi* LS1)' implies that in line d of verse 6, L and S1 erroneously read *kyi* while all the other texts are consistent with the correct reading, *kyis*. '+Skt' indicates that that is the literal Tibetan translation of the established Sanskrit text. Some forty-odd evident misprints of no interest are omitted.

Translators' homage: *Oṃ* ADGK, omitted JLT.
1a *dpa' mo* (*dpal mo* AD). 1d *bye* (*phye* T).
2b *gang ba* (*gang ma* A).
3a *gser* 'gold' (*ser* 'yellow' GK).
5a *tuttā ra* (*tuttā re* AJ); *yi ges* (*yi ge* JL). 5c *bdun* (*gsum* $S_4$).

6d *kyis* (*kyi* $LS_1$).

7a *traṭ* $ADS_1S_4$+Skt, *trad* GKLQT (*ṭat* J). 7c *bskum* $AJLQS_1S_4T$, *bskums* DGK; *brkyang* $AJLQS_1S_4T$, *brkyangs* DGK. 7d *'khrug* $ADGJKS_1$, *'khrugs* $LQS_4T$; *pa* ADGJKLQ, *ma* $S_1S_4$.

(8 and 9 interchanged $S_4$). 8a *tu re* (*tu res* $S_1$); *chen mo* (*chen po* $KS_1$). 8d *ma lus* (*rab tu* $S_4$).

9a *rgya'i* (*rgya* $S_4$). 9d *'khrug* $ADGJKLS_4T$, *'khrugs* $QS_1$.

10a *dga' ba* (*dga' bas* $S_1$, *dga' bar* $S_4$). 10b *phreng* $AGJKLQS_1S_4$, *'phreng* DT. 10c *tuttā ra* $ADKLS_4T$ (*tuttā re* $S_1$, *tāre* G).

11b *nus pa* $ADJQS_1S_4$, *nus ma* KLT. 11c *g.yo ba'i* $ADKLQS_1T$, *g.yo ba* $JS_4$. 11d *phongs* $ADJKLQS_4$, *'phongs* $GS_1T$; *rnam par* (*rab tu* $S_4$).

12a *dum bus* $AJKLS_1S_4T$+Skt, *rtse mos* DGQ; *brgyan* $AGJKLS_4T$, *rgyan* $DQS_1$+Skt. 12c *khrod na* DJKL, *khrod nas* $AQS_1$, *khur na* $GS_4T$+Skt. 12d *ni* $ADGLS_1$ (→ Skt *kiraṇadhruve*), *rab* $JKQS_4$ (→ *kiraṇoddhruve*).

13a *bskal pa'i* $KS_1$, *bskal ba'i* A, *skal ba'i* Q, *bskal pa* $JLS_4T$, *bskal ba* DG; *tha* $ADJKQS_1S_4$, *mtha'* GLT. 13b *phreng* $AGJKLQS_1S_4$, *'phreng* DT; *gnas* (*bzhugs* J). 13c *brkyang* $AJLS_1S_4T$ (*brgyad* Q), *brkyangs* DGK; *bskum* $AJLS_4T$, *bskums* DGK; *dga'* $DGJS_1$, *dga'i* KQ (*kun 'khor dga' ba'i* $S_4$), *dgas* LT.

14b *brdung* $ADGKLS_1$, *brdungs* $S_4$, *rdung* JQT. 14c *can mdzad* (*spyan mdzad* K, *dun mdzad* Q, *g.yo ba'i* $S_4$). 14d *'gems* (*'gegs* $S_4$, *'gengs* J).

15b *zhi* (*shing* $S_4$). 15c *ldan pas* DGKLT, *ldan ma* $JQS_1S_4$+Skt, *ldan mas* A.

16a *rab* (*bar* $S_1$); *dga' ba'i* $ADGKLQS_1S_4$, *dga' bas* JT. 16b *lus* (*dpung* $S_4$); *rab tu* $ADGLQS_1S_4T$+Skt, *rnam par* JK. 16c *bcu pa'i* (*bcu po'i* T); *bkod pa'i* ADGJKLQT, *bkod pas* $S_1S_4$. 16d *rig pa* (*rig pa'i* $S_1$); *sgrol ma* $ADGJKQS_1S_4T$, *sgron ma* L (= *dīpa*).

17a *tu re* $JKQS_4$, *tu re'i* $ADGLS_1T$; *ni* (*kyis* $S_4$). 17b *gi* ADGJKLQT, *yig* $S_1$+Skt. 17c *manda ra* $JQS_1$, *man da ra* DT, *man dā ra* AL, *mandha ra* $GKS_4$. 17d *gsum rnams* (*gsum po* J).

18b *bsnams* $ADGJKLS_4T$, *gnas* $QS_1$+Skt. 18c *tā ra* (*tā re* QT). 18d *par* $ADGJLQS_1T$, *pa* $KS_4$.

19a *rnams rgyal po* AKLQT, *kyi rgyal po* $JS_1$, *rgyal po dang* $DGS_4$.

20c *ha ra* (*hā ra* D, *tā ra* $S_4$); *tuttā ra* (*tuttā rā* J, *tuttā re* $S_1$). 20d *nad* ADGJKL, *ni* $QS_1S_4T$.

21a *pas* $ADLS_1S_4T$, *pa'i* GJQ. 21d *tu re* (*tu re'i* $S_1$).

22a *kyi* AGLT, *kyis* DGJK (G quotes the line twice). 22c *pa'i* ADLT, *pas* GJK. 22d *dad* GJLT, *dang* ADK; *de* AK, *pas* DGJL, *pa* T.

23c *zhi ba* ADJLT, *zhi bas* GK. 23d *do* ADGJLT (*thob* K).

24c *'di las* ADKLT, *'di la* GJ+Skt; *thob* ADGKLT, *'thob* J.

25a *de yi* (*de yis* J). 25d *thob* ADGJLT, *'thob* K.

26b *spong* ADGT, *spang* L, *spangs* JK.

27b *thob* ADGT, *'thob* JKL. 27c *te* ADGJLT, *la* K.

Colophon: that reproduced above is from L. T is similar but omits *yang dag par rdzogs pa'i sangs rgyas kyis bstod pa*. J: *bCom ldan 'das ma sgrol ma la yang dag par rdzogs pa'i sangs rgyas rnam par snang mdzad chen pos bstod pa gsungs pa/*, K the same but starting *rJe btsun 'phags ma sgrol ma la* and adding *rdzogs so* at the end. J adds: *slob dpon 'phags pa klu sgrub nas brgyud pa lo tsā ba gnyan gyis bsgyur ba/ rje btsun chen po grags pa rgyal mtshan gyis gtan la phab pa'o//*. The other texts do not give a colophon for the *Praise*.

# *Appendix 2 English Phonetics and Translation of the Tibetan Version of the Praise in Twenty-one Homages*

OṂ! Je-tsün-ma p'ak-ma dröl-ma-la ch'ak-ts'äl-lo!
OṂ! Homage to the Venerable Ārya-Tārā!

1 Ch'ak-ts'äl! Dröl-ma! nyur-ma! pa-mo!
Homage! Tārā, swift, heroic!

chän-ni kä-chik lok-d'ang dra-ma!
Eyes like lightning instantaneous!

Jik-ten sum-gön ch'u-kye zhäl-gy'i
Sprung from op'ning stamens of the

g'e-sar j'e-wa-lä-ni j'ung-ma!
Lord of Three Worlds' tear-born lotus!

2 Ch'ak-ts'äl! Tön-käi da-wa kün-tu
Homage! She whose face combines a

g'ang-wa gya-ni tsek-päi zhäl-ma!
hundred autumn moons at fullest!

Kar-ma tong-tr'ak ts'ok-pa-nam-kyi
Blazing with light-rays resplendent

rap-tu ch'e-wäi ö rap-bar-ma!
as a thousand-star collection!

3 Ch'ak-ts'äl! Ser-ngo ch'u-nä kye-kyi
Homage! Golden blue one, lotus,

pä-mä ch'ak-ni nam-par gyän-ma!
water-born, in hand adornèd!

Jin-pa tsön-drü ka-t'up zhi-wa
Giving, Effort, Calm, Austerities,

zö-pa sam-tän chö-yül-nyi-ma!
Patience, Meditation Her field!

4 Ch'ak-ts'äl! D'e-zhin-shek-päi tsuk-tor
Homage! Crown of *Tathāgatas,*

t'a-yä nam-par gyäl-war chö-ma!
She who goes in endless triumph!

Ma-lü p'a-röl-ch'in-pa t'op-päi
Honoured much by Conqu'rors' Offspring,

gyäl-wäi sä-kyi shin-tu ten-ma!
having reached ev'ry Perfection!

5 Ch'ak-ts'äl! TUTTĀRA HŪṂ yi-g'e
Homage! Filling with TUTTĀRA,

dö-d'ang ch'ok-d'ang nam-k'a g'ang-ma!
HŪṂ, Desire, Direction and Space!

Jik-ten dün-po zhap-kyi nän-te
Trampling with Her feet the sev'n worlds,

lü-pa me-par guk-par nü-ma!
able to draw forth all [beings]!

6 Ch'ak-ts'äl! Gya-j'in Me-lha Ts'ang-pa
Homage! Worshipped by the All-Lord(s),

Lung-lha Na-ts'ok wang-ch'uk ch'ö-ma!
Śakra, Agni, Brahmā, Marut!

Jung-po ro-lang dr'i-za-nam-d'ang
Honoured by the hosts of spirits,

nö-jin ts'ok-kyi dün-nä tö-ma!
corpse-raisers, *gandharvas, yakṣas*!

7 Ch'ak-ts'äl! TRÄṬ-che-j'a-d'ang PHÄṬ-kyi
Homage! With Her TRAṬ and PHAṬ sounds

p'a-röl tr'ül-k'or rap-tu jom-ma!
crusher of foes' magic diagrams!

Yä-kum yön-kyang zhap-kyi nän-te
Putting Her feet left out, right back,

me-bar tr'uk-pa shin-tu bar-ma!
blazing up in raging fire-blaze!

8 Ch'ak-ts'äl! TURE! jik-pa ch'en-mo!
Homage! Ture, very dreadful!

dü-kyi pa-wo nam-par jom-ma!
Destroyer of Māra's champions!

Ch'u-kye zhäl-ni tr'o-nyer dän-dzä
She with frowning lotus visage

dra-wo t'am-chä ma-lü sö-ma!
who is slayer of all enemies!

9 Ch'ak-ts'äl! Kön-ch'ok sum-ts'ön ch'ak-gyäi
Homage! She adorned with fingers,

sor-mö t'uk-kar nam-par gyän-ma!
at Her heart, in Three-Jewel *mudrā*!

Ma-lü ch'ok-kyi k'or-lö gyän-päi
She with universal wheels adornèd,

rang-g'i ö-kyi ts'ok-nam tr'uk-ma!
warring masses of their own light!

10 Ch'ak-ts'äl! Rap-tu ga-wa ji-päi
Homage! She of Great Joy, shining,

u-gyän ö-kyi tr'eng-wa pel-ma!
diadem emitting light-wreaths!

Zhä-pa rap-zhä TUTTĀRA-yi
Mirthful, laughing with TUTTĀRE,

dü-d'ang jik-ten wang-d'u dzä-ma!
Subjugating *māras, devas*!

11 Ch'ak-ts'äl! sa-zhi kyong-wäi ts'ok-nam
Homage! She able to summon

t'am-chä guk-par nü-pa-nyi-ma!
all earth-guardians and their trains!

Tr'o-nyer yo-wäi yi-g'e HŪṂ-g'i
Shaking, frowning, with Her HŪṂ-sign

p'ong-pa t'am-chä nam-par dröl-ma!
saving from ev'ry misfortune!

12 Ch'ak-ts'äl! Da-wäi d'um-b'ü u-gyän
Homage! Crown adorned with crescent

gyän-pa t'am-chä shin-tu bar-ma!
moon, all ornaments most shining!

Räl-päi tr'ö-na Ö-pak-me-lä
Producing, from Amitābha

tak-par shin-tů ö-ni dzä-ma!
in Her hair-mass, always much light!

13 Ch'ak-ts'äl! Käl-päi t'a-mäi me-tar
Homage! She 'mid wreath ablaze like

bar-wäi tr'eng-wäi ü-na nä-ma!
eon-ending fire abiding!

Yä-kyang yön-kum kün-nä kor ga
Right stretched, left bent, turning-glad ones'

dra-yi pung-ni nam-par jom-ma!
troops of enemies destroying!

14 Ch'ak-ts'äl! Sa-zhi ngö-la ch'ak-g'i
Homage! She who smites the ground with

t'il-gy'i nün-ching zhap-kyi dung-ma!
Her palm, and with Her foot beats it!

Tr'o-nyer chän-dzä yi-g'e HŪṂ-g'i
Frowning, with the letter HŪṂ the

rim-pa dün-po-nam-ni gem-ma!
seven underworlds She conquers!

15 Ch'ak-ts'äl! De-ma! ge-ma! zhi-ma!
Homage! Happy, Virtuous, Peaceful!

Nya-ngän-dä-zhi chö-yül-nyi-ma!
She whose field is Peace, *Nirvāṇa*!

SVĀHĀ OṂ-d'ang yang-d'ak-dän-pä
With that having OṂ and SVĀHĀ,

dik-pa ch'en-po jom-pa-nyi-ma!
of the great downfall destroyer!

16 Ch'ak-ts'äl! Kün-nä kor rap-ga-wäi
Homage! Of those glad at turning

dra-yi lü-ni rap-tu gem-ma!
tearing foes' bodies asunder!

Yi-g'e chu-päi ngak-ni kö-päi
Liberating with HŪṂ-mantra,

rik-pa HŪṂ-lä dröl-ma-nyi-ma!
word-array of the ten syllables!

17 Ch'ak-ts'äl! TURE! zhap-ni dap-pä
Homage! Swift One! The foot-stamper

HŪṂ-g'i nam-päi sa-b'ön-nyi-ma!
with for seed the letter HŪṂ's shape!

Ri-rap Mändara-d'ang Bik-j'e
She who shakes the triple world and

jik-ten sum-nam yo-wa-nyi-ma!
Meru, Mandara and Vindhya!

18 Ch'ak-ts'äl! Lha-yi ts'o-yi nam-päi
Homage! Holding in Her hand the

ri-d'ak-tak-chän ch'ak-na nam-ma!
deer-marked moon, of *deva*-lake form!

TĀRA nyi-jö PHÄṬ-kyi yi-g'e
With twice-spoken TĀRĀ and PHAṬ,

d'uk-nam ma-lü-par-ni sel-ma!
totally dispelling poison!

19 Ch'ak-ts'äl! Lha-yi ts'ok-nam gyäl-po
Homage! She whom god-host rulers,

lha-d'ang mi-am-chi-yi ten-ma!
gods and *Kinnaras* do honour!

Kün-nä g'o-ch'a ga-wäi ji-kyi
She whose joyful splendour dispels

tsö-d'ang mi-lam ngän-pa sel-ma!
armoured ones' bad dreams and conflicts!

20 Ch'ak-ts'äl! Nyi-ma da-wa gyä-päi
Homage! She whose eyes are bright with

chän-nyi-po-la ö rap-säl-ma!
radiance of sun or full moon!

ḤARA nyi-jö TUTTĀRA-yi
With twice HARA and TUTTĀRE

shin-tu dr'ak-pöi rim-nä sel-ma!
Driver-out of chronic fever!

21 Ch'ak-ts'äl! D'e-nyi sum-nam kö-pä
Homage! Full of liberating

zhi-wäi t'u-d'ang yang-d'ak-dän-ma!
power by set of three Realities!

Dön-d'ang ro-lang nö-jin ts'ok-nam
Crushing crowds of spirits, *yakṣas*

jom-pa! TURE! Rap-ch'ok-nyi-ma!
and corpse-raisers! Supreme! TURE!

22 Tsa-wäi ngak-kyi tö-pa di-d'ang
This praise of the root mantras and

ch'ak-ts'äl-wa-ni nyi-shu-tsa-chik*
twenty-one-fold homage* — for one

Lha-mo-la g'ü yang-d'ak-dän-päi
Who recites it, wise and pious,

lo-dän g'ang-g'i rap-d'ä jö-d'e,
full of faith towards the Goddess,

* At this point, the Tibetans generally break off their recitation.

23 Sö-d'ang t'o-rang lang-par j'ä-nä
And remembers it at even

dr'än-pä, mi-jik t'am-chä rap-ter,
and at dawn on rising, it grants

Dik-pa t'am-chä rap-tu zhi-wa,
Ev'ry fearlessness, quells all sins,

ngän-dro t'am-chä jom-pa-nyi-d'o.
and destroys all bad migrations.

24 Gyäl-wa j'e-wa-tr'ak-dün-nam-kyi
Quickly he'll be consecrated

nyur-d'u wang-ni kur-war gyur-la;
by sev'n times ten million Conqu'rors.

Di-lä ch'e-wa-nyi-ni t'op-ching,
Thereby gaining greatness, he will

sang-gyä g'o-p'ang t'ar-t'uk d'er dro.
reach at last the rank of Buddha.

25 D'e-yi d'uk-ni dr'ak-po ch'en-po,
The most dreadful poison, whether

tän-nä-pa-am zhän-yang dro-wa,
animal, or plant or min'ral,

Zö-pa d'ang-ni t'ung-pa-nyi-kyang,
Whether he's devoured or drunk it,

dr'än-pä rap-tu sel-wa-nyi t'op.
meets its end through his rememb'ring.

26 Dön-d'ang rim-d'ang d'uk-g'i zir-wäi
It completely stops the pain of

duk-ngäl ts'ok-ni nam-par pong-te,
those whom spirits, fevers, poisons

Sem-chän zhän-pa-nam-la yang-ngo.
Afflict—other beings' also.

Nyi-sum dün-d'u ngön-par jö-na,
On reciting twice three sevens,

27 B'u-dö-pä-ni b'u t'op-gyur-zhing,
One who wants a child will get one,

nor-dö-pä-ni nor-nam-nyi t'op,
one desiring wealth will find wealth,

Dö-pa t'am-chä t'op-par gyur-te,
One obtains all one's desires; no

gek-nam me-ching so-sor jom-gyur.
hindrances, each will be subdued.

The speech of all Buddhas and Bodhisattvas, the praise of the Lady Ārya-Tārā by the Complete and Perfect Buddha (Mahā-Vairocana[JK]), the Praise in Twenty-one Homages, from the Tantra teaching all the rites of Tārā, is complete.[L(T)]

It was translated [into Tibetan] by the translator Nyän, of the lineage of Master Ārya-Nāgārjuna, and revised by the great Jetsün Dr'ak-pa gyäl-ts'än.[J]

# *Appendix 3*
# *The Lineages from Sūryagupta*

1 Lineage of Tārā with Seventeen Deities, according to Bu-tön Rinpoche (Bu ston Rin po che, 1290–1364). (*Collected Works, 16* (MA), 14.7–15.2. Given as prayer entirely in Sanskrit.)

2 Lineage of the *maṇḍala* of Tārā with Seventeen Deities, according to P'ak-pa ('Phags pa bLo gros rgyal mtshan dPal bzang po, 1235–80). (*Sa skya pa'i bka' 'bum, 6,* 266.3.1-3. Names mostly in Tibetan.)

3 Lineage of Vajra-tārā *Sādhana*, according to P'ak-pa. (Ib., 267.4.3–4. Names all in Sanskrit.)

4 Lineage of the Mäl-gyo translation of Sūryagupta's Tārā cycle (S1 and S2), according to Gö Lotsawa ('Gos Lo tsā ba, 1392–1481). (*BA* 1051.) Six names following Rong pa rGwa lo have been omitted.

5 Lineage of the Tr'o-p'u Lotsawa (Khro phu Lo tsā ba) translation of Sūryagupta's Tārā cycle (S4), according to the colophon of S4 (P2560).

6 The same, according to Gö Lotsawa. (*BA* 1051.)

(1)

ĀRYA-TĀRĀ
|
Nāgārjuna
|
SŪRYAGUPTA
|
Dāna-śrī
|
Mañjuśrī
|
Ratnakīrti
|
Grags pa rgyal mtshan (1147–1216)
|
bSod nams rtse mo (1142–82)
|
Shes rab grags
|
Tshul khrims brtan pa
|
Yon tan blo gros
|
Shes rab gzhon nu

(2, 3)

Śākyamuni[3]
|
ĀRYA-TĀRĀ
|
RAVIGUPTA
|
Candragarbha
|
Jetāri
|
Vāgīśvara-kīrti
|
Śraddhākara-varman
|
Tathāgata-rakṣita
|
Dāna-śrī
|
Mañjuśrī
|
Mal gyo Lo tsā ba bLo gros grags pa
|
Pu tser Lo tsā ba
|
dBang phyug rin chen dpal[2]
dBang phyug grags pa[3]
|
Chos kyi seng ge
|
bLo gros brtan pa
|
Nam mkha' grags
|
'Phags pa bLo gros rgyal mtshan dPal bzang po (1235–80)

(4)

TĀRĀ
SŪRYAGUPTA
Candragarbha
Jetāri
Vāgīśvara
Śraddhākara
Tathāgata-rakṣita
Dāna-śīla
Mal gyo Lo tsā ba
Sa chen Kun dga' snying po (1092–1158)
bSod nams rtse mo (1142–82)
rJe btsun Grags pa rgyal mtshan (1147–1216)
'Chims chos seng
Dharmasvāmin 'Jam gsar
Rong pa rGwa lo
'Gos Lo tsā ba (1392–1481)

(5, 6)

TĀRĀ
Ven. Ānanda
Arhant Madhyāntika
Arhant Śāṇavāsa
Arhant Kṛṣṇavāsa
SŪRYAGUPTA of Kashmir
Rāhula-śrī
Vinada-śrī
Mahāpaṇḍita Śākya-śrī-bhadra of Kashmir (1127–1225)
Khro phu Lo tsā ba Byams pa dpal
bLa ma bSod nams rgyal mtshan[5]
bLa chen bSod dbang[6]
Rin po che pa
Tshad ma'i skyes bu
Bu ston Rin po che (1290–1364)

In the chart, the names of those believed to be Indian are given in Sanskrit, and of those believed to be Tibetan in Tibetan – in transliteration, since here it is correct identification that counts, not pronunciation. The vertical spacing has been adjusted so that a horizontal line should cut each lineage at approximately the same time, e.g. Shes rab grags (1) may be expected to be more or less contemporary with Chos kyi seng ge (2, 3), who in turn could well be the same person as 'Chims Chos seng (4).

Dates are given when known, after *BA* or Tucci. Some other information on the Indians appearing follows.

*The Arhants Madhyāntika and Śāṇavāsa* are reputed to have introduced Buddhism to Kashmir in the first century after the *Nirvāṇa*, or at any rate no later than the time of Aśoka (272–236 BC). Śāṇavāsa, 'Hempen Robe', is so called because all his life he wore a hempen robe he is supposed to have been born with; Hiuan-tsang saw it at a monastery near Bāmiyān. (Lamotte, *Histoire*, 226–232).

*Arhant Kṛṣṇavāsa* must be the *Ārya* Kṛṣṇa who, according to Tāranātha, combatted the personalist heresy in Kashmir in the time of Aśoka and reintroduced the Dharma to Ceylon (*HBI* 70–72; Lamotte, *Histoire*, 771).

*Sūryagupta/Ravigupta*: see above, pp. 238ff.

*Candragarbha* is obviously not the Prince Candragarbha who became Atīśa. I find no mention of him elsewhere, nor of Rāhula-śrī and Vinada-śrī (*BA*: Vinda-śrī).

*Jetāri*: according to *HBI* 290–2, Jetāri the elder was born in the reign of King Vanapāla (probably c.870). Although as a result of practising Mañjughoṣa when he was seven he acquired all branches of learning effortlessly, he did not receive his *paṇḍita* degree until the time of King Mahāpāla (c.930?). Tārā, in a vision, told him to compose treatises on Mahāyāna. The Jetāri who was a teacher of Atīśa c.1010 (*BA* 243) was presumably the younger one.

*Vāgīśvara-kīrti*: may be the Vāgīśvara-kīrti also known as Piṇḍo *ācārya*, who heard the Kālacakra system from its introducer Tsi-lu-pa (tenth century) (*BA* 757–8). There was also a Vāgīśvara-kīrti who was one of the Gate-keeper Scholars of Vikramaśīla (c.1000), probably a different person (*BA* 763); one in Nepāl, c.1070, also called Pham mthing pa (*BA* 227); and yet another in the fourteenth century (*BA* 801, see Chart 2, p. 177).

*Śraddhākara(-varman)* gave an empowerment of Guhyasamāja to the great Translator Rin chen bzang po (958–1055) (*BA* 373, 328), so may be dated in the tenth century.

*Tathāgata-rakṣita*: Tantric Master at Vikramaśīla, apparently around 950 AD according to Tāranātha's data (*HBI* 327).

*Dāna-śīla or Dāna-śrī* was a disciple of Nāro-pa (956–1040). He was one of Atīśa's teachers (c.1010) (*BA* 243) and also a teacher of Atīśa's younger contemporary Khyung po rnal 'byor (*BA* 729). *BA* calls him 'the great Dā' (Dā chen po). He is sometimes confused with other Dāna-śīlas, one of whom went to Tibet in the early ninth century and collaborated on the *Mahāvyutpatti* dictionary and many translations (*HBI* 259). Another is reported in Tibet in the 1250's (*BA* 962, 1058).

*Mañjuśrī* was the Indian *upādhyāya* who worked with Mal gyo (colophons of S1 and S2), evidently c.1100 AD.

*Ratnakīrti*: the logician of this name flourished c.1000–1050 (Mimaki, p.6) and was teacher of Ratnākara-śānti, one of the Gate-keeper Scholars (c.1000) (Vidyabhusana, 338). A Ratnakīrti of the late fourteenth century is also known (*BA* 801, 803; see Chart 2).

# *List of abbreviations*

| | |
|---|---|
| Ā. | *Ātmanepada* |
| Acad. | Academy |
| acc. | accusative |
| *AdK* | *Abhidharma-kośa*, tr. La Vallée Poussin |
| attrib. | attributed to |
| B | Bu-ston, *Collected Works, 16*, 430ff. |
| b. | born |
| *BA* | Roerich (tr.), *The Blue Annals* |
| C | century |
| c. | *circa* |
| caus. | causative |
| CD | Chandra Das, *Tibetan-English Dictionary* |
| Ch | dGe bshes Chos kyi grags pa, *brDa dag ming tshig gsal ba.* |
| Chap. | Chapter |
| Coll. | College |
| Colln | Collection |
| D | Derge (sDe dge) edition of Kg; Ngül-ch'u Dharmabhadra; Dagyab, *Tibetan Dictionary.* |
| d. | died |
| Dat. | dative |
| dictt. | dictionaries |
| E | Edgerton, *Buddhist Hybrid Sanskrit Dictionary;* East |

| | |
|---|---|
| ed. | edited, edition, editor |
| *EHNI* | Chattopadhyaya, *Early History of North India* |
| Eng | English |
| esp. | especially |
| fem. | feminine |
| Fig. | Figure |
| fl. | flourished |
| Fr | French |
| fr. | from |
| G | Ge-dün dr'up-pa, see. p. 111. |
| Gen. | Genitive |
| GL | Geshe Thubten Lodan |
| *GR* | Tāranātha's *The Golden Rosary* |
| *HBI* | Tāranātha's *History of Buddhism in India*, tr. Chimpa & Chattopadhyaya |
| ib. | *ibīdem*, in the same place |
| impv. | imperative |
| Ind. | Indian |
| Inst. | Institute, Institut |
| Int. | International |
| J | Jetsün Dr'ak-pa gyäl-ts'än, see p. 111 |
| Kg | Kangyur (*bKa' 'gyur*) |
| L | Lhasa edition of Kg |
| lit. | literally |
| M | Godefroy de Blonay, *Matériaux* |
| *MA* | Candrakīrti, *Madhyamakâvatāra* |
| masc. | masculine |
| *MMK* | *Mañjuśrī-mūla-kalpa* |
| *MN* | *Majjhima-nikāya* (Pali Text Soc. ed.) |
| *Mppś* | Lamotte, *Traité* (*Mahā-prajñā-pāramitā-śāstra*) |
| *MSA* | *Mahāyāna-sūtrâlaṃkāra*, ed. & tr. Lévi |
| *MT* | Datta (ed.), *Mystic Tales of Lāma Tāranātha* |
| *Mvy* | *Mahā-vyutpatti* (quoted in Lokesh Chandra's *Dictionary*) |
| MW | Monier-Williams, *Sanskrit-English Dictionary* |
| N | Nar-t'ang (sNar thang) edition of Kg; North |
| n. | name; note |
| n.d. | no date |
| NLD | Nando lal Dey, *Geographical Dictionary* |
| no. | number |

| | |
|---|---|
| nom. | nominative |
| NY | New York |
| P | D.T. Suzuki (ed.): *The Tibetan Tripiṭaka, Peking Edition* – kept in the library of the Otani University, Kyoto. Tokyo-Kyoto, Tibetan Tripitaka Research Inst., 1957. |
| p. | page |
| part. | participle |
| pbk. | paperback |
| pf. | perfect |
| pl. | plural |
| pp. | pages |
| pres. | present |
| pron. | pronounced |
| Pubg, Pubn | Publishing, Publication |
| Q | Quadrilingual blockprint, see p. 109 |
| repr. | reprinted |
| rev. | revised |
| rG | *rGyud 'bum, rGyud 'grel* |
| rg | reigned |
| S | Sūryagupta; South |
| S1 . . . S5 | Texts of Sūryagupta's Tārā cycle, see pp. 109–11 |
| Ser. | Series |
| sing. | singular |
| Skt | Sanskrit |
| Soc. | Society |
| T | Tog Palace manuscript of Kg |
| Tg | Tängyur (*bsTan 'gyur*) |
| Tib | Tibetan |
| tr. | translation, translated, translator |
| Univ. | University |
| V1, V2, V3 | *Vajra-tārā-sādhanas*, P4308, P4309 and P4312. |
| Vol. | Volume |
| W | West |

# Notes

*Notes to Introduction*

1 See the fine study by Mallar Ghosh, *Development of Buddhist Iconography in Eastern India*, particularly Chap. II.
2 This group remained popular for several centuries; Ghosh illustrates many examples.
3 Ghosh, 22–24.
4 See p. 96 and Ghosh, Chap. II.
5 Toynbee 295–7. Cybele was a Queen-bee-goddess whose priests, swarming round her, ecstatically castrated themselves.
6 Graves, *The White Goddess*, esp. pp. 424, 394–8. The orgiastic rites seem to have centred on 'Mary Gipsy', or St Mary of Egypt, a prostitute turned desert anchorite who became identified with a whole string of pagan goddesses. For the importance of the Virgin Mary in the Middle Ages see Adams, *Mont-St-Michel and Chartres*.
7 Apuleius, *The Golden Ass*, tr. William Adlington (1566) (quoted by Graves, 72).
8 Graves, 386, after John Skelton; Neumann, 319.
9 Graves, 24, 70, etc.
10 Neumann, *The Great Mother*.
11 Neumann, 233.
12 *Hevajra-tantra*, II.iv.32. My tr.
13 Typically, earth: Locanā; water: Māmakī; fire: Pāṇḍara-

vāsinī; air: Tārā.

14 *Hevajra-tantra*, II.ii. 53–57.

15 Lama Yeshe, 173–4.

16 Neumann, 330.

17 Van der Post, 158.

18 Neumann, 55–59.

19 Graves, 476.

20 See Graves, Chap. 26; Van der Post; Neumann, xlii, etc.

21 Occasionally a problem may arise because the descriptions in the Sūtras concern male Buddhas. The obvious case is that of one of the thirty-two Marks of a Great Being, 'His male organ is hidden in a sheath like that of an elephant.' Since Tārā has certainly collected the causes for this Mark, She may be deemed to possess it latently in case She should ever wish to assume a male body; or perhaps She has some corresponding peculiarity with the same significance, viz. having many spiritual offspring (see Conze, *Large Sutra*, 660 (13)).

22 In *Kriyā-tantra*, where there is no Action Family, Tārā belongs to the Lotus Family of Amitābha.

23 See *Cullavagga*, X.1 (tr. Horner, *Book of the Discipline*, 5, 352–6); Bu-ston, ii. 78–9, for Theravādin and Mūlasarvāstivādin versions respectively.

24 *Bahudhātuka-sutta, MN, III*, 65.

25 Bhikkhu Bodhi (tr.), *The Discourse on the All-Embracing Net of Views*, 262.

26 Kern, 252; Paul, 189.

27 Kern, 417; Paul, 169–70.

28 Including goddesses and *nāgīs* as well as human women.

29 See for example Rhie.

30 Nam-mkha'i snying-po, *Mother of Knowledge*, tr. Tarthang Tulku, 102.

31 Gega Lama, 15, 27–8, 36–7; *BA* 219.

32 By Nam-mkha'i snying-po, see n. 30.

33 *gCod*, see Tucci 87–92. Two versions of Ma-chik's biography, with next to nothing in common: *BA* 219–226, Allione 150–187. The prophecy: Nam-mkha'i snying-po, 102.

34 *Sa skya pa'i bka' 'bum*, 4, 83.2.5.

35 To translate *yakṣa* as 'harm-giver' or *nāga* as 'dragon', because in Tibet the Indian *yakṣa* was identified with a Tibetan spirit called a 'harm-giver' and in China the Indian *nāga* was held to correspond with the Chinese

dragon, is also thoroughly misleading in Indian texts, especially as the unsuspecting reader is likely to take 'harm-giver' literally – *yakṣas* are usually beneficent.

36 Note that the aspirates *g', j', d', b'* are in fact voiceless, like *k', ch', t', p'*, from which they differ only in tone.

## *Notes to the Prologue*

1 Tib. *sNa tshogs pa'i 'od*. Some of the proper names in this text are given by Tāranātha in transliterated Sanskrit, and for some others the Skt. original is known from other texts (source in Lokesh Chandra's dictionary, unless otherwise stated). For others in this section, as here, the original is uncertain, so they will simply be translated into English.

Buddhist cosmology asserts the existence of countless different universes, or world-systems (*loka-dhātu*); our own, according to the Sūtras, is the universe called Sahā. It also asserts that time has no beginning, but every cosmical period or eon (*kalpa*) was preceded by an earlier eon.

2 Tib. *Ye shes zla ba*, probably = *Jñāna-candrā*.

3 Tāranātha gives both the Skt. and its Tib. translation, *rNam par rgyas pa*.

4 Highest heaven of the Realm of Desire, ruled by Māra, the Buddhist Satan who tempts those seeking Enlightenment.

5 Tib. *gDung ma* = *Vatsalā* (Lokesh Chandra: *gdung ba*, 15).

6 Tib. *Myur ma* = *Turā* (see *Praise in Twenty-one Homages*).

7 Tib. *dPa' mo* = *Vīrā* (ib.)

8 Tib. *Thogs pa med pa* = *Apratibaddha, Apratigha*.

9 Tib. *Dri ma med pa'i 'od kyi snang ba*. Many possible Skt forms, such as *Vimala-jyotiṣ-prabha*.

10 Tib. *bZang po chen po*.

11 This refers to a chronological division of the teaching of Tantra into six 'encouragements' (*dbugs dbyung*), taught in the Heruka Tantra.

12 This title, given to Tārā in the Tantra which we translate below, identifies Her with Prajñā-pāramitā, the Perfection of Wisdom, who is called 'Mother of the Conquerors' (*jināna mātā*) in *Ratna-guṇa-saṃcaya-gāthā* I.15 (Yuyama, 207), probably the earliest Perfection of Wisdom Sūtra.

13 Tāranātha's principal Guru was the Indian master, Buddhagupta.

14 *mKha 'gro ma gsang ba'i thig le*. Apparently not included in the Kangyur (Tibetan canon).
15 Śākyamuni Buddha.
16 For *mthag*, read *'thag*.
17 *Alakāvatī*, *Aṭakāvatī* or *Aḍakavatī* (Tib. *lCang lo can*) is the Pure Land of Vajrapāṇi, 'the great *yakṣa*' (Conze (tr), *The Perfection of Wisdom in Eight Thousand Lines*, 205), said to be on the south slope of Mount Meru (*BA* 1041).
18 Indrabhūti was a king of Oḍḍiyāna in the eighth century, renowned as a *siddha* and tantric commentator (*Blue Annals*, pp. 359–363).

*Notes to 'Tārā in the Mañjuśrī-mūla-kalpa'*

1 Ghosh, p. 10.
2 Tajima, *Étude sur le Mahāvairoċana-sūtra*.
3 Ghosh, p. 11.
4 The following information is drawn from Ariane Macdonald's introduction to her *Le Maṇḍala du Mañjuśrī-mūla-kalpa*. She shows that Benoytosh Bhattacharyya's arguments for dating much of *MMK* as early as c. 200 AD are baseless.
5 'Dānaśīla, Dharmakīrti, dPal brtsegs of sKa ba, kLu'i rgyal mtshan of Cog ro, kLu dbang srung ba, Ye shes sde and others translated the *Mañjuśrī-mūla-tantra*, . . . the Tantra of Tārā and many others.' Toussaint (tr.), *Le Dict de Padma*, p. 333, see also pp. 355–6.
6 Macdonald, 107–8.
7 Translated from the Skt as quoted by Ghosh, pp. 11–12, except for words in square brackets, which come from the Tibetan, Tog Kg, 353–5.
8 *Ratna*; Tib. 'red' = *rakta*.
9 *Pravāla*, also means 'coral' as in the Tib.
10 *Śubham*, also means 'beautiful'.
11 'The mother of': *mātā* + gen. If we read *matā*, 'esteemed by', it would be closer to the Tib.
12 Title missing in Tib., where this chapter runs straight into the next, without its own colophon, as part of Chapter 36.
13 See quotations in Bu ston, ii. 111–122.
14 Ghosh, p. 12. Words in square brackets are absent from this quotation and have been supplied from the Tib.

15 Tog Kg, 920–2.

16 Harikela, according to Edgerton's Dictionary, is possibly Bengal. Kāmarūpa is Assam. Ghosh suggests that Kalaśa could be Kalasan in Java. I have not identified Karmaraṅga, which in the Tib. is given as Kadaraṅ.

*Notes to Tārā's Tantra, the Origin of all Rites*

1 *GR* 10.

2 This date is quoted by Beyer, 13.

3 Lessing & Wayman, 126–7.

4 Beyer, 476.

5 See Ghosh, pp. 74–90 and plates, for descriptions and for photographs of a fine model of Her *maṇḍala* found near the ruins of what is believed to be Vikramaśīla.

6 Ghosh, 81.

7 Colin Wilson in his worthwhile study *Mysteries* gives a recent example (p. 59).

8 See *BA* 160–7. From *BA* 706 one can deduce that a disciple of his was born in 1054.

9 *BA* 859, 856.

10 Beyer, 476.

11 Bu-tön, ii. 222. Date from *BA* 103 etc.

12 *BA* 1056.

13 Part 16 (MA), 430–435. *sGrol ma las sna tshogs 'byung ba zhes bya ba'i rgyud sngags.*

14 *Mātani* PT, *mātanī* L.

15 Kurukullā and Parṇa-śabarī are transcendent deities, goddesses already free from *saṃsāra*, who came to be considered aspects of Tārā. Brahmā and Śakra (whom the Hindus call Indra), however, though rulers of heavenly realms, are mere worldly gods, still subject to saṃsāric rebirth – see the unforgettable fable of Indra and the ants with which Zimmer opens his *Myths and Symbols in Indian Art and Civilization.*

16 Cf. Heart Sutra, IV (Conze, *Buddhist Wisdom Books,* 85–89). *'Grib pa med pa/ 'phel ba med pa,* 'without decrease or increase', could be translating *anūnā anutkarṣāḥ,* 'without deficiency or excess', or 'neither inferior nor superior'; cf. also Conze, *Short Prajñāpāramitā Texts,* p. 82.

All *dharmas* lack production, cessation etc. in an ultimate sense, although they may be said to be produced and to cease on a merely conventional level.

17 Or 'She is *saṃsāra* and *Nirvāṇa*,' but this is harder to interpret.

18 Probably Tārā's ten-syllable mantra (Geshe Kayang).

19 'Rites' (*las*): LNT omit, present in D and P. To practise them 'severally', according to Geshe Kayang, means not doing a fierce rite when a peaceful one is required, and so forth.

20 *Viśuddh°* (x2) BNT, *śuddh°* . . . *viśuddh°* L, *śuddh°* (x2) DP. The endings vary – here and elsewhere, we shall not normally give variant readings when there is no doubt as to the correct reading.

21 The Four Immeasurables are Loving-kindness, wishing all beings to be happy; Compassion, wishing them to be free of suffering; Joy, rejoicing in the prospect of their temporal and ultimate happiness; and Equanimity, wishing that all see each other equally, without attachment or aversion (see Rabten, *Essential Nectar*, verses 27–34 and commentary). The text is suggesting particular ways to develop them in meditation. 'From a womb', etc., are the four ways of birth that encompass all living beings. Birth, aging, sickness and death are the four main sufferings of human beings (*Essential Nectar*, verses 266–273). Emptiness, Signlessness and Wishlessness constitute the Three Doors of Deliverance (*AdK* VIII, pp. 184–7; *MSA* XVIII, 77–80; *MA* VI, 208–9). 'The Signless' is a name for *Nirvāṇa*; Wishlessness implies abandonment of clinging to conditioned things. Cultivating Joy with regard to them no doubt means concentrating on such thoughts as 'How wonderful it would be if all beings realized these three!'

22 *Utpādaya* BT, *utapādaya* N, *utabādaya* L, *utpadāya* D, *udpatāya* P. May be 1st sing. Ā. caus. impv. *utpādayai* with irregular *saṃdhi*, or an optative form (cf. Edgerton, *Grammar* §29.35).

23 *Phye ma phur ma* = *cūrṇa-puṭa*: according to E, *puṭa* in this context means the calices of flowers, strewn as an offering; but Tib. dictionaries explain it as a synonym of *thum bu* 'piece' (Ch), 'incense powder made into pieces' (D).

24 Verses 3 to 6 apparently identify Tārā, the Genetrix of the

Conquerors, with the Mothers of four of the five Families (cf. Chapters 12–16). Possibly verse 2 is meant to imply the fifth. Verses 2 to 7 make the standard series of offerings – flowers, incense, lamps, perfume, food and music (the first two here interchanged) – as in the *sādhanas* of Part Six.

25 'Soft foods' (*bhojanīya*) include boiled grain, sour gruel (or sweets?), cakes, meat and fish, while 'hard foods' (*khādanīya*) include roots, stems (such as sugar cane), leaves, flowers and fruits (Ch; D; Vajirañāṇavarorasa, 131–2).

26 Geese are as much admired in India as swans are in the West.

27 The pearl hangings (*dra ba dra ba phyed pa = hārârdha-hāra*) can be seen in the diagram of the *maṇḍala* palace (p. 62). The pearls are of course magically created, without killing any oysters.

28 The mantras correspond in order to verses 2 to 7. The editions are divided as to whether the key words (incense, flowers, etc.) should be in stem form (-*a*) or in the feminine vocative singular (-*e*) (see Beyer, 148): *dhūpa* B, *dhūpe* DLPT (*dhupe* N); *puṣpa* BDNT, *puṣpe* LP; *āloka* BDNT, *āloke* LP; *gandha* BNT, *gandhe* DLP; *naividya* LN, *naividye* BDT (*nividye* P); *śabda* D (*śapta* B, *śapda* LNT, *śabta* P). Considering that by force of habit a Tibetan scribe would be very likely to copy *puṣpa* as *puṣpe*, but not the reverse, -*a* is probably correct. Beyer (150–1) takes -*e*. The exact interpretation is uncertain.

29 *Sūkasaṃ* BLNT, *sukasaṃ* D, *spukasaṃ* P (obscure, I am suggesting *sūkasāṃ* as G.pl. of a hypothetical *sūkas* after *śūka* 'compassion'); *namaḥ* BDLNPT (classical Skt. *namas*); *tārāyai* D, *tāraye* BLNPT; *tāramitā* BT, *tāramita* D, *tār(a)mimitā* LN, *tāramitāra* P.

30 The complete list of variants among the different editions of this *Praise* runs to several pages. If we standardize the arbitrary conventions of spelling, ignore readings found only in the Nepalese MSS (M – de Blonay's *Matériaux*) or Wayman's edition, and correct obvious errors to the nearest reading worth considering, the points where a real choice exists are as follows. BDLNPT: see page 49. Q: Skt text from the Quadrilingual blockprint (p. 109). Brackets indicate resort to 'correction', e.g. *kṣaṇair* DP(LNT):

Derge & Peking actually read *kṣaṇair*, while Lhasa, Nart'ang and Tog read *kṣaṇaira*, which must be corrected to *kṣaṇair*.

1b *kṣaṇair* DP(LNT), *kṣaṇa* MQ, *kṣaṇe* B. 1d *keśar°* BDLNPT, *kesar°* MQ.

3c *śānti* BDLNPT, *śānte* Q. 3d *titikṣā* MPQ, *titikṣa* BDLNT.

4b *cāriṇi* DMPQ(B), *cāriṇī* LNT. 4c *pāramitā* BDMQT, *pāramita* LNP; *prāpta* BDMPT (LN), *prāpte* Q. 4d *niṣevite* BM(Q), *nisevite* DLP(NT).

5c *kramākrānti* BDT(LMN), *kramākrāntair* Q. 5d *aśeṣā°* BLMNPQT, *niḥśeṣā°* D.

6d *gaṇa* BLMNQT(P), *gaṇair* D; *puras* BMPQ, *pūras* DLNT.

7c *nyāse* DMQ(LNT), *nyāsa* BP. 7d *jvāl°* BLMNPQT, *jval°* D; *°ekṣaṇe* DT, *°a-kṣaṇe* LN, *°ojjvale* M(BPQ) + Tib.

8c *vaktr°* LMNQ(P), *vāktr°* DT(B). 8d *niṣūdani* Q, *nisūdani* BDLMNPT.

10c *prahasat* BDLMNPT, *prahasa* Q; *tuttāre* DLMNQT, *tuttāra* BP.

11a *pāla* DLNPT(B), *pāle* Q. 11b *°ākarṣaṇa* BDLNQ(MP), *°ākarṣaṇe* T.

12d *bhāsure* BNQT(L), *bhāsvare* DM(P); *kiraṇa* MQ, *kiraṇo* BDLNT, *karaṇa* P.

13b *jvālā* DLMQ, *jvāla* N, *jvalā* T(BP). 13c *bandha* DLNT, *baddha* BMPQ. 13d *vināśani* BNQ(T), *vināsani* DL, *vināsini* P.

14b *caraṇāhata* BDM(PQ), *caraṇa-hata* LN(T).

15d *pātaka* MNQT, *pāpaka* DL; *nāśani* BNQT, *nāsani* DLP.

16a *bandha* DLNPT, *baddha* MQ. 16c *nyāsa* BPT, *nyāse* DMQ(LN).

17a *pad°* BQ, *pād°* DLMNPT. 17c *mandara* BLNPQ, *mandāra* DT.

18c *tāra* BPQ + Tib, *tārā* NT, *hara* M, *hāra* D, *hārā* L; *phaṭ* BMQ(P) + Tib, *sphuṭ* D(LNT). 18d *nāśani* BNTQ, *nāsani* DLP.

19c *ābandha* DNT(L), *ābaddha* MQ. 19d *nāśani* BNT(Q), *nāsani* DLP.

20b *bhāsure* LNT, *bhāsvare* BDMP. 20c *tuttāre* DLNQT(P), *tuttāra* B. 20d *nāśani* BNT(Q), *nāsani* DP(L).

21a *vinyāsa* BDLNPT, *vinyāse* M(Q). 21d *nāśani*

LMNQT, *nāśanī* BDP.

22c *prayato* B(P), *prayatna* LNT, *prasanna* (D). 22d *devyā* BLMNP, *devyāṃ* D.

23a *sāyaṃ* B, *śayam DLNT; utthāya* BMP, *utthāyaḥ* DN, *utthāpyaḥ* (LT). 23c *praśamanaṃ* DLM(B), *praśamani* NPT. 23d *nāśanam* DLM(B), *nāśinaṃ* NT, *nāśani* P.

24d *bauddha* DLM, *bauddhaṃ* BN(PT); *padaṃ* BDLMN(P), *pade* T; *vrajet* DM, *prajet* B(LNPT).

25a *ghauraṃ* LNPT, *ghoraṃ* BDM; 25b *sthāvaraṃ* BM(T), *sthavaraṃ* DLNP. 25d *khāditaṃ* BD, *khāhitaṃ* LNPT.

26b *arti* N(LT), *ārti* DM(BP); *vināśanaṃ* BLMNT, *vināśanāṃ* DP. 26c *caiva* DM(P), *ceva* BLNT. 26d *dvis* DLNPT, *dvi* BM; °*vartinaṃ* N(LT), °*vartināṃ* MP(BD).

Of these variations, only those at 7d, 18c and 22c make much difference.

31 *Tārā* D, *Tāra* BLNP (*Tara* T); *bhagavatīyaṃ* D (Gen. in -*īyaṃ*: see Edgerton, *Grammar*, §10.141), *bhagavateya* BN, (*ghabagavateya* T), *bhagavateyaṃ* LP; *sūtraṃ* D, *sutra* NT, *sutraṃ* LP, *putraṃ* B; *saṃbuddha* BDLNT, *sabuddhā* P; *bhāṣitaṃ* D, *bhaṣitaṃ* L, *baśetraṃ* BNPT.

32 *Samayā* DLNPT, *samaya* B; *ulakaraye* BDLT, *ulkaraye* NP (perhaps *ulkā-raye* 'meteor-swift').

33 *Dharmaṇi* DLNT, °*ni* BP; *tāraye* DLNPT, *tārāyai* B.

34 Though the original was doubtless phrased in the singular, I have rendered this paragraph using the plural throughout for the sake of euphony.

35 °*buddhāya* B, °*budhāya* P, °*buddhaya* DLN, °*buddhā* T; *treyate* DLN, *treyaṃte* P, *treyatre* B, *traiyate* T (perhaps Dat. sing. pres. part. from *TRAI*, 'save'); *dhārate* D, *tārate* BP, *trārate* L, *trayate trarate* NT; *tu tāra* BDLNPT.

36 *Aṃ-dhātu* D, *aṃ-dhatu* L, *aṃ-dhabu* B, *aṃ-dharbu* P, *ā-dhātu* N, *āṃ-dhātu* T. Could it be *andha-pu* 'purifying darkness'?

37 *Prakṣa* BD, *brakṣa* P, *pakṣa* L, *pākṣa* NT.

38 *Tathāgata* BDNPT, *tathāgatā* L; *viśuddha* BDLNT, *śuddha* P.

39 Hibiscus flowers: *tarani* L, *tvaraṇa* T – possibly an error for *toraṇa*, festooned decorations over the doorways.

40 According to Geshe Kayang, the *vajras* produced from the light-rays touch each other to form an immense, impenetrable sphere. The entire lower half of the sphere is filled with the elements produced from the seed-

syllables; these elements should be visualized as solid, so that one can walk on them. In the centre of the sphere is the *maṇḍala*-palace, surrounded by a circular *vajra* wall at least as big as Switzerland. The palace itself is square, with a gate with two pillars in each wall (p. 62), very large and extremely precious.

41 These are standard similes for Emptiness (*śūnyatā*), explained further on (210–11). Comparable lists are found in the sūtras, e.g. *Daśa-bhūmika-sūtra*, VI; Conze, *Buddhist Texts Through the Ages*, nos. 183–4.

42 The text is ambiguous as to whether the four wrathful Tārās are sitting or standing, but they are normally depicted standing (e.g. Ghosh, plates 32g to j).

43 The reflection of the moon in water (*udaka-candra, chu zla*) arises dependent on the presence of the moon and the water surface and the correct positioning of the observer.

44 I.e. a fairy city appearing momentarily in a cloud.

45 *A taṃ ahaṃ* DLP, *a taṃ* B, *taṃ* NT; 2nd *stana* BDP, *tana* LNT. Obscure; A and TAṂ seem to be seed-syllables.

46 *Cintāmaṇi* D, *cintamaṇi* BLNT, *cindhamani* P.

47 'Said' (*smras pa*) T, 'asked' (*gsol ba*) L.

48 In the mantras of this chapter, we shall print in lower case italics the words quoted from the *Praise in Twenty-one Homages* of Chapter 3, adding the appropriate punctuation and verse numbers. The quotations are heavily garbled, but differently in the different editions, so that most of the deviations from the Chapter 3 text give every appearance of being mere errors and will not be listed here. D tends to be close to or identical with the Chapter 3 text, while P's distortions are often more extreme than those of the other editions (P also has *tudtāre* for *tuttāre* throughout). Outside the quotations, I have normally followed D, which in Chapter 3 was much the most accurate edition.

49 *Traiyadhva* D, *traiyadhvi* B, *traiyaddhā* P, *tyadhva* NT, *traidhva* L; *tārāyai* DNT(B), *tārāye* L, *tāraye* P.

50 1b *kṣaṇa* B (*kṣāṇa* NT), *kṣaṇe* DP (*kṣāṇe* L). 1d *vikasat* BNT(L), *vikaśat* D(P); *keśar°* BN(T), *kesar°* DLP.

3d *titikṣā* D, *titikṣa* BLNT(P).

4a *namas tath°* D(B), *namaḥ sarva-tath°* LNPT. 4d *niṣevite*? (*ṇasevite* D, *nite* T, *nitre* LN, *netra* BP).

51 *Ture ture* D, *ture* B, *tāre ture* P, *tu tāre ture* LN, *tu tāre* T.

52 *Ture ture* DLNT, *ture tu* BP.

53 1st *tāre* BDLNT (*ture* P); 2nd *tāre* BDP (*tare* LNT).

54 *Tāre* BDLNT (*ture* P).

55 *Tāre tāre tuttāre* DL, *tuttāre tāre ture* B(P), *tuttāre tāre* NT. 5d *aśeṣâ°* D, *abhiṣa-* LNPT (= *abhīṣaṭ* 'by force'?) (*ābaśi* B). *Hrīḥ* DLN (*hriḥ* BT, *hūṃ* P).

Taking this mantra and the next three together, the commonest readings are: 5b *dig-antare* DL, *degaṃ-* or *tegaṃ-cari* BNPT; 5d *karṣaṇa* BD, *karaśana* LNPT; *kṣami* BDLNPT. Errors of quantity abound in *kāra*, *pūritāśā* and *kramākrānti*.

56 BNT insert *ture* after *tuttāre*, *tu* P, omitted DL. *Svāhā* BDLP, omitted NT. 5d *aśeṣa* BDLNPT. *Ho* DLNPT, *hoḥ* B.

57 *Tāre tuttāre* DL, *tuttāre tura* B, *tuttāre tu* NT, *tudtāre* P. *Uṣṇīṣa* BDT, *uṣṇiṣa* LNP; *alika-rayā°* D(P), *avika-rayā°* B, *akarṣaya* LNT.

58 *Tāre tāre* D, one *tāre* BLNPT. *Aśeṣa* P(BLNT), *niḥ-aśeṣa* D; *karṣaṇa-kṣami* (DLNPT), *rakṣāmi* B.

59 *Ture* DLT(BN), omitted P. 6b *rudraiś* D, *rudriś* L, *roddheśe* BN, *roddheśi* P, *roddheśer* T. 6d *puras-kṛte* D, *bīrasa-kṛte* L, *duṣe* BNPT.

7a *phaṭ* DL, *triteva* NT, *tritevat* B, *tritevad* P; *kāra* DL, *kari* BNPT. 7d *śikhi* BDL, *nekhi* NPT; *jvālâkuli* D, *jvala-kuli* L, *jvala-jvala-kuli* B, *jala-jala-kuli* NPT; *jaliri* BDLPT, *jalari* N.

8a *ghori* BDLP, *ghore* T.

60 *Nairṛtyai* (*nairityai* D, *nairṭi* B, *nairiti* P, *nairitaye* LNT); *rakṣase* DLN, *rākṣase* BPT; *sūrya-* BLNPT, *sūryāya* D; *uti-aya* BDLNPT; *bumiye* DP (*bumiyi* B), *bhumiye* LNT.

Indra, etc. are the Protectors of the eight directions: E, S, W, N, SE, NW, SW, NE respectively.

*A-kāro mukhaṃ* . . . is the beginning of the *Arapacana* alphabet in the *Prajñā-pāramitā-sūtra* (Conze, *Large Sutra on Perfect Wisdom*, pp. 160–162.)

61 T omits 'sandalwood' and the 'white' of 'white *maṇḍala*'; it also omits the 'white' in the next sentence, and 'five grains' and 'five essences' later in the paragraph. All these words are present in L.

62 Only twelve of these twenty substances occur in the list of twenty-five flask substances for a Tārā rite quoted by Beyer (p. 290). The five medicines included there are not mentioned here, but are referred to in Chapter 8.

63 Benares cloth (*ka shi ka'i ras* = *kāśikâṃśuka*) can be either silk or fine muslin. The phrase can also be read as 'a silken upper garment'.

64 T omits 'five'.

65 Casket: *ga'u* = *saṃpuṭa*, a round, covered box or casket, also a hemispherical bowl (MW).

66 *Ture* D, *tu* B, omitted LT.

67 'Sun and moon' (*nyi zla*) L, 'sun' (*nyi ma*) T.

68 'With its stem' present L, omitted T.

69 *Ture* DLT, *tāre* B.

70 What mantra? What ending? What is this 'doubled consonants' (or perhaps 'the two consonants')? With neither commentary nor oral instructions, we are evidently not meant to understand.

71 'Beautifully adorned' L, 'beautified' T.

72 *Nag pa* or *gnag pa* = *kṛṣṇa*, dark blue or black. Succeeding chapters make clear that this is the right face, the next is the left and the last is the rear one.

73 I.e. the Buddhas of the Five Families – Akṣobhya etc. Note the Mothers of the other Families have only four Buddhas on the crown – similar variation occurs in descriptions of Vajra-tārā in the *Sādhana-mālā* (Ghosh, 76–7).

74 These emblems and gestures are identical to those of Vajra-tārā as described in *Sādhana* 94 of the *Sādhana-mālā* (Ghosh, 76) except that the third right hand holds a lance (*mdung*) instead of a conch-shell (*dung*), which could well be a misprint. See Ghosh, pp. 82–3, for explanation of them. Like her, I take it that the threatening forefinger gesture (*tarjanī-mudrā*) is displayed by the hand that holds the noose, though the text is ambiguous.

The facial colours also correspond to that form of Vajra-tārā, except that those of the front and rear faces are interchanged so as to keep the front face the same colour as the body.

75 Combining the common parts of the long mantras of Chapters 12 to 16: *vyūha* NT, B (except 12), D14–16, *vyuha* L, D12–13; *arhate* BNT, *arhatebhyaḥ* DL; *āryāvalokiteśvarāya* D, B14–16, L13 & 16, T16, *ārya-avalokiteśvarāya* L12 & 15, T12–15. Occasionally *namo* or *namaḥ* for *nama*, °*aya* for °*āya*. The plural *arhatebhyaḥ* alters the meaning considerably.

This chapter only: *akṣobhya* NT, *akṣobhyaḥ* BDL.

76 T omits 'reciting'.

77 *Hulu'i.*

78 A *Vajra-tārā-sādhana* from the *Sādhana-mālā*, found in three versions in the Peking edition of the Tängyur, threw much light on the extraordinarily garbled short mantras of Chapters 12, 13, 15 and 16. V1: P4308; V2: P4309; V3: P4312 (by Ratnākara-śānti). In the *sādhanas*, all the mantras start OṂ TĀRE TUTTĀRE TURE instead of just OṂ, while some phrases are left out.

*Amukaṃ* DLNPT$V_3$, *amuka* B, *amuki* $V_1V_2$; *vaśam* BDP$V_1$($V_2$), *śam* LNT (very confusing), *vasam* $V_3$; *ānaya* $V_1V_2V_3$, *anaya* DLNPT, *anāya* B.

The *sādhanas* say: 'If you make burnt-offering of a hundred and eight *utpalas*, reciting this mantra, you will subjugate whomever you want to.' Thus it is a mantra for subjugating and should not be in this chapter at all. The driving-away mantra required here is given in Chapter 16.

79 *Amitābha-deva* L(D), *amita-deva* T, *amitābhā* B; *ture* BDL, *ture tu* T. See also n.75.

80 General consensus of the Kangyur readings alone yields: OṂ AMUKA-AMITANAṂ KUMĀRI MAHĀM U(RI)DRAVAHENA DASYA PITA PAYAC(CH)ATU HŪṂ HRĪḤ! When the readings from V are added, there is no real doubt as to the correct wording.

The *sādhanas* explain:

'Make five thousand burnt off'rings
with narcotic *caṇḍālī* seeds
And likewise narcotic fruits
and the flowers of the *aśoka*.
Make burnt off'ring of honey, ghee
and sugar. Apply for seven days
This mantra for attaining girls
and you will get the girl you want.'

And if that fails, the next charm 'will summon even a king's daughter.'

81 The phrase NAMA ĀRYÂVALOKITÊŚVARĀYA ... -KĀRUṆIKĀYA is present in B but omitted in DLT.

82 LAṂ is the seed-syllable of the earth element. This mantra is not included in the *Vajra-tārā-sādhanas*.

83 Blue: *mthing kha* or *mthing ga* = *nīla*, dark blue or black.

84 T adds *Oṃ* at beginning; *ratnasaṃbhava* BT, *saṃbhava* DLN; *ture* DLT, *tu* B.

85 First phrase absent in V. *Abhidhānam: ibiṭānaṃ* D, *ibiṭanaṃ* LP, *ibiḍanaṃ* BNT; *mayeva* BDT(P), *mameva* $V_3(V_2)$, *mayaiva* LN; *savanaṃ*: *sabana* D, *sabanan* B, *sabhanan* P, *svabanaṃ* L, *svabnan* NT, *svapnaṃ* $V_2$, *svasnaṃ* $V_1V_3$; *kathaya* $V_1V_2V_3$, *katha* DLNPT(B); *hrīḥ* BDLP(NT), *phaṭ* $V_1V_2V_3$.

The enigmatic rite in the *Tantra* may well not be meant to go with this mantra, for the *sādhanas'* instructions are quite different:

'On a cloth stained with wild flowers, draw the Lady [Tārā], one-faced and two-armed, holding a hook and an *utpala* and noose. Make offering before Her with

'With these excellent heavenly flowers . . .

Then, meditating, recite [this mantra] five thousand times, and [the desired woman] will come.

'With her neck bound by the noose,
lacerated by the hook,
And her feet completely tied
by the *utpala*, she is dragged
Right 'neath your soles: so meditate,
and you'll enjoy her as your slave.'

(Verses translated from the Skt quoted by Ghosh, p.81 – the Tib. translation is in prose. Ghosh, understandably finding them so 'horrible' that she refrains from translating them, does point out that the same *Sādhana*, beside 'these gross and . . . cruel magical rites, embodies . . . certain sublime aspects of Mahāyāna.')

86 *Ture* BDT, *tāre* L.

87 *dNgul rdo* = *rūpya-mākṣika*, hepatic pyrites of iron, or *tārkṣya-śaila*, a sort of collyrium (MW). Or according to Tib. dictt., a silver ore.

88 This wittily substituted mantra is the driving-away mantra that should be in Chapter 12. Only the first sentence is common to the *Sādhana* version, OṂ TĀRE TUTTĀRE TURE CALA . . . UCCĀṬAYA HŪṂ PHAṬ!

'If you recite this mantra thirty-two times on a raven's feather and hide it in the enemy's house, it will drive him away in seven days.'

The text is doubtful in several places: *gami* DLNPT, *gamini* $V_3$, *gāmi* B, *gāmini* $V_2$ (*ghamini* $V_1$); *amukaṃ* BD, *amukhaṃ* LNPT; *vasanaṃ* BLNT, *vasānāṃ* D, *pasanāṃ* P; *nayana* LNT, *nayin(a)* D, *nayaṃ na* BP; *mahāri* BDNT, *mahari* P, *mahāra* L; *had(a)te* D, *hadte* P, *hadde* BLNT; *svāhā* BDLP, omitted NT.

89 *Cu tse* L, *cu rtse* T: possibly the same as *ci tse*, *ci tshe* or *ce tse* = *kodrava*, 'a species of grain eaten by the poor (*Paspalum scrobiculatum*).'

90 *Tathāgata* BDNT, *tathāgatā* L.

91 This paragraph is no doubt a fragment of the burnt-offering for fierce rites. Perhaps in the original 'the fire house' could have been read with 'anoints'?

92 Nine compartments: i.e. an eight-spoked wheel, with a central hub and eight spaces between the spokes. 'Compartments' is throughout written *ling tshe* in D & L, *le tse* in T.

93 'If', 'will be' D, omitted LT.

94 *Oṃ* LT, omitted D.

95 *Kun la* DL, *ku* T.

96 L adds TURE.

97 D. LT omit 'having the ending'.

98 LT; 'the circle that protects against all obstacles' D.

99 Eight U's L, four D, 'U Ū U U' T, 'U Ū U Ū U Ū U Ū' B.

100 'U and U' DL, 'U and Ū' T.

101 This order BDLT – normally Ṛ Ṝ Ḷ Ḹ come between Ū and E.

102 *Svāhā* D, omitted LT.

103 *Svāhā* DL, omitted T.

104 Probably incense, flowers, light, perfume and food, see Chapter 2.

105 White DL, red T.

106 *Gi wang* D, *gi hang* T, *ghi wang* L = *go-rocanā*.

107 Lit. 'each mutually to right and left'.

108 'Theft' (*rku*) DL, 'foods with strong bad smell' (*dku*) T.

*Notes to The Sūtra of Ārya-Tārā Who Saves from the Eight Fears*

1 Here and in verses 24–25, the *-a re* construction (*spyad da re*, *'khor ra re*, etc.) clearly has negative force, although this meaning does not appear in dictionaries.

2 Reading *skyes bus* for *skyes bu'i*.

3 Obscure line (*Bya cha'i rnam pa rang bzhin rdzogs gyur nas*).

4 The first part of this *dhāraṇī appears in the Dhāraṇī of Ārya-tārā* (P393) and elsewhere (e.g. Beyer, p. 280), thus its text is adequately established. The second part is less certain, as besides the Peking edition's rendering I have only that in Bu-tön Rinpoche's *Collected Works*, Part 16 (MA), 436.6–7. The two are practically identical except for the opening of the second part, *Nama āryāvalokabhayā* B, *mama āryāvalo-bhayā* P. This leaves the text a little odd in places, although the endings masc. nom. pl. in *-āni* and acc. pl. in *-e* are both recorded in Edgerton's *Grammar*, and the translation is doubtful.

5 Reading *kyi mthus* for *kyis su*.

6 *mTshan ldan*, lit. 'endowed with the mark(s)', presumably the marks of maidenly beauty.

*Notes to the Hundred and Eight Names*

0 Because if a deity's secret name became known, enemies could do destructive magic with it (Graves, 49).

1 The other is the *Tārā-devī-nāmâṣṭa-śataka* (Tib: see Bibliography. Chinese: Taishō 1105, cf. Blonay pp.3–4). The Names there are either long and elaborate or tangled up with extensive comments.

2 For an account of what is known of Shambhala see Bernbaum, *The Way to Shambhala*.

3 Cf. Graves, *The White Goddess*, p. 481: 'The Goddess is no townswoman: she is the Lady of the Wild Things, haunting the wooded hilltops.'

4 *HBI* 281–2.

5 Blonay, ix-x.

6 Ghosh's list (p. 20) includes four more I have not counted because they come in the part of Blonay's text I have excluded.

7 Ghosh, p. 17.

8 A disciple of Rong-zom Lotsawa, see *BA* 162–3.

9 Named in the contents (*dKar chag*) of the De-ge Kangyur. He was a teacher of Bu-tön Rinpoche (1290–1364) (Bu-tön ii. 224).

10 Conze (ed.), *Buddhist Texts Through the Ages*, no. *176*.

11 *Bhaṭṭārikā* Skt(L), *bhadra* NT; *stotra* Skt, omitted LNT.

12 I.e. elephants in rut (*matta*) – Indian poets seem unable to

mention an elephant without its being in this condition. I have taken the liberty of reading *pāda* 3d before 3c and 4b before 4a, as this makes much more sense.

13 'Knowledge' in 'Knowledge-holder' (*vidyā-dhara*) and 'Queen of Knowledge' (*vidyā-rājñī*) implies understanding of the Tantras.

14 Hayagrīva's close connection with Tārā is attested by two carvings illustrated by Ghosh (plates 42, 44), which show Avalokiteśvara with Tārā, Bhṛkuṭī and Hayagrīva.

15 The *guhyakas*, a class of beings attendant on Kubera, seem here to be identified with the *yakṣas*, since the Bodhisattva Vajrapāṇi was a leading *yakṣa*.

16 'Vow of Amitābha', as T2, is less forced than Conze's 'Listen to Amitābha', with Amitābha supposedly speaking through Avalokiteśvara, but *mamâjñā* can be read in several ways, none very convincing; T2 has 'known by me (as the Mother of the World).'

17 Here and elsewhere, whether through corruption of the source, incompetence, or subsequent errors of copying (e.g. *mchog* for *phyogs*), T2 changes the words, damaging the meaning. Here we have a redundant 'all human beings' in place of 'Tārās' and 'trees'.

18 *Tārayiṣyāmi.*

19 'She who leads across', 'the Saviouress'.

20 T2 transfers this phrase incongruously to verse 16, in Tārā's speech.

21 'Great in wisdom' can also be taken as within the speech, as T2.

22 In the Skt we find here a prose *dhāraṇī*, absent from both Tib. versions (T2 just has OṂ, T1 nothing). Printed as four 'verses', it might at first sight appear to include part of the list of Names:

> 'OṂ. Bright one, you of the beautiful eyes, Tārā, shining joy, compassionate towards all beings,/ Saviour of all beings, thousand-armed, thousand-eyed,// OṂ. Homage to the Blessed Lady! Look down, look down/ On all beings, and on me, PHAṬ SVĀHĀ! OṂ TĀRE TUTTĀRE TURE SVĀHA!// OṂ. Pure, quite pure, cleanser, purifier,/ *Sugatas'* Daughter, essence of friendliness, immaculate, green, appearing as green,// Great in wisdom, most excellent, most excellently adorned, invincible,/ Very terrible, taking all forms, of great power!'

However, the style is different, the names are in the vocative case instead of the nominative, and some are repeated in the verses. Furthermore, the Names in the verses (27–39) are straightforwardly counted as one hundred and eight without including any of this *dhāraṇī*. Therefore we may safely dismiss it as a later interpolation that only disrupts the flow.

This leaves a Skt text of fifty-three stanzas. Both Tibetan versions, and the numbering of two half-stanzas as whole ones in Blonay's manuscripts, give reason to believe that a few lines may have gone missing. Most likely there were originally fifty-four stanzas, bringing the number of half-stanzas to the magic figure of a hundred and eight.

23 *dPal ldan dge ma* T1, *dge ba can* T2 = *kalyāṇi* (*kalpâgni* 'cosmic fire' Skt).

24 Here the Skt adds another OṂ, absent in T1 and T2.

25 She of the conch: *śaṃkhinī* after T1, T2 (*sakhinī* 'friend' Skt).

26 'Intensely brilliant' (*mahā-gaurī*), 'very white' (*mahā-śvetā*) are both translated *dkar mo che* 'Great White One' in T1 and T2.

27 *Mahā-māyā* – name of the Buddha's mother, and also a name of Durgā.

28 *Kāla-rātrī*: can mean 'dark night' (as T1, T2), but here *kāla* more likely means 'time' than 'dark', referring to the night of destruction at the end of the world. A name of Durgā.

29 *Vibhāvinī* (*'dra ba'i lding* T2, *'gro lding ma* = *dramilā*?? T1).

30 *Brāhmaṇī* (i.e. brahman woman) Skt and T1, *tshangs pa ma* = *Brahmāṇī* (name of a Hindu goddess, daughter and wife of Brahmā) T2.

31 'Auspicious' (*śaṅkarī*) Skt, *ri khrod ma* = *śavarī* T1, *don byed* = *artha-karī* T2.

32 *Shugs chen (mo)* = *mahāvegā*, as Skt text B.

33 Should 'true' be taken with the preceding word (T1), with the following word (Conze), or on its own (T2, Blonay)? The last is best, for each of the three Names thus formed is known to be a name of Durgā, and Graves (*The White Goddess*, p. 448) confirms that even in Europe, Truth is a name of The Goddess.

34 *Sārthavāhā kṛpā-dṛṣṭī*: Ghosh (p. 24) plausibly amends to *sārthavāha-kṛpā-dṛṣṭī* 'She who looks with compassion on caravan-leaders (i.e. merchants)', an allusion to Tārā's early popularity with the merchant community whom She

protected in their travels. T1, T2 unintelligible.

35 *Ri khrod ma* T1, T2 = *śabarī* (*śavalī* Skt).

36 *Kun 'gro rjes 'gro ma* T2 confirms the reading *sarvatra-cânugā* of Blonay's text C.

37 Name of Mahā-prajāpatī (Gautama Buddha's aunt and foster-mother, the first nun); also of Durgā.

38 *'Jigs pa kun las* T2 ([*sarva-pāpāny*] 'all evils' Skt).

39 According to Conze, 'the demons who torment people in hell'.

40 These two verses list classes of potentially harmful supernatural beings. Verse 49 is very different in T2, six lines long and with only three names in common with the Skt.

41 T2 omits 51ab.

42 Concluding couplet of T1 – perhaps the translator's précis of the benefit verses, perhaps lost lines from the Skt.

43 T2; 'spoken by the Buddha' Skt; omitted T1.

*Notes to the Praise in Twenty-one Homages*

1 Wayman's (1959) edition was based on M and D. He goes astray at the point most crucial to his rather weird theory (*tritatā* for *tri-tattva* at 21a) and in verse 26, but otherwise his differences from my more widely-based edition are fairly minor.

2 D'ar-ma-dr'ak of Nyän, recorded as having attended a congress of translators in 1076 (*BA* 71, 328). Bu-tön (ii. 219) says he lived twelve years in India. He translated Prajñā-karamati's great commentary on the *Bodhi-caryâvatāra*, texts on Kālacakra and Tārā, and other works.

3 There is a sharp contradiction at 1c, see note on *vaktrâb-ja*.

4 See pp. 238–241.

5 Lessing and Wayman edition, pp. 126–7.

6 See p. 290.

7 See pp. 297–8.

8 *sGrol ma phyag 'tshal nyer gcig gi ṭīkka Rin po che'i phreng ba.*

9 See p. 299.

10 *sGrol mar phyag 'tshal nyer gcig gis bstod pa'i rnam bshad Yid 'phrog utpa la'i chun po zhes bya ba.*

11 See Appendix 3.

12 *Phyag 'tshal nyer gcig gi bstod pa'i sa bcad.*

13 *bsTod pa'i rnam bshad gsal ba'i 'od zer.*

14 Colophon from M.

15 Beyer, pp. 469–70, n. 11.

16 Translator of *Kālacakra-tantra* and other texts, lived 1276–1342. See *BA* 785–7.

17 Wayman misinterprets his quotation from this rite. One performs it when definite signs occur that one is about to die. As it is a once-in-a-lifetime opportunity, one must take all the steps necessary to ensure success, so that one will in fact be reborn in the Pure Land. One of these is to collect merit by such means as giving life to sentient beings (e.g. buying animals to save them from slaughter) and giving away one's possessions.

18 See pp. 280–281 and the praises by Nāgārjuna and Gedün-dr'up.

19 Another possibility is perhaps *āpūrya* 'fulfilling'.

20 Wayman's 'delighted in the circular band', which he equates to a protective circle, loses whatever credibility it had when one notes he has been misled by the wrong numbering of the chapters in S2 – the protective circle goes with the next verse.

21 The Fourth Panchen Lama interprets line d, *rig pa hūṃ las sgrol ma nyid ma*, as 'the only Tārā born from the mantric syllable HŪṂ', i.e. the only one of the twenty-one to belong to the Family of Akṣobhya. His other assignments are: Family of Ratnasambhava: nos. 3, 7, 11 and 21; of Amitābha: 2, 5, 6, 13, 15 and 18; of Amoghasiddhi: 4, 8, 9 (Tārā Granter of Boons), 10, 14, 17 and 20; of Vairocana: 1, 12 and 19. (*Sādhana-mālā of the Paṇchen Lama*, Part 2, 145–162).

22 See the article by John Snelling, *The Middle Way*, *56*, 33–35, 1981.

23 Mandara or Mandāra-giri is a hill near Bansi in Bihar, 50 km south of Bhagalpur, supposed to have served Viṣṇu as a churning-stick for churning the milk-ocean. It is covered with temples of Hindus, Buddhists and Jains, though it is not clear why it should be sacred to Buddhists (NLD; M.S. Pandey, 49–51).

24 The verb SPHUṬ (imperative *sphuṭa*) = 'dispel (poison)': *Hevajra Tantra* II.ii. 46.

25 See note 1.

26 Followers of a Śaivite cult of *śakti* would of course read

*śiva-śakti* as 'female energy of Śiva'. On this basis Wayman (1959) elaborated the theory that the *Praise in Twenty-one Homages* originated among people trying to practise a combination of Śaivism and Buddhism. In this light, the Buddha's *uṣṇīṣa* (4) 'reminds us of Rudra' and his matted hair, the fingers at Tārā's heart (9) become an erect *liṅgaṃ*, and Tārā (= 'stars') is revealed as the Milky Way, the heavenly Gaṅgā flowing from the matted locks of Śiva's stand-in, Amitābha (12). Alas, outright blunders aside, the present phrase and these far-fetched analogies constitute virtually Wayman's entire argument. Even so, it is not impossible that *śiva-śakti-samanvite* represents some connection with Śāktism, like the names of Durgā (a principal focus of Śāktism) among Tārā's hundred and eight Names.

27 See note 16.

*Notes on Tāranātha's 'Golden Rosary'*

1 See introductions to *HBI* and *MT*.

2 See Tucci, *The Religions of Tibet*, 67–70.

3 Usually abbreviated to *bKa' babs bdun ldan*.

4 *rTag brtan phun tshogs gling*, renamed *dGa' ldan phun tshogs gling* after its forcible acquisition by the Ge-luk-pas (*HBI* ix).

5 Another is the *Ārya-tārā-kurukulle-kalpa*, whose introduction states: 'The text and ritual (*kalpa*) of the *Tantra of the Ocean of Yoga of the Origin of Tārā* have been damaged and disappeared, and the *Principal Tantra Called the Concentration of the Origin of Tārā* (**Tārā-bhava-samādhi-nāma-parama-tantra*) has also disappeared, but this *Kalpa* is extant. It was taught by Lokeśvara.' (Tog Kg, rG NGA, 833).

6 Pandey, 21. Conze (*Buddhism*, table of dates) quotes 770–815.

7 *HBI* 110.

8 Lamotte, *Mppś I*, pp. X–XIV; see also Lamotte, *Histoire du Bouddhisme Indien*, 379–80.

9 See pp. 279–80.

10 Guenther (ed. & tr.), *The Life and Teaching of Nāropa*, 100.

11 Ib., 2nd p. of Introduction, n.

12 *BA* 404.

13 *BA* 399–400.
14 Chattopadhyaya, *Atīśa and Tibet*, 412–3.
15 Guenther, loc. cit., 4th p. of Introduction.
16 Historical data in this paragraph and the next mainly from T. Ling, *Buddhism, Imperialism and War*, Chap. 1.
17 Seckel, 57.
18 *HBI* 331, *BA* 797–805.
19 See n.11 to Prologue.
20 Bu-tön (ii. 96–101) presents conflicting traditions on the third Council. Some (like the Theravādins) say it took place under Aśoka, 160 years after the *Nirvāṇa* according to them; others date it at 210 or 360 years after the *Nirvāṇa*. But the tradition favoured by both Bu-tön and Tāranātha (*HBI* 91–95) is that it happened at Jālandhara in Kashmir under King Kaniṣka, 300 years after the Nirvāṇa. In fact, Kaniṣka reigned c.128–151 AD (Lamotte, *Histoire*, 648; but cf. Chattopadhyaya, *EHNI*, Chap. V, who prefers c.78–101 AD). The grand *stūpa* he built at his capital, Puruṣapura (Peshāwār) has been much admired.
21 *mDo sde phal che ba* could mean specifically the *Avataṃsaka-sūtra*, but here the wider sense seems more appropriate.
22 The Yogācāra and Madhyamaka are two schools of the Great Vehicle. Neither the 'five hundred masters' nor the 'eight *mahātmas*' are recognized sets of specific teachers.
23 Tāranātha mentions these kings again in *HBI* (108 & 117), placing them in the time of Nāgarjūna. A tenth-century King Muñja and an eleventh-century Bhojadeva of Mālava are known.
24 This would be Parṇa-śabarī, an aspect of Tārā mentioned in the Tantra (p. 51).
25 *Rin po che'i gling* = *Ratna-dvīpa*, according to NLD a name for Ceylon.
26 Saṃmatīyas would have been called Śrāvaka because they were Hīnayānist and Saindhava because they were particularly numerous in Sindhu (cf. Joshi, 43–44; Bareau, 121).
27 There are several places in India called Kumāra or Kumārī, but I cannot find a Kumāra-kṣetra. Perhaps Kuru-kṣetra, the area just north of Delhi, or Kūrmakṣetra, on the east coast near Srikakulam (84 E, 18 N)?

28 *Śarabha*: a fabulous animal with eight legs, living in snowy mountains and said to be stronger than a lion or an elephant (MW).

29 At 30.4, 30.5, 31.4 and 36.13, for *skos* or *bskos* read *rkos* or *brkos*.

30 As note 24.

31 A King Jaya-candra of Kanauj ruled Vārāṇasī and as far east as Gayā in the second half of the twelfth century, until his defeat by Muhammed Ghuri (Pandey 25, NLD 24). Tāranātha also mentions (*HBI* 117) a King Jaya-candra, great-nephew of the Haricandra of *GR* 16, about the time the Muslim religion first appeared.

32 See pp. 222–3.

33 See pp. 256–7 and *HBI* 221–2.

34 See *HBI* 252–4. When a poisonous snake swallowed some of his disciples, bit others and made many more faint with its poisonous breath, A-svabhāva saved them all by reciting a long praise of Tārā.

35 *bLo gros brtan pa*. See *HBI* 179–181 and Bu-tön ii.147–8. He saw Tārā when, as a child, he offered some beans to Her image in a temple.

36 *sGyu 'phrul*. Māyā-purī (or -pura), modern Hardwar, was sacred to the Hindus, but here perhaps Lumbinī, where the Buddha was born of Queen Māyā, may be meant.

37 The Phalgu, or Nairañjana, is the united stream of two branches that unite about a mile (1.6 km) below Bodhgayā (NLD).

38 This story and the next also appear in the biography of Ch'ak Lotsāwa, who visited the region in 1234–6. (Roerich, *Biography of Dharmasvāmin*, 19–20 (text), 74–76 (tr.).) According to that version,

> 'Tārā appeared in the middle of the river, said "When you are happy and well-off you don't think of me. Now you are distressed and in need you say 'Tārā, Tārā!' Get out here!" and showed him the way with Her right hand . . . He got out and glanced back – the Goddess was still in the river . . . Turned into a stone image, She was put in the Tārā temple.'

This story certainly rings true – compare the experience of a geologist, Blofeld's *Compassion Yoga*, 30–33.

Ch'ak's biography continues:

'There is also a Hulu[hulu]-tā[rā], or 'Laughing Tārā', a

miraculously-created image of Tārā with Her right hand over Her mouth, laughing derisively at Māra's attempts to hinder the Enlightenment of the Complete and Perfect Buddha. This still exists.

'Again, once a man afflicted by an evil spirit performed meditation and recitations of Tārā. Tārā appeared before him and said "Ha ha ha ha!" Straight away all his illness ceased. As in the above case, She survives, turned into a stone image of Tārā, and is known as the Ha-ha Tārā.'

Can we hope these evidences of the Goddess with a sense of humour will some day be rediscovered?

39 Reigned c. 783 to 815 or 819 (Pandey, cf. note 6).

40 See also *MT* 53. Geshe Jampa Tekchok thinks this *Dharma-cakra* ('Wheel of the Doctrine') may have been a rotating wheel containing mantras, like a Tibetan prayer-wheel, possibly water-driven.

41 See above, pp. 170–172.

42 'Gone forth' (*pravrajita*, Tib. *rab tu byung ba*): having given up the life of a householder and adopted the life of a Buddhist monk, by taking ordination. At ordination, distinctions of caste are left behind.

43 The Vehicle of the Perfections (*pāramitā-yāna*), as opposed to the Tantra.

44 *Lag na rdo rje mchog tu gsang ba'i rgyud*, 'Supremely Secret Tantra of Vajrapāṇi'.

45 *He ru ka bskyed pa zhes bya ba'i rgyud*, 'Tantra Called the Generation of Heruka'.

46 *bsDus pa dag* (with a plural particle) must mean the shorter *Prajñā-pāramitā-sūtras* in general, not just the Verse Collection, [*Ratna-guṇa-*]*saṃcaya-gāthā*, known in Tib. as the *sDud pa*.

47 *Rab tu dga' ba* – a name of Kubera. Other possible Skt equivalents are Pramudita, Praharṣa, Praharṣin, etc.

48 Saraha, also known as Rāhula, Rāhula-bhadra or the Great Brahman (*HBI* 102–5), was the root *Guru* of the *siddha* Nāgārjuna, so naturally Tāranātha says this other teacher of Nāgārjuna's, Hayaghoṣa, was of the same time. According to Joshi, pp. 270–1, he probably flourished in the latter half of the eighth century. According to Rä-ch'ung-pa, however, the Buddha passed into *Nirvāṇa* in 1983 BC and Saraha appeared 300 years later and lived at

least 2700 years (*BA* 451)!

49 Tāranātha's biography of Nāgārjuna is in *MT*. For Āryadeva, see *HBI* 123–6.

50 *Asma-* makes little sense, no doubt *Aśma-* or even *Uṣma-* is meant.

51 This quotation from the colophon of *Prasanna-padā* appears at greater length in Bu-tön, ii.135, and in Hopkins, *Meditation on Emptiness*, p. 592 (cf. his notes 516 and 523; Tāranātha's version differs somewhat). Tāranātha's point must be that this Rāhula-bhadra, a disciple of a disciple of Nāgārjuna, cannot possibly be the Rāhula-bhadra who was Nāgārjuna's *guru* (see n. 48).

In *BA* 371 a third Rāhula-bhadra is mentioned, a disciple of Buddha-śrī-jñāna. He must be a different one because he was a *kṣatriya*, not a *śūdra* (*HBI* 280).

52 *Nyi ma sbas pa*, can also be Ravi-gupta. See pp. 238–9.

53 These include the five texts used in Part Two (see pp. 109–10), indeed the *maṇḍala-vidhi* is no doubt Chap. 10 of S2.

54 Tāranātha is evidently referring to P2562, *Ārya-tārā-stotra*, attributed to Master Nyi ma sbas pa (Sūryagupta or Ravigupta) of Kashmir. Its tenth stanza gives as the example of Tārā saving from water Candragomin's rescue from the Ganges, which suggests the author is unlikely to have been quite contemporary with Candragomin. Verse 6 shows it cannot be by Tāranātha's Sūryagupta, for it tells of the latter's disciple Sarvajña[-mitra] being saved from a king's sacrificial fire. The dedicatory verse (24) implies the author is a Nyi ma sbas pa, disciple of Nāgārjuna.

55 *Thams cad mkhyen pa'i bshes gnyen*. Author of the famous *Sragdharā-stotra*, see Part Four.

56 *sGeg pa'i rdo rje*, sometimes also rendered as Līlā-vajra. Of the several individuals of these names, this must be the one who taught Buddha-jñāna in Oḍḍiyāna, contemporary with Haribhadra, the expert on the Perfection of Wisdom literature (*BA* 367, *MT* 51) – middle to late eighth century.

57 *sNgon gyi slob dpon rnams kyi rabs dang gtam gyi tshig bcad*, apparently the name of a text.

58 Misprinted as *Ya ma ra sing ha*, but the name of the author of the *Amara-koṣa* is well known.

59 To express respect for him and his royal protector.

60 Misspelt in our text *Bi bri karma dit*. Vikramāditya, coins show, was a title of Candra-gupta II, who reigned from 375 to between 412 and 416, by which time he governed a major part of North India. His capital was originally Pāṭaliputra, but he is supposed to have moved it to Ujjayinī. There his court (or that of one of his descendants who took the same title) was renowned for nine great men of letters who flourished there, the 'nine jewels', who included Amarasiṃha and the poet Kālidāsa. Amara was certainly acquainted with Kālidāsa's work and with Mahāyāna Buddhism; in view of the uncertainty as to which king it was, he is placed between 400 and 600 AD. (Pandey 18; Chattopadhyaya, *EHNI*, 202ff; Stutley & Stutley; MW 955, 531).

61 *Lha'i seng ge*.

62 Text *Hri Harsha de ba*. The mention of the Ghaznavid Turks shows this was not the great Emperor Harṣa of North India (reigned 606–47) but a late-eleventh-century king of Kashmir.

63 'Persians' (*stag gzigs* = *Tajik*) might mean the Ghori Muslims from what is now central Afghanistan, who a hundred years later were to conquer all northern India. Since he describes the same king first as Persian and later as *Turuṣka*, literally 'Turkish', it would seem Tāranātha does not discriminate clearly between the different Muslim races. Later on (*GR* 72), he mentions a Mongolian (or Mughal) king in Delhi, which at that date – the eleventh century – also appears implausible.

64 There were two great Vimuktisenas expert in the *Prajñāpāramitā*. Ārya Vimuktisena, according to Conze (*The Prajñāpāramitā Literature*, 122), flourished around 450 AD, and Bhadanta Vimuktisena around 580. The former studied with Vasubandhu, or with his disciple Saṅgharakṣita. Tāranātha (*HBI* 196, 210–1) makes them contemporary with Sūryagupta and Sarvajña-mitra respectively, i.e. middle and late seventh century.

65 While there was a town of Dhanapura near Ghazipur on the Ganges, more probably the celebrated monastery of Odantapurī or Daṇapura is meant. *HBI* (177, 188) mentions a Buddhadāsa, disciple of Asaṅga and uncle of Ārya-Vimuktisena, but he would have lived centuries before Odantapurī was founded.

66 *dKon mchog gsum gyi 'bangs.* Also mentioned *HBI* 190–1.

67 Diṅ-nāga, or Dignāga, a disciple of Vasubandhu, worked c. 450 AD and was the founder of Buddhist systematic logic.

68 Utkala is another name for the country Orissa (MW, NLD). The old capital was Chauduar, near modern Cuttack. The many images of Tārā found in this area show it was a major centre of Her cult. They include the earliest known image from East India of Tārā Saving from the Eight Great Fears, a glorious carving of the late eighth century, from Ratnagiri (Ghosh, p. 40 ff, Ill.9, etc.).

69 In fact it would have been the Mahānadī, 'Great River' – an understandable error since this is also a name of the Ganges.

70 *Ye shes lha.*

71 C. 700 AD, celebrated author of the *Bodhisattva-caryâvatāra* and compiler of the *Śikṣā-samuccaya.* See Bu-tön ii.161–6, *HBI* 215–20 and p. 251 here.

72 Perhaps Trimalla (Tirumala, AP: 79E, 14N); Trimalaya, the birthplace of Dharmakīrti (*HBI* 228); or more likely, the country of Dramila = Drāviḍa, whose capital was the early Buddhist centre of Kāñcī (Lamotte, *Histoire*, 383).

73 The list of eight *siddhis*, or magical attainments, is subject to considerable variation. See Beyer, 245–255.

74 A son of Kubera, lord of the *yakṣas.*

75 See n.39 and pp. 171–2.

76 Same as the Buddha-śrī-jñāna already mentioned (*GR* 39); see pp. 271–2.

77 *Nyi 'og gi rgyal khams*: this enigmatic phrase, lit. 'the country under the sun', is explained as 'East India' in Geshe Chos grags's dictionary, in agreement with Tāranātha's usage – *HBI* 256 and 330 say it includes Magadha, Bengal and Oḍiviśa. But in *HBI* it is translated (following CD) as *Aparāntaka*. This is extremely confusing, as Indian sources always place Aparāntaka on the *western* seaboard, and indeed since *aparânta* means 'western limit' it is hard to see how it could be applied to the east.

78 [*De nyid*] *'dus pa*, the 'Collection of Categories', the fundamental Yoga Tantra. See Lessing & Wayman, 214ff.

79 *gDan bzhi las kyi phreng ba.*

80 The cremation ground in the Cool Wood (*Śīta-vana*) at Rājagṛha, where the Buddha often dwelt. Directions to

the probable site may be found in Sen, 38.

81 *MT* 41–2 explains Tilli-pa was born in the east and became a monk. He took a consort, was expelled from the monastery and worked with her pounding sesame (*tila*), thus receiving the name Tilli.

82 *sNgo sangs* = *śyāma,* which can mean any dark colour – black, dark blue, brown, grey, green – but is the usual word for the colour of Green Tārā (*Śyāma-tārā*).

83 This evidently refers to secret signs by which a *yogin* and *yoginī* of the same Tantric family are to recognize one another, like those described in *Hevajra-tantra,* I.vii. None such are given in the *Tārā-viśvakarma-bhava-tantra* we have.

84 *MT* 41–50 gives Tāranātha's biographies for Tilli, Nāro, Śrī-Ḍombī, Kuśali-bhadra (= Kusala) the Younger, Asitaghana and Jñāna-mitra. *MT* 82–103 gives an extensive account of Śānti-gupta.

85 *BA* 382, 384.

86 *rNam gnon tshul.* At *GR* 72 the name is transliterated, *Bi ka ma la shri la.*

87 This could well result from his having meditated on Cakrasaṃvara in a previous life.

88 Tib. *'Khor lo bde mchog,* whereas Cakrasaṃvara with a plain *s* is *'Khor lo sdom pa.*

89 Neyapāla, or Nayapāla, succeeded Mahīpāla c.1032 (Pandey. 24). Atīśa's letter to him from Nepāl (1041) survives in Tib. translation.

90 Tib. *bem po* = Skt. *kanthā,* of which *kandhari* would be a vernacular form. This kind of garment was worn by certain ascetics.

91 Cf. E, under *nagna* and *mahānagna.*

92 *Mi thub zla ba.* A disciple of Dombhī-Heruka (*BA* 206) and *Tantra-ācārya* at Vikramaśīla, c. 930 AD (*HBI* 327).

93 Doubtless the Nīlgiri in Tamil Nadu.There is another Nīlaparvata (Nīlgiri or Nīlācal) in Distt. Puri, Orissa, but this is only a low sandhill, incapable of offering a great abyss.

94 'Reversed' means the practitioner visualizes herself as the *Prajñā* or female aspect of the deity.

95 Abhayākara-gupta (cf. Chart 2), a prominent scholar of Nālandā and Vikramaśīla, who wrote many books on Kālacakra and other subjects, see *MT* 64–7. He flourished

in the time of King Rāmapāla, c.1077–1130 (Ruegg, in *Prajñāpāramitā and Related Systems*, 284).

96 Text *Pī la badzra* (68.14), *La li badzra* (77.1). Certainly a different person from the late eighth or early ninth century Lalitavajra of 48.2 – he is mentioned as *Rol pa'i rdo rje*, *MT* 43, *BA* 1030.

97 See pp. 288–290.

98 It is clear from *HBI* 330 that Tāranātha's *Ra khang* is Arakan in Burma. Tāranātha says it includes *Pu khang*, plainly the great Buddhist city of Pagán. The next country to the east is that of the *Mu nyang*, i.e. Mòn. This includes Haṃsavatī (now Pegu: MW, NLD). Haripuñjaya was in fact in Mòn territory, see p. 176 above.

99 See p. 176. Could possibly read *Cigla-rājā*.

100 *Kam po dza* is as close a Tib. transcription of Kampuchea/ Cambodia as one could hope for. The Kāmboja in Gilgit or N. or E. Afghanistan is obviously not meant here or at *HBI* 330.

101 'Outer Secret Mantra' is *Kriyā-* and *Caryā-tantra*, 'inner Secret Mantra' is the two higher levels of Tantra (Gonsar Rinpoche).

102 *Padminī*, 'lotus-woman', is the best of the four classes of women. Cf. this description from *Hevajra-tantra*, II. viii. 2–5, of Mahā-mudrā in her conventional aspect:

2 'Not too tall and not too short,
not quite black and not quite white,
Like a lotus leaf she's dark:
sweetly perfumed is her breath,
3 And her perspiration has
a scent as beautiful as musk.
Her "lotus" (sexual organ) momently evolves
a smell like lotuses blue or red.
4 In her genital secretions
wisdom notes a pleasant scent,
Redolent of the *utpala*
or like the fragrant aloe-wood.
5 Calm she is, and steady too,
charming, sweet of speech, with three
Folds in her midriff, and lovely hair;
she's commonly classed as *padminī*.
Of the nature of Innate Joy,
having won her one gains *siddhi*.'

See *BA* 221 for more remarkable sings of a *padminī* (in this cas an incarnation of Tārā), such as a mark on the navel resemblin a red lotus with three roots.

103 More on Ratigupta (or Rātigupta): *MT* 81–2. He was born in South India and travelled widely. His teachers included Ratnakīrti and Asita-ghana (cf. Charts 2 and 3).

Śrī-tanu-pāla may perhaps be named after the Mòn territory of Tanu-śrī (now Tenasserim, Lower Burma).

104 Or Loka-pradha (69.8, 88.14).

105 *Kā-dzi,* Indian pron. of Arabic *qāḍī,* actually a civil judge.

106 The petrifying gaze (*stambhanā-dṛṣṭi*) is one of four gazes taught in *Hevajra-tantra,* I.xi.

107 At this period (eleventh century), permanent Muslim domination extended to the Indus basin and the Muslims made occasional raids as far as Gujarat (Toynbee, 410).

108 *Ma si ta,* from Arabic *masgid.*

109 *Padma gar dbang dbugs dbyung ba.*

110 An absurdly large quantity, around 300 bushels, or 100 hl.

111 A *tola* is of the order of 13 g, presumably of silver.

112 The rite of *grong 'jug* is discussed by Evans-Wentz, *Tibetan Yoga,* 253–9.

113 *Chos 'byung zhi ba.*

114 *Nyi ma dpal.* A disciple – or some say a teacher – of Dharmâkara-śānti (*BA* 764).

115 This Saṅgha-śrī is evidently later than Dharmâkara-śānti, and therefore later than the Nāyaka-śrī of Chart 2, suggesting the Tārā lineage may well be out of order here (cf. pp. 174–6).

116 *Mi'i nyi ma.* Mentioned *BA* 798 as a great *paṇḍita* in Kaliṅga, who in about 1410 composed a verse in praise of Vanaratna.

117 'Receiving': *mnos pa,* pf. of *nod pa* or *mnod pa.*

118 Appears to have been altered from 'queen'.

119 'Wanderer': *rGyal khams pa,* see dictionaries D, Ch.

*Notes to Praises Attributed to Mātṛceṭa.*

1 *HBI* 123–6, 130-6. Bu-ston (ii.130, 136) also mentions him as a pupil of Āryadeva but declines to give his biography.

2 *HBI* 133.

3 Joshi, *Buddhistic Culture,* 130. Date after Grousset, p. 248.

4 *HBI* 131–2.
5 Joshi, 85, 131.
6 See *HBI* 391–2 and Lamotte, *Histoire*, 655.
7 Lamotte, *Histoire*, 655.
8 Ib., 656.
9 *HBI* 390–1.
10 Python, *Upāli-paripṛcchā*, 156n. Python gives a French translation of Mātṛceṭa's *Praise of the Thirty-five Sugatas*, surely a Mahāyāna work (it mentions, for example, the *trikāya* doctrine), which could possibly be by the same author as our *Praise of Ārya-Tārā*.
11 Ghosh, 22–4.
12 Vāgindra, presumably = Vāgīśvara, a title of Mañjuśrī.
13 I.e. the two obscurations – *kleśâvaraṇa*, which obstruct Liberation, and *jñeyâvaraṇa*, which obstruct the attainment of perfect Buddhahood. For an explanation of these terms, see Kochumuttom, 14–16.
14 Usually the hair of Green Tārā is described as black; perhaps the adjective has become misplaced and should apply to Her complexion.
15 Of the five *Jinas*, Tārā is generally connected with either Amitābha or Amoghasiddhi – here, for example, She is assigned in the next verse to Amoghasiddhi's Action Family (*karma-kula*) – but a link with Vairocana is attested by the colophons of some versions of the *Praise in Twenty-one Homages*.
16 *Sattva* (*sems dpa'*): lit. 'being', but here perhaps an unorthodox abbreviation for *Bodhisattva*.
17 Three points needing no guard (*arakṣya*): the Buddha's conduct is automatically pure, so she does not need to be on guard in body, speech and mind. (E)

The three Special Awarenesses, or Applications of Mindfulness (*āveṇika-smṛty-upasthāna*) of a Buddha are that she is neither elated nor depressed when her audience is responsive, unresponsive or partly both. (E).
18 Four Fearlessnesses: see p. 408, n.16. Four Purities: Purity of Body, Deeds, Enjoyments and Place. (D)
19 See Lessing & Wayman, 28–35.
20 *Zag zad* = *āsrava-kṣaya*, 'the contaminations being exhausted'.
21 Guardians of the ten directions. Bhūta must stand for Nairṛti.

22 Wandering ascetics (*parivrājaka*) used to carry three staves tied together, as an emblem of their control over body, speech and mind.

23 In fact, Tārā is called 'goer by night' (*niśācarī*) in the *Hundred and Eight Names* (verse 32). 'All times' is virtually illegible in the text.

24 *Dud pa'i dka' thub*, probably the practice of adopting animal-like behaviour.

25 *sKung ba'i*? The text has been rather clumsily retouched in several places round here (15–17), often incorrectly.

26 Missing line, required to make up a four-line stanza mentioning all the eight Masteries.

27 Sitā (Tib. *ka ra*) perhaps for Sītā, a Vedic earth goddess, and Śama (*śam*) for Śamī-devī?

28 Perhaps a line connecting these Buddhist Goddesses with the rest of the text has gone astray.

29 Activities of the four elements: cf. *Abhidharma-kośa*, I, p. 22.

30 Siṃha-nāda-tārā, Tārā of the Lion's Roar, is a rare form of Tārā discussed and illustrated by Ghosh, pp. 53–4.

31 These emblems are exactly those of Vajra-tārā in Her usual form, golden in colour, with four faces and eight arms. See Ghosh, 74–90.

32 Reading *dri'i* for *dril bu'i*.

33 I.e. the Tārās of the *Vajra*, Jewel, Lotus and Action Families; the Incense, Flower, Lamp and Perfume Tārās; and the Tārās with Elephant-hook, Noose, Chain and Bell. All these Tārās are two-armed and hold the appropriate emblem in the right hand, or in both hands.

34 Lokeśvara, a name of Avalokiteśvara.

35 This and the next two lines may refer to Avalokiteśvara.

36 Maheśvara: name of a Bodhisattva (E).

37 *rDo rje chos chen.*

38 *De nyid don mchog.*

39 *'Jig rten dbang rab.*

40 *rDo rje spyan rgyas.*

41 *Bud med sgyu 'phrul.*

42 *rGyud gsum = tri-saṃtati*, possibly the continuum of body, speech and mind (E); but CD mentions three forms of descent (*rgyud pa gsum*), through one's children, one's own rebirths, and one's disciples (which could in fact be considered as descent through the body, mind and speech

respectively).

43 Fasting: lit. 'truly abiding in the keeping of the fast', probably implying keeping the eight fast-day vows.

*Notes to Praises by Candragomin*

1 Mainly *HBI* 199–209, Bu-ston ii.132–134. See also Roerich, *Biography of Dharmasvāmin*, 30–32 and 91–93.
2 According to NLD, the chief town of Varendra was Mahāsthāna, 11 km (7 miles) north of Bogra, now in Bangla Desh. The kingdom extended west to the Malda district in Indian Bengal.
3 See Chattopadhyaya, *Atīśa and Tibet*, pp. 303–311.
4 Beyer, p. 10.
5 See Beyer, pp. 245–255.
6 The meaning of this line is debatable. *rGyab phyogs* = *parāṅ-mukha*, with such meanings as 'turning the back upon, avoiding; hostile (to), unfavourable; a spell or magical formula pronounced over weapons' etc. (MW); but in modern Tibetan it can also mean 'backing, support'.
7 Reading *bsgrogs* for *bsgrod*.
8 Worldly *ḍākinīs* are the equivalent of witches, some of them malevolent. For a story of a *ṛṣi's* curse, overcome by the wiles of a courtesan, see *Mppś* 1009–1012; Frank, *Histoires qui sont maintenant du passé*, VII.
9 These four are all the possible ways of birth, according to Buddhist views. HŪLU-HŪLU is presumably equivalent to *hulu-hulu*, which is an exclamation of joy (cf. verse 37). I do not recall seeing it in a Tārā mantra.
10 The eight Masteries (*aiśvarya*) of a Buddha are sometimes listed (cf. p. 217, v. 18 above) as those of Body, Speech, Mind, Qualities, Omnipresence, Place (*gnas*), Magical Power (*ṛddhi*), and producing or appearing as whatever one wishes. Here the Buddha's activities, the ten Powers (*daśa-bala*) of a Tathāgata (see *MN* I.69–71, *MA* XI B.19–31), and the six or ten Perfections (*pāramitā*) are included.
11 I take this to mean that the *Buddha-kāyas* encompass all phenomena, principally in that they are omniscient. Alternatively *shes bya'i dkyil 'khor* could be construed with the next line and interpreted differently.

12 *Ghande*, read *ghaṇṭā*; could also read *gaṇḍī*, 'gong'.

13 'Objects of six classes' (*tshogs drug yul*) I take to mean sentient beings of the six destinies. If it means the objects of the six types of consciousness (five sensory and one mental), we could put:

'Proclaims the objects of six classes empty,
without inherent existence'.

14 Reading *mthon mthing* for *'thon 'thing* (?).

15 The wishing and engaging thoughts (*smon 'jug*) are the two kinds of *Bodhicitta* (see *Bodhicaryāvatāra* I.15–19): the wish to become Enlightened so as to benefit all sentient beings, and the vow actually to engage in the Bodhisattva conduct, the Perfections, through which Enlightenment is attained.

16 The four Fearlessnesses (*vaiśāradya*) of a Buddha are that when She or He pronounces the four theses: 'I am perfectly and fully enlightened with respect to all *dharmas*,' 'I have exhausted all contaminations,' 'I have explained unfailingly and truly the hindering *dharmas*,' and 'The Path I have taught leads to Deliverance,' there is no-one with any ground to say it is not so (*MN* I.71–72, *MA-bhāṣya* to VI.210, etc.).

17 Mahāyāna sources typically give twenty wrong views of the personality (*satkāya-dṛṣṭi*), e.g. *MA* VI.144. The sixty-two wrong views are discussed in the *Brahmajāla-sutta* of the *Dīgha Nikāya* (translation of Sutta, commentaries and related exegetical treatises: Bhikkhu Bodhi, *The Discourse on the All-Embracing Net of Views*).

18 Becoming (*bhava*) is that one of the twelve links of Dependent Arising that is immediately responsible for the taking of saṃsāric rebirth. Thus Candragomin is saying that to hear Tārā's name at the moment of death cuts off the process that would normally lead to rebirth.

19 *Hulu-hulu*: an expression of joy. *Hulu-hulu-tārā*: see n.38, pp. 397–8.

20 I.e. in a Pure Land.

21 *Ma rmongs pa*: the translation of this colophon in Chattopadhyaya's *Atīśa and Tibet*, p. 476, goes astray mainly through neglecting this *ma*.

22 Title of text A = P4870, which this translation follows. Two other versions exist, differing in many minor details: B = P4490 *Ārya-tārā-stotra-dvādaśa-gāthā*, C = P4493 *Ārya-tārā-devī-stava-nāma*.

23 BC: to the Venerable Ārya-Tārā.
24 *rNo ba'i* A, *rna ba'i* C; but *rmongs pa'i* B ('stupid').
25 On sight A; from one who bows to You B, from one who praises You C.
26 Overpoweringly: *'dul bas* A. But BC *du bas*, 'with smoke'.
27 *Khri* A, *khro* B, *'gro* C. B → 'burning angrily'.
28 Whole: *ma lus* AB; *ma rungs* C 'intractable'.
29 Venomous: *dug ma can* A, *dug mang can* C; *dug mig can* B 'with poison-eye'.
30 *'Gro ba* B; *grol ba* A (?); *'dral ba* C '(cut and) rend'.
31 Just through remembering Your name BC.
32 *Khyod kyi 'bangs ni* AC; *khyod kyis 'phangs nas* B 'saved by You'.
33 AB; just by praising You C.
34 A; by remembering You B; by praising You C.
35 AC; Begging hungry ghost migrators B.
36 *gDungs* BC; *gdong* A.
37 AB; by praising You C.
38 Pure One A; with faith B; mentally C.
39 *'Jigs byed pa* AC; *'jigs med pa* B.
40 Gain happiness A; reach Sukhāvatī BC.
41 Anecdote only in A.
42 Title of P4871. The other version, P4491 *Ārya-tārā-stotra-viśvakarma-sādhana-nāma*, includes line 3d and verse 7, missing in P4871, and shortens verse 10 to four lines.
43 Special deity (*yi dam*): i.e. the author's own tutelary deity.
44 'Sun' P4871, 'moon' P4491.
45 *Viśva-karman*, see Chapter 11 of the Tantra.
46 So the Tängyur title, but the catalogue has *Ārya-aṣṭa-mahā-bhayôttārā-tārā-stava*.
47 *Zla ba sbas pa*.
48 Advances: *rnam par gnon pa* = *vikramate*, mistranslated by Beyer as 'trampled beneath the feet'. Traveller: *lam du zhugs pa* = *adhva-gat*.
49 The subject, evidently a rutting elephant (cf. verse 12 of the *Sragdharā Praise*), is not mentioned explicitly in our Tibetan text.
50 *Grong khyer*, literally 'city': if not an actual abbreviation for 'citizen', it is a figure of speech for people in the city.
51 *Ri sul* = *darī*, 'hole in the ground, cave'; or else = *nikuñja*, 'thicket'.
52 Reading *dregs pa* for *dreg pa*. Beyer apparently reads *dug pa*,

which he then mistranslates as if it were the same word as *dug*.

53 I.e. a king etc.

54 By Buddhist convention, shipwreck is due to the ship's being over-turned by sea-monsters. The Skt. surely read this way, with 'by', but the Tib. has *zhig gyur pa* where I would prefer *zhig byed pa*. Beyer fails dismally; among other errors, how can he imagine that a Tibetan translator would refer to Tārā's holy Body by the non-honorific *lus*?

55 Reading *skems* for *skams*; other possibilities are *skam* 'dried up', *skom(s)* 'thirsty'.

56 *dPal bTsun zla ba* (cf. *Mvy* 3493).

*Notes to the Praise by Sūryagupta.*

1 Appendix 3 (1).

2 Appendix 3 (3).

3 The *Nyāya-mañjarī* of Jayanta. See Vidyabhusana, 322.

4 *GR* 46–7, *HBI* 196–8 and 222.

5 De Blonay, 21.

6 *BA* 346 gives a lineage for the *Pramāṇa-vārtika*, including the sequence: Prajñākara-gupta – Ravigupta – Yamāri – Jñāna-śrī-mitra. From *HBI* 289–290 it follows that Prajñākaragupta lived in the early tenth century; while Jñāna-śrī-mitra was one of the gate-keeper scholars of Vikramaśīla, c.1000 AD. However, Mimaki (p. 6) estimates that Prajñākaragupta lived around the eighth century, which like several of his other dates is inconsistent with this lineage.

7 *HBI* 197.

8 I.e. from the realization of the ultimate True Nature of things, in Yogācārin terms their Emptiness of subject-object distinction. Compassion operates in the sphere of conventional truths; only a Buddha (such as Amitābha) can observe both ultimate and conventional truths simultaneously.

9 *Jambudvīpa*, the southern 'continent', here obviously not referring merely to India.

10 Lit. 'wrathful kings and wrathful female [deities]'.

11 Reading *du* for *'du*. If *'du* stands, the phrase means 'not coming together with or separating from in the three times'.

12 In brief: Awakened Female, Omniscient and seeing Ultimate and conventional truths without any wrong projections.

13 The ten 'samenesses' (*samatā*) of *dharmas* are ways in which they are all the same in their Ultimate Nature, taught in Chap. VI of the *Daśabhūmika-sūtra*. Thus this verse is again praising Tārā as a fully enlightened being who perceives both Ultimate and conventional levels at once, but the emphasis is now on Her compassionate action in the relative sphere.

14 *rJe* 'chief', *blon ma* = *nāyikā* 'guide'; perhaps read *rjes blon ma* = *anunāyikā* 'conciliator'?

15 *Thabs*? or *thags*, 'web'?

16 Reading *snang* for *nang*. Objects appear, but are empty, or void; their appearance and their Emptiness are inseparable.

17 The five lines of sentient beings (*rgyud lnga*) are said to be gods (including *asuras*), human beings, animals, *pretas* and hell beings.

18 Reading *rig* for *rigs*, as the sense of the verse requires.

19 Lit. 'one with seven horses' – the chariot of the sun is drawn by seven horses, corresponding to the seven days of the week.

20 Reading *bdun* for *bdud*.

21 'Hare-bearer' = moon. 'Pleasant' makes the line two syllables too long and may be an interpolation.

22 *Lha bran* = *deva-dāsa*.

23 For *drod rtag*, 'constant heat', reading *drod rtags* = **uṣma-liṅga*, as in verse 49. Heat is a particular level of realization, the first stage of the Path of Preparation (*prayoga-mārga*), so called because it is the first sign of the approaching *Ārya* Path, which will burn up one's defilements like a fire (*AdK* VI, p. 163). Tārā is of course far beyond this stage; perhaps 'heat' is here a metaphor for perseverance in meditation, in which case *rtag* could stand.

24 Syllable missing: read [*bung*] *ba'i*.

25 The verse seems to interpret this as implying a lioness.

26 Reading *mche sder* or *mchu sder*. An apt simile for Indian (or Tibetan) debate.

27 *Rab brtan ma* = *supratiṣṭhitā*, *sudṛḍhā*, *susthirā*: perhaps there is some legend concerning a person of this name that would elucidate this verse, but I cannot find one.

28 The four 'feet' (or bases) of psychic power (*ṛddhi-pāda*) –

desire-to-act, energy, thought and investigation – are taught at length in the *Hīnayāna* Sūtras and in Abhidharma texts; e.g. Book VII of the *Mahāvagga* (*Kindred Sayings, V,* 225–60). They are included in the thirty-seven Aids to Enlightenment.

29 Indian tradition credits peacocks with the ability to eat poison unharmed, so why not peahens; but to allow the female the gorgeous colouring of the male is sheer poetic licence.

30 Reading *stong pa* for *stong pa'i.*

31 Reading *rtog pa'i* for *rtogs pa'i.* Subduing *nāgas* is a feat normally reserved for *garuḍas,* the most powerful of birds, and surely beyond an ordinary *kalaviṅka* (Indian cuckoo).

32 *mDzes ston ma?*

33 According to Asaṅga's version of Yogācārin doctrine, every sentient being has an *ālaya* or 'receptacle' consciousness, which carries the imprints (*vāsanā*) of past actions and experiences. These imprints act as the seeds of all the being's future experiences. Eliminating them by yogic practice leads to *Nirvāṇa.* See *Mahāyāna-saṃgraha,* Chap. I (tr. Lamotte, *La Somme du Grand Véhicule, II,* 12–86) and Kochumuttom, *A Buddhist Doctrine of Experience,* 147–151.

34 I.e. Emptiness (*śūnyatā*) as one of the three Deliverances (*vimokṣa*), also called Doors of Deliverance (*vimokṣa-mukha*). Heaps: see n. 36.

35 Illegible, perhaps *khung.* A 'sign' (*nimitta*) is an object of false perception, see Conze, *Buddhist Wisdom Books,* 27.

36 Ordinary beings are addicted to wrong views, especially the grasping of a real Personality (*satkāya*) where there is in fact no more than the five 'heaps' (*skandha*) of forms, feelings, recognitions, volitions and consciousnesses, and the 'extreme views' of permanence and annihilation. We also perversely imagine the body to be pure, although analysis reveals that it is filthy through and through. Such false views are a kind of death, but by realizing Right View – that nothing is produced or ceases in ultimate reality – we can awaken.

37 *rTsod dus lnga brgya'i*: perhaps the 'five hundred' stands for the last five hundred years before the Buddha's Doctrine disappears; if so, the degree of abbreviation is excessive.

38 I.e. the eight unfree states (*a-kṣaṇa*), where one has no opportunity to practise the Dharma – birth in non-human

realms, or human birth in an irreligious country, mentally defective, etc.

39 An outrageous over-abbreviation even for Tibetan.

40 I.e. take the eight fast-day vows before dawn: that until sunrise the next day one will not kill, steal, engage in sexual activity, lie, drink alcohol, use an excessively high or luxurious bed or seat, eat food (apart from a single meal before midday), or wear perfumes, cosmetics, garlands or ornaments or sing, dance or play music.

41 Reading *zad* for *sad*.

42 *Lha srin sde brgyad*: many different lists of eight classes of supernatural beings are found in Tibetan sources (see Beyer 294, CD 718).

43 Line partially illegible.

44 One will come to understand the falsity of conventional truth (*vyavahāra-satya*), and the workings of Dependent Arising (*pratītya-samutpāda*) will become clear. By meditational practice, one will reach the stage of Heat (see note 23) and progressively realize virtues.

*Notes to Sarvajñamitra's Sragdharā Praise.*

1 Blonay, 21.

2 *HBI* 220.

3 Blonay, 23 – the colophon also describes him as a king's *guru*.

4 *HBI* 220–2.

5 Blonay, 63.

6 Blonay, 30–31.

7 See *BA* 341–3.

8 *Kara-puṭa-mukuṭâtopa*: commentary *hastâñjalinā kirīṭe yogena* 'through union in a crest by hands in the gesture of salutation', i.e. joined and slightly hollowed. A 'pressed down by crest of joined palms', B 'joined palms placed on the crown', C 'beautified by a palm crest'.

9 Himâlaya, personified as husband of Menā, fathered two daughters, of whom the elder, Gaṅgā, is here meant. The younger is Pārvatī, 'Daughter of the Mountain'.

10 Tib. all translate *dhātrī* as *yum*, 'Mother'.

11 Cf. Candra-kumāra's rendering of this verse, p. 255.

12 Creeper: *vallī*. A agrees, but BC *yal ga*, usually 'branch'.

13 C: 'When the vow of Perfect Buddhahood/ is arising in my mind,/Tārā, I ask [You] to assist [me].'

14 *Vāhyamāno* V, Tib.; *vākyamāno* (Y) is a misprint.

15 Read *abhinuti* with V and Tib. (Y *abhibhūti).*

16 'Sky': *gamana* (V) is a misprint for *gagana.*

17 *Vallī.* J:= 'branches' (*yaṣṭi*). B 'offerings' (= *bali*).

18 'Dazzling, noisy': or (J) 'of immense splendour'.

19 'Undertakings': *ārambha;* so AB, but J 'arrogance'.

20 'Pent-up streams': *baddha-dhārā;* J little help. The 'darkness' may be from the elephants' point of view, their vision being obscured by rut-fluid in the eyes.

21 *Vādī*: 'of the eloquent' C, 'of disputants' AB (i.e. by overcoming non-Buddhists in debate).

22 According to V, this refers to the custom of leaving beds outside for low-caste men to rid them of vermin.

23 'Fortune': *daiva.* A *phongs* 'misfortune', B '*phya* 'censure'.

24 The wheel, wife, etc. are the seven jewels of a Universal Monarch.

25 'Pleasure grove': *madhu-vana. Madhu* (related to English *mead*) evokes sweetness, springtime and love. The Malaya grove is in the realm of the gods, thus in place of 'lovers' C specifies 'goddesses'.

26 'Bar': *pratigha,* an iron bar for locking a gate–his arms being so powerful. Tib. 'wooden pestle'.

27 I.e. the sword is so bright that the arms seem dark by comparison. Tib. absurdly 'green'.

28 Text of this line uncertain; reading *druma-madhura* with Tib. J has the awning raised 'by female bees'; or it could be 'by shaking (of the trees) by a pleasant breeze'.

29 I.e. long-lived gods.

30 'The Garden of Joy', in the heaven governed by Śakra (Indra).

31 'Sluggishly going', a river in heaven – also the celestial Gaṅgā or Milky Way. A translates it straight, B has 'sluggishly flowing Ganges', and C tibetanizes it to 'heavenly Tsang-po'.

32 *Dāntā* (Y) is a misprint for *kāntā.*

33 The translations disagree on this phrase, but the general idea seems to be some kind of vigorous splashing. *Chaṭa* 'splash' (J), 'drop' (A), also 'mass'. 'Unsluggish' (*a-manda*) is a play on the name *Mandākinī,* which immediately precedes it.

34 The mention of Śakra's (Indra's) wife Śacī, 'Divine Power', proves that he is the subject of this verse–the Indian reader would have guessed this already. You too, dear Tārā practitioner, can be a Śakra for a while, if Divine Power is what you want above all else.

35 *Hīra*, 'diamond, thunderbolt', must here refer to the *vajra* as Indra's magical weapon.

36 This interpretation follows C: 'For the Buddha and the Doctrine,/jewels and flowers rest on Your crown,/covered with canopy of the sky's splendour.' Several others are possible

37 B has: 'with Your arm-collection, connected with the light-rays of Your implements, filling the interior of space.' I cannot reconcile this with the Skt.

38 'Those dwelling on the earth' (*bhū*[*-stha*]), e.g. human beings; 'those dwelling in the earth's surface' (*bhū-tala-stha*), i.e. underground, e.g. *nāgas*. 'At ease' (*sva-stha*), according to the Tib., stands for *svaḥ-stha*, 'dwelling in heaven', i.e. the gods. These three make up the three worlds.

39 'Refreshing' Y, A; 'beauteous' V; 'satisfying' B.

40 B interprets the verse rather differently: '...Grant Your satisfying vision to me, whose mind has been purified in the water of Your praises...dispel my internal darkness, because I know the praise of Your virtues alone is useful, the sole abode of most excellent bliss for all beings in the world'

41 I.e. Avalokiteśvara.

42 Colophon from V's MS 'A'.

*Notes to Praises by Akṣobhya-vajra and Dīpaṃkara-bhadra*

1 Bu-ston, ii.159–60; *BA* 367–74; *HBI* 276 etc; *MT* 51ff; Dargyay, *Rise of Esoteric Buddhism in Tibet*, 18, 21, 27.

2 Tucci, *The Religions of Tibet*.

3 C. 770 according to Conze, *Prajñāpāramitā Literature*, 122.

4 *GR* 65.

5 See *MT* 54; Chattopadhyaya, *Atīśa and Tibet*, 45–49; *HBI* 325.

6 Lama Govinda: *Creative Meditation and Multi-Dimensional Consciousness*, 75.

7 *dbYings* = [*Dharma*]*dhātu*, the realm or sphere of Ultimate

Nature, or Emptiness of inherent existence.

8 Knowledge (*rig pa* = *vidyā*) here implies realization of Emptiness.

9 *sPros med* = *aprapañca*, 'without elaboration', not imagining conventional objects.

10 Ultimate *Bodhicitta* is another term for the realization of Emptiness.

11 I.e. the ten Powers of a Tathāgata, which are Powers of Knowing (*jñāna-bala*).

12 Or: of the thirst for becoming.

13 The Tib. words translated here and in verse 19 by 'speech', 'phrases', 'words', 'sounds', etc. overlap as regards the Skt. words they may stand for and their English meanings; it would be unwise to analyse these two stanzas in too much detail.

14 **Bhāvâbhāvâdyapaśyanti*: 'or other' implies the two possibilities: both real and unreal, or neither real nor unreal. A similar 'etc.' is present in the next line but omitted in the translation for metrical reasons.

15 'Free of object': *dmigs med* = *anālambana*, having no mental support or object perceived as inherently existent.

16 To make this line grammatical, I have been forced to read *g.yon par* for *g.yon pas* and *rtags* for *rtag*.

17 *Mar me mdzad bzang po.*

18 *Bhud ta ka ra bar ma, dGe slong Chos kyi ye shes.* I can find no information on when these two translators lived; five other translations are attributed to Buddhākara-varman in the Tängyur, and one to Ch'ökyi Ye-she.

*Notes to Praises by Nāgārjuna and Candrakīrti*

1 Nāgārjuna – Śavarī – Lui-pāda – Ḍombī – Tilli-pa. Quoted by Joshi (p. 266) from Tāranātha's *MT*.

2 *BA* 380.

3 See Joshi, 266–273. But Joshi's theory (263–4) that Nāgārjuna was the author of the *Guhyasamāja-tantra* itself is far-fetched; it ignores the existence of the other commentarial tradition, Buddha-jñāna's.

4 *BA* 358–367.

5 Walleser, *The Life of Nāgārjuna*, 4.

6 Ib., 10.

7 Passages from some of these can be found translated in Beyer, pp. 80, 246, 254, 255, and 287.
8 Beyer, pp. xiii, 470.
9 *BA* 359–60.
10 See Wayman, *Yoga of the Guhyasamāja-tantra*, passim.
11 Ghosh, 74.
12 Ghosh, 66–68.
13 *Uḍumbara, Ficus glomerata.*
14 Reading for *taṃ po, dam po* = *gāḍha* 'pressed together, close', or *kaṭu* 'pungent, sharp in taste'.
15 For *mtshongs*, read *mchongs. Dom dred* may indicate two species of bear.
16 ? *Khri snyan.*
17 For *'gur chu*, read *mgur chu.*
18 Padmapāṇi, = Avalokiteśvara.
19 Reading *byi'i rje* for *bi'i rje*. Perhaps means a cat?
20 A circle of hair between the eyebrows, one of the thirty-two Marks.
21 I find no recorded explanation of the significance of Tārā's milk. A medieval Italian miniature reproduced by Neumann (*The Great Mother,* Pl. 174) shows philosophers sucking milk of spiritual nourishment from the breasts of the goddess of Wisdom; nothing like this appears in Buddhist sources.
22 Reading *spyan mo. Vṛṣa-pakṣma-netra* is one of the thirty-two Marks of a Buddha, see *Ratna-gotra-vibhāga* III.23 (Takasaki, p. 346).
23 Such a birthmark was shown by Tārā's emanation Ma-chik Lap-drön-ma (*BA* 221).
24 Or jasmine (*jātī*).
25 *Tsam pa* = *campaka.*
26 *Gru grub*: or perhaps a boat perfected by the Sage's Teachings.
27 *sNying po yis//nags su gzigs so*: obscure.
28 Reading *phyi.*
29 Reading *gzhan gyi[s] mi bskyod sku* (blank patch in text).
30 Or self-liberated.
31 Mārīcī, or Aśoka-kāntā, carries a branch of an *aśoka* tree in the left hand and sometimes a *vajra* in the right; Ekajaṭā holds a *kartṛ* (chopper) in the right hand and a skull-cup in the left (cf. Ghosh, 64–5).
32 *Rigs rgyal*, probably for *rig [pa'i] rgyal [mo].*

33 Reading *mi zad* for *mi bzad.*
34 *Pāramitā,* cf. verse 8.
35 Or Moon of Wisdom-knowledge: Tārā's name as Bodhisattva-princess, see Prologue (*GR* 4).
36 I.e. the three Deliverances (*vimokṣa*), of Emptiness, Signlessness and Wishlessness.
37 'Pleasure', the land of Akṣobhya, in the east.
38 The *ḍākinīs* mentioned in verses 4 to 7 are illustrated in Lokesh Chandra's *Dictionary*, pp. 292–3. Each has three eyes and two arms, and stands on her left leg, holding in the right hand her emblem (*vajra*, jewel, lotus, sword) and in the left a skull-cup, with a *khatvāṅga* staff in the fold of her left arm.
39 *dPal dang ldan pa* = Śrīmat or Ketumat.
40 Presumably implies *Prajñā-pāramitā.*

*Notes to Praise by Atīśa*

1 Sources: *BA*, Book V; Bu-ston, ii. 213–4; and Chattopadhyaya's most useful study, *Atīśa and Tibet.* Like Chattopadhyaya (330–1), I follow Gö Lotsawa as regards the dating of Atīśa, since this renowned historian goes out of his way to express his great confidence in it (*BA* 261) and the other tradition, which places the main events of Atīśa's life all two years earlier, is harder to reconcile with other sources.
2 In Dacca District, Bangla Desh; see NLD, 19–20. Popular tradition, according to Chattopadhyaya (60), points out his birthplace in the village Vajrayoginī of Vikramapura.
3 Kelsang et al., *Atisha*, pp. 4–5.
4 Also appears as Śrī-dīpaṃkara-jñāna, Dīpaṃkara-jñāna-pāda, Dīpaṃkara-jñāna, just Dīpaṃkara, and other forms (Chattopadhyaya, 32).
5 See Chattopadhyaya, Chap. 10.
6 *BA* 245, Bu-ston ii.212. Tucci (16–17) gives other examples.
7 The *Bodhi-patha-pradīpa*, 'Lamp on the Path to Enlightenment', yet awaits a really satisfactory translation by someone familiar with its teachings. Of the versions published so far, Sherburne's is the most useful, since it includes the author's commentary, but the translator, a Jesuit, has but shaky understanding and introduces misinformation here and there.

8 *BA* 251, 264. Tucci (35) gives his dates as 1003–63 or 64.
9 *BA* 245, 247.
10 *BA* 260.
11 *BA* 261.
12 *rGyud bla ma: BA* 271.
13 *BA* 260.
14 *BA* 261 and 218–30: instructive reading for anyone interested in what an incarnation of a deity is like. Tucci (33) gives Machik's dates as 1055–1145.

*Notes to Song by Gedün-dr'up*

1 Biographical information from: Khetsun Sangpo, *Biographical Dictionary, VI,* 270–8; Richardson, *The Dalai Lamas;* Petech; Schulemann, *Geschichte der Dalai-Lamas,* 182–193; Mullin, *Bridging the Sutras and Tantras,* 9–13.
2 'The man from Onion Valley' (Tsong-k'a, his birthplace). Unaccountably, the practice has grown up of printing the name in two words as 'Tsong Khapa', which is about as sensible as writing 'Ber Liner' instead of 'Berliner' – this form would mean 'Onion Number Two' or 'the Onion Lawyer'.
3 Schmid, *Saviours of Mankind.* See Thanka VII.
4 Translation: Mullin, *Meditations upon Arya Tara,* 21–26.
5 Information from the Preface to Vol. *1* of the *Collected Works of Dṅul-chu Dharma-bhadra.* The commentary is in Vol. *2,* 627–646.
6 *Legs bris ma,* from the first word *Legs bris.*
7 A literal translation of this verse would be incomprehensible.

*Devas*: lit. 'auspiciously drawn': the gods, and their chief, Śakra, are so-called because they have auspicious drawings on their neck, feet and hands.[D]

Lakṣmī's husband: Viṣṇu.

Gold-hatched Brahmā: lit. 'Golden Womb' – Brahmā emerged from a golden egg in the creation of the world.

Bṛhaspati: lit. 'Guru of the gods', since Śakra appointed him as teacher of the young *devas.*[D]

Gaṇeśa: lit. 'Elephant-face'.

Śiva: lit. 'Splendid Throat' – from the story of his throat

being turned blue by poison during the churning of the ocean of milk.

Sūrya: lit. 'Friend of the Lotus'.

8 I.e. they bow their heads to the lotus on which Tārā's lowest part, Her [right] foot, rests.[D]

9 Avalokiteśvara.

10 The right leg symbolizes Method and the left Wisdom.[D]

11 The *mudrā* of Giving Refuge – thumb and ring finger joined, with the other three fingers raised – shows that She is the ultimate Refuge, combining all the Three Jewels: Her Mind is Buddha, Her Speech Dharma and Her Body Saṅgha.[D]

12 Personified as Viśvakarman.[D]

13 So D, but possibly 'wish-granting gems of the gods [who live in] aerial palaces (*vimāna*)'.

14 That could be lifted with a finger, but if spread out would cover a thrice-thousandfold world-system.[D]

15 'Five-coloured [cloth]'.[D]

16 Lit, 'robbing the sky of its beauty', i.e. of its colour.

17 *Drug ldan glu: drug ldan = ṣaḍ-ja*, the first note of the Indian musical scale (SHA), while *glu* according to CD can = *ṛṣabha*, the second note (RI), thus Gedün-dr'up may well have meant 'skilled in SHA RI [GA MA . . .],' which is to say, in music itself. However, D interprets the phrase as 'skilled in singing from the mouth songs with six elements: thin, thick, changing, driven out (?*khugs* = *niṣkāsita*), raising, putting down.'

18 Eightfold rain of Dharma: rain is eightfold by being clear, cool, light, soft, sweet in smell and taste, good for the throat, and not harmful to the stomach. The Dharma is eightfold since it is the Teaching of the Eightfold Noble Path.[D]

19 *rLabs*, lit. 'waves', but D: 'wave trains coming every seven days, which can in no way be averted,' suggests some tidal phenomenon must be meant. As we say, 'time and tide wait for no man.'

20 I.e. the sufferings that come from the eight great fears described in 20–27.[D]

21 Despite D's gloss, I take *zhabs* as merely honorific.

22 Wrong views of selfhood (*jig tshogs lta ba = satkāya-dṛṣṭi*): twenty such views are enumerated and likened to a range of mountains in *Madhyamakâvatāra*, VI, 144–5.

23 D illustrates verses 20 to 27 with stories from Tāranātha (*GR* 18–26).
24 I.e. non-Buddhist practices such as the five fires.[D]
25 The extreme views of eternality and annihilation.
26 *Piśāca* (see Glossary).
27 Even without training in the hundreds of arduous practices of Bodhisattvas.[D]
28 The Five Eyes and Six Superknowledges are varieties of clairvoyant vision, and a magical power of manifestation.
29 *Byang chub chen po'i dben gnas Theg chen pho brang.*

*Notes to Songs by Lo-dr'ö gyats'o*

1 Vol. *V.* p. 635.
2 Beyer, 334–5.
3 This scheme is described at length in Geshe Rabten, *The Essential Nectar.*
4 This verse is numbered zero to facilitate comparison of the next twenty-one verses with the *Praise in Twenty-one Homages.*
5 *Grub gnyis*: ordinary and supreme *siddhis.*
6 *Siddhi: rig 'dzin,* lit. *vidyādhara,* 'Knowledge-holder', but used here in the sense of 'realization'.
7 A standard example, cf. *The Essential Nectar,* verse 285 and Appendix 3.
8 I.e. the *Praise in Twenty-one Homages,* taught in Tārā's Tantra. See above, pp. 55–59.
9 The outer fears are lions, elephants, etc. and the inner are pride, delusion, etc. See the song by Gedün-dr'up, verses 20 to 27.
10 Powerful Conduct: the Perfections, practised by Bodhisattvas.
11 All-Seeing: *kun gzigs* = *Samanta-darśin* or *Nikhila-darśin,* names of past Buddhas.
12 *Byang chub snying po* = *bodhi-maṇḍa,* often used in a physical sense referring to the seat under the *Bodhi* tree where the Buddha gained Enlightenment.
13 The colophon shows that this refers to Tsongk'a-pa, considered to be an emanation of Mañjuśrī, or Mañjughoṣa.
14 I.e. the six root defilements (*mūla-kleśa*) (alternatively counted as ten) and the twenty secondary defilements

(*upakleśa*), listed and defined in *Abhidharma-samuccaya* (tr. Rahula, pp. 7–14, items [19]-[28] and [29]-[48]).

15 I.e. Buddhahood.

*Notes to Song by Lozang tänpä gyälts'än*

1 Vol. *V*, p. 586.

2 Beyer, 60–63.

3 Read this way, the line is pointing out the sin against the Dharma of seeking to trade its eternal truth for mere transitory wealth. Alternatively one could read *brtag* for *rtag* to give 'Selling Dharma without checking qualifications,' i.e. regardless of whether the student is fitted to receive that teaching.

4 The eight worldly *dharmas* (*'jig rten (gyi) chos brgyad*) are concern with gain and loss, fame and disgrace, praise and blame, and pleasure and pain.

5 'Friends' (*bshes*) here implies Spiritual Friends, i.e. *gurus*.

6 It is considered that even a *guru* who is fully Enlightened cannot greatly benefit a disciple unless a karmic connection (*las 'brel*) has been established between them by some action by either party in a previous life. For example, the Buddha in a previous life as a Bodhisattva gave his body to feed a starving tigress and her cubs; this established the link that enabled the cubs, reborn as men, to become His first disciples after His Enlightenment.

7 *Chos srung*, Dharma-protectors. Some of them are Enlightened or highly realized (and thus fit objects of Refuge), but may be able to do little for us for lack of karmic connection. Others are powerful samsaric beings who sometimes help competent practitioners but should not be taken as objects of Refuge. The last two lines refer to these.

8 *Nor*, 'riches', also means 'error'.

9 'Jewel' is also *nor*. The *Āryas'* seven Jewels, or Treasures, are faith, morality, etc., see Glossary.

10 'Two extremes': *rtag chad*, lit. 'eternalism and annihilationism'. Right View is the Middle Way between them, so hard to define philosophically that countless books have been written arguing over its nuances, and also hard to realize in meditation.

11 Observing all the moral precepts taught for Hearers (*śrā-*

*vaka*) or practitioners of the Hīnayāna, in particular the code of monastic discipline, while keeping one's Tantric practice secret.

12 No doubt the second Tibetan month, when a display of miraculous powers by the Buddha is celebrated.

13 4 February 1979. The edited transcript of these teachings has been published: Lama Yeshe, *Cittamani Tara*, 196–202. The quotation is from the unedited transcript.

*Notes to Part Six: Sādhanas*

1 For a more extensive, systematic account of the preparatory practices, see the relevant chapter of Geshe Rabten's *The Essential Nectar*. There they are described in the context of Guru Yoga; here, in Deity Yoga, the main difference is that the central figure of the visualization is now Tārā instead of Śākyamuni Buddha.

2 See *The Essential Nectar*, p. 32: five reasons for cleaning the room.

3 Teachings on the Stages of the Path (*Lam rim*) treat Refuge in detail. E.g. *The Essential Nectar*, sGam-po-pa's *The Jewel Ornament of Liberation* (tr. Guenther), Geshe Loden's *The Graduated Path to Enlightenment*, etc.

4 The Theravādin approach (see Buddhaghosa, *The Path of Purification*, Chapter IX) is popular even among Mahāyānists. This starts with the example of oneself, following the Buddha's maxim,

'Who loves himself will never harm another,'

and gradually widens the object. If one tries to start with 'all sentient beings', there is a danger that the meditation can become so abstract as to be meaningless.

5 See Beyer, pp. 143–167.

6 Guenther, *The Life and Teaching of Nāropa*, p. 83. For the standard chants used to offer a *maṇḍala*, see my booklet *Common Prayers*.

7 See Beyer, index, under 'torma', for further information and drawings.

8 Reading *'jig* for *'jigs*.

9 I.e. obscurations (*sgrib-pa*).

10 *Chu shel* = *candra-kānta*, a gem supposed to be formed from the moon's rays.

11 I.e. *anusvāra*, a dot above the TA-letter, standing for M, the last letter of the fifth group of consonants in the Sanskrit alphabet.
12 Illegible in text, reading *phan pa'i phyir.*
13 Text unclear.
14 Mārīcī and Pratisarā are two of a set of five Protective Goddesses (*Pañca-rakṣā*), said to be personifications of mantras (Edgerton, s.v. *rakṣā*).
15 Text unclear, reading *'dun pa'i.*
16 The *palāśa* tree is identified as *Butea monosperma*, 'the flame of the forest', which bears masses of brilliant orange flowers.
17 *Gri gug* = *kartari*: a tantric knife with curved blade.
18 JAḤ HŪṂ BAṂ HOḤ: see Atīśa's longer *sādhana*, also Beyer pp. 101–2.
19 Number missing in text, but must be four or five.
20 Reading *snod* for *gnod.*
21 Mantra of the *Arapacana* alphabet, representing the forty-three *Dhāraṇī*-doors. See Conze, *Large Sutra*, pp. 160–162.
22 Reading *gdod ma* for *gdon ma.*
23 Reading *stan* for *bstan.*
24 Reading ĀḤ for A, the accuracy of the mantras in this text being such that one might as well take one as the other.
25 Reading *mdun* for *bdun.*
26 Reading *bdug spos kyi* for *bdag po'i.*
27 See p. 266 verse 24 and Beyer 151–3.
28 Reading *mchog* for *mchod.*
29 Reading *'dod rgu* for *'dod sku.*
30 This suggests that the practice is being done on behalf of another person; but there is no hint of that elsewhere in the *sādhana.*
31 'Service': Derge reportedly *bsten*; Peking *brtan*, 'firm'.
32 *dGyes pa byas.* More often, HOḤ is considered as making the Wisdom-knowledge Being dissolve inseparably into the Symbolic Being (cf. Beyer, p. 101).
33 The 'Three Secrets' are the Body, Speech and Mind of a Buddha.

# *Glossary*

The terms are defined according to the ways they are used in this book; many have other meanings also. The explanations try to give a first, rough idea of the meaning, not aiming at great rigour or depth, and avoiding such complications as differences between schools. Sources used include MW, E, D, Stutley & Stutley, teachings I have received, *AdK* and various other texts. The botanical names come from MW, published in 1899; it is possible some may be outdated.

In the Sanskrit and Tibetan equivalents, syllables enclosed in brackets were sometimes omitted in the texts translated. Where only the Tibetan was encountered, the Sanskrit has been supplied if possible from Lokesh Chandra's dictionary or other reliable sources.

Abhidharma (*(chos) mngon pa*): branch of Buddhist literature and practice concerned with the analysis of phenomena into their elementary constituents (*dharma*).

*Ācārya* (*slob dpon*): Master.

Acceptance that *dharmas* are unproduced (*anutpattika-dharma-kṣānti, mi skye ba'i chos la bzod pa*): an important realization gained on entry to the eighth Bodhisattva Stage.

Accumulations, the two (*saṃbhāra, tshogs*): the accumulations of merits and of Wisdom-knowledge that one must gather by practising the Perfections so as to achieve Enlightenment.

Action, act, activity, rite (*karman; las, phrin las, 'phrin las*): for the activity of a Buddha, or for Tantric rites, Tib. often uses the honorific *(')phrin las*, which I have sometimes translated as 'divine action' or 'divine activity'. The 'four activities' or 'four rites' are Pacifying or Calming, Increasing, Subjugating or Subduing, and Fierceness. See also *karma*.

Action Family (*karma-kula, las kyi rigs (tshogs)*): the Family of Amoghasiddhi.

Adamantine, Concentration called (*vajrôpamo nāma samādhiḥ, rdo rje lta bu zhes bya ba'i ting nge 'dzin*): the concentration in which Liberation or the Enlightenment of a Buddha is attained. Called 'destroyer of hostile forces' (*para-sainya-pramardin*) since it eliminates the last obstructions.

Age of Destruction (*'jig dus*): when seven suns blaze and the whole world is consumed in a firestorm.

Age of Strife (*kali-yuga, rtsod dus*): the present world-age.

Agitation and fading (*ḷayauddhatya, bying rgod*): faults of meditation.

Agni (*agni, anala; me lha*): the Vedic god of fire, guardian of the south-eastern direction.

Aids to *Bodhi*, or to Enlightenment (*bodhi-pākṣika-dharma, byang chub phyogs chos*): a series of seven groups of qualities – thirty-seven in all – to be practised at successive stages of the Path. See *Mppś III*, chap. XXXI.

Akṣobhya (*mi bskyod pa*): 'Imperturbable', n. of a Buddha, Lord of the Vajra Family.

*Ālīḍha* (*gYas brkyang (ba) gYon bskum (pa)*): a posture, either sitting or standing, in which the left leg is bent more sharply than the right.

Amitābha (*'od dpag med (pa), a mi de ba*): 'Measureless Light', n. of a Buddha, Lord of the Lotus Family and of the Sukhāvatī Pure Land. Usually red in colour.

Amoghasiddhi (*don (yod) grub (pa)*): 'Unfailing Accomplishment', n. of a Buddha, Lord of the Action Family.

*Amṛta (bdud rtsi*): lit. 'deathless': nectar, ambrosia (conferring immortality or other powers).

*Anuṣṭubh*: 'praise', n. of a Skt verse metre, see p.108.

*Anuttara* Vehicle (*theg pa bla na med pa*): = next.

*Anuttara-yoga-tantra* (*(rnal 'byor) bla med (kyi) rgyud*): 'Highest Yoga Tantra', highest of the four levels of Tantra.

*Ardha-paryaṅka* (*skyil (mo) krung phyed pa*): 'half-cross-legged' position, as Tārās 8 and 21 (Part Two).

*Arhant* (*dgra bcom pa*), fem. *Arhantī* (*dgra bcom ma*): one who has attained *Nirvāṇa*. Pali *Arahant*.

*Ārya* (*'phags pa*): a Noble Being, or Saint – one who has realized the Path of direct Insight into Ultimate Reality.

*Āryā* (*'phags ma*): feminine of *Ārya*.

*Āryas'* seven Treasures (*dhana*, *'phags (pa'i) nor*): faith, morality, conscience, consideration, learning, generosity and wisdom.

*Aśoka* (*mya ngan med pa*, *mya ngan 'tshang*): the tree *Jonesia asoka*, with magnificent red flowers. Lit. 'sorrowless'.

*Asura* (*lha ma yin*, *lha min*): a class of beings slightly inferior to *devas*, who live within sight of a *deva* realm and are plagued by envy of their neighbours.

Attractions, four (*saṃgraha*, *bsdu ba*) or Means of Attraction (*saṃgraha-vastu*, *bsdu (ba'i) dngos (po)*): giving, pleasant speech, helping, and consistency.

Avalokita (*spyan ras gzigs*): 'He who looks down from on high', n. of a Bodhisattva, often called Avalokiteśvara (*spyan ras gzigs dbang phyugs*) 'Lord Avalokita', Āryâvalokiteśvara 'Noble Lord A.', etc.

Avīci (*mnar med*): the hottest hell.

Awakening (*bodhi*, *byang chub*): = Enlightenment.

*Bandhuka*: the flower *Pentapetes phoenicia*.

*Bardo* (Tib. *bar do*): the intermediate state between death and the next rebirth.

Becoming (*bhava*, *srid (pa)*): synonym for *saṃsāra*. The three becomings (or states of existence) are the Desire Realm, Form Realm and Formless Realm.

Beings: usually for 'migrating beings' (*'gro ba*) or 'sentient beings' (*sattva*, *sems can*) – it excludes Enlightened Beings unless written with a capital B.

Bell (*ghaṇṭā dril bu*): as a Tantric implement, symbolizes the Wisdom that directly comprehends Emptiness. It is held in the left hand (female side), while the *vajra* is held in the right.

*Bhagavan* (*bcom ldan 'das*): 'Lord', 'Blessed One'; fem. *Bhagavatī*: a title of Buddhas.

*Bhikṣu* (*dge slong*): a fully-ordained Buddhist monk, observing 253 rules (or thereabouts).

*Bimpala* tree (*shing bim pa la*): perhaps an error for *bimbā*,

*Momordica monadelpha*, a plant with bright red gourd fruits.

Birth, four doors of (*skye sgo bzhi*): birth from a womb, from an egg, from moist heat, or miraculously.

Blessed One (*bhagavant*, fem. *bhagavatī*): Buddha.

*Bodhi* (*byang chub*): Awakening to Buddhahood, Enlightenment.

*Bodhicitta*, *Bodhi*-mind (*byang chub (kyi) sems, sems bskyed*): determination to attain Enlightenment for the benefit of all sentient beings.

*Bodhisattva* (*byang chub sems dpa'*): one who has realized the generation of *Bodhicitta* and whose sole aim is thus to benefit others.

Body (of a Buddha) (*kāya, sku*): see *Kāya*.

Boon-granting (*vara-da, mchog sbyin (pa)*): gesture in which the arm is outstretched with all the fingers extended and the palm outwards.

Brahmā (*tshangs pa*): the ruler of the gods of the Realm of Form. He has four faces.

Brahman (*brāhmaṇa, bram ze*): member of the priestly caste.

*Brahma-rākṣasa* (*tshangs pa'i srin po*): a type of demoniac spirit.

Brahmic voice, tones of Brahmā, etc. (*brahma-ghoṣa, tshangs (pa'i) dbyangs*): common description of a Buddha's speech.

Buddha (*sangs rgyas*): Enlightened or Awakened One, Who has completely abandoned all obscurations and perfected every good quality.

*Buddhā* (*sangs rgyas ma*): female Buddha.

Buddha-child, Buddha-son (*jina-putra, rgyal sras*): Bodhisattva.

Buddha-dharma: the Buddhist Doctrine.

Buddha-family: see Family.

Buddha-locanā (*sangs rgyas spyan*): = Locanā.

Calm and Insight, Quietude and Insight (*śamatha-vipaśyanā, zhi (gnas) lhag (mthong)*): one-pointed concentrated meditation, and analytical meditation on Emptiness.

*Caṇḍāla* (Skt): outcaste.

*Caryā-tantra* (*spyod rgyud*): second of the four levels of Tantra.

Complete and Perfect Buddha (*samyak-saṃbuddha, yang dag par rdzogs pa'i sangs rgyas*).

Completing Stage (*utpanna-krama, rdzogs (pa'i) rim (pa)*): second of the Two Stages of *Anuttara-yoga-tantra*.

Concentration (*samādhi, ting (nge) 'dzin*).

Conceptualizations, conceptions, concepts (*(vi)kalpa, (rnam (par)) rtog (pa)*): conceptual thoughts.

Conqueror (*jina, rgyal ba*): = Buddha.

Conquerors' Offspring or Son (*jina-putra, rgyal (ba'i) sras*): Bodhisattva.

Contamination (*āsrava, zag pa*).

Corpse-raiser, corpse-raising spirit (*vetāla, ro langs*): a kind of demon or spirit that occupies dead bodies.

Countless (*asaṃkhya, asaṃkhyeya; grangs med (pa)*): a very large finite number.

Cow-products, five (*pañca-gavya, ba'i rnam lnga*): milk, sour milk or yogurt, butter, dung, urine.

*Ḍākinī* (*mkha 'gro ma*): beings of the form of women, of many types from witches and fiends, through various grades of guardians of the Doctrine, to fully Enlightened deities.

*Ḍamaru* (Tib *ḍāmaru* or *cang te'u*): Tantric drum.

*Datura* (Skt *dhattūra*, Tib *da du ra* or *dha du ra*): the white thorn-apple, *Datura alba*, mentioned in commentary to *MA* VI.25 as a drug that distorts the perceptions.

Defilement (*kleśa, nyon mongs (pa)*): negative emotions involving one or more of the three poisons (greed, hate and delusion), under whose influence we create actions that cause us to be reborn in *saṃsāra*. They include six root defilements – ignorance, attachment, aversion, pride, defiled doubt and wrong view – and secondary defilements, sometimes counted as twenty.

Degenerate age, times of decline, etc. (*snyigs dus*): the present age, when the five degenerations are rife – those of lifetime, the era, beings, views and defilements.

Deity (*deva, lha*; fem. *devī, lha mo*): Enlightened Being taken as an object of practice.

Delusion (*moha, gti mug* or *rmongs (pa)*): most important of the three poisons.

Demon of disease or sickness (*graha, gdon*).

Demons of rotting corpses (*kaṭapūtana, lus srul po*): a kind of *preta*.

Dependent Arising (*pratītya-samutpāda, rten (cing) 'brel ((bar) 'byung (ba))*): the essential dependence of things on each other, whereby they are empty of independent self-existence;

causality, expressed in a formula of twelve links.

Desire Realm (*kāma-dhātu, 'dod khams*): set of samsaric states of rebirth in which it is possible for gross defilements such as greed and hatred to manifest, including the hell, *preta*, animal and human states and the lower *deva* states.

Destiny, migration (*gati, 'gro ba*): state of existence into which beings are born under the influence of their karma and defilements. The six destinies comprise three ill destinies, or bad migrations (*dur-gati, ngan 'gro* or *ngan song*) – hell-beings, *pretas* and animals – and three good destinies (*su-gati, bde 'gro*) – gods, *asuras* and human beings. When five are spoken of, the gods and *asuras* are counted together.

*Deva* (*lha*): 'god', samsaric being temporarily enjoying a heavenly state of existence.

Developing Stage (*utpatti-krama, bskyed rim*): first of the two Stages of *Anuttara-yoga-tantra*.

*Dhāraṇī* (*gzungs (sngags)*): a long mantra.

*Dharma* (*chos*): 1. *dharmas* are elementary constituent events into which the world is broken down, what we see as the Person or Self being no more than a collection of *dharmas*, without ultimate reality. In the higher schools of Buddhist philosophy it is shown that *dharmas* themselves have no ultimate existence: their Suchness, or true nature, is to be Empty (or pure) of true existence. 2. The Dharma that is one of the Three Jewels of Refuge (Buddha, Dharma and Saṅgha) is the realizations and abandonments in the mind of a Buddha. 3. 'The Dharma' frequently means the Doctrine of the Buddha, Truth, what is right.

*Dharma-dhātu* (*chos (kyi) dbyings*): the Universal Law, the fact that phenomena do not exist as they are apprehended by consciousness adhering to their true existence. The *Dharmadhātu* Wisdom is the Wisdom-knowledge directly cognizing this.

*Dharma-kāya* (*chos sku*): the Buddha's Omniscient Mind.

Dharma-protector (*chos srung*): guardian of the Doctrine.

*Dhyāna* (*bsam gtan*): meditative absorption, concentration meditation, n. of the fifth Perfection. Four form and four formless *dhyānas* are taught.

Directions, the ten (*daśa-diś, phyogs bcu*): i.e. all space. They are enumerated as the four cardinal and four intermediate points plus up and down.

Divine activity (*karman, 'phrin las*): see Action.

Doors, three (*sgo gsum*): body, speech and mind.

Doors of Deliverance, three (*vimokṣa-mukha, rnam par thar pa'i sgo*): Emptiness, Signlessness, Wishlessness.

Earth-owning spirits (*sa bdag*).

Effort, Energy (*vīrya, brtson 'grus*): n. of fourth Perfection, joy in the practice of virtue.

Elements, eighteen (*dhātu, khams*): a sentient being can be regarded as made up of eighteen e., three for each sense – visual object e., visual faculty e., visual consciousness e., etc. . . . mental object e., mental faculty e., mental consciousness e.

Elements, four (*bhūta, 'byung ba*): earth, water, fire, air.

Emperor (*cakravartin, 'khor lo bsgyur (ba'i) rgyal (po)*): see Universal Monarch.

Empowerment (*abhiṣeka, dbang (bskur (ba))*): the four empowerments, consecrations or initiations are the Flask, Secret, Wisdom-knowledge and Word Empowerments of *Anuttara-yoga-tantra*.

Emptiness (*śūnyatā, stong (pa) nyid*): the Ultimate Mode of Being of all things.

Emptiness, Signlessness and Wishlessness (*śūnyatā, animitta, apraṇihita*): the three Deliverances, or Doors of Deliverance.

Energy: see Effort.

Enlightenment, Awakening (*bodhi, byang chub*): Awakening to Buddhahood from the sleep of ignorance, perfect knowledge.

Eon (*kalpa, bskal pa*): world-age, cosmic cycle.

Eternity and destruction (*rtag dang chad pa*): = the two Extreme views.

Evil, sin (*pāpa, sdig (pa)*): unwholesome karma.

Evil spirit (*graha, gdon*).

Extremes, two (*anta, mtha'*; or *rtag chad*): the wrong views of eternalism (*śāśvata-dṛṣṭi*) and annihilationism (*uccheda-dṛṣṭi*), lit. that the personal self is eternal or that it truly ceases to exist, but often generalized to include all over- or under-estimation of just how much anything can be said to exist.

Families, five (*kula, rigs*): see pp.46–7. 'Six F.' are obtained by adding Vajrasattva (*Hevajra-tantra* II. iv. 100–102).

Fearlessnesses, four (*vaiśāradya, mi 'jigs (pa)*): see p. 408, n.16.

Formations (*saṃskāra, 'du byed*): 'this life's f.' will mean everything making up one's present personality, formed by a coming-together of causes and conditions. However, the same word is also used for volitions, the karmic motivations created in this life that contribute to shaping future lives.

Form-body (*rūpa-kāya, gzugs sku*): a *Saṃbhoga-kāya* or *Nirmāṇa-kāya* of a Buddha – what we would call Her 'Body' as contrasted with the *Dharmakāya*, which is Her Mind.

Form Realm (*rūpa-dhātu, gzugs khams*): a subtle divine state of samsaric existence, where sense of smell, sense of taste and sexual organs are absent, and physical suffering, mental distress and unwholesome mental factors such as attachment cannot arise.

Formless Realm (*ārūpya-dhātu, gzugs med khams*): the most subtle state of samsaric existence, without anything physical at all; lacking even mental pleasure, its beings dwell in unchanging equanimity.

Fragrant aloe-wood (*agaru*): *Agallochum, Amyris agallocha.*

Freedom (*mokṣa, thar pa*): = Liberation.

Friendliness, Loving-kindness, Love (*maitrī, byams pa*): wishing all sentient beings to be happy.

Friendly-minded (*maitrī-citta, byams sems*): = Bodhisattva.

*Gandharva* (*dri za*): class of celestial spirits, noted for their musical talents. They have healing powers but can also cause insanity. A 'city of the *gandharvas*' (*gandharva-nagara, dri za'i grong khyer*) is an imaginary city in the sky, like a fairy castle in the clouds.

Gaṇeśa (*tshogs bdag*): n. of a Hindu god with an elephant's head, who both creates and removes obstacles, lord (*īśa*) of the troop (*gaṇa*) of subordinate gods attendant on Śiva. His title *Vināyaka* 'Remover (of obstacles)' is deliberately misinterpreted by Buddhists as 'Leader-astray' (Tib. *log 'dren*).

*Garuḍa* (*nam mkha' lding*): a large mythical bird, which eats snakes.

Ghosts (*mi min*).

Giving Refuge (*abhaya-mudrā, skyabs sbyin (pa)*): hand gesture similar to Boon-granting but with the hand the other way up, i.e. palm outward, fingers extended parallel pointing upwards.

Gnosis (*jñāna, ye shes*): = Wisdom-knowledge.

God (*deva, sura; lha*): see *Deva*.

Goddess (*devī, lha mo*): 'the Goddess' is of course Tārā.

Graceful (*līlā, lalita; 'gying bag (can), rol pa*): *lalitâsana* is a name for Green Tārā's usual sitting posture (right leg lowered), but this meaning is not always applicable in the texts translated here.

Granting boons: = boon-granting.

Greed (*rāga, chags (pa)*): one of the three poisons.

Guide (*nāyaka, 'dren pa*): common epithet of a Buddha.

Guru (*bla ma*): Spiritual Teacher.

Half-cross-legged: see *Ardha-paryaṅka*.

Happy realm (*bde 'gro*): = good destiny, see Destiny.

Hate, hatred (*dveṣa, (zhe) sdang*): one of the three poisons.

Heaps, five (*skandha, phung po*): see p. 412, n.36.

Hero (*vīra, dpa' bo*): a grade of Tantric adept.

Heroine (*vīrā, dpa' mo,* also *dpa' mdzad ma*): fem. of above.

High rebirth (*svarga, mtho ris*): rebirth as a god or human being.

Hīnayāna (*theg dman*): the 'Lesser Vehicle' – the Buddhist practices of those who have taken Refuge in the Three Jewels but are not and do not aspire to be Bodhisattvas, and the schools advocating such an attitude.

Hindrance, hindering demon (*vighna, bgegs*): Tibetans tend to attribute many, if not most hindrances to demons, sentient beings of the *preta* class.

Hungry ghost (*preta, yi dvags*): see *preta*.

Ignorance, unknowing (*avidyā, ma rig (pa)*): through i. of good and evil one is reborn in ill destinies; through i. of Ultimate Truth one is reborn in *saṃsāra* in general.

Ill destinies, ill migrations: see Destiny.

Immeasurables, Four (*apramāṇa, tshad med (pa)*): see p. 334.

Immediate, five (*ānantarya, mtshams med (pa)*): the five immediate karmas, sins or evil acts are killing one's mother, one's father, or an *Arhant*; causing schism in the Saṅgha of *bhikṣus*; and drawing blood from a *Tathāgata* with evil intent. The five close to or approaching them (*de dang nye ba lnga*) are defiling one's mother who is an *Arhantī*; killing a Bodhisattva on the Definite Stage (*niyata-bhūmi*); killing an *Ārya* on the Path of Training (i.e. not yet an *Arhant*); robbing the Saṅgha of means of livelihood; and destroying a *stūpa*.

Imprints, impressions (*vāsanā, bag chags*): the imprints of actions and defilements, which are carried from life to life and can ripen as a persistence of the same defilement or as the various forms of karmic results.

Indra (*dbang (po)*): Vedic god of rain, who became considered lord of all the gods. In Buddhist *sūtras* he is usually called Śakra.

Insight: 1. see Calm and Insight. 2. Path of I. (*darśana-mārga, mthong lam*): the realization of direct insight into Ultimate Reality, whereby one becomes an *Ārya*. 3. What is abandoned by I. (*darśana-heya, mthong spang*): many defilements, with the mental and non-mental factors associated with them, are eliminated by this realization.

Īśvara (*dbang phyug*): 'Lord', Hindu non-sectarian term for 'God', but sometimes treated as synonymous with Śiva.

Jambu river (*'dzam bu chu bo*): a mythical river formed by the juice of the fruits of the immense *jambu* tree (rose-apple tree, *Eugenia jambolana*) growing on Mount Meru, with golden sand.

Jambudvīpa (*'dzam (bu) gling*): the Southern Continent of Indian mythical geography, often identified with the Indian subcontinent; but from the point of view of the characteristics of its human inhabitants, all this Earth is classed as Jambudvīpa. I have usually translated it as 'India' or 'our world' according to the context.

Jewels, the Three (*ratna, (dkon) mchog*): the three Objects of Refuge – Buddha, Dharma and Saṅgha.

*Jina* (*rgyal ba*): 'Conqueror', = Buddha. The five *Jinas* (*(rgyal ba) rigs lnga*) are the Lords of the Five Families.

Joy (*dga' (ba)*): in the set Loving-kindness, Compassion, Joy and Equanimity – the Four Immeasurables – it is Skt. *muditā* and implies joy in the virtues and happiness of others.

*Kākhorda* (*byad*): 'a kind of evil spirit, often associated with *vetālas*' (E).

*Kalaviṅka*, fem. *kalaviṅkā* (*ka la bing ka mā*): the Indian cuckoo, to whose sweet song the Buddha's voice is often compared.

Kangyur (*bka' 'gyur*), often pron. 'Kanjur': 'the Translated Word (of the Buddha)', the Tibetan canon of scriptures, comprising the Vinaya, several collections of Sūtras, and the Tantras.

Karma (*karman, las*): in Skt the word is wider (see Action), but in English it means a willed action of body, speech or mind, and the impression or seed this leaves on one's personal continuum, which must eventually ripen and produce a result.

Karmic result, karmically governed rebirth (*vipāka, (las kyi) rnam par smin pa*): that result of an action which consists of a particular state of rebirth.

*Kāya* (*sku*): the 'Bodies' of a Buddha, usually counted as three, see pp. 272–3. Sometimes, to make four *Kāyas*, the *Dharmakāya* is divided into two, the *Jñāna-dharma-kāya* or *Dharmakāya* of Wisdom-knowledge and the *Svābhāvika-kāya* or 'Natural Body', respectively the Buddha's Mind and its Ultimate Nature.

*Khadira* (*seng ldeng*): *Acacia catechu*, a tree with very hard wood used for the points of ploughshares, the axle-pins of chariots, amulets, etc. Its resin is used medicinally.

*Khaṭvāṅga*: a staff surmounted by a freshly-severed head, a withered one and a skull, and a triple point, carried by Tantric adepts and representing the secret consort.

*Kinnara* (*kiṃnara, mi 'am ci*): mythical beings with a horse's head and a human body (or vice versa). They became celebrated as celestial musicians, along with the *gandharvas*.

*Kleśa* (*nyon mongs*): see Defilement. The five *kleśa* and their relation to the Buddhas of the Five Families and their Wisdom-knowledges are given in *Hevajra-tantra* II.ii.52–59 and II.iv.101 and its commentaries as follows. Hatred when purified is Akṣobhya and his *Dharmadhātu* Wisdom-knowledge; delusion, Vairocana and the Mirror Wisdom-knowledge; avarice, Ratnasaṃbhava and the Wisdom-knowledge of Equality; greed, Amitābha and the Discriminating Wisdom-knowledge; and envy, Amoghasiddhi and the Wisdom-knowledge of Doing What Is to be Done.

Knife (*kartṛ, kartari; gri gug*): a Tantric chopping knife with an almost semicircular blade slightly hooked at one end and a *vajra* handle in the middle.

Knowledge-holder, Bearer of Knowledge (*vidyā-dhara, rig 'dzin*; fem. *vidyā-dharī, rig 'dzin ma*): see *Vidyādhara*.

*Kriyā-tantra* (*bya rgyud*): lowest of the four levels of Tantra.

*Krodha-rāja* (*khro (mo'i) rgyal (po)*): 'wrathful king', a title of fierce deities.

*Kṣatriya* (*rgyal rigs*): a member of the military or governing caste.

*Kumuda*: the edible white water-lily, *Nymphæa esculenta*.

Kurukullā (*ku ru kulle*): female deity considered a form of Tārā, whose particular function is subjugating, hence Her red colour.

Lady (*bhagavatī, bcom ldan 'das ma*): a title of female Buddhas.

Lapis lazuli (*rājāvarta, mu men*) (meaning confirmed by Jackson & Jackson).

Lay follower, layman (*upāsaka, dge bsnyen*): one who has taken Refuge in the Three Jewels and vows of pure moral conduct — to abandon killing, stealing, sexual misconduct, lying and drinking alcohol.

League (*yojana, dpag tshad*): about 8000 yd, or 7.4 km, according to *Adk* III, p. 178.

Leisureless states, the eight (*a-kṣaṇa, mi khom pa*): the states in which there is no opportunity to practise the Dharma, namely being born in hell, as an animal, as a *preta*, among the long-lived gods, or in a barbaric country where there are no Buddhist monastics or lay followers; being dull-witted, deaf and dumb; being addicted to perverse views such as disbelief in rebirth or Liberation; and when no Buddha has appeared and taught the Dharma.

Liberation, Freedom (*mokṣa, thar pa*): release from the bondage of *saṃsāra*, whether as an *Arhant* or as a Buddha, the latter being 'Great L.'

*Liṅgaṃ*: male organ, especially as emblem of Śiva.

Locanā, Buddha-locanā (*(sangs rgyas) spyan*): first of the four Sublime Mothers (*yum (mchog)*), the female aspects of the *Tathāgatas* of the Five Families.

Lokeśvara (*'jig rten dbang phyug*): 'Lord of the World', a title of the Bodhisattva Lord Avalokita.

Lord (*bhagavan, bcom ldan 'das*): a title of male Buddhas.

Lotus Family (*padma-kula, padma'i rigs*): the Family of Amitābha.

Love, Loving-kindness (*maitrī, byams pa*): see Friendliness; 'Love' also translates *brtse (ba)*, which includes compassion or mercy.

Madhyamaka (*dbu ma*): 'Middle Way System', highest philosophical system of Indian Buddhism.

Mahābrahmā (*tshangs pa chen po*): 'Great Brahmā', = Brahmā.

Mahādeva (*lha chen*): a form of Śiva.

*Mahāsattva*: 'Great Being', standard epithet of Bodhisattvas.

*Mahāsiddha* (*grub chen*): 'great perfected one', realized Tantric practitioner.

*Mahātma* (*bdag nyid chen po*): one of noble nature, exceedingly wise, etc.

Mahāyāna (*theg (pa) chen (po)*): the 'Great Vehicle' – the way of a Bodhisattva, and the schools that emphasize it in their teaching.

*Mahoraga* (*lto 'phye chen po*): 'great serpent', a class of demons.

Maitreya (*byams pa*): 'the Friendly', n. of a Bodhisattva now residing in Tuṣita, who is to appear on Earth as the next Universal Buddha.

Māmakī: second of the four Sublime Mothers (see Locanā).

*Maṇḍala* (*dkyil 'khor, 'khor lo, maṇḍal*): 'circle, disk,' esp. the 'circle' composed of a deity and her or his emanations, attendants and environment; also the disk of an entire universe visualized as an offering, and the round plate or tray that serves as physical support for this practice.

*Mandāra, mandārava*: the coral tree, *Erythrina indica*, one of the five trees of paradise, with brilliant scarlet flowers.

Mañjughoṣa (*'jam dbyangs*): 'the Sweet-voiced', a form of Mañjuśrī.

Mañjuśrī (*'jam dpal*): n. of a Bodhisattva, who represents particularly Wisdom and is depicted flourishing a blazing wisdom sword in the right hand and holding a lotus that supports a book in the left. He is called 'the Youthful' (*kumāra(-bhūta), gzhon nu(r gyur pa)*) because of his everlastingly youthful appearance; the same title is sometimes taken to mean 'Crown Prince'.

Mantra (*mantra, (rig) sngags; vidyā, rig pa; guhya-mantra, gsang sngags*): because mantras play such a key role in its practice, Tantra or Vajrayāna is often called Mantra, or the M. Vehicle. Their nature is discussed in many books, such as Lama Govinda's.

Māra (*bdud*): lit. 'death'. 1. The Evil One, a powerful god ruling the highest heaven of the Desire Realm, who habitually tries to distract and hinder Buddhas and Bodhisattvas. Since each world-system has its own set of heavens, it is possible to speak of infinitely many such Evil Ones. 2. The four *māras* or obstructions to practice of the Dharma: those of defilements, death and the aggregates, and the god Māra (= 1). 3. Māra's whole army of followers are also called Māras or *māras* after him; they act as evil spirits, obstructing Dharma practice.

Marks and Signs (*lakṣaṇânuvyañjana, mtshan (dang) dpe (byad)*): the thirty-two characteristic Marks and eighty minor Signs of a Great Being (a Universal Monarch or a Buddha), such as thousand-spoked wheels on the palms and soles, the hairs of the body pointing upwards, and copper-coloured nails. See Conze, *Large Sutra*, Appendix II.

Marut (*rlung lha*): perhaps 'flashing or shining one' (MW): Brahmanical god of the wind, and the numerous Vedic storm-gods.

Master (*ācārya, slob dpon*): title given to spiritual teachers and learned scholars.

Means, Method (*upāya, thabs*): the conventional aspect of the practice of Dharma, equivalent to Compassion, as contrasted with the ultimate aspect, Wisdom. In Tantra, it is symbolized by the *vajra* and the male aspect. Also counted as seventh of the ten Perfections.

Meditation (*dhyāna, bsam gtan*): the fifth Perfection, see *Dhyāna*; (*dhyāna, mnyam bzhag*): gesture of both hands flat with palms upward, right fingers resting on the left, thumbs slightly bent with the tips touching.

Merit (*puṇya, bsod nams*; sometimes *dge ba*); Field of (Accumulation of) M. (*tshogs zhing*); Merits and Wisdom (*tshogs (gnyis)*): see Accumulations.

Meru, Mount (*ri rab (lhun po), lhun po*): giant mountain at the centre of the world, where the two lowest classes of gods of the Desire Realm live. It is said to rise 84000 leagues above sea-level.

Method: see Means.

Migration: see Destiny.

Migrators, migrating beings (*jagat, 'gro (ba)* or *'gro rnams*): sentient beings, wandering continually from one samsaric existence to another.

*Mleccha* (*kla klo*): barbarian, one ignorant of Sanskrit.

Mode of Existence (*saṃniveśa?, gnas lugs*): a synonym for Ultimate Truth.

Morality (*śīla, tshul khrims*): the second Perfection.

Mother-tantra (*ma rgyud*): Tantras of the *Anuttara-yoga* class are divided into Father-tantras such as the *Guhyasamāja*, which emphasize the Method side, the practice of the Illusory Body; and Mother-tantras such as the *Saṃvara* and *Hevajra*, which emphasize more the Wisdom side, the indivisibility of Bliss and Emptiness. See Lessing & Wayman, 260–267.

*Mṛdaṅga* (*rdza rnga*): a kind of large drum.

*Mudrā* (*phyag rgya*): lit. 'seal, token'. 1. A symbolic hand gesture, endowed with power not unlike a mantra. 2. A tantric consort.

*Nāga* (*klu*), fem. *nāgī* (*klu mo*): beings of the underworld and the waters, classed as animals. They generally live in the form of snakes, but many can change into human form and they are often depicted as human from the waist up with a serpent's tail below. They are supposed to control the weather, especially rain.

*Nāga-puṣpa*: n. of several plants – *Mesua roxburghii, Rottlera tinctoria* and *Michelia champaka* – or may = *nāga-puṣpikā*, yellow jasmine.

*Naiyāyika*: following the Nyāya system of Brahmanical philosophy.

Nectar (*amṛta, bdud rtsi*): see *Amṛta*.

Nimb (*nimba, nim pa*): a tree with bitter fruit, *Azadirachta indica*. Every part of it is used for magical purposes.

*Nirmāṇa-kāya* (*sprul (pa'i) sku*): Emanation Body of a Buddha, see p. 273.

*Nirvāṇa* (*mya ngan (las) 'das (pa)*, in compounds *zhi*): the cessation of everything samsaric such as ignorance and suffering, the Liberation of an *Arhant* or a Buddha. Hīnayāna *Nirvāṇa* is supremely blissful but unhelpful to others, and the *Arhant* must eventually abandon that self-absorbed state and enter the Mahāyāna. '*Nirvāṇa*' is also used for the passing away of a Buddha (and sometimes for that of other, presumably saintly persons), 'the *N*.' being the passing of 'the Buddha', Śākyamuni; when we ask Buddhas not to enter *N*., they are of course in *N*. already in one sense, but we want them to continue manifesting themselves, not to pass away.

Non-conceptual (*nirvikalpa, rnam par mi rtog (pa)*).

Non-self (*nairātmya, bdag med*): the lack of true, independent self-existence.

Novice (*śramaṇera, dge tshul*): monk and nun novices alike are bound by a somewhat less severe version of the *bhikṣu*'s discipline. While *bhikṣu* ordination cannot be taken before the age of twenty, novice ordination can be taken younger; the vows are taken for life.

Obscurations, the two (*āvaraṇa, sgrib (pa)*): those of defilements (*kleśa*) and of knowables (*jñeya*), see p. 405, n.13.

Offspring (*suta, putra; sras*) of the Buddhas or Conquerors: Bodhisattvas.

Omniscience (*sarva-jña(tā); kun mkhyen, thams cad mkhyen pa, rnam mkhyen sa*): Buddhahood.

Opportune, fortunate rebirth (*dal 'byor*): the human existence with all necessary conditions for Dharma practice – free of the eight leisureless states, and with ten factors of good fortune (Rabten, *The Essential Nectar*, n.35).

*Pāda*: a half-line of Skt verse (usually becoming a whole line in Tib. translation).

*Pañcalika*: a kind of cloth worn by *devas*; according to Dharmabhadra and Ch, 'five-coloured'.

Pāṇḍara-vāsinī (*gos dkar (mo), na bza' dkar*): third of the four Sublime Mothers (see Locanā), 'the White-robed Goddess', red in colour and the consort of Amitābha.

*Paṇḍita*: scholar, learned man.

*Pāramitā* (*pha rol phyin*): Perfection.

*Paryaṅka* (*skyil mo krung*): a particular sitting position, some say one leg on top of the other with the soles almost hidden.

Path (*mārga, lam*): several usages, all relating to the universal metaphor of the spiritual journey towards the Goal.

1. Expressions such as 'the perfect P.' (*yang dag lam*) are self-explanatory. 2. Choice of routes: 'the common P.' is the practices that both Sūtra and Tantra practitioners should follow, whereas 'the uncommon P.' is those specific to Tantra; 'the Two-Stage P.' is *Anuttara-yoga-tantra* practice. 3. The five P. are successive segments of one person's route, demarcated by particular realizations and each to be traversed by a particular method of practice. In order, they are: (a) the P. of Accumulation (*saṃbhāra-mārga, tshogs lam*); (b) the P. of Preparation (*prayoga-mārga, sbyor lam*); (c) the P. of Insight (*darśana-mārga, mthong lam*); (d) the P. of Meditation (*bhāvana-mārga, sgom lam*); and (e) the P. Beyond Learning (*aśaikṣa-mārga, mi slob lam*), i.e. Liberation.

Patience (*kṣānti, titikṣā; bzod pa*): the third Perfection.

Peace (*śānti, zhi (ba)*): *Nirvāṇa.*

Pe-cha (*dpe cha*): a Tibetan-style book, made of long strips of paper, unbound, in imitation of the Indian palm-leaf manuscripts.

Perfect Buddha (*(samyak)-saṃbuddha, (yang dag) rdzogs sangs rgyas*).

Perfection (*pāramitā; pha rol (tu) phyin pa, phar phyin*): for most purposes, there are six P. a Bodhisattva must practise – Giving, Morality, Patience, Joyous Energy, Meditative absorption (*dhyāna*) and Wisdom. In the scheme of the *Daśa-bhūmika-sūtra*, the list is extended to ten by the addition of Skill in Means, Vow, Power and Wisdom-knowledge, but very little is taught of these extra four. Overwhelmingly the most important is the P. of Wisdom (*prajñā-pāramitā*), to which a major branch of the Sūtra and commentarial literature has been devoted.

Perverse view (*mithyā-dṛṣṭi, log lta*): e.g. disbelief in rebirth and the laws of actions and results.

*Piśāca* (*sha za*): a class of fierce, malignant, goblin-like demons, belonging to the *preta* realm, said to eat human flesh.

*Piṭaka* (*sde snod*): 'basket', collection of the Buddhist scriptures. There are three – Vinaya, Sūtra and Abhidharma.

Places, three (*gnas gsum*): head (= body), throat (= speech), heart (= mind).

Planets (*graha, gza'*): the seven p. are the familiar Sun, Moon, Mars, Mercury, Jupiter, Venus and Saturn; the eighth is the fictitious and malevolent Rāhu, causer of eclipses. Often a ninth is added, Ketu, the comet, likewise evil and fictitious.

Pledge (*samaya, dam tshig*): besides the Bodhisattva vows and (in the higher classes of Tantra) the Tantric vows, one receiving a Tantric empowerment has to take numerous pledges, which must be kept purely if the practice is to be successful. See Tsong-ka-pa, *The Yoga of Tibet*, 69–76; Beyer, 406–7.

Poisons, three (*viṣa, dug*): greed, hate, delusion.

Polluting demons (*chāyā, grib gnon*): Skt. lit. 'shadow', 'shade'.

Powers, ten (*bala, stobs*): ten aspects of the Omniscience of a Buddha, understanding karmic causes etc. See p. 407, n.10.

*Prajñā-pāramitā* (*shes rab kyi pha rol tu phyin pa, phar phyin*): the Perfection of Wisdom, esp. as a branch of literature and study; (*sher phyin ma*): the Perfection of Wisdom as a female deity.

*Prātimokṣa* (*so (sor) thar (pa)*): vowed discipline common to followers of all three Vehicles. It is of eight types: (a) the eight fasting vows, taken for one day only; (b, c) the five vows of laymen and laywomen; (d, e) the vows of male and female novices; (f) additional vows taken by probationer nuns as a step towards becoming full nuns; (g) the discipline of the full nun (*bhikṣuṇī*); (h) that of the full monk (*bhikṣu*).

*Pratyālīḍha* (*gYas bskum gYon brkyang*): 'counter-*ālīḍha*' posture – sitting or standing with the right leg bent more sharply than the left.

*Pratyeka-buddha* (*rang sangs rgyas*): a Hīnayāna *Arhant* who attains *Nirvāṇa* without needing teachings in that lifetime, but lacks the complete realization of a Buddha so cannot benefit limitless sentient beings as a Buddha does.

Preceptor (*upādhyāya, mkhan po*): principal officiant at the ordination of a monk or nun.

Predispositions (*anuśaya, bag la nyal*): unwholesome tendencies, much the same as defilements.

*Preta* (*yi dvags*): lit. 'departed', i.e. the spirit of a dead person, one of the six destinies of samsaric beings, often called 'hungry ghosts' because of their main form of suffering. They are of many kinds; those that dwell in our world are normally invisible to humans, but may be seen by animals.

Protector (usually *nātha, mgon (po)*): a title of deities.

*Punnāga* tree (*punnāga-vṛkṣa, shing pun na ga*): *Rottleria tinctoria* or *Calophyllum inophyllum*.

Pure Land (*zhing khams, zhing mchog, dag pa'i zhing*): a realm inhabited entirely by *Ārya* Bodhisattvas, where Buddhas teach in *Saṃbhoga-kāya* form.

Queen of Knowledge (*vidyā-rājñī, rig pa'i rgyal mo*): or 'Queen of Mantra'.

Quietude and Insight: see Calm and Insight.

*Rāga*: lit. 'tint, colour': a mode in Indian classical music.

Rainbow body (*'ja' lus*): passing away in a mass of rainbow light and leaving no corpse behind.

*Rākṣasa* (*rakṣas, rākṣasa; srin po*): 'guarding; to be guarded against': an evil being or demon. Some say there are also benevolent *rākṣasas*, of a semi-divine nature like the *yakṣas*.

Ratna-saṃbhava (*rin 'byung*): n. of a Buddha, Lord of the Jewel Family.

Realms, three (*dhātu, khams; bhava, srid (pa)*): Desire R., Form R., Formless R.

Realms of woe: = the three ill destinies, see Destiny.

Refuge (*śaraṇa, skyabs*): see p. 334.

Renunciation (*niḥsaraṇa, nges 'byung*): escape from the world, in that one understands so well the faults of even the best of samsaric life that it arouses no attachment in one.

Rinpoche (*rin po che*, pron. 'rim-po-ch'é'): 'Precious One', Tib. title for someone identified as the rebirth of an earlier distinguished Dharma practitioner. Also called Tülku (*sprul sku*), lit. *Nirmāṇa-kāya* but in most cases simply a courtesy title.

Rite: see Action.

*Ṛṣi* (*drang srong*): 'seer', inspired Vedic sage, Brahmanical ascetic with magical powers.

Rudra (*drag po*): 'Roarer, Howler': Vedic god of tempests, who later became known by the euphemistic title of Śiva, 'benevolent, auspicious'.

Rut-fluid (*mada, dānaṃbhas; myos (pa'i) chu, myos byed chu po*): fluid that exudes from bumps on the temples of a male elephant when he is in rut.

Śacī (*bde sogs, legs brjod ma*): 'Divine Power', wife of Śakra or Indra.

Sacred thread (*brahma-sūtra, tshangs skud*): thread worn over the shoulder by brahmans.

*Sādhana* (*sgrub thabs*): Tantric rite for deity practice, see pp. 331–6.

Sage, the Great (*mahā-muni, thub (pa) chen po*): epithet of the Buddha Śākya-muni ('the Sage of the Śākyas').

Śakra (*brgya byin*): ruler of the gods of the lower heavens of the Desire Realm, who dwells in the immense Vaijayanta palace on the summit of Mount Meru. Sometimes referred to as Indra.

*Śakti*: divine energy or power, personified as female in Hindu Tantra. The term is never used for female deities in Buddhist Tantra, and would for most of them be inappropriate, though Tārā might be an exception.

Śākyamuni (*Shākya thub pa*): 'the Sage of the Śākyas', n. of the historical Buddha.

*Samādhi* (*ting (nge) 'dzin*): concentration of the mind on a single object.

*Sama-paryaṅka* (*mnyam pa'i skyil mo krung*): 'even cross-legged posture', according to Geshe Kayang 'the ordinary cross-legged posture'; perhaps the same as *sattva-paryaṇka.*

*Saṃbhoga-kāya* (*longs (spyod rdzogs pa'i) sku, longs spyod*): 'Enjoyment Body', the Body endowed with the thirty-two Marks and eighty minor Signs that a Buddha displays to *Ārya*-Bodhisattvas in a Pure Land, teaching the Mahāyāna until the end of *saṃsāra.*

Saṃmatīya: prominent Hīnayānist school, to which in the seventh century more than a quarter of the Buddhist monks in India were counted as belonging. They were notorious for their heretical, 'Personalist' views and often their bigotry and moral depravity.

*Saṃsāra* (*'khor (ba);* also *bhava, srid (pa)*): the state of continually having to take rebirth under the control of karma and defilements.

Saṅgha (*dge 'dun*): 'community, congregation'. The Saṅgha in which one takes Refuge is the Community of Saints, or *Ārya* Beings – those of the Hīnayāna, the *Śrāvaka* and *Pratyeka-buddha Āryas*; those of the Mahāyāna, the *Ārya* Bodhisattvas and Buddhas; and those of the Vajrayāna, the Heroes, *Ḍākinīs*, etc. This is Ultimate Saṅgha; Relative Saṅgha is the community of ordained monks and nuns, which should be honoured as representing the actual Saṅgha Refuge just as Buddha-images and sacred texts should be revered as representing the actual Buddha and Dharma.

Sarasvatī (*dbyangs can (ma)*): Vedic goddess of a now dried-up river, who became patron deity of poetry, music, science and all the creative arts, and in much this form was adopted into the Buddhist pantheon, with Mañjuśrī as Her consort.

Sarvāstivāda (*thams cad yod par smra ba*): 'pan-realism', a prominent and influential Hīnayānist school named after their assertion that a *dharma* exists during all time, wandering from the future to the present when it seems to arise and transferred into the past when it perishes.

*Sattva-paryaṅka* (*sems dpa'i skyil (mo) krung*): cross-legged sitting posture with the shins flat on the ground forming virtually a straight line, right ankle on top of the left.

Sciences, the five (*vidyā-sthāna, rig pa'i gnas*): grammar, dialectics, medicine, arts and crafts, and religious philosophy.

Secret Mantra (*guhya-mantra, gsang sngags*): Tantra.

Self-grasping (*ātma-grāha, bdag 'dzin*): a mind apprehending an independently existent self-nature of a person or of *dharmas*; the misconception of a truly-existing self.

Selflessness: = Non-self.

Sentient beings (*sattva, sems can*; also *jagat, 'gro (ba)*): any beings who have not yet attained Buddhahood.

*Siddha* (*grub thob, grub pa*): perfected one, realized one, adept who has attained *siddhi*.

*Siddhi* (*dngos grub*): success, attainment, esp. magical attainment such as flying in the sky, becoming invisible, everlasting youth, or powers of transmutation. They are divided into supreme *s.* (*mchog gi dngos grub*) and ordinary or common *s.* (*mthun mong gi dngos grub*), see Beyer 245–255.

Signs, eighty (*anuvyañjana, dpe byad*): see Marks and Signs.

Simple (*niṣ-prapañca, spros (pa (dang)) bral (ba)*): 'free of elaboration', i.e. devoid of conventional objects, which are mere mental projections.

Sin: see Evil.

*Skanda* (*skem byed*): Skanda is the Brahmanical god of war, leader of demons that cause illness in children, and the god of thieves. 'The *skandas*' are no doubt these demons, however the Tib. name, which means 'drier-up', is puzzling.

*Skandha* (*phung po*): see p. 412, n.36.

Sky-soarer (*khe-cara, mkha' (la) spyod (pa)*): 'one who goes in the air', deity, *ḍākinī*; also conceivably Kha-sarpaṇa, a form of Avalokiteśvara.

*Śloka* (Tib. *shlo ka*): a stanza, esp. one of four eight-syllable *pādas*; as a unit of length of prose, 32 syllables.

Spirits (*bhūta, 'byung po*; also *graha, gdon; mi ma yin*): malignant beings of the *preta* class, ghosts etc.

Spiritual Friend (*kalyāṇa-mitra, dge ba'i bshes gnyen* or *bshes gnyen dam pa*): Guru.

*Śrāvaka* (*nyan thos*): 'Hearer, Disciple (of a Buddha)': a Hīnayāna *Arhant* who attains *Nirvāṇa* under the guidance of a teacher; or someone practising to become such an *Arhant*, a Hīnayānist.

*Śrī* (*dpal*): 'glorious, holy', a respectful title.

Stages, Ten (*bhūmi, sa*): the successive steps in the career of an *Ārya*-Bodhisattva; Buddhahood is attained from the Tenth Stage. A Master of the T.S. is thus an *Ārya*-Bodhisattva or a Buddha.

Stages, two (*krama, rim (pa)*): *Anuttara-yoga-tantra* is divided into two main Stages, first the Stage of Generation, then when that is perfected, the Completing Stage.

Stains (*mala, dri ma*): sometimes = the three poisons.

*Stūpa* (*mchod rten*): a dome-shaped monument housing relics of the Buddha or some revered person, embodying in its form an elaborate symbolism.

Subjugating, subduing (*vaśya, dbang (du bsdu ba)*): rite for summoning or controlling another person.

Suchness (*tattva, de kho na nyid*): Ultimate Nature, lack of true existence.

*Śūdra* caste (*dmangs rigs*): the menial classes.

*Sugata* (*bde (bar) gshegs (pa), bder gshegs*): 'one who has fared well', i.e. a Buddha.

*Sugatas'* Offspring (*sugata-suta, bde gshegs sras po*): Bodhisattva.

Sukhāvatī (*bde ba can*): 'Blissful', n. of Amitābha's Pure Land.

Sumeru, Mount (*ri rab*): = Meru.

Superknowledges, five or six (*abhijñā, mngon shes*): the s. of magical power (of levitation, transmutation and control of one's feelings), divine hearing, knowing others' thoughts, remembering past lives, and knowing the death and rebirth of sentient beings; and (in *Arhants* and Buddhas only) knowledge of the exhaustion of the contaminations. See *Mppś*, Chap. XLIII.

*Śūrpa-vīṇā* (*dgu po rgyud mang*): a kind of *vīṇā*.

Sūtra (*mdo (sde)*): a Discourse of the Buddha, scripture of the Sūtra *Piṭaka*; also, all exoteric teachings of Buddhism (the three *Piṭakas* and their commentaries) as opposed to the esoteric, Tantric teachings.

Symbolic Being (*samaya-sattva, dam tshig sems dpa'*): visualized image of the deity, with which the Tantric practitioner identifies herself.

Tän-gyur (*bstan 'gyur*); often pron. 'Tänjur': 'the Translated Treatises', the collection of Tib. translations of the Indian Buddhist literature other than the actual Buddha-Word – commentaries, treatises, hymns, rituals, dictionaries, medical texts, etc. – amounting to over two hundred volumes, or about twice the length of the Kangyur.

Tantra (*rgyud*): a canonical scripture of the esoteric class; the whole set of practices taught in such scriptures and their commentaries, involving identification of oneself with a fully Enlightened deity, the Vajrayāna; a subset of such Tantric teachings, centred on a particular deity (e.g. 'the T. of Heruka') or of a particular level (*Kriyā-tantra, Caryā-tantra, Yoga-tantra, Anuttara-yoga-tantra*).

*Tantra-ācārya*: professor of Tantric studies.

Tantric vows (*mantra-saṃvara, sngags kyi sdom pa*): set of twenty-two prohibitions that anyone receiving an empowerment of *Yoga-tantra* or *Anuttara-yoga-tantra* must undertake to observe. See Lessing & Wayman, 328–9.

Tārā (*sgrol ma*): the Saviouress, She Who Takes (beings) Across (the Ocean of *Saṃsāra*); also means 'Star'.

*Tāraka*: 'star, meteor': a type of demon, presumably the followers of the *daitya* (or *asura*) Tāraka.

*Tathāgata* (*de bzhin gshegs pa*): 'thus gone' or 'thus come', a Buddha.

*Thang-ka* (Tib, pron. t'ang-ka) (Skt *paṭa*): a painting on cloth.

Threatening forefinger (*tarjanī, sdigs mdzub*): a gesture of threat, pointing the forefinger.

*Ṭīkā*: a commentary (esp. on another commentary).

Times, the three (*dus gsum*): past, present, future.

Times of decline: = degenerate age.

*Tīrthika* (*mu stegs*): an adherent of a non-Buddhist religion, esp. a Hindu, Jain or Lokāyata (Materialist).

Training, threefold (*tri-śikṣā, bslab pa gsum*): the trainings relating to Morality, to Concentration, and to Wisdom.

Triple Gem (*tri-ratna, dkon mchog gsum*): the Buddha, Dharma and Saṅgha Refuges.

True Dharma (*sad-dharma, dam chos*): the Law of the Buddhas.

True Goal (*bhūta-koṭi, yang dag pa'i mtha'*): Ultimate Truth, Emptiness.

True Nature (*dharmatā, chos nyid;* also *gnas lugs*): ditto.

Truths, the two (*satya, bden*): Ultimate and conventional.

Tuṣita (*dga' ldan*): 'the Joyous', n. of the Pure Land of the thousand Buddhas of this eon, inhabited only by Bodhisattvas and Buddhas.

Tutelary deity (*thugs dam, yi dam*): Enlightened deity on whom one's Tantric practice is centred.

Ultimate (*paramārtha, don dam (pa)*):

Umā (*U ma*): a mother-goddess, identified with Pārvatī, Durgā, etc.; it is prophesied that she will one day be reborn as the Buddha Umeśvara.

Unconditioned (*a-saṃskṛta, 'dus ma byas pa*): e.g. space, temporary absence of defilements, final cessation of obscurations, Emptiness, *Nirvāṇa*.

Uncontaminated, uncontaminate, unpolluted (*an-āsrava, zag med*).

Union, Unification (*yuganaddha, zung 'jug*): Union of the Illusory Body and Clear Light, final section of the Completing Stage. The U. of the Four *Kāyas*, or U. Beyond Learning, is Buddhahood.

Universal Monarch, emperor (*cakravartin, 'khor lo(s) (b)sgyur ba'i rgyal po*): one who rules over the four continents of human beings. He bears the thirty-two Marks of a Great Being, and is assisted in his rule by the Seven precious Things (*sapta-ratna*), listed in Sarvajña-mitra's verse 24, the precious wheel etc. These have remarkable magical properties, and are also interpreted as symbolic of the seven Enlightenment factors (*bodhyaṅga, byang chub kyi yan lag*), mindfulness etc.

Unknowing: see Ignorance.

Unvirtue, unwholesome (*a-kuśala, mi dge (ba)*): the ten unwholesome acts are killing, stealing, sexual misconduct, lying, harsh speech, slander, vain speech, covetousness, ill-will, and wrong view.

*Upādhyāya* (*mkhan po*): a teacher, in certain instructional or ritual functions such as advising a translator or giving ordination (see also Preceptor).

*Upāsaka* (*dge bsnyen*): a Buddhist layman, bound by the five vows (to avoid killing, stealing, sexual misconduct, intoxicating liquor and lying). Fem. *upāsikā*.

Upper rebirth (*svarga, mtho ris*): rebirth as a god or human being.

*Uśīra* (*pu shel tse*): 'the fragrant root of the plant *Andropogon muricatus*' (MW).

*Utpala*: Tārā's flower, the blue lotus, whose earthly representative is *Nymphæa caerulea*.

Vairocana (*rnam (par) snang (mdzad)*): 'the Sun-like', n. of a Buddha, Lord of the Tathāgata Family.

*Vaiṣṇava*: a follower of Viṣṇu.

*Vajra* (*rdo rje*): 1. The magical weapon of the Vedic god Indra, made of metal and very hard and sharp. 2. A thunderbolt. 3. A Tantric implement symbolizing Method (Compassion), held in the right hand (male side), cf. Bell. Also a part of various other Tantric implements, e.g. *v.* hook, a hook with *v.*-shaped knobs on. 4. As a description of anything that is supposed to be impenetrably hard (*v.* wall, *v.* tent) or indestructible (Vajrayāna and just about everything involved in it) – adamantine.

Vajrapāṇi (*phyag na rdo rje*): 'He who holds a *vajra* in his hand', n. of a Bodhisattva and Tantric deity, a *yakṣa* prince.

*Vajra-paryaṅka* (*rdo rje('i) skyil (mo) krung*): the *vajra* cross-legged position, like the 'lotus position' of Hindu *yoga* but reversed.

Vajrayāna (*rdo rje theg pa*): the 'Adamantine Vehicle' – also called the Mantra Vehicle, or Tantra.

Varuṇa (*chu lha*): Vedic god of the sky, 'the Encompassing', lord of light and darkness, celestial order, morality, and the primordial waters. Later relegated to overlordship of the terrestrial oceans, hence the Tib. translation of his name, 'water-god'. Guardian of the western quarter.

Vāyu (*rlung lha*): Vedic god of the wind, guardian of the north-west quarter.

Veda (*rig byed*): the books of 'sacred knowledge' – hymns and rituals – of the Āryans who invaded India c. 1700 BC, completed by about 800 BC.

Vehicle (*yāna, theg pa*): a means to Liberation; in the 'Lotus

Sūtra' (*Sad-dharma-puṇḍarīka-sūtra*) the various V. are compared to carts of different sizes. 'Both V.' (*theg pa che chung*, lit. 'the Great and Small V.') means the Hīnayāna and Mahāyāna, the latter being also called the V. of the Perfect Buddhas. 'The Supreme V.' (*theg mchog*) is Tantra, the Vajrayāna, strictly speaking included in the Mahāyāna. The three V., in the present book, are Hīnayāna, (non-tantric) Mahāyāna, and Vajrayāna.

Venerable (usually *bhaṭṭārikā, rje btsun (ma)*): common title of Tārā.

*Vetāla* (*ro langs*): see Corpse-raiser.

*Vidyā* (*rig ma*): 'knowledge-woman, mantra-woman', a *yogin*'s consort in Tantric sexual practices.

*Vidyā-dhara* (*rig (pa) 'dzin (pa)*): 'knowledge-bearer, mantra-bearer', a kind of supernatural being, possessed of magical power; usually depicted flying in the air in beautiful human form, sometimes with the lower half of the body bird-like. Fem. *vidyā-dharī*.

*Vidyā-mantra-dhara* (*rig sngags 'chang ba*): one learned in the profound mantric lore (D).

View (*dṛṣṭi, lta (ba)*): used several times in the sense of the Right View of Emptiness.

*Vihāra* (*gtsug lag khang*): a Buddhist monastery or monastic college.

*Vīṇā* (*pi bang, pi wang*): a type of stringed instrument, Indian lute.

Vinaya (*'dul ba*): 'basket' of the scriptures (see *Piṭaka*) concerned with monastic discipline, the rules for the behaviour of monks and nuns and the conduct of their communal business.

Viṣṇu (*khyab 'jug*): probably 'the Pervader'; as preserver of the universe, he forms part of the Hindu triad of gods, with Brahmā the creator and Śiva the destroyer.

Voice of sixty qualities, of sixty melodious aspects (*gsung dbyangs yan lag drug cu*): sixty qualities are ascribed to the Buddha's voice in a Sūtra.

Vow (*praṇidhāna, smon lam*): the eighth Perfection; (*saṃvara, sdom (pa)*): the sets of vowed discipline – *Prātimokṣa*, Bodhisattva and Tantric vows.

Wholesome (*kuśala, dge (ba)*).

Wisdom (*prajñā, shes rab* or *mkhyen (rab)*; also *mati, blo gros*):

1. direct intuitive apprehension of Ultimate Truth, i.e. of Emptiness; the sixth Perfection. The Path combines W. and Method; Tantric symbolism centres on the union of the two, W. being the female aspect and Method, or Means, the male. 2. The wisdoms of listening, thinking and meditation are steps towards this W. 3. In verse, 'Wisdom' is sometimes short for 'Wisdom-knowledge'.

Wisdom-knowledge (*jñāna, ye shes*): 'the perfect, absolute, heavenly, divine wisdom, which will suddenly break forth from the bodies of terrifying gods in the shape of fire' (Jäschke), the transcendant knowledge of Buddhas and Bodhisattvas beyond the Seventh Stage; the tenth Perfection. Five W.-k.: see *Kleśa*.

World-element (*loka-dhātu, 'jig rten gyi khams*): generally means a world or world-system.

Worlds, the three (*loka, 'jig rten*): see p. 415, n.39.

Worshipful: = Venerable.

*Yakṣa* (*gnod sbyin*); fem. *yakṣī* (*gnod sbyin mo*): a class of semi-divine beings, generally beneficent but sometimes malignant so that it is well to propitiate them with offerings. Many are local divinities of the countryside, often dwelling in sacred trees and guarding the treasure buried nearby. Others live on Mount Meru, guarding the realm of the gods. They are ruled by Kubera, the god of wealth and guardian of the northern quarter.

Yama (*gshin rje*; Skt also *kīnāśa*): the terrible judge of the dead, king of the *pretas* in the underground Yama-world (*yama-loka*) and also guardian of the southern quarter. The 'Yamas' are either the *pretas* or his servants who on his orders throw sinners into hell (*AdK*, III pp. 153, 156).

Yogācārin: pertaining to the Yogācāra, a Mahāyāna philosophical school also known as Citta-mātra.

*Yoga-tantra* (*rnal 'byor rgyud*): third of the four levels of Tantra.

*Yogin* (*rnal 'byor pa*), fem. *yoginī* (*rnal 'byor ma*): an ascetic, a practitioner of *yoga*, i.e. of Tantra; esp. one who engages in sexual and other Tantric practices incompatible with keeping monastic vows.

*Yojana* (*dpag tshad*): Indian measure of distance equal to 16000 cubits, or about 4.5 miles (7.4 km); definitions differing by a factor of two are also given.

*Yoni* (*skye gnas*): the female genitals.

# *Bibliography*

## 1 KANGYUR TEXTS. *By Sanskrit title.*

*Ārya-tārā-kurukulle-kalpa*. Tib: 'Phags ma sgrol ma ku ru kulle'i rtog pa. Tr. Ind. *upādhyāya* Kṛṣṇa-Paṇḍita & *Lo tsā ba* Tshul khrims rgyal ba. Tog: rG NGA 832–869. sDe dge: Toh. 437.

*Ārya-tārā-bhaṭṭārikā-nāmâṣṭôttara-śataka-stotra*. Skt: ed. Blonay, *Matériaux* (1895), pp. 48–53.

Tib: T1: Bhaṭa-tārā-aṣṭa-śadaka-nāma, rJe btsun sgrol ma'i mtshan brgya rtsa brgyad pa zhes bya ba. Tr. Kashmiri *paṇḍita* Buddha-ākara & Tib. tr. Ga rub Chos kyi shes rab. Tog: rG MA 251–253. (Names only).

T2: Ārya-tārā-bhaṭṭārikā-nāmâṣṭa-śataka(ṃ), rJe btsun ma 'phags ma sgrol ma'i mtshan brgya rtsa brgyad pa. Tr. not given, attrib. Thar pa lo tsa ba Nyi ma rgyal mtshan. sDe dge: Toh.727. Lhasa: rG PHA 75b–79a. sNar thang: rG PHA 480a–483a. Peking: P391, Vol.*8*, 155.5.8–156.5.6, rG TSA 74a–76b. Tog: rG MA 238–243.

Fr: G. de Blonay (1895), 54–57.

Eng: E1: E.Conze, *Buddhist Texts through the Ages* (1954), 196–202. The 108 Names of the Holy Tara.

E2: here, 98–104. The Hundred and Eight Names of the Venerable Ārya-Tārā.

*Ārya-tārā-aṣṭaghora-tāraṇī-sūtra*. Tib: 'Phags ma sgrol ma 'jigs pa brgyad las skyob pa'i mdo. Tr. not given. Peking:

P395, Vol.8, 158.2.2–159.1.5, rGTSA 80a–82a. sDe dge: Toh. 731. Lhasa: rG NA 473b-476a. Not in Tog dkar chag.

Eng: here, 89–93. The Sūtra of Ārya-Tārā Who Saves from the Eight Fears.

*Ārya-Mañjuśrī-mūla-kalpa*. Skt: extracts quoted by Ghosh fr. ed. of P.L. Vaidya, Buddhist Skt Texts, no.18, Darbhanga, 1964.

Tib: Ārya-Mañjuśrī-mūla-tantra, 'Phags pa 'Jam dpal gyi rtsa ba'i rgyud. Tr. dGe slong Shākya blo gros. Tog: rG DA 218–951 (Chap. 2: pp. 278–331; Chap. 4: pp. 334–357; Chap. 36: pp. 820–950).

Fr (Chap. 2): A. Macdonald.

Eng: short extracts here, 41–43.

*Tārā-devī-nāmâṣṭa-śataka*. Tib: Lha mo sgrol ma'i mtshan brgya rtsa brgyad pa. Tr. not given. sDe dge: Toh.728. Peking: P392, Vol.*8*, 156.5.6–158.1.8, rG TSA 76b–79b. Tog: rG MA, 243–251.

*Bhagavaty-ārya-tārā-devyā namaskāraikaviṃśati-stotraṃ guṇa-hita-sahitam*. Skt: Sources: D, L, N, P, T in Chap. 3 of *Sarva-tathāgata-mātṛ-tārā-viśvakarma-bhava-tantra* in Kg. B in Bu ston Rin po che, *sGrol ma las sna tshogs 'byung ba zhes bya ba'i rgyud sngags*. M in G. de Blonay, *Matériaux*, 58–60.

Editions: Wayman (1959) (from D & M); here, 55–58 (fr. all above sources).

Tib: sGrol ma la phyag 'tshal nyi shu rtsa gcig gi bstod pa phan yon dang bcas pa. Tr. not given, according to rJe btsun Grags pa rgyal mtshan tr. gNyan Lo tsā ba (Dhar ma grags) and rev. rJe btsun Grags pa rgyal mtshan. Lhasa Kg: rG NGA, 299b–301b. sDe dge: Toh. 438. Peking: P77. Other versions and edited text: Appendix 1.

Eng: here, 113–6. The Praise in Twenty-one Homages to Our Lady, the Goddess Ārya-Tārā, with its Benefits (fr. Skt). Also Appendix 2 (fr. Tib).

Commentaries: see Part Two.

*Sarva-tathāgata-mātṛ-tārā-viśvakarma-bhava-tantra-nāma*. Tib: De bzhin gshegs pa thams cad kyi yum sgrol ma las sna tshogs 'byung ba zhes bya ba'i rgyud. Tr. Ind. *upādhyāya* Dharmaśrīmitra & *Lo tsa ba* dge slong Chos kyi bzang po. sDe dge: Toh.726, rG TSHA 202a–217a. Lhasa: rG PHA 51a–75b. sNar thang: rG PHA 457b–483a. Peking: P390, Vol.*8*, 149.3.5–155.5.8, rG TSA 58a–74a. Tog: rG MA 195–237.

Eng: here, 51–85. The Tantra called the Origin of All Rites of Tārā, Mother of All the Tathāgatas.

*Hevajra-tantra*. Skt: Śrī-Hevajra-(ḍākinī-jāla-saṃvara-)mahā-tantra-rāja. Ed. in D.L.Snellgrove: *The Hevajra Tantra. A critical study*. London, Oxford Univ. Press, 1959. 2 parts.

Tib: Hevajra-tantra-rāja-nāma, Kye'i rdo rje zhes bya ba rgyud kyi rgyal po. Ed. in Snellgrove, Part 2.

Eng: Snellgrove, Part 1.

## 2 TÄNGYUR TEXTS. *By author.*

(Anonymous): (V1, V2) *Vajra-tārā-sādhana*. Skt: in *Sādhana-mālā*, quoted by Ghosh.

Tib: rDo rje sgrol ma'i sgrub thabs. Tr. Grags pa rgyal mtshan. V1: P4308, Vol.*80*, 286.2.4–287.2.3, rG DU 170a–172b. V2: P4309, Vol. *80*, 287.2.3–288.3.2, rG DU 172b–175b.

Akṣobhya-vajra (= Buddha-jñāna-pāda): *Ārya-tārā-stotra*. Tib: 'Phags ma sgrol ma la bstod pa. Tr. not given. P4875, Vol.*86*, 126.4.1–127.1.3, rG ZU 186a–187a.

Eng: here, 274–276. Praise of Ārya-Tārā.

Candrakīrti: *Madhyamakâvatāra*. Tib: dbU ma la 'jug pa. Ed. with author's commentary by L. de La Vallée Poussin, Bibliotheca Buddhica, *IX*, 1907–12.

Fr: tr. La Vallée Poussin, Le Muséon, *8*, 249–317, 1907; *11*, 271–358, 1910; *12*, 235–328, 1911. Introduction au Traité du Milieu (first three-quarters, with author's commentary).

Eng: Willson, to be published. Introduction to the Middle Way (complete root text with Gedün-dr'up's commentary).

Candrakīrti (Zla ba grags pa): *Vajravārāhī-tārā-stotra*. Tib: rDo rje phag mo sgrol ma la bstod pa. Tr. not given. P2595, Vol. *59*, 90.5.6–91.1.5, rG LA 106b–107a.

Eng: here, 286–287. Praise of Vajravārāhī Tārā.

Candragomin: *Ārya-tārā-devī-stotra-muktikā-mālā-nāma*. Tib: 'Phags ma lha mo sgrol ma la bstod pa Mu tig 'phreng ba zhes bya ba. Tr. Ind. *upādhyāya* Dīpaṃkara-śrī-jñāna & *Lo tsā ba* Nag tsho Tshul khrims rgyal ba, at Vikramaśīla *vihāra*. P4869, Vol. *86*, 123.4.6–124.4.8, rG ZU 178b–181a.

Eng: here, 226–231. The Pearl Garland, a Praise of the Goddess Ārya-Tārā.

Candragomin (dPal btsun zla ba): *Ārya-tārā-mahā-aṣṭabhayôt-*

*tārā-stava* (cat. as Ārya-aṣṭa-mahābhayottārā-tārā-stava). Tib: 'Phags ma sgrol ma 'jigs pa chen po brgyad las sgrol ba'i bstod pa. Tr. not given. P4873, Vol. *86*, 126.1.1–2.5, rG ZU 184b–185a.

Eng: here, 236–237. Praise of Ārya-Tārā Who Saves from the Eight Great Fears.

Candragomin: *Ārya-tārā-aṣṭabhaya-trāta-nāma-sādhana* (cat. as Ārya-aṣṭabhaya-trāta-nāma-tārā-sādhana). Tib: 'Phags ma sgrol ma 'jigs pa brgyad las skyob pa zhes bya ba'i sgrub thabs. Tr. Ind. *upādhyāya* Dīpaṃkara-śrī-jñāna & *Lo tsā ba* Tshul khrims rgyal ba, rev. Ind. *upādhyāya* Bodhisattva Dāna-śrī & *Lo tsā ba* Mal gyi bLo gros grags pa. P4494, Vol. *81*, 74.1.1–5.4, rG DU 373a–375a.

Eng: here, 337–342. Sādhana of Ārya-Tārā called Protection from the Eight Fears.

Candragomin: *Ārya-tārā-stotra-praṇidhāna-siddhi-nāma*. Tib: A: Ārya-tārā-stotra-praṇidhāna-nāma, 'Phags ma sgrol ma la bstod pa smon lam grub pa zhes bya ba. Tr. not given. P4871, Vol. *86*, 125.1.5–2.8, rG ZU 182a-b.

B: Ārya-tārā-stotra-viśvakarma-sādhana-nāma, 'Phags ma sgrol ma'i bstod pa phrin las sgrub pa zhes bya ba. Tr. not given. P4491, Vol. *81*, 72.4.1–5.5, rG DU 369b–370a.

Eng: here, 234–235. A Praise of Ārya-Tārā, called the Accomplisher of Vows.

Candragomin: *Ārya-devī-tārā-stotra*. Tib: A: (Skt as above), 'Phags ma lha mo sgrol ma'i bstod pa. Tr. not given. P4870, Vol. *86*, 124.5.1–125.1.4, rG ZU 181b–182a.

B: Ārya-tārā-stotra-dvādaśa-gāthā, 'Phags ma sgrol ma la bstod pa tshigs su bcad pa bcu gnyis pa. Tr. not given, P4490, Vol. *81*, 72.2.6–3.8, rG DU 368b–369a.

C: Ārya-tārādevī-stava-nāma, 'Phags ma lha mo sgrol ma la bstod pa zhes bya ba. Tr. not given. P4493, Vol. *81*, 73.4.7–5.8, rG DU 372a-b.

Eng: here, 232–233. Praise of the Noble Goddess Tārā (follows A).

Dīpaṃkara-bhadra (Mar me mdzad bzang po): *Ārya-tārā-stotra*. Tib: 'Phags ma sgrol ma la bstod pa. Tr. Kashmiri *upādhyāya* Buddhākara-varman & *Lo tsā ba* dGe slong Chos kyi ye shes. P4874, Vol. *86*, 126.2.6–3.8, rG ZU 185a-b.

Eng: here, 277–278. Praise of Ārya-Tārā.

Dīpaṃkara-śrī-jñāna (dPal mar me mdzad ye shes, = Atīśa): [*Aṣṭa-bhaya-trāṇa*]. Tib: 'Jigs pa brgyad las skyob pa. Tr.

not given; index: author & Nag tsho Tshul khrims rgyal ba. P4510, Vol. *81*, 94.4.2–5.5, rG DU 424b–425a.

Eng: here, 343–344. Protecting from the Eight Fears.

Dīpaṃkara-śrī-jñāna (= Atīśa): *Ārya-tārā-stotra*. Tib: 'Phags ma sgrol ma la bstod pa. Tr. author & *Lo tsā ba* Tshul khrims rgyal ba. P4511, Vol. *81*, 94.5.6–95.1.8, rG DU 425a-b.

Eng: here, 293–294. Praise of Ārya-Tārā.

Dīpaṃkara-śrī-jñāna (dPal mar me mdzad ye shes, = Atīśa): [*Tārā-bhaṭṭārikā-sādhana*]. Tib: rJe btsun sgrol ma'i sgrub thabs. Tr. Ind. *upādhyāya* Dīpaṃkara-śrī-jñāna (= author) & Tib. tr. dGe ba'i blo gros. P4508, Vol. *81*, 90.4.5–91.5.7, rG DU 414b–417b.

Eng: here, 345–350. Sādhana of the Venerable Tārā.

Nāgārjuna ('Phags pa klu [s]grub): *Khadiravaṇī-tārā-stotra*. Tib: Seng ldeng nags kyi sgrol ma la bstod pa. Tr. not given. P4481, Vol. *86*, 130.1.7–4.1, rG ZU 194b–196a.

Eng: here, 282–285. Praise of Khadiravaṇī Tārā.

Mātṛceṭa: *Ārya-tārādevī-stotra-Sarvârtha-sādhana-nāma-stotra-rāja*. Tib: 'Phags ma lha mo sgrol ma'i bstod pa Don thams cad grub pa zhes bya ba bstod pa'i rgyal po. Tr. not given. P2574, Vol. *59*, 75.4.2–76.4.8, rG LA 68b–71a.

Eng: here, 214–221. The King of Praises called the Fulfiller of All Aims, a Praise of the *Ārya* Goddess Tārā.

Mātṛceṭa: *Ārya-tārā-stotra*. Tib: 'Phags ma sgrol ma la bstod pa. Tr. not given. P4516, Vol. *81*, 97.1.5–2.7, rG DU 430b–431a.

Eng: here, 212–213. Praise of Ārya-Tārā.

Ratnākara-śānti: (V3) *Vajra-tārā-sādhana*. Tib: rDo rje sgrol ma'i sgrub thabs. Tr. Grags pa rgyal mtshan. P4312, Vol. *80*, 290.1.6–292.5.4, rG DU 179b–186b.

Sarvajña-mitra (Thams cad mkhyen pa'i bshes gnyen): *Ārya-tārā-sragdharā-stotra*. Skt: ed. G. de Blonay, *Matériaux* (1895), 34–40; ed. Vidyabhusana (1908), see p.255.

Tib: A: Phreng ba 'dzin pa'i bstod pa. Tr. not given; is a version of the Kanakavarman & Pa tshab tr. P2563, Vol. *59*, 67.1.6–68.5.7, rG LA 47a–51b.

B: Me tog phreng 'dzin gyi bstod pa. Tr. Ind. *upādhyāya* Kanakavarman & Tib. *lo tsā ba* Pa tshab Nyi ma grags, later slightly corrected with *paṇḍita* Maṇika-śrī-jñāna by *lo tsā ba* Chos rje dpal of Phyag. P2564, Vol. *59*, 68.5.7–70.4.8, rG LA 51b–56a.

C: 'Phags ma sgrol ma'i me tog phreng ba 'dzin pa'i bstod

pa. Tr. Zla ba gzhon nu. P2565, Vol. *59*, 70.4.8–72.3.3, rG LA 56a–60b.

Fr: G. de Blonay (1895), 41–47 (fr. Skt).

Eng: here, 258–270. Sragdharā Praise of Ārya-Tārā (fr. Skt).

Sūryagupta (Kha che Nyi ma sbas pa): [*Ārya-tārā-bhaṭṭārikā-nāma-dvātriṃśatka-stotra Sarvârtha-sādhaka-ratna-alaṃkāra-saṃnibha-nāma*]. Tib: rJe btsun ma 'phags ma sgrol ma la mtshan sum cu rtsa gnyis kyi bstod pa Don thams cad grub par byed pa Rin chen brgyan 'dra zhes bya ba. Tr. not given. P4879, Vol. *86*, 128.3.4–129.4.3, rG ZU 190b–193b.

Eng: here, 242–250. Praise of the Thirty-two Names of the Venerable Ārya-Tārā called the Jewel-ornament-like Fulfiller of All Aims.

Sūryagupta: (S2) [*Ārya-tārā-bhaṭṭārikā-sādhana-sakalpa-ekaviṃśaka-karma-saṃkṣepa-nāma*]. Tib: rJe btsun ma 'phags ma sgrol ma'i sgrub thabs nyi shu rtsa gcig pa'i las kyi yan lag dang bcas pa mdor bsdus pa zhes bya ba. Tr. Ind. *upādhyāya* Mañjuśrī & Tib. *lo tsā ba* Mal gyo bLo gros grags pa, at Vikramaśīla *mahāvihāra*. P2558, Vol. *59*, 53.1.1–59.5.4, rG LA 12a–29a.

Sūryagupta: *Ārya-tārā-stotra*. Tib: 'Phags ma sgrol ma la bstod pa. Tr. Ind. *paṇḍita* Sādhukīrti & Tib. *lo tsā ba* 'Dan ma Tshul khrims seng ge, later corrected at Sa skya *vihāra*. P2562, Vol. *59*, 66.3.5–67.1.6, rG LA 45b–47a.

Sūryagupta: (S1) *Tārādevī-stotra-ekaviṃśatika-sādhana-nāma*. Tib: Lha mo sgrol ma'i bstod pa nyi shu rtsa gcig pa'i sgrub thabs zhes bya ba. Tr. *paṇḍita* Mañjuśri & Tib. *lo tsā ba* Mal gyi (read 'gyo') bLo gros grags pa. P2557, Vol. *59*, 51.2.6–53.1.1, rG LA 7b–12a.

Sūryagupta-pāda: (S3) *Tārā-sādhana-upadeśa-krama*. Tib: sGrol ma'i sgrub thabs man ngag gi rim pa. Tr. later at Sa skya fr. a copy brought to Tibet by the *paṇḍita* [Śākyaśrībhadra] of Kashmir. P2559, Vol. *59*, 59.5.4–60.2.8, rG LA 29a–30a.

Eng: Willson, unpublished. Method of Instruction on the Accomplishment of Tārā.

Sūryagupta-pāda: (S5) *Devītārā-ekaviṃśati-stotra-Viśuddha-cūḍāmaṇi-nāma*. Tib: Lha mo sgrol ma nyi shu rtsa gcig la bstod pa, rNam dag gtsug gi nor bu zhes bya ba. Tr. not given, cat. as tr. by rGya lo tsā ba brTson 'grus seng ge.

P2561, Vol. *59*, 64.4.7–66.3.5, rG LA 41a–45b.
Eng: quotations in Part Two.

Sūryagupta-pāda: (S4) *Bhagavatī-tārā-devī-ekaviṃśati-stotra-upāyika*. Tib: bCom ldan 'das ma sgrol ma la bstod pa nyi shu rtsa gcig pa'i sgrub thabs. Tr. Śākyaśrībhadra of Kashmir & *Lo tsā ba* Byams pa'i dpal. P2560, Vol. *59*, 60.2.8–64.4.7, rG LA 30a–41a.
Eng: quotations in Part Two.

## 3 TIBETAN TEXTS. *By author.*

Grags pa rgyal mtshan, rJe btsun: *Phyag 'tshal nyer gcig gi bstod pa sa bcad*. In *Sa skya pa'i bka' 'bum. The Complete Works of the Great Masters of the Sa-skya Sect of Tibetan Buddhism*, compiled by bSod nams rgya mtsho. Tokyo, Toyo Bunko, 1968. Vol. *4*, 92.1.2–2.3. ('Outlines of the Praise in Twenty-one Homages.')

Grags pa rgyal mtshan, rJe btsun: *bsTod pa'i rnam bshad gsal ba'i 'od zer*. In *Sa skya pa'i bka' 'bum*, Vol. *4*, 92.2.3–94.2.2. ('Clear Light Explanation of the Praise.')

Grags pa rgyal mtshan, rJe btsun: *Nyi ma sbas pas mdzad pa'i rgya gzhung gi las tshogs kyi bsdus don*. In *Sa skya pa'i bka' 'bum*, Vol. *4*, 83.2.3–86.1.4. ('Epitome of the Set of Rites in the Indian Text by Sūryagupta.')

dGe 'dūn grub pa, First Dalai Lama: *sGrol ma phyag 'tshal nyer gcig gi ṭīkka Rin po che'i phreng ba*. In *The Collected Works (gSuṅ 'Bum) of the First Dalai Lama dGe 'dun grub pa*, Gangtok 1981, Vol. *6* (CHA), 59–73. ('The Precious Garland, a *Ṭīkā* on the Twenty-one Homages to Tārā.')

dGe 'dun grub pa dpal bzang po, First Dalai Lama: *rJe btsun bcom ldan 'das ma seng ldeng nags kyi sgrol ma la bstod pa mKhas pa'i gtsug rgyan zhes bya ba* (known as *Legs bris ma*). Manuscript pe-cha.
Eng: here, 301–306. Praise of the Venerable Lady Khadira-vaṇī Tārā called the Crown Jewel of the Wise.

dNgul chu Dharmabhadra: *sGrol mar phyag 'tshal nyer gcig gis bstod pa'i rnam bshad Yid 'phrog utpa la'i chun po zhes bya ba*. In *Collected Works (gSuṅ 'bum) of Dṅul-chu Dharmabhadra*, New Delhi, 1973. Vol. *2*, 583–606. ('The Bunch of Captivating *Utpalas*, an Explanation of the Praise in Twenty-one Homages to Tārā.')

dNgul chu Dharmabhadra: *rJe btsun sengs ldeng nags kyi sgrol ma'i bstod pa Legs bris mar grags pa'i 'grel pa nyung ngu rnam gsal zhes bya ba.* In *Collected Works*, Vol. 2, 627–646. ('Illuminating Small Commentary on the Praise of the Venerable Khadiravaṇī Tārā known as the *Legs bris ma*.')

Chos kyi grags pa, dGe bshes: (Ch) *brDa dag ming tshig gsal ba.* Lhasa 1949; with Chinese translations added 1957, repr. Peking, Mi rigs dpe skrun khang, 1981.

Tāranātha: *bKa' babs bdun ldan = bKa' babs bdun ldan gyi brgyud pa'i rnam thar ngo mtshar rmad byung rin po che*, 1600.
German: Grünwedel.
Eng: Datta (*MT*).

Tāranātha: *sGrol ma'i rgyud kyi byung khungs gsal bar byed pa'i lo rgyus gSer gyi phreng ba zhes bya ba*, 1604. Repr. in India as small lithographed booklet, n.d.
Eng: here, 33–36, 178–206. The Golden Rosary: A History Illuminating the Origin of the Tantra of Tārā.

Tāranātha: *rGya gar chos 'byung*, 1608. Eng: see section 4.

bDud 'joms Rin po che 'Jigs bral ye shes rdo rje: *'Phags ma nor rgyun ma'i rgyun khyer*. Manuscript.

Paṇ chen bsTan pa'i nyi ma Phyogs las rnam rgyal, Fourth Paṇchen Lama: *Sādhana-mālā of the Paṇchen Lama* (*Yi dam rgya mtsho'i sgrub thabs rin chen 'byung gnas kyi lhan thabs: rin 'byung don gsal*). 2 parts. New Delhi, Int. Acad. Ind. Culture, 1974 (Śatapiṭaka Ser. No. 210).

'Phags pa bLo gros rgyal mtshan, Chos rgyal: *sGrol ma lha bcu bdun ma'i dkyil 'khor gyi sgrub thabs.* In bSod nams rgya mtsho (compiled), *Sa skya pa'i bka' 'bum. The Complete Works of the Great Masters of the Sa-skya Sect of Tibetan Buddhism*, Tokyo, Toyo Bunko, 1968. Vol. 6, 263.4–266.3.6. ('*Sādhana* of the *Maṇḍala* of Tārā with Seventeen Deities.')

'Phags pa bLo gros rgyal mtshan, Chos rgyal: *rDo rje sgrol ma'i* sgrub thabs. In *Sa skya pa'i bka' 'bum*, Vol. 6, 267.1.3–4.5. ('*Sādhana* of Vajra-tārā.')

Bu ston Rin po che: *Chos 'byung*. Eng: see section 4.

Bu ston Rin po che: *sGrol ma bcu bdun ma'i brgyud pa.* In *Collected Works of Bu-ston*. Ed. by Dr Lokesh Chandra, from the collections of Dr Raghu Vira. New Delhi, Int. Acad. Ind. Culture, 1969. Part 16 (MA), 14.7–15.2. ('Lineage of Tārā with Seventeen Deities.')

Bu ston Rin po che: *sGrol ma las sna tshogs 'byung ba zhes bya ba'i rgyud sngags.* In *Collected Works of Bu-ston*, Part 16 (MA),

430–435. ('Mantras of the *Tārā-viśvakarma-bhava-tantra*.')

Brag gYab, bLo ldan shes rab: (D) *Bod brda'i tshig mdzod* (Tibetan Dictionary). Dharamsala, 1977.

bLo gros rgya mtsho: *rJe btsun sgrol ma'i gdung 'bod Ratna'i phreng [ba] zhes bya ba*. Manuscript pe-cha.

Eng: here, 318–321. The Garland of Jewels, A Song of Longing for Venerable Ārya-Tārā.

bLo gros rgya mtsho (Matisāra): *rJe btsun ma phyag 'tshal nyer gcig gi lha tshogs la bstod cing gsol ba 'debs pa*. Small pe-cha, 7 leaves, no publication details.

Eng: here, 309–317. Praises and Requests to the Assembly of Deities of the Venerable Mother of the Twenty-one Homages.

bLo bzang bstan pa'i rgyal mtshan: *rJe btsun sgrol ma'i gdung 'bod* (= *gDung 'bod bslu med ma*). Manuscript pe-cha.

Eng: here, 324–328. A Song of Longing for Tārā, the Infallible.

## 4 GENERAL

Adams, Henry: *Mont-Saint-Michel and Chartres*. Privately printed 1904, published 1913; repr. NY, Mentor Books, 1961.

Allione, Tsultrim: *Women of Wisdom*. London, Routledge & Kegan Paul, 1984.

Bareau, André: *Les Sectes Bouddhiques du Petit Véhicule*. Paris, École Française d'Extrême-Orient, 1955 (Pubns E.F.E.O., *XXXVIII*).

Bernbaum, Edwin: *The Way to Shambhala*. Garden City, NY, Anchor Books, 1980.

Beyer, Stephan: *The Cult of Tārā*. Magic and Ritual in Tibet. Berkeley, Univ. Cal. Press, 1973, pbk. ed. 1978.

Blofeld, John: *Compassion Yoga*. The Mystical Cult of Kuan Yin. London, Unwin Pbks, 1977.

Blonay, Godefroy de: *Matériaux pour Servir à l'Histoire de la Déesse Buddhique Tārā*. Paris, Librairie Émile Bouillon, 1895 (Bibliothèque de l'École des Hautes Études, *107*).

Bodhi, Bhikkhu (tr.): *The Discourse on the All-Embracing Net of Views*. The *Brahmajāla Sutta* and its commentarial exegesis, tr. from the Pali. Kandy, Buddhist Pubn Soc., 1978.

Buddhaghosa, Bhadantācariya: *The Path of Purification (Visuddhimagga)*. Tr. fr. the Pali by Bhikkhu Ñāṇamoli. Sri Lanka,

1956, 1964; repr. in 2 vol., Berkeley, Shambhala, 1976.
Bu-ston (Bu-tön): *History of Buddhism (Chos 'byung)*. Tr. fr. the Tib. by Dr E. Obermiller. Two parts, Heidelberg 1931–2, repr. in one vol. Japan, Suzuki Research Foundation, Repr. Ser., 5.
Chandra, Lokesh: *Tibetan-Sanskrit Dictionary*, based on a close comparative study of Skt originals and Tib translations of several texts. New Delhi, Int. Acad. of Ind. Culture, 1959–1961 (12 vols), repr. in 2 vols Kyoto, Rinsen, 1971, and in one vol., ib., 1982.
Chattopadhyaya, Alaka: *Atīśa and Tibet*. Life and Works of Dīpaṃkara Śrījñāna in relation to the History and Religion of Tibet. With Tib. sources tr. under the direction of Prof. Lama Chimpa. Calcutta, 1967, repr. Delhi, Motilal Banarsidass, 1981.
Chattopadhyaya, Debiprasad (ed.): *Tāranātha's History of Buddhism in India*: see Tāranātha.
Chattopadhyaya, Sudhakar: (*EHNI*) *Early History of North India* (from the fall of the Mauryas to the death of Harṣa). 3rd rev. ed., Delhi, Motilal Banarsidass, 1976.
Conze, Edward: *Buddhism: its essence and development*. Oxford, Bruno Cassirer, 1951; repr. NY, Harper Torchbooks, 1959.
Conze, Edward (ed.): *Buddhist Texts Through the Ages*. Tr. fr. Pali, Skt, Chinese, Tib, Japanese and Apabhramsa. Oxford, Bruno Cassirer, 1954, repr. NY, Harper Torchbooks, 1964.
Conze, Edward (tr. & explained): *Buddhist Wisdom Books*. Containing the Diamond Sutra and the Heart Sutra. London, Allen & Unwin, 1958; repr. NY, Harper Torchbooks, 1972.
Conze, Edward (tr.): *The Short Prajñāpāramitā Texts*. London, Luzac, 1973.
Conze, Edward (tr.): *The Perfection of Wisdom in Eight Thousand Lines and its Verse Summary*. Bolinas, Cal., Four Seasons Foundation, 1973.
Conze, Edward (tr. & ed.): *The Large Sutra on Perfect Wisdom*, with the divisions of the Abhisamayālaṃkāra. Berkeley, Univ. Cal. Press, 1975 (repr. Delhi, Motilal Banarsidass, 1979).
Conze, Edward: *The Prajñāpāramitā Literature*. 2nd ed., rev. & enlarged, Tokyo, The Reiyukai, 1978.
Dagyab, L.S.: see section 3, Brag gYab.
Dargyay, Eva M.: *The Rise of Esoteric Buddhism in Tibet*. Delhi, Motilal Banarsidass, 2nd rev. ed., 1979.

Das, Sarat Chandra: (CD) *A Tibetan-English Dictionary with Sanskrit Synonyms.* Rev. & ed. by Graham Sandberg & A. William Hyde. Calcutta 1902, repr. Kyoto, Rinsen, 1979.

Datta, Bhupendranath (tr.): (*MT*) *Mystic Tales of Lāmā Tārānātha.* A Religio-sociological History of Mahāyāna Buddhism. Calcutta, Ramakrishna Vedanta Math, 1944, repr. 1957 (Eng. abstract of Grünwedel's German tr.).

Dey, Nando lal: (NLD) *The Geographical Dictionary of Ancient and Mediaeval India.* 2nd ed. 1927, repr. New Delhi, Cosmo Pubns, 1979.

Edgerton, Franklin: (E) *Buddhist Hybrid Sanskrit Grammar & Dictionary.* 2 vols (Vol. I: Grammar; Vol. II: Dictionary). New Haven, Yale Univ. Press, 1953; repr. Delhi, Motilal Banarsidass, 1970.

Evans-Wentz, W. Y. (ed.): *Tibetan Yoga and Secret Doctrines;* Or Seven Books of Wisdom of the Great Path, according to the late Lāma Kazi Dawa-Samdup's English rendering. 2nd ed., London, Oxford Univ. Press, 1958.

Frank, Bernard (tr.): *Histoires qui sont maintenant du passé* (*Konjaku monogatari shû*). Paris, Gallimard, 1968 (Colln Connaissance de l'Orient, Vol. 26; Colln UNESCO d'Œuvres Représentatives).

Gega lama (dGe dga' bla ma): *Principles of Tibetan Art.* Illustrations and explanations of Buddhist iconography and iconometry according to the Karma Gardri School. In Tib with Eng tr. by Richard Barron. Antwerp, Karma Sonam Gyamtso Ling, 1985.

Ghosh, Mallar: *Development of Buddhist Iconography in Eastern India*: A Study of Tārā, Prajñās of Five Tathāgatas and Bhṛkuṭī. New Delhi, Munshiram Manoharlal, 1980.

Goldstein, Melvyn C. (ed.): *Tibetan-English Dictionary of Modern Tibetan.* Kathmandu, Ratna Pustak Bhandar, 1978 (Bibliotheca Himalayica, Ser. II, Vol. 7).

Govinda, Lama Anagarika: *Foundations of Tibetan Mysticism.* According to the Esoteric Teachings of the Great Mantra OṂ MAṆI PADME HŪṂ. London, Rider, 1960.

Govinda, Lama Anagarika: *Creative Meditation and Multi-Dimensional Consciousness.* Wheaton, Ill., Theosophical Pubg House, 1976.

Graves, Robert: *The White Goddess.* A historical grammar of poetic myth. Amended & enlarged ed., London, Faber & Faber, 1961.

Grousset, René: *Sur les Traces du Bouddha*. 1957, repr. Paris, Librairie Académique Perrin, 1977.

Grünwedel, Albert (tr.): *Tāranātha's Edelsteinmine*, das Buch von den Vermittlern der Sieben Inspirationen (*bKa' 'babs bdun ldan*). Aus dem Tibetischen übersetzt. Petrograd, Acad. Impériale des Sciences, 1914 (Bibliotheca Buddhica XVIII).

Guenther, H.V. (tr. & annotated): *The Jewel Ornament of Liberation*, by sGam po pa. London, Rider, 1959, 1970; Berkeley, Shambhala, 1971.

Guenther, H.V. (tr. & introduced): *The Life and Teaching of Nāropa*. Oxford Univ. Press, 1963.

Hopkins, Jeffrey: *Meditation on Emptiness*. London, Wisdom Pubns, 1983.

Jackson, David P. & Janice A.: *Tibetan Thangka Painting*. Methods & Materials. London, Serindia Pubns, 1984.

Jäschke, H.A.: *Tibetan-English Dictionary*. London, 1881.

Joshi, Lal Mani: *Studies in the Buddhistic Culture of India* (During the 7th and 8th centuries A.D.). Delhi, Motilal Banarsidass, 2nd rev. ed., 1977.

Kelsang, Lama Thubten, et al: *Atisha*. A biography of the renowned Buddhist sage. Bangkok, Social Science Association Press, 1974; repr. New Delhi, Mahayana Pubns, 1983.

Kern, H. (tr.): *Saddharma-puṇḍarīka, or The Lotus of the True Law*. Oxford, 1884, repr. NY, Dover Pubns, 1963 (Sacred Books of the East, Vol. XXI).

Khetsun Sangpo: *Biographical Dictionary of Tibet and Tibetan Buddhism*. Vols V & VI: The bKa' gdams pa Tradition. (In Tib). Dharamsala, Library of Tibetan Works & Archives, 1973–1975.

Kochumuttom, Thomas A.: *A Buddhist Doctrine of Experience*. A New Translation and Interpretation of the Works of Vasubandhu the Yogācārin. Delhi, Motilal Banarsidass, 1982.

Lamotte, Étienne: *Histoire du Bouddhisme Indien*. Des Origines à l'Ère Śaka. Louvain-la-Neuve, Inst. Orientaliste, 1976.

Lamotte, Étienne: *La Somme du Grand Véhicule d'Asaṅga (Mahāyānasaṃgraha)*. 2 vols, Louvain 1938, repr. Louvain-la-Neuve, Inst. Orientaliste, 1973.

Lamotte, Étienne (tr. & annotated): *Le Traité de la Grande Vertu de Sagesse, de Nāgārjuna (Mahāprajñāpāramitāśāstra)*. 5 tomes. Louvain(-la-Neuve), Inst. Orientaliste, 1944–80.

La Vallée Poussin, Louis de (tr. & annotated): *L'Abhidhar-*

*makośa de Vasubandhu.* 6 tomes, Paris, 1923–31; repr. Bruxelles, Inst. Belge des Hautes Études Chinoises, 1971, 1980 (Mélanges Chinois et Bouddhiques, Vol. XVI).

Lessing, F.D. & A. Wayman (tr.): *Introduction to the Buddhist Tantric Systems.* Tr. fr. mKhas grub rJe's *rGyud sde spyi'i rnam par gzhag pa rgyas par brjod.* With original text and annotation. 2nd ed., Delhi, Motilal Banarsidass, 1978.

Lévi, Sylvain (tr.): *Asaṅga: Mahāyāna-sūtrālaṃkāra.* Exposé de la Doctrine du Grand Véhicule selon le Système Yogācāra. Tome II: Traduction. Paris, Librairie Honoré Champion, 1911. (Bibliothèque de l'École des Hautes Études, *190*).

Ling, Trevor: *Buddhism, Imperialism and War.* Burma and Thailand in modern history. London, George Allen & Unwin, 1979.

Loden, Geshe Thubten: *The Graduated Path to Enlightenment.* Ed. by Tony Duff. Australia, Tib. Buddhist Loden Mahāyāna Friendship Soc., 1980.

Macdonald, Ariane: *Le Maṇḍala du Mañjuśrīmūlakalpa.* Paris, Adrien-Maisonneuve, 1962 (Colln Jean Przyluski, Tome III).

Mimaki, Katsumi: *La Réfutation Bouddhique de la Permanence des Choses (Sthira-siddhi-dūṣaṇa) et la Preuve de la Momentanéité des Choses (Kṣaṇa-bhaṅga-siddhi).* Paris, Inst. de Civilisation Indienne, 1976. (Pubns de l'I.C.I., Sér. in-8°, Fasc. 41).

Monier-Williams, Sir Monier: *A Sanskrit-English Dictionary.* Etymologically and philologically arranged with special reference to cognate Indo-European languages. New ed., Oxford, 1899, repr. Delhi, Motilal Banarsidass, 1979.

Mullin, Glenn H.: *Meditations upon Arya Tara* by the First, Fifth and Seventh Dalai Lamas. Dharamsala, Dharmakaya Book, 1978 (small pe-cha).

Mullin, Glenn H.: (compiled & tr.): *Bridging the Sutras and Tantras.* A collection of ten minor works by Gyalwa Gendun Drub the First Dalai Lama. Dharamsala, Tushita Books, 1981.

Nam-mkha'i snying-po: *Mother of Knowledge*: The Enlightenment of Ye-shes mTsho-rgyal. Oral tr. by Tarthang Tulku, ed. by Jane Wilhelms. Berkeley, Dharma Pubg, 1983.

Neumann, Erich: *The Great Mother.* An Analysis of the Archetype. Tr. fr. the German by Ralph Manheim. Princeton Univ. Press, 2nd ed. 1963, repr. Bollingen Ser. XLVII, 1972.

Paṇdey, Mithila Sharan: *The Historical Geography and Topo-*

*graphy of Bihar*. Delhi, Motilal Banarsidass, 1963.
Paul, Diana Y.: *Women in Buddhism*. Images of the Feminine in Mahāyāna Tradition. With contributions by Frances Wilson. Berkeley, Asian Humanities Press, 1979.
Petech, Luciano: *The Dalai-lamas and Regents of Tibet: A Chronological Study*. In: T'oung Pao, Vol. XLVII, Leiden, E.J. Brill, 1959, pp. 368–394.
Python, Pierre (ed. & tr.): *Vinaya-viniścaya-Upāli-paripṛcchā*. Enquête d'Upāli pour une Exégèse de la Discipline. Tr. du sanscrit, du tib. et du chinois, avec introduction, éd. critique des fragments sanscrits et de la version tib., notes et glossaires. Paris, Adrien-Maisonneuve, 1973 (Colln Jean Przyluski, Tome V).
Rabten, Geshe: *The Essential Nectar*. Meditations on the Buddhist Path. An explanation of the Lam rim text of Yeshe Tsöndrü entitled The Essential Nectar of the Holy Doctrine, and the text itself. Ed. & verse tr. Martin Willson. London, Wisdom Pubns, 1984.
Rahula, Walpola (tr. & annotated): *Le Compendium de la Superdoctrine (Philosophie) (Abhidharmasamuccaya) d'Asaṅga*. Paris, École Française d'Extrême-Orient, 1971, 2nd ed. 1980 (Pubns E.F.E.O., *LXXVIII*).
Rhie, Marylin et al.: *The Bodhisattva and the Goddess*. Deities of Compassion in Buddhist and Hindu Art. Cat. of exhibition, Northampton, Mass., Smith Coll. Museum of Art, 1980.
Richardson, H.E.: *The Dalai Lamas*. In: *Shambhala*, Occasional Papers of the Inst. of Tib. Studies, No. 1, Jan. 1971, 18–30.
Roerich, George N. (tr.): *The Blue Annals*. Calcutta, 1949; 2nd ed. Delhi, Motilal Banarsidass, 1976 (tr. of 'Gos lo tsā ba gZhon nu dpal: *Bod kyi yul du chos dang chos smra ba ji ltar byung ba'i rim pa Deb ther sngon po*. Finished at Chos rdzong, 1478).
Roerich, G. (tr.): *Biography of Dharmasvāmin* (Chag lo-tsa-ba Chos-rje-dpal), A Tibetan Monk Pilgrim. Original Tib. text deciphered & tr. Patna, K.P. Jayaswal Research Inst., 1959.
Ruegg, D.Seyfort: *The* gotra, ekayāna *and* tathāgatagarbha *theories of the Prajñāpāramitā according to Dharmamitra and Abhayākaragupta*. In: L. Lancaster (ed.), *Prajñāpāramitā and Related Systems*, Berkeley Buddhist Studies Ser., *1*, 1977, 283–312.
Schmid, Toni: *Saviours of Mankind*. Dalai Lamas and Former Incarnations of Avalokiteśvara. Stockholm, Statens Etnogra-

fiska Museum, 1961 (Sino-Swedish Expedition, Pubn 45; XIII. 9).

Schulemann, Günther: *Geschichte der Dalai-Lamas.* Leipzig, Otto Harassowitz, 1958.

Seckel, Dietrich: *The Art of Buddhism.* London, Methuen, 1964.

Sen, A.C. (ed.): *Buddhist Remains in India.* New Delhi, Ind. Council for Cultural Relations, 1956.

Stutley, Margaret & James: *A Dictionary of Hinduism.* Its Mythology, Folklore and Development 1500 B.C.—A.D. 1500. Bombay, Allied Publishers, 1977.

Tajima, R.: *Étude sur le Mahāvairocana-sutra (Dainichikyō).* Avec la Traduction Commentée du Premier Chapitre. Paris, Adrien-Maisonneuve, 1936.

Takasaki, Jikido: *A Study on the Ratnagotravibhāga* (*Uttaratantra*). Serie Orientale Roma, *XXXIII*, 1966.

Tāranātha: (*HBI*) *History of Buddhism in India.* Tr. fr. the Tib. (*rGya gar chos 'byung*, 1608) by Lama Chimpa & Alaka Chattopadhyaya, ed. Debiprasad Chattopadhyaya. Simla, Ind. Inst. of Advanced Study, 1970.

Toussaint, Gustave-Charles (tr.): *Le Dict de Padma (Padma Thaṅ Yig).* Paris, 1933; repr. as *Le Grand Guru Padmasambhava*: Histoire de ses Existences, Paris, Éditions Orientales, 1979.

Toynbee, Arnold: *Mankind and Mother Earth.* 1976, repr. London, Granada Pubg, 1978.

Tsong-ka-pa: *The Yoga of Tibet.* The Great Exposition of Secret Mantra: 2 & 3. Introduced by H.H. Tenzin Gyatso, XIV Dalai Lama. Tr. & ed. by Jeffrey Hopkins. London, George Allen & Unwin, 1981 (The Wisdom of Tibet Ser., 4).

Tucci, Giuseppe: *The Religions of Tibet.* Tr. fr. the German and Italian by Geoffrey Samuel. London, Routledge & Kegan Paul, 1980.

Vajirañāṇavarorasa, Somdet Phra Mahā Samaṇa Chao Krom Phrayā: *The Entrance to the Vinaya (Vinayamukha)*, Vol. II. Tr. Khantipālo Bhikkhu et al. Bangkok, Mahāmakut Rājavidyālaya Press, 1973.

Van der Post, Laurens: *Jung and the Story of Our Time.* London, Hogarth Press, 1976.

Vidyābhūṣaṇa, Satis Chandra: *A History of Indian Logic* (Ancient, Medieval and Modern Schools) (Nyāya-śāstrasya itihāsaḥ). Calcutta, 1920, repr. Delhi, Motilal Banarsidass, 1971.

Walleser, M.: *The Life of Nāgārjuna from Tibetan and Chinese*

*Sources*. London, 1922, repr. Delhi, Nag, 1979.

Wayman, Alex: *The Twenty-one Praises of Tārā, a Syncretism of Śaivism and Buddhism*. Journal of Bihar Research Soc., *45*, 36–43, 1959.

Wayman, Alex: *Yoga of the Guhyasamājatantra*. The Arcane Lore of Forty Verses. A Buddhist Tantra Commentary. Delhi, Motilal Banarsidass, 1977.

Willson, Martin (tr. & ed.): *Common Prayers*. A collection of shorter and widely used prayers of the Tibetan Gelukpa tradition. London, Wisdom Pubns, 1984; repr. in *Rites and Prayers*: An FPMT Manual, ib., 1985.

Wilson, Colin. *Mysteries*. An investigation into the occult, the paranormal and the supernatural. London, Granada Pubg (Panther Books), 1979.

Yeshe, Lama Thubten: *Cittamani Tara*. A Commentary on the Anuttarayoga-tantra Method of Cittamani Tara. Arnstorf, 1980, repr. London, Wisdom Pubns, 1984.

Yuyama, Akira: *The First Two Chapters of the* Prajñā-pāramitā-ratna-guṇa-saṃcaya-gāthā (*Rgs*). In: L. Lancaster (ed.), *Prajñāpāramitā and Related Systems*, Berkeley Buddhist Studies Ser., *1*, 1977, 203–218.

Zimmer, Heinrich: *Myths and Symbols in Indian Art and Civilization*. Ed. by Joseph Campbell. NY, Pantheon Books, 1946, repr. Harper Torchbooks, 1962.

# *Index*

* refers to an entry in the Glossary. Figures in italics refer to actual translations of relevant works, or to illustrations. C8: 8th century CE; C-2: 2nd century BC; (80E 17N): longitude and latitude to nearest degree – for countries and rivers, the reference is to where the name is on the map (pp.8–9); n: note, v: verse. Translated texts are indexed in the Bibliography, only short or abbreviated titles being included here.

109–12, 118–9, 307, 353, quoted and illus. 121–61; lineages from, 367–71; *Praise* (P2562), 189, 239, 399 n.54
Sūrya-śrī, C12, 205
Sūtra*, 23, 222, etc.
*Sūtra of Ārya-Tārā Who Saves from the Eight Fears, 89–93*
Suvarṇa-dvīpa, 289
Swat, *see* Oḍḍiyāna

Takṣaśīla (73E 34N), 271
Tak-tän (rTag brtan phun tshogs gling), 169
Tängyur*, 209, etc.
Tantra*, 19, 174, 240–41; books of, 35, 197; burnt, 186; corrupt in Tibet, 289; history of, 39, 169–206; practice of, 17, 18, 22, 316, 320; Three Jewels in, 322–3; *See also* Mantra Vehicle; Tārā, Tantras of; Vajrayāna
Tanu-śrī (99E 12N), 404 n.103
Tārā* (f. deity), 11–15 and *passim*; as bodhisattva, 11–14, 20–21, 24, 25, 34; as Buddha, 20–21, 24; colours of, 269; fierce, 73–74, 119, 248 v.38, 268 v.31; Green, *2*, *121*, 139, 234, 298, 333, 402 n.82; incarnations of, 24–25, 417 n.23; Laughing, 397–8; of the Lion's Roar, 219 v.29; mantras, 48, 67–69, 75–84, 91, 151–3; miracles and visions of, 177, 179–205, 209, 222–3, 233, 239, 256–7, 288–91, 370; miraculous images of, 186, 223, 233, 397–8; Mother of All the Buddhas, 12–13, 35, 51–55, 217, 244, 309–13, 347, 377 n.12; as Mother goddess, 14–20, 25, 96; Names of, 12–13, 35, 94–104, 240–50, 314; as old woman, 95; origin of, 33–36, 99, 123–5, 283 v.6, 301 v.2; pledges of, 84; reciting mantra of, 341, 344, 349; reciting praises of, 331–2; Saving from the Eight Great Fears, (described) 179–82, 190–93, 232–3, 236–7, 261–3, 304–6, (illustrated) *see* 9, (lists) 93, 217, 234, 249, 340, (other mentions) 13–14, 22, 35, 74, 88, 210, 218, 224–5, 286, 299, 314, 401 n.68; Saviouress, 13–14, 34, 210, 244, 248, 260; with seventeen deities, 238, 367; as Sublime Mother, 348, 376 n.13; Tantras of, 35–36, 44, *51–85*, 170–206, 314 v.28, 333, 366; as Tantric deity, 17, 18, 20–25; Tantric practice of, 332; Twenty-one, 110, 117–20, 280, 307, (individually) 123–61, 309–13; of wealth, 227, 334; White, 21, 298, 332, 347. *See also* Khadiravaṇī-tārā, Vajratārā, etc.
Tārā (wife of Candragomin), 222

# ABOUT THE AUTHOR

Martin Willson was born in England in 1946. After receiving his Ph.D. in radioastronomy from the University of Cambridge in 1971, he went to Australia and conducted research in physics for several years, this time in the field of climatology. Then, realising that scientific research would not cure the world's most pressing problems, he left to explore alternative ways of life. Soon he was living at Chenrezig Institute, a Tibetan Buddhist centre in the Queensland bush, where in 1977 he took ordination as a novice monk. He studied there for three years under Geshe Thubten Lodan and Lama Zasep Tulku, and with their encouragement began to translate texts that were needed for the teaching programme. He then returned to Europe and spent three years at Tharpa Choeling, the late Geshe Rabten's centre for Western monks in Switzerland (now Rabten Choeling), and two at Nalanda Monastery in France.

After twelve years as a Buddhist monk, he is now married and lives in Weymouth, England, where he continues to work in Buddhist translation. His hobbies include walking, environmental campaigning, and classical music.

His other works include The Essential Nectar with Geshe Rabten's teachings; Rebirth and the Western Buddhist, an examination of the evidence for rebirth; and translations of numerous rites and prayers.

## Publisher's Acknowledgment

The publisher gratefully acknowledges the generous help of the Hershey Family Foundation in sponsoring the production of this book.

# WISDOM PUBLICATIONS

WISDOM PUBLICATIONS is a non-profit publisher of books on Buddhism, Tibet, and related East-West themes. We publish our titles with the appreciation of Buddhism as a living philosophy and the special commitment of preserving and transmitting important works from all the major Buddhist traditions.

If you would like more information, a copy of our mail order catalogue, or to be kept informed about our future publications, please write or call us at:


361 Newbury Street
Boston, Massachusetts 02115
USA
Telephone: (617) 536–3358
Fax: (617) 536–1897


# THE WISDOM TRUST

As a non-profit publisher, Wisdom is dedicated to the publication of fine Dharma books for the benefit of all sentient beings. We depend upon sponsors in order to publish books like the one you are holding in your hand.

If you would like to make a donation to the Wisdom Trust Fund to help us continue our Dharma work, or to receive information about opportunities for planned giving, please write to our Boston office.

Thank you so much.

# The Foundation for the Preservation of the Mahayana Tradition

The Foundation for the Preservation of the Mahayana Tradition (FPMT) is an international network of Buddhist centers and activities dedicated to the transmission of Mahayana Buddhism as a practiced and living tradition. The FPMT was founded in 1975 by Lama Thubten Yeshe and Lama Thubten Zopa Rinpoche. It is composed of monasteries, retreat centers, communities, publishing houses and healing centers, all functioning as a means to benefit others. Teachings, such as those presented in Transforming Problems Into Happiness, are given at many of the centers.

To receive a complete listing of these centers as well as news about the activities throughout this global network, please write requesting a complimentary copy of the Mandala journal:


FPMT Central Office
P.O. Box 1778
Soquel, California 95073
Telephone: (408) 476–8435.
Fax: (408) 476–4823.

# Care of Dharma Books

Dharma books contain the teachings of the Buddha; they have the power to protect against lower rebirth and to point the way to liberation. Therefore, they should be treated with respect—kept off the floor and places where people sit or walk—and not stepped over. They should be covered or protected for transporting and kept in a high, clean place separate from more "mundane" materials. Other objects should not be placed on top of Dharma books and materials. Licking the fingers to turn pages is considered bad form (and negative karma). If it is necessary to dispose of Dharma materials, they should be burned rather than thrown in the trash. When burning Dharma texts, it is considered skillful to first recite a prayer or mantra, such as OM, AH, HUNG. Then, you can visualize the letters of the texts (to be burned) absorbing into the AH, and the AH absorbing into you. After that, you can burn the texts.

These considerations may also be kept in mind for Dharma artwork, as well as the written teachings and artwork of other religions.

# Also by Wisdom Publications

## TARA, THE LIBERATOR
Lama Zopa Rinpoche

This small volume contains a teaching on Tara, Mother of all Buddhas, by Lama Thubten Zopa Rinpoche, combining two lectures given in May 1987 at Kopan Monastery and at the Himalaya Yogic Institute, both in Nepal. Tara, an enlightened being in female form, has been a familiar figure in Tibetan Buddhism since its inception. This book explains vividly to practitioners and newcomers alike the qualities and characteristics of Tara and how one can engage in her practice.

$4.00, 32 pages

## CITTAMANI TARA
*An Extended Sadhana*
Translated by Martin Willson

This booklet contains the extended sadhana of Cittamani Tara, the highest yoga tantra aspect of Arya Tara, compassionate Mother of all the Buddhas. The sadhana has been translated from the Tibetan consulting the teachings and draft translation by Lama Yeshe, from Kopan, Nepal in 1979.

$5.50, 66 pages

## CONDENSED FOUR-MANDALA RITUAL OF CITTAMANI TARA
*Gadan Trijang Rinpoche*
Translated and edited by Martin Willson

This small volume contains Gadan Trijang Rinpoche's four-mandala offering prayer to Cittamani Tara, translated with advice from Geshe Jampa Tekchok. Included in this highest yoga tantra practice is a new version of the "Praise to Tara in Twenty-one Homages."

$5.50, 58 pages

## How to Meditate
*A Practical Guide*
Kathleen McDonald

What is meditation? Why practice it? Which technique is best for me? How do I do it? The answers to these often-asked questions are contained in this down-to-earth book compiled and written by Kathleen McDonald, a Western Buddhist nun with solid experience in both the practice and teaching of meditation. *How to Meditate* contains a wealth of practical advice on a variety of authentic and proven techniques.
"An excellent introduction... refreshingly readable... clarity without oversimplification."— *Buddhist Studies Review*

$12.95, 224 pages, 0-86171-009-6

## Enlightened Beings
*Life Stories from the Ganden Oral Tradition*
Translated, annotated, and introduced by Janice D. Willis

Here are the sacred biographies of six great tantric meditators from the Gelukpa school of Tibetan Buddhism. These life stories—or namtar—are actually tales of liberation. Part of a distinct tradition in Tibetan Buddhism, they are meant not only to inspire but also to instruct others on the path to enlightenment. You will gain valuable insights into the religious and political worlds in which these early Tibetan masters studied, practiced, and became enlightened beings in their lifetimes.

$18.00, 288 pages, 0-86171-068-1

## BUDDHIST SYMBOLS IN TIBETAN CULTURE
Dagyab Rinpoche

The Queen's Earrings. The Fur-Bearing Fish. The Endless Knot. Tibetan Buddhism is filled with rich, colorful symbols. But what do they all mean? In this fascinating study, Dagyab Rinpoche not only explains the nine best-known groups of Tibetan Buddhist symbols, but also shows how they serve as bridges between our inner and outer worlds. As such, they can be used to point the way to ultimate reality, and to transmit a reservoir of deep knowledge formed over thousands of years.

"Symbolism is the language of the human spirit, and this book is the most systematic study of its Tibetan idiom that has yet appeared."
—Huston Smith, author of *The World's Religions*

$14.95, 168 pages, 0-86171-047-9

## DRINKING THE MOUNTAIN STREAM
*Songs of Tibet's Beloved Saint, Milarepa*
Translated by Lama Kunga and Brian Cutillo

Here is a rare collection of sacred songs by one of the world's most celebrated spiritual teachers. Known for his penetrating insights, wry sense of humor, and ability to render any lesson into spontaneous song, Milarepa wandered the rugged terrain of eleventh-century Tibet and Nepal guiding countless followers along the Buddhist path through his songs of liberation. *Drinking the Mountain Stream* reveals Milarepa's actions as scathingly direct, and his humor and wisdom acutely penetrating as he cuts through the veil of illusion.

$14.95, 200 pages, 0-86171-063-0